Portals:

Portals: Pedagogy, Practice, and Architecture's Future Imaginary (RISD 2020)

Editors: Amy Catania Kulper,
Kevin Crouse, Jennifer Liese

Department of Architecture,
Rhode Island School of Design,
Providence

This book is dedicated to RISD alumnus Rex Siu Han Wong (B.Arch. '03), in gratitude for his generous support of the department and our students, and without whom this publication would not be possible.

Portals: Pedagogy, Practice, and Architecture's Future Imaginary (RISD 2020)

Contents

Kent Kleinman

Foreword

The work in this volume was produced in extraordinary times. Though initiated under normal studio circumstances at the beginning of RISD's spring semester, it continued as the world became unmoored roughly halfway through the semester. On March 30, 2020, the novel coronavirus forced the evacuation of the RISD campus, students and faculty scrambling to find a foothold and adopt a teaching mode foreign to this institution. The projects were developed, completed, and reviewed under conditions we had never imagined.

However, it is worth noting that the projects presented here originated well before the pandemic upended the college. The thematic frames devised by the studio critics and the theses authored by the individual students reflect dedication to a project that RISD Architecture has been incubating for some time. The core elements of this project can be easily discerned in the work: an abiding interest in sustainability and the nested issues of environmental and social justice (see Peter Niels Heller's thesis *Climate Resilience for a Neighborhood Without Privilege*); an embrace of the quotidian as an instantiation of architecture (see Eamon Wagner's thesis *Uncanny Genericism*); substantive engagement with scholars beyond the discipline (architect Rachely Rotem paired up with historian and professor Ijlal Muzaffar; architect Daniel Ibañez paired up with sociologist and professor Damian White); an unwillingness to accept normative techniques of representation (see Nathalie d'Hennezel's thesis *Acoustic Signatures*, or almost all the projects developed under the tutelage of David Gersten); and an expanded conception of expertise and agency (see Sophie Weston Chien's thesis *Practice: A Designer-Organizer Framework for Community Power*). Collectively, RISD Architecture has staked out a broad agenda, one that is arguably better prepared than most for the two overlapping imperatives of our time: the inevitable consequences of climate change and the desperate call for social justice. And this before the advent of Covid-19, and before the murder of George Floyd.

This publication is very different from the many published collections of student projects that typically serve to document a curricular project at a particular moment in time. Instead, you are holding something akin to the printout of a seismograph. The tracks of the pre-pandemic agenda are very much a part of the work, and it is essential to appreciate this curricular trajectory as a baseline vector. However, the abrupt jolt of the pandemic will be readily legible to those familiar with RISD's studio culture as a conspicuous discontinuity. Absent are the large material constructs that were often the embodiment of a project. Missing are rough process drawings that could be as revelatory as any polished image. The productive frictions that come with direct material engagement are smoothed out. And less apparent but enormously important: gone is the common ground provided by the RISD campus and community that normally serves as a creative safe haven for our students. These disruptions are encoded in the projects included in this publication. But also inscribed in the work are the signs of multiple futures. Collaborations occurred across time and space. Authorship became distributed across virtual communities of shared expertise. Habitual practices came under critical review as ways of working were forced to adapt. Digital tools were discovered that allowed remarkably fluid exchanges; other digital tools were exposed as biased or inflexible.

RISD Architecture, under the leadership of Department Head Amy Catania Kulper and Graduate Program Director Carl Lostritto, embraced the challenge thrust upon them with the elan for which the department is renowned, and the work collected here charts not just a possible future pedagogy, but a probable one. What will the studio become when afforded both embodied and virtual contexts in a post-pandemic world? I am confident of two things. First, propinquity has never been more highly valued. Second, the studio has changed forever.

Amy Catania Kulper

Introduction

When the academic year began at RISD Architecture in September 2019, none of us, neither students nor instructors, could have imagined how the year would conclude. There were seven cohorts—six thesis studios and one directed research studio—all under the supervision of our fearless coordinator, Daniel Ibañez. Hansy Better Barraza, David Gersten, Ryan McCaffrey, Ben Pell, Rachely Rotem, and I each taught thesis sections, while Dani taught a directed research studio that was more explicit in its methodological framing. We began the semester with a colloquium, inviting four guests to join us in Providence at the Bayard Ewing Building to do workshops with students and faculty in the morning, and then to present and participate in a conversation about the nature of theses and directed research projects. We were joined by Timothy Hyde from MIT, Ang Li of Northeastern University, Jamie Vanucchi from Cornell, and Jason Young from the University of Tennessee. The workshops were replete with substantive exchanges and the colloquium was packed with wonderful insights and takeaways for our students. We were off to a great start.

RISD has a five-week Wintersession, and while the directed research students pursued an independent study, the thesis students were enrolled in the Thesis Discursive Workshop. This is a relatively new part of the thesis curriculum, and for the past three years Jacqueline Shaw, a member of the RISD Architecture faculty, has developed it into a robust course focused on the crafting of the thesis book and the disciplinary positioning of the students' thesis projects. One of the distinguishing features of this course is a workshop on book design with guests from RISD's renowned Graphic Design department.

The spring semester was off to a solid start when news of the Covid-19 pandemic began to dominate the daily headlines, and by the end of March, RISD, like so many other colleges across the country, had made the difficult decision to send our students home and finish the semester remotely. For our B.Arch students who had been imagining the culmination of their degree projects for five years, and for the graduate students anticipating the consummation of two or three years of advanced study in architecture, this was a crushing blow. I remember sitting around the long table in my office with my ten thesis students and sharing the news. At that time, none of us imagined that just six months later, to assemble around that same table would require face masks and a room twice the size to accommodate social distancing protocols. As the students hastily packed their belongings and frantically booked flights, we waited in anxious anticipation for news of their safe arrival home. Our preoccupation gradually shifted from safe passage to: What now? How, with just six weeks left in the semester, would our students be able to continue the work they began in RISD Architecture's fourth-floor studio and successfully complete it from the cramped interiors of quickly leased apartments or their childhood bedroom in their parents' home?

In rapid succession we all downloaded Zoom (which would become the primary medium through which we communicated remotely), we set up Slack channels for the department, we used Miro boards and Cargo sites as ersatz pin-up spaces, and we designed protocols for accessing RISD's shop and computer lab remotely. Tentatively at first, but then with more confidence, we became acquainted with the ebbs and flows of remote pedagogy. The students resiliently leaned into their agility as designers, mapping out how they would complete their work given the economies of remoteness in which they were operating. There was an elusive missing ingredient in these early weeks of remote pedagogy, however, as we struggled to imagine how we might capture the camaraderie and peer-to-peer learning that studio culture offers.

Still, we had final reviews to plan and a Super Jury—a group of critics invited to engage in a high-level conversation across thesis and design research sections—to organize, so we set our sights on imagining some concrete form of closure for our students at a moment when all of our engagements were virtual and ephemeral. Ramon Tejada, a member of RISD's Graphic Design faculty, visited a graduate seminar I was teaching and shared a wonderful essay that the Indian novelist Arundhati Roy wrote about the pandemic in the *Financial Times*. Roy, whose novels brilliantly capture the details that often fly beneath our experiential radars, poignantly conveyed feelings of helplessness and despair over the tragedy, the surreal state of suspension that is the hallmark of such a crisis, and the slightest glimmer of hope that this global pandemic is a portal offering each of us ethical choices to make as we pass through it. The department had recently received a generous gift from alumnus Rex Siu Han Wong (B.Arch '03), so Daniel Ibañez, Carl Lostritto, the Graduate Program Director, and I, discussed the possibility of using this gift to create a book in honor of our graduating class. We crafted a prompt, and when we invited critics to the Super Jury, we asked them to contribute an essay or interview to the book. Inspired by Arundhati Roy's writing, the prompt (right) asked our critics to speculate about how the discipline of architecture might be reconfigured on the other side of this portal.

ARCHITECTURE'S PORTAL:
IMAGINING ANOTHER WORLD

"Whatever it is, coronavirus has made the mighty kneel and brought the world to a halt like nothing else could. Our minds are still racing back and forth, longing for a return to "normality," trying to stitch our future to our past and refusing to acknowledge the rupture. But the rupture exists. And in the midst of this terrible despair, it offers us a chance to rethink the doomsday machine we have built for ourselves. Nothing could be worse than a return to normality.

Historically, pandemics have forced humans to break with the past and imagine their world anew. This one is no different. It is a portal, a gateway between one world and the next.

We can choose to walk through it, dragging the carcasses of our prejudice and hatred, our avarice, our data banks and dead ideas, our dead rivers and smoky skies behind us. Or we can walk through lightly, with little luggage, ready to imagine another world. And ready to fight for it."

Arundhati Roy, "The Pandemic Is a Portal," *Financial Times* (April 3, 2020)

RISD Architecture's class of 2020 consists of undergraduate and graduate students undertaking the design of theses and directed research projects amid drastically uncertain times. Like their colleagues in schools of architecture across the globe, they are being asked to work remotely, to produce compelling design proposals in less-than-favorable conditions, and to lean into the constraints that have been so capriciously thrust upon them and their work.

Inevitably, as Indian novelist Arundhati Roy suggests, this global pandemic creates a temporal threshold between this world and the next, between a past that made this previously unthinkable scenario unavoidable, and a future that will constantly reference and be forever shaped by its occurrence. As a discipline, architecture is also likely to be indelibly transformed by these circumstances. The implications for new practice models, advocacy for social justice, innovative material sourcing, collaborative digital workflows, and environmentally responsible design are myriad.

In order to both commemorate this transformative disciplinary moment and to celebrate the resilient work of our graduating students, we are commissioning our Super Jury participants to submit essays (5,000 to 7,000 words) for inclusion in an Actar publication, documenting the student work at RISD Architecture, creating a discursive context around it, and projecting speculative futures for the discipline of architecture through this lens. Inspired by the insights of Arundhati Roy, we ask each of you to imagine another world for architecture, and to be prepared to craft a polemic that fights for it.

This book is a response to this set of diverse circumstances, inspirations, and imperatives. It consists of essays contributed by guests to the Super Jury; interviews conducted by Kevin Crouse and RISD faculty members Ijlal Muzaffar, Carl Lostritto, Ryan McCaffrey, Jacqueline Shaw, and myself; introductions to the framing of the Thesis and Directed Research Studios by Hansy Better Barraza, David Gersten, Daniel Ibañez, Ryan McCaffrey, Ben Pell, Rachely Rotem, and myself; and, of course, the student work of the RISD Architecture class of 2020, introduced in their own words.

The essays, like the Super Jury conversations that preceded them, cover a broad range of topics, offering salient speculations on architecture's disciplinary futures. Carl Lostritto's "Digital Hypnic Jerk" compares the digital situation of architecture's transition to remote pedagogy to a hypnic jerk, that hazy transitional territory separating sleep from wakefulness. His essay questions whether the discipline of architecture might emerge from this drowsy state of hibernation, fully embracing digital technology in our practices. My own essay, "Framed: The Aesthetics of Remoteness and the Ethics of Deferral," compares the Zoom frame to the larger economy of architectural, aesthetic, and technological frames. Arguing that the operations of the Zoom frame are different from others because they are temporal, the essay questions whether and how they might catalyze an ethics of deferral in our discipline. Daniel Barber's "The Great Age of Doors Is Behind Us!" posits doors and portals as objects of architectural design, metaphorically aligning their function with enduring gatekeeping habits in architectural pedagogy and practice. Barber prompts us to reconsider the portal's access to privilege—to open the door, or to dismantle it altogether—challenging architecture's uneven distribution of comfort and its protracted legacy of social and environmental injustice. Iñaki Alday's essay, "Becoming Accountable: The Project as Thesis," examines the critical components of thesis work—technical competence, a hot topic, contribution to the field, and subjective expression—formulating an appeal to invigorate the thesis by making it more accountable. For Alday, this accountability can best be achieved by an epistemological commitment to producing new knowledge through the work.

Peggy Deamer's essay, "Teaching Architecture in the Time of Covid-19," argues that architectural pedagogy must be more responsive to our current crises and suggests broadening disciplinary intent by designing scenarios rather than objects. This expansive lens situates resource procurement and labor processes within the scope of an architectural project, positioning architecture as a bridge to the communities we hope to serve. In his essay "The Difficult Whole Is Full of Difficult Holes," Kiel Moe critiques the false complexity and inclusion of Robert Venturi's "difficult whole," arguing instead for a new, terrestrial, antiracist whole. Moe highlights the importance of questioning basic disciplinary assumptions and routines, introducing Steve Jackson's "broken world thinking" as an alternative starting point for architectural design. Ana Miljački's essay, "Future-Catching in Our Times," utilizes the framework of speculative fiction to position students of architecture as future-catchers, hearing whispers from the future while producing work with the quality of sincere irony. For Miljački, the architectural effect of sincere irony is born of the recognition of operating within global ecosystems with disciplinary scales of gesture that are wholly inadequate to this task. Sean Canty's "New Adjacencies of Discourse and Practice" considers the work of digital tools and formal typologies, positioning métier and skillfulness as vehicles of disciplinary transformation. Georgeen Theodore's "Creative Collaboration in the Time of Covid-19" challenges the myth of the heroic architect toiling in isolation, arguing instead that creative collaboration is essential to contemporary architectural practice. For Theodore, collaborative practice allows for the coexistence of different voices, perspectives, and experiences, lending the capacity to ameliorate economic and racial segregation and political and cultural isolationism. Regarding the RISD Architecture thesis and directed research projects, Timothy Hyde notes "actions of irresolution" that he characterizes as the manifestation of a "compelling form of stillness." Hyde's essay, "Action and Stillness," positions stillness as neither inaction nor a withdrawal into disciplinary introspection, but rather as a tool to recalibrate certain aspects of disciplinary thinking.

The interviews in this volume took place in late July and early August, so several weeks had passed since the RISD Architecture Super Jury, leaving time for reflection about architecture's place within this global crisis had elapsed. In his interview with Kevin Crouse and myself, Jason Young observes a pluralism and unevenness in the student work that, for him, is indicative of an active questioning of disciplinary legacies of consolidation and reduction. Young claims that design education should be more invested in acquiring vulnerabilities than manifesting expertise. In her conversation with Jacqueline Shaw and Crouse, Dr. Mabel O. Wilson also alludes to disciplinary vulnerabilities, in this case, vulnerabilities in the built environment that constitute a "pastness," exposing legacies of colonialism, imperialism, deep resource extraction, and labor exploitation. For Wilson, these conditions are obfuscated by architecture's claim to a universal truth through idealized diagrams that purportedly represent every human, when in reality their operations are highly exclusive.

In Crouse and Carl Lostritto's interview with Nicholas de Monchaux, the conversation focuses on his desire to archive as much as the discipline of architecture can at this moment, so that we can find a democratic, inclusive, and expansive way forward. In Crouse and Ryan McCaffrey's interview with Lola Sheppard and Mason White, professional partners in Lateral Office, Sheppard notes, like Young, the pluralism in the students' design research and thesis work, suggesting that the projects recognized history as more complex than a singular narrative. On the topic of design research, White unexpectedly frames research as listening—perhaps listening to these alternative narratives—concluding that this is what makes architecture a discipline and not a mere service industry. In Crouse and Ijlal Muzaffar's interview with Mario Gooden, the conversation returned to the idea of the disciplinary universal subject that was also discussed in the Wilson interview. For Gooden, this universal subject obfuscates the fact that architecture is complicit in a division of labor that is often highly racialized and socially stratified. Gooden argues instead for a performative architectural subject, noting that designing with multiple people and purposes in mind opens architecture up to be more inclusive and more imaginative.

Sandwiched between these provocative essays and stimulating interviews are the theses and directed research projects of the RISD Architecture class of 2020. Of the sixty-five students who presented their work remotely in our final reviews in June, only forty-four are captured in these pages, which is an indication of the extreme situations our students continued to navigate after graduation. It is our hope that this book represents the herculean efforts of the entire class, capturing their spirit, their collegiality, and their heroic support of each other under difficult circumstances. Each studio, denoted by color, is introduced by the faculty advisor in a brief text delineating the pedagogical framing of the work that follows. The student work is a testimony to the incredible resilience, agility, and necessary innovation involved in its remote completion. Some students accessed RISD's shop and computer lab remotely; others jerry-rigged construction projects in their backyards; some outsourced the fabrication of various components; others pivoted to different media and alternative forms of representation available to them. As a body, this work speaks to the nimbleness and creativity of RISD Architecture students and to their willingness to reflect critically upon their discipline in a moment of global crisis, while continuing to produce explorative and meaningful projects. Against all odds, this cohort of students designed projects that were strategic in their disciplinary positioning, pluralistic in the topics they addressed and the media they deployed, and speculative in their crafting of a plausible future imaginary for architecture. They did this while they were scattered across the globe, working in cramped spaces without access to resources and materials, but more importantly, with only remote access to each other. Still, they supported each other remotely, through the anxiety of isolation and the disillusion of the unceremonious end of an important year in their lives.

The work contained within these pages is tangible evidence of this cohort's entanglements with adversity and documented proof of their continued spatial advocacy and activism through architectural practice. For them, the pandemic is a portal, as they design new forms of practice and create new knowledge that addresses the racial and environmental inequalities they have inherited. I am confident that they will undertake this future work with the same enthusiasm, resourcefulness, empathy, and creativity that has fueled the work in this book. While the professional road ahead for them is arduous, steep, and full of thorny obstacles, as we collectively endeavor to undertake a disciplinary course correction, making architecture more inclusive, equitable, and just, I hope that they will draw strength from this experience, demonstrating the confidence of architects who understand that design is central to this future that we imagine.

Though this book documents an affair internal to RISD Architecture, the conversations and contributions in these pages represent architect-scholars from more than a dozen institutions reflecting on the transition to remote pedagogy and what it portends for the future of our discipline. In the months of this book's production, the pandemic has foregrounded the racial, social, and environmental injustice underwriting various aspects of architectural practice. The book thus documents a first wave of resulting disciplinary course correction. In this sense, it analyzes a period and set of experiences shared by many schools of architecture, serving as an important case study of this transition. As a case study, the student projects, essays, and interviews in this volume demonstrate resilience and agility in the face of immense challenges, seizing upon them as opportunities to reposition the ethics of architectural practice and to reconsider the constituencies we serve as architects. Consequently, this book offers a view *of* and *through* the portal of the pandemic, pointing toward what must come next, not just at RISD, but in the discipline.

Carl Lostritto

Digital Hypnic Jerk

The Least Relaxing Summer Ever

It's early June in Rhode Island. The mornings are cool; the ocean breezes bring a saltiness to the air. At RISD Architecture, just a few miles from the confluence of a river and a bay—close enough to the ocean that dolphins swim upriver with the tide to feed—thesis presentations have concluded. Very shortly, we'll turn our attention to the students enrolled for the summer term, and then the fall. Usually, the upcoming start of a semester is one of the few fixed conditions we can count on amid the otherwise open-ended territory we intellectually inhabit as an academic community. Normally, for example, graduation marks a clean break from student to alumni status. Not this year. Instead, we'll be celebrating the class of 2020 in the fall with a planned Grad Show and the launch of this book, which sees us engaging our alumni-students as curatorial collaborators.

We are anxious. Among faculty and staff, there are collectively tens of thousands of hours of planning, advising, editing, and debating ahead of us. The parameters are regularly changing, and we are tackling a problem that we know, even in the best-case scenario, can't be solved by us. Our students are even more anxious. Not yet comfortable with the notion of a "day off," we might take a nap under the sun. Maybe we set an alarm, so we don't sleep through the whole afternoon. As we drift off, we enter a state of hypnagogia, the confluence between consciousness and unconsciousness at the onset of sleep. Mild hallucinations are common in this state, and students will sympathize with my observation that images from the day's work can creep in, regardless of whether we want them to. This phenomenon is well documented. Researchers have coined it the "Tetris effect," wherein after repetitive gameplay, images "intrude" into our perception as we drift off.[1] For us, it's probably the cells of a spreadsheet, line weights, or a contradictory corner condition that would have left enough mental residue to make an appearance well after we've closed our laptops.

As consciousness slips away and the hallucinations intermingle with images of clouds and the sounds of seagulls, our muscles spasm. Briefly, we feel a dreamlike sensation of falling, or like we've tripped and lost our balance. This in turn causes us to wake up, just a little bit, or at least to become briefly aware of our transition to sleep, and our body gives a little twitch. This involuntary event, known as the "hypnic jerk," is quite common. When it occurs, we feel no alarm, we don't sit up, and we certainly don't cancel the nap.

Portal within a Portal

This blip at the threshold of consciousness is one way to temporarily make some productive sense about how the Covid-19 pandemic will change RISD Architecture's relationship to digital media. If the pandemic is a portal, it's a relatively thin one, durationally speaking, compared with the thick portal of technological change in the discipline. At the same time, as of this writing, the virus and the shift to online learning have no end in

1 Robert Stickgold, April Malia, Denise Maguire, David Roddenberry, Margaret O'Connor, "Replaying the Game: Hypnagogic Images in Normals and Amnesics," *Science* 290, no. 5490 (2000): 350–53.

sight, and therefore there's no limit to the ways they will change the department, the discipline, and each of our lives.

Before we tackle what it means to experience the disciplinary digital hypnic jerk brought on by Covid, let's extend our metaphor so that being digital is akin to being asleep. Let's then acknowledge that there are two general reasons to avoid fixation on the "digital" as a modifier to "architecture." You might think "digital architecture" is a redundant term. All architecture is digital architecture now and it has been this way for, by the most conservative measure, two decades. You'd be right to think that. On the other hand, it may be asserted that architecture itself is not and cannot be digital. Representations and media are digital, but architecture is always material and one to one. This is a tired argument, but one so dependent on myth, idealism, and a rejection of disciplinary traditions that it helps with our metaphor. Being "non-digital" is as silly as declaring that one "doesn't sleep." Appealing—perhaps—but certainly impossible. We need digital media, just like we need sleep. Have you ever noticed that those who insist on marginalizing digital media are cranky? Have you ever noticed that if you don't get enough sleep you become murderous? No? Oh, well, in *Star Trek* that happens.[2]

But there are times in which we really do not want to be asleep.[3] Being asleep is to be isolated from reality even as our dream world samples from reality. If that wasn't obvious enough, we should also observe here that it's really hard to be "woke" and asleep. This is where our metaphor is uncomfortable, cautionary, and fitting. Digital architecture is a little like dreaming—the laws of physics, time, scale, and even object permanence are all figments of our data. It's certainly true that just as every dream is not an allegory of our wakeful state not everything that's digital is meant to be fabricated or materialized. Doing so would be to take the most boring and unimaginative view possible of both dreams and digital media. To complete our exploration of this aspect of our metaphor, let's not kid ourselves: like dreaming, existing in digital media, even networked online digital media, is isolating and tends to overemphasize the individual. Like sleep, digital spaces can be tantalizingly escapist. For many of us—myself included—debugging a digital script is much easier than directly confronting the finally foregrounded racism that will define our 2020 reality as much as the pandemic.

Acknowledge You're Sleeping, Enjoy Being Awake

One key implication of the hypnic jerk is that it disrupts the smooth trajectory toward unconsciousness. Our body reminds us that we are going to sleep, and we are aware, even if for a brief moment, of the process. In this context we might treat the hypnic jerk as a modest stepping stone toward lucid dreaming, where being aware that one is dreaming can lead to control over the dream. Here, our web-based presentations, online classes, and large group video conferences are jarring but salient reminders that our discipline is becoming even more deeply digital. It's not because of the pandemic, but the pandemic makes that obvious. This moment gives us agency to influence how we digitally dream in the future, but only if we start training ourselves now to control our dreams.

OMG, I'm Falling; Oh Wait, It's Fine

A medical professional will reassure you that regular hypnic jerks are nothing to worry about.[4] Most people won't even bother to ask their doctor about them because they are so common. Their effects are not at all the same as waking up from a nightmare in a cold sweat with disturbing imagery that lingers for days. To be clear, the pandemic is much more than a metaphorical hypnic jerk. The pandemic is much more than even a nightmare. It's only the abruptly digital transition to remote education, remote critique, remote event, and remote community that warrants this comparison. Consider that as recently as 2019, online education at RISD was a rarity—a special case, a risky experiment that sounded to many like a threat to our fundamental values. How quaint those debates now seem. But maybe it was just that we were overtired and uncertain about our reality. Maybe we were sleepwalking. Regardless, this hypnic jerk reminded us that our discipline is becoming entirely digital, and that's okay, as long as we know it.

2 Shari Goodhartz, Pamela Douglas, and Jeri Taylor, "Night Terrors," *Star Trek: The Next Generation* 4, no. 17, March 18, 1991. I wouldn't dare not find a way to conjure a *Star Trek* reference. In this episode, one of many that deal with dreaming, the crew has encountered a space anomaly that disrupts their sleep. Dr. Beverly Crusher informs her colleagues that the violence and paranoia experienced throughout the ship is the direct result of the crew not dreaming.

3 Jean Lousie Matthias, Ron Wilkerson, and Brannon Braga, "Schisms," *Star Trek: The Next Generation* 6, no. 5, October 19, 1992. In this alien abduction–themed episode, sleep resistance saves the day. More accurately, Commander William Riker saves the day with the help of drugs that keep him awake. It's also one of the rare episodes in which Counselor Deanna Troi uses her professional expertise in the main storyline—in the holodeck no less. Truly chilling.

4 I'm a professor, not a doctor! (Yes, this is also a thinly veiled, ironic *Star Trek* reference.)

Being "non-digital" is as silly as declaring that one "doesn't sleep." Appealing—perhaps—but certainly impossible. We need digital media, just like we need sleep. But there are times in which we really do not want to be asleep. Being asleep is to be isolated from reality even as our dream world samples from reality. It's really hard to be "woke" and asleep.

What We Owe to the Class of 2020

I'm writing from a faculty perspective, but I also saw the effect of the digital hypnic jerk on student projects. Whether it was turning a backyard into a design-build site for a time-lapse digital video, transforming a portfolio website into a presentation tool, or performing a web conference call alone to record a presentation, these relatively inconsequential moves can lead to some important lessons. First, that it might be the case we overemphasize the positive and negative impacts of digital technology. At reviews this spring, the fact that all work was represented via pixels was less consequential than the fact that everyone was looking at slightly different pixels thanks to variations in resolution, compression, bandwidth, etc. Relatedly, the digitization of sound was less an issue than the selective playback of one audio stream at time. In other words, we interrupted each other a lot.

Students: your digital hypnic jerks were conducted under observation. You went to sleep while on stage, and with this metaphor now at its breaking point, I hope it may suffice to conclude with an observation: While it's the case that no semester and no other graduating class will be comparable to you, it's also true that every subsequent class will have learned better, stranger, and healthier digital habits thanks to you.

Amy Catania Kulper

Framed: The Aesthetics of Remoteness and the Ethics of Deferral

Seamless: The Continuous Interior, Presentism, and Zoom

How best to describe architectural education, or what we might call its aesthetics of remoteness, in the emerging Zoom economy? The scene is all too familiar by now. The classroom is swapped for an overcrowded computer desktop. The critics appear in a grid. Their countenances are serious. Their attention is engaged. Their black clothing appears to be the same as it was pre-pandemic, but we see much less of it now: shirt collars, jacket shoulders, the occasional necklace—head and shoulders only, no torsos in sight. Slight movements signal active listening to the student who shares screen to present her work. The grid of faces, critics and student, becomes a line overlaid across a constellation of architectural representations. The student presents from her living room in Dallas, Texas. The critics are geographically scattered—Cambridge, MA; Muncie, IN; Providence, RI—yet their perceptually continuous domestic scenography is seamless. White walls, mid-century modern furniture, and impressive collections of books merge into a relentless interior sprawl. It is tempting to appropriate a description by German philosopher and cultural theorist Peter Sloterdijk to describe this Zoom diorama, as one which "already [anticipates] an integral, experience-oriented, popular capitalism in which no less than the comprehensive absorption of the outside world in a fully calculated interior [is] at stake."[1] If Sloterdijk were to continue to embellish upon the description of this laptop spectacle, he might add that it "[invokes] the idea of an enclosure so spacious that one might never have to leave it."[2] This is the reality of the current Zoom economy of architectural education, in which our virtual connectedness and digital simultaneity conspire to evoke a picture of ubiquitous interiority.

The contemporary illusion of a seamless and continuous interior finds its temporal corollary in the historical concept of presentism. Recognized through current cultural tropes such as the 24/7 news cycle, the currency of Tweets as a source for the dissemination of information and disinformation, and surreptitious iPhone videos simultaneously recording and publishing events, presentism describes a condition in which the past and the future are instrumentalized in order to validate the immanent, the immediate, and the contemporary. A byproduct of the simultaneity of an experience with its recording, archiving, chronicling, or documenting, presentism implicitly prohibits distance—reflective distance, temporal distance, aesthetic distance, critical distance, distance of any kind. In his 2003 book *Regimes of Historicity: Presentism and Experiences of Time*, historiographer François Hartog describes the phenomenon in this way: "It is a candid expression of our collective inability to shake off what is generally called 'short-termism' and which I prefer to call 'presentism,' the sense that only the present exists, a present characterized at once by the tyranny of the instant and by the treadmill

1 Peter Sloterdijk, *In the World Interior of Capital*, trans. Wieland Hoban (Cambridge: Polity Press, 2013), 169–70. Sloterdijk is describing Joseph Paxton's Crystal Palace (1851), using its structure, with its artificial climate control and apparent immateriality, as the instantiation of an "aesthetics of immersion" that signals the emergence of modern cosmopolitanism.

2 Sloterdijk, 175.

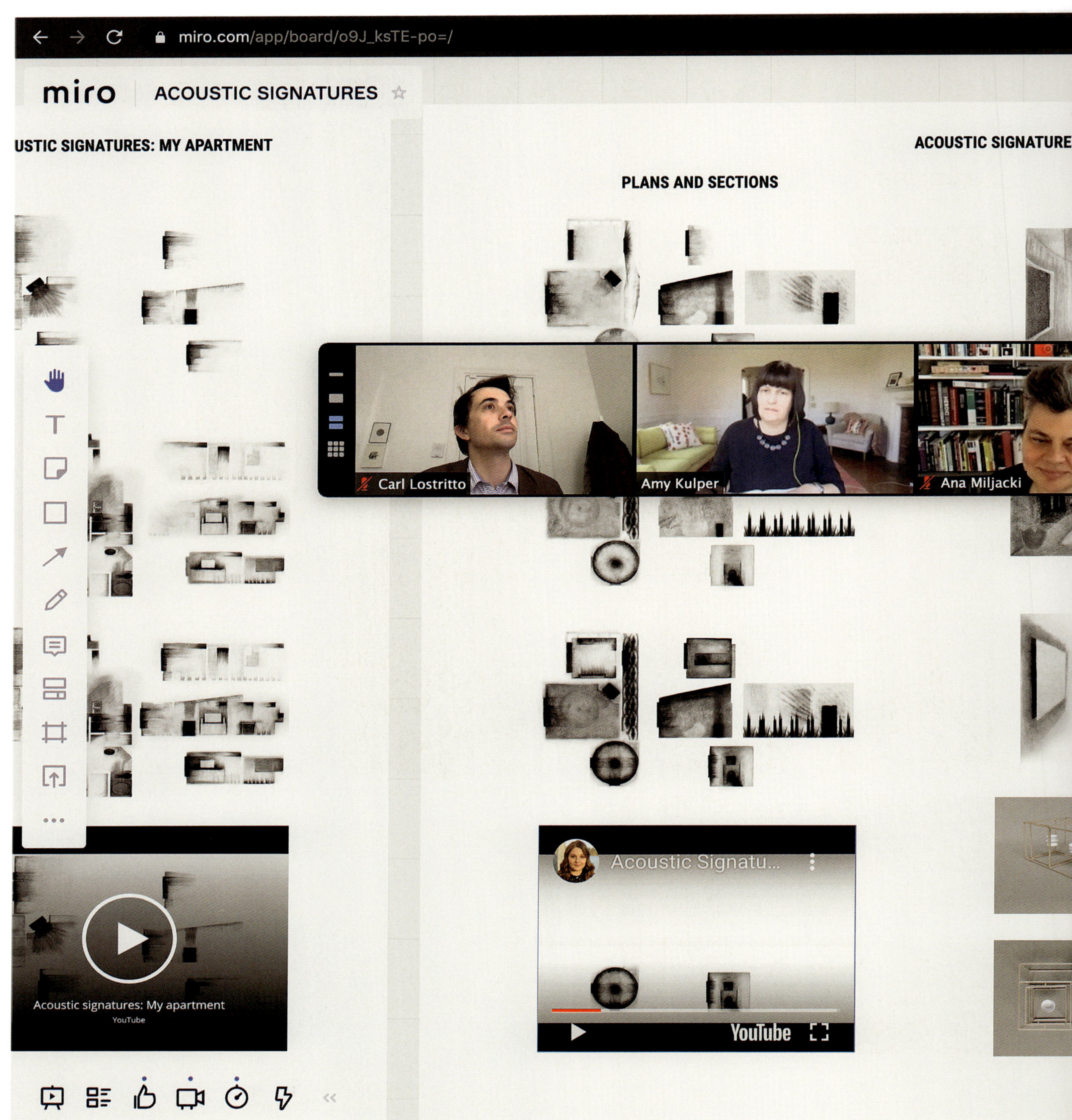
miro.com/app/board/o9J_ksTE-po=/
miro
ACOUSTIC SIGNATURES
USTIC SIGNATURES: MY APARTMENT
ACOUSTIC SIGNATURES
PLANS AND SECTIONS
Carl Lostritto
Amy Kulper
Ana Miljacki
Acoustic signatures: My apartment
YouTube
Acoustic Signatu...
YouTube

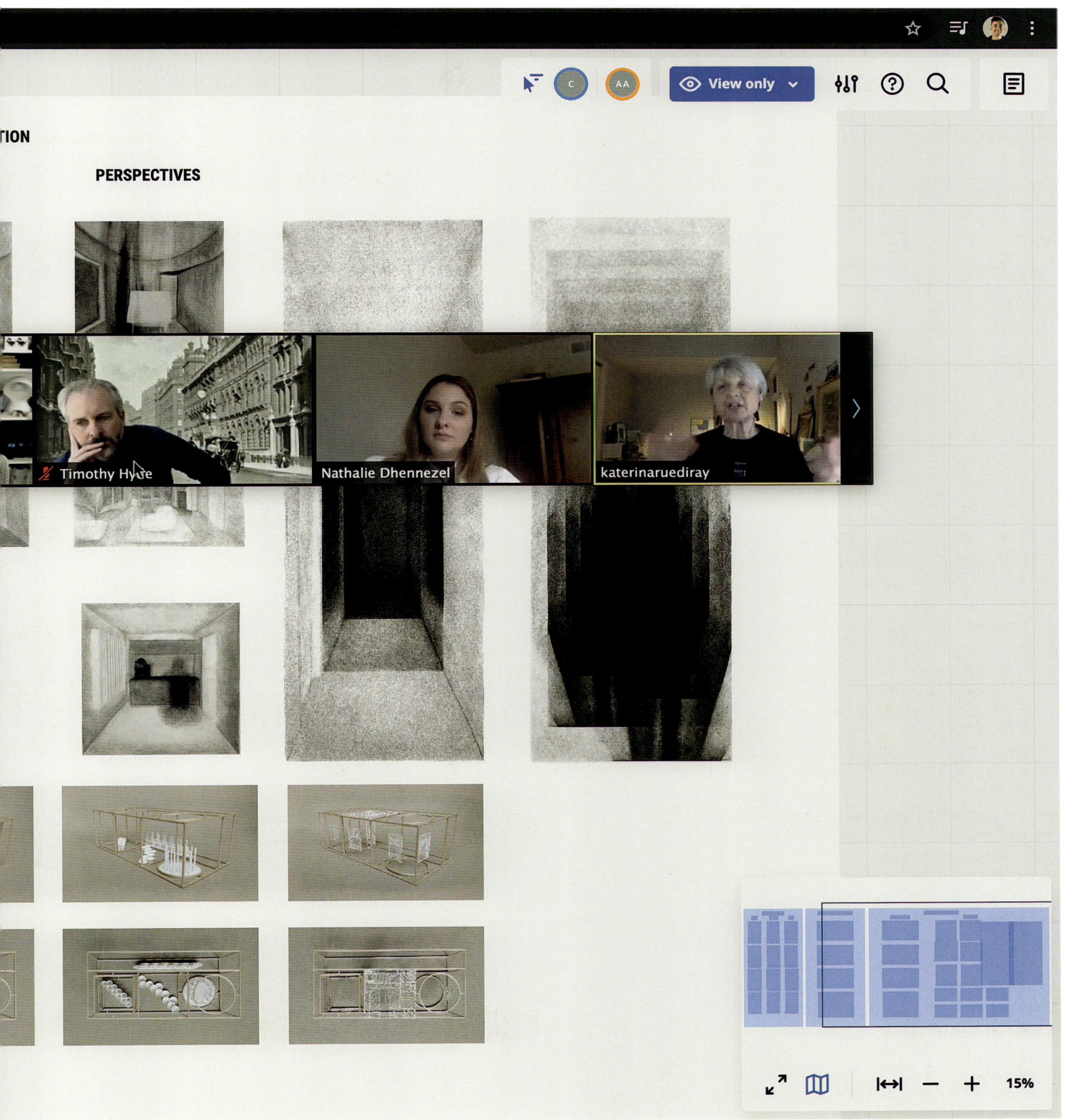
View only
TION
PERSPECTIVES
Timothy Hyde
Nathalie Dhennezel
katerinaruediray
15%

of the unending now."[3] Through its conflation of disparate places, times, and forms of representation and its insistence upon continuous interiority, the scenography of Zoom captures exactly both "the tyranny of the instant and the treadmill of the unending now." In fact, Zoom critiques are the epitome of presentism—just ask anyone who has lost track of time, location, or even their bodily needs while participating in their virtual economies.

Eluding Presentism: Gaps, Rifts, and Fault Lines

Hartog diagnoses the smooth, seamless, continuous presentism that we currently occupy by identifying disorienting temporal moments from the early twentieth century—gaps, rifts, fault lines, breaches, returns, ridges, joints, cracks, a veritable taxonomy of ruptures—that the relentless ooze of an omnipresent present sought to fill, culminating in the hegemony of contemporaneity. Among the historical moments that signaled the advent of presentism: the 1968 protests against capitalistic progress, the emergence of heritage as a historical category in 1972, and the fall of the Berlin Wall in 1989, to name a few. In each instance, the historical categories of past, present, and future are suspended, providing fertile ground for presentism to take root like a historically invasive species.

For Hartog, lines from a 1935 lecture by Paul Valéry depict this state of "broken continuity": "On the one hand, there is the past that can neither be abolished nor forgotten, but from which we can derive almost nothing that will orient us in the present or help us imagine the future. On the other hand, there is the future without the least shape."[4] Hartog identifies another such gap in Hannah Arendt's *Between Past and Future*, in which the author describes an "odd in-between period … during which one becomes aware of an interval in time which is entirely determined by things that are no longer and by things that are not yet."[5] Arendt's "interval in time" is an indicator, signaling a suspension, a pause, an interruption—more absence than presence, more inactive than proactive—a perfect Petri dish in which to cultivate presentism's relentless proliferation. Decontextualized, these passages detailing the conceptualization of a moment of equipoise between the "no longer and the not yet" or a "future without shape" could easily be mistaken for descriptions of what it feels like to live through the current pandemic. Indeed, the coronavirus pandemic is a sort of temporal rupture in the early twenty-first century, echoing the temporal discontinuities described by Valéry and Arendt in the previous century.

What role does architecture play in relation to these gaps, rifts, and fault lines? Perhaps one of the most intriguing inclusions in Hartog's book, which is essentially an argument about historiography, or how historians construct their narratives, is the presence of architecture. His earliest reference dates to 1909, in the context of Italian architect Filippo Tommaso Marinetti's "Manifesto of Futurism." Within Marinetti's writing, Hartog notes a slippage in which the future he describes is simultaneously already a presentism: "Time and Space died yesterday. We are *already* living in a world of the absolute, since we have already created eternal, omnipresent speed."[6] It is as if in the Futurist's embrace of speed, past, present, and future are elided, like the visual blur of a speeding train, into one comprehensive historical category. In this first example, Hartog illustrates architectural theory's capacity to anticipate the phenomenon of presentism, however, his second example demonstrates architecture's facility in resisting presentism. Here, he characterizes Berlin of the 1990s, after the fall of the wall—the West, a territory with all of the appurtenances of a modern city; the East, a stultification of urban practice in the form of a crumbling relic—in these words: "In Berlin more than elsewhere time was a visible and a tangible problem that could not be eluded."[7] Against this background, Hartog introduces the German architect Hans Scharoun, a member of the city's planning and architecture commission after the war best known for his design of the Berlin Philharmonic. On the dilemma of the temporal disjuncture in East and West Berlin, Scharoun remarked: "One cannot hope to build a new society and to rebuild old buildings."[8] Scharoun's observation, a direct reference to places like Warsaw, which rebuilt its demolished pre-war city

3 François Hartog, *Regimes of Historicity: Presentism and Experiences of Time* (New York: Columbia University Press, 2003), xv.

4 Hartog, 3. Hartog references Paul Valéry, *History and Politics*, trans. Denise Folliot and Jackson Mathews (New York: Bollingen Foundation, 1962), 28–29.

5 Hartog, 5. The passage references Hannah Arendt, *Between Past and Future: Eight Exercises in Political Thought* (New York: Penguin, 1993), 9.

6 Hartog, 108. This passage references Giovanni Lista, *Le Futurisme* (Paris: Terrail, 2001), 29, 30, 38, and Umberto Boccioni, Carlo Carrà, Luigi Russolo, Giacomo Balla, and Gino Severini, "Manifesto of the Futurist Painters 1910," *Futurist Manifestos*, trans. Robert Brain et al., ed. Umbro Apollonio (New York: Viking, 1973), 24–26.

7 Hartog, 10.

8 Hartog, 10.

through techniques of historic preservation, acknowledges the roles architecture plays in indexing historical continuity, actively embodying urban categories of past, present, and future. Thus Hartog positions architecture as a presence that can potentially resist, or even thwart, the invasive proliferation of presentism through its historical specificity and cultural permanence as urban fabric.

In contrast, Hartog's third architectural example, Dutch architect Rem Koolhaas's conceptualization of "Junkspace," is offered as a cautionary tale. Junkspace appears in generic cities as a byproduct of modernization; Koolhaas describes it as "the product of an encounter between escalator and air-conditioning, conceived in an incubator of Sheetrock."[9] In its articulation, Junkspace uncannily resembles the continuous interiority of the contemporary Zoom experience, as Koolhaas's further description suggests: "Continuity is the essence of Junkspace; it exploits any invention that enables expansion, deploys the infrastructure of seamlessness: escalator, air-conditioning, sprinkler, fire shutter, hot-air curtain. … It is always interior, so extensive that you rarely perceive limits; it promotes disorientation by any means (mirror, polish, echo)."[10] In his evocation of Koolhaas's concept of Junkspace, Hartog is describing a condition in our built environment that propagates presentism. By extension, it is easy then to speculate that architectural pedagogy via Zoom is similarly deploying an infrastructure of seamlessness with the potential for limitless expansion. If, indeed, the Zoom economy is a virtual Junkspace, proliferating the temporality of presentism, we must ask ourselves: How might the aesthetics of remoteness make a space for the discipline of architecture to *resist* such temptations?

Framed: Pictures, Screens, and Windows

A predominant feature of the aesthetics of remoteness in the Zoom economy is the appearance of the frame: the frame of the computer screen that stages the encounter and the grid of smaller frames that constitutes the continuous interior of a specific conversation. The chartreuse frame around each active speaker's image mitigates against this economy of "reception in distraction," as Walter Benjamin might describe it, drawing our attention to one person's discursive contributions.[11] Prior to a Zoom utterance and the appearance of this frame, we experience this virtual Junkspace through reception in distraction. Importantly, Benjamin utilizes the experience of architecture as a primary example of reception in distraction, juxtaposing this habitual understanding from the optical reception of space, a corollary to the chartreuse frame. While the Zoom frames knit together disparate individuals and their domestic interiors, the Miro frames interweave individual drawings, models, and animations into larger aggregations such as projects and studios. In Zoom's continuous interior, the Miro board serves as an ersatz gallery, extending the nesting of frames within frames like a virtual Russian doll.

We can see then that the computer screen during a remote architectural review is rife with frames, but what, precisely, are these frames doing? While these virtual frames appear to do the work that analog frames have done historically, their operations differ. Philosopher Karsten Harries describes the historical aesthetic operations of the frame in this way: "Frames re-present what they frame. Such re-presentation invites us to take a second look, bids us to take leave from our usual interests and concerns and to attend to what is thus re-presented. … Frames may be understood as objectifications of the aesthetic attitude. Paintings are thus often given frames. The frame helps present the painting as an aesthetic object."[12] When the frame cordons off a picture, it sets it apart from direct engagement through the introduction of aesthetic distance. The function of a frame in an aesthetic context then is to distinguish the aesthetic from the experiential, while, paradoxically, once in a frame, the experiential becomes aesthetic.

If, as Harries argues, the picture frame invites us to take a second look by physically displacing the object of contemplation, then what work do the Zoom and Miro frames do in the context of the remote architectural review? Contrary to the aesthetic distancing of their analog predecessors, these digital frames draw critics, students, and works into a strangely intimate proximity. Like property lines that exist on a drawing but have no

9 Rem Koolhaas, "Junkspace," *October* 100, Obsolescence (Spring, 2002): 175.

10 Koolhaas, 175.

11 Walter Benjamin, "The Work of Art in the Age of Mechanical Reproduction," in *Illuminations*, ed., Hannah Arendt (New York: First Mariner Books, 2019), 192.

12 Karsten Harries, *The Broken Frame: Three Lectures* (Washington, DC: The Catholic University of America Press, 1989), 67.

physical manifestations on an actual site, or clothing seams—an inevitable byproduct of garment construction, but rarely a feature—these frames are present but ineffable, enabling the continuous interior to emerge. Abetted by Zoom's technologies of communication, the digital frame's ability to distance is transgressed by the collective capacity of the occupants to collaborate (share screen), to chat (type notes in a field), to make judgments (thumbs up or thumbs down), or to approve (clap hands). These technologies, however, only produce the *effects* of intimate proximity, masking the infinitely extendable interior of remote pedagogy.

If Zoom countermands the traditional work of frames, propagating presentism's illusion of a ubiquitous continuous interior, then do architectural frames behave more like analog picture frames or their virtual corollaries? As a discipline, architecture is rife with frames—the Chicago frame, the balloon frame, windows, doors, thresholds, curtain walls, and enfilades—so it is not a stretch to make the leap from picture frame to picture window, but what distinctions are lost in this translation? Historically, architectural frames delineate between interior and exterior or between different elements of architectural program. But beyond this task of making boundaries, transitions, and thresholds and pictorializing what lies ahead, they also have the capacity to influence and shape the spatial occupant. For example, the punched window of nineteenth-century bearing wall construction anticipates a static viewer gazing from the interior to a framed scene beyond, whereas the early twentieth-century strip window envisages a mobile viewer encountering the landscape almost cinematically. While these examples allude to operations of architectural frames that transcend the pictorial, they are not yet explicit about what criteria differentiates them from purely aesthetic frames. In his essay "Figures, Doors, and Passages," architect and historian Robin Evans compares how paintings and architecture frame events. His conclusion is equal parts unsurprising and profound: "Yet architecture is quite distinct from painting … because it encompasses everyday reality, and in so doing, provides a format for social life."[13]

Evans's assertion suggests that implicit in architecture's propensity for framing resides an ethical dimension of spatial practice. In designing architecture for a range of human practices and social engagements, the disciplinary aspiration transcends the aesthetic.

Hold on, you might argue, Junkspace is designed for a range of human practices and social engagements, but nobody ever accused *it* of being ethical. Rampant in shopping malls and airports, with their iterative thresholds of store entries and airline gates and their continuous polished interiors primed for capitalist consumption, the allure of Junkspace resides in its capacity to mask transitions and obscure boundaries. Its infrastructure of seamlessness is supported by innocuous technologies like air conditioning, escalators, air curtains, and elevators. Lulled into a comatose sense of complacency, Junkspace occupants are unaware of these spatial sleights-of-hand that mask architectural transitions and frames beneath a veneer of perennial boredom. They are too busy humming along to the piped-in Muzak to notice. So, the infrastructure of seamlessness reverses the distancing, reflection-inducing operations of the frame in two proliferating environments central to architectural pedagogy and practice: the Zoom critique and architectural Junkspace. This is our new reality: we are living a good part of our lives in paradoxically borderless frames. Benjamin used the term *reception in distraction* to describe the immersive quality of both early twentieth-century architecture and film. Here, it can aptly be applied to the enticement of Zoom's borderless interiority and its invitation to live in perennial distraction from our lives, from the spaces we occupy and the people we engage, beyond the scenography of Zoom.

Framed: The Affordances of the Pandemic as Portal

Returning for a moment to Valéry's characterization of "a future without shape" and Arendt's evocation of a time determined by things that are "no longer" and "not yet"—again, descriptions that perfectly capture the experience of living through a pandemic—we might posit that the pandemic itself is a rupture, a frame, a threshold, or as Roy describes it, a portal.[14] In fact, the pandemic has opened up a temporal portal—a yawning expanse of unexpected and

13 Robin Evans, *Translations from Drawing to Building and Other Essays* (London: Architectural Association, 2003), 89.

14 Arundhati Roy, "The Pandemic Is a Portal," *The Financial Times* (April 3, 2020).

unprogrammed time, challenging and resisting presentism's tyranny of the instant with every stretch of boredom and each moment of tedious monotony quarantine serves up. The pandemic as portal occasions the opportunity to reference a totally different, entirely contradictory, connotation of frame, one captured in the colloquial expression *I've been framed*. This expression encapsulates a certain tension or conflict between an event and the evidence of it happening, or, put differently, things appear one way, but actually occurred another. Could the Zoom frame conceivably be a wolf in sheep's clothing? Is it possible that its appearance, so closely resembling a picture frame, leads us to believe that it promises one thing, aesthetic distance, when actually it delivers another, instrumentalizing us as its technological subject?

To answer this question, we must return to the context of the Zoom critique and ask the critical question: What role *do* these frames play? They neither function like aesthetic frames (distancing) nor like architectural frames (associating). Perhaps their operations are best comprehended in the extended context of technology. Consider, for example, a biologist examining a specimen through the lens of a microscope. In this scenario, the specimen on the glass slide is instrumentalized—captured through the magnification of the lens—but this is not the full extent of the instrumentalization. The representation of the specimen, captured in a circular frame in order to preserve the instrumentality of the microscope, perpetuates the technological frame long after the memory of the laboratory practice and its instruments are forgotten. As Canadian philosopher and media theorist Marshall McLuhan so astutely observed: "It is the framework which changes with each new technology and not just the picture within the frame."[15] Further, simply by gazing into the microscope, by implicitly succumbing to its regimes of visualization and its practices of imaging, the biologist is instrumentalized. Applying this scientific model to the Zoom frame, we can see its capacity for instrumentalization. First, consider the elaborate ritual of the Zoom setup: laptop camera at eye level, positioned so that the occupant is facing a flattering lighting source; watch your flank—everything within the scope of the laptop camera is immaculate, everything outside of its scope, chaos; click *join the meeting with video on*, then scurry to tame your stray hairs and smile widely to make sure nothing is stuck in your teeth. In the blink of an eye, your living room or home office has become a pedagogical stage set and you its spotlighted occupant. The instrumentality of the Zoom camera has the capacity to surreptitiously reconfigure the spaces of our everyday lives. It also has the facility to transform its digital subjects from passive participants to self-aware poseurs, gaming the platform's artifice while simultaneously transforming ourselves into complicit avatars of its virtual economies. Zoom appears to offer us aesthetic frames, benign in their introduction of distance, when in reality, it is entangling us in technological frames with the capacity to instrumentalize us as its digital subjects, and the very spaces we occupy.

Architectural educators, meet the wolf!

The Aesthetics of Remoteness and the Ethics of Deferral

So here we are. The pandemic produced a global need for Zoom and its obsessively framed aesthetics of remoteness. Zoom's siren call to its potential users encourages us to keep in touch while in quarantine, and the platform's capacity to do just that is considerable. The question however, as we sign in and prepare to click on "start meeting," is how self-aware can we be when using Zoom, especially as architects engaged in the design of the one thing that seems capable of thwarting the relentless advance of presentism?

Right now, for a brief moment of time in the enculturation of Zoom technologies, its frames can make us aware of this profound moment of global transformation and cognizant of the rituals of participation that will soon become unreflective habit. The Zoom frame is still open for interpretation. We can choose to ignore its encroachments into our daily lives, continuing to stage our interiors on the way to becoming the docile body avatars it assumes us to be. But to do so is to look the other way as Zoom's instrumentality is hidden behind its innocuous chartreuse frame, to succumb to presentism's tyranny of the instant, and to accelerate the propagation of this virtual Junkspace. Instead, what if we acknowledge

15 Marshall McLuhan and Frank Zingrone, eds., *The Essential McLuhan* (New York: Basic Books, 1995), 273.

the Zoom frame's capacity to instrumentalize us as its digital subjects and … resist? In this scenario, our self-awareness of the incursions of Zoom might coincide with the suspension, pause, or interruption of presentism's proliferation by the pandemic. Zoom's frame might become the signifier of what we might call temporal deferral, a resistance to the continuously accelerating forces of presentism. This resistance, this temporal deferral, need not be just broadly cultural. It can apply directly to the discipline of architecture. The Zoom frame can become a trapdoor to escape the infinitely expandable virtual interiority of capitalist Junkspace, a way to resist the enticement of constantly doing, making, problem-solving, accomplishing, producing. It might allow us to utilize time, instead, to do nothing, to choose inaction, and to fully contemplate the global predicament we find ourselves in.

Indeed, the Zoom critique's aesthetics of remoteness did give rise to an ethics of deferral in the thesis and directed research projects of the RISD Architecture students in spring 2020. With the help of friends and colleagues who so thoughtfully shaped the discourse around the student work in their final reviews—and in the student work itself—I saw it was possible to both *design* and *defer* simultaneously. Ijlal Muzaffar introduced the idea of an ethics of deferral in the projects, noting that when architects are working on problems at the scale of a global pandemic or climate change, they must pause to ask the thorny question: Who gets left behind? For Mario Gooden, deferral was less an opportunity for reflection and more an occasion for active resistance. He posited deferral as the opportunity to ask both how architecture can reclaim its cultural agency and who gets served. For Timothy Hyde, the ethics of deferral took the form of purposeful inaction. Understanding the value of inaction, he posed the question: Can architecture embrace this state of deferral as a decision, as something potentially productive? Ana Miljački witnessed in the student work a deferral through the effect of "sincere irony" and asked: At what scale do we operate? Daniel A. Barber posited deferral as an overall resistance to urgency and turn toward our work as discursive agents. He asked: might we say that deferral creates a space for architecture to theorize its activity? Nicholas de Monchaux seized upon this notion of temporal deferral as an opportunity for theorization and speculation. He returned to the question of inaction through the lens of Jenny O'Dell's book, *How to Do Nothing: Resisting the Attention Economy.*[16] Paraphrasing O'Dell, he argued that the right to say—or perhaps *do*—nothing is crucial because then and only then is there a chance of framing the rare and essential thing that might be worth doing.

The enticement for architects to continuously design projects, problem-solve, and add value to the built environment is our disciplinary corollary to presentism. Only when we refuse to engage with presentism's tyranny can we address the ethical dilemmas of our work—tacit and explicit exclusions and environmental destruction among them. Each contributor to the reviews acknowledged the breakneck speed of presentism within which students of architecture are currently operating, and each found integrity and promise in how their projects counterbalanced these pressures with temporal deferral. Collectively, the ethics of deferral in the student work allowed them to address critical architectural questions, to operate both *in* and *on* the discipline. Perhaps then through its nested portals, its frames within frames, Zoom pedagogy offered us a reprieve amid the rupture. Here again is Roy: "Our minds are still racing back and forth, longing for a return to 'normality,' trying to stitch our future to our past and refusing to acknowledge the rupture. But the rupture exists. And in the midst of this terrible despair, it offers us a chance to rethink the doomsday machine we have built for ourselves. Nothing could be worse than a return to normality."[17] That was in April 2020, at the start of the pandemic. The spring and summer carried us farther and farther from "normality," making its return less and less imaginable. And less and less desirable. If, as Roy conjectures, the pandemic is a portal, then architecture finally has its chance to intentionally step off of presentism's treadmill of the unending now, to pass lightly through this portal, leaving our disciplinary baggage behind us, and to ethically reorient our efforts through deferral. Business as usual is simply not an option. *Framing* the things that are worth doing is our only recourse.

16 Jenny Odell, *How to Do Nothing: Resisting the Attention Economy* (New York: Melville House, 2019).

17 Roy, "The Pandemic Is a Portal."

Transcalar Feedback Loops
Introduction

Primary Advisor **Daniel Ibañez, Professor, Department of Architecture, RISD**
Secondary Advisor **Damian White, Dean, Liberal Arts, RISD**

Students **Ece Cetin (B.Arch), Anya Drozd (B.Arch), Sung Hyun Hong (B.Arch), Min Jin (MJ) Kook (M.Arch), Taylor McCabe (M.Arch), Elizabeth Parker (M.Arch), Yangchuan (Niko) Tian (M.Arch), Diyi Zhang (B.Arch)**

In recent years architecture education has begun to address essential socioecological and sociopolitical issues, yet the methodologies utilized for this task have fallen behind. Can design research become the methodological foundation for addressing them more effectively? The Directed Research path's goal is to research, speculate toward, and design alternative architectural scenarios through design research methodologies to address the societal and ecological demands associated with the metabolism of contemporary urbanization. Compared with the thesis path, directed research is tightly delimited, and the methods of research, design, and documentation are more explicit. Its outcomes—design research projects—can stand simultaneously as design propositions and as forms of disciplinary knowledge. There is no common theme or topic; each student selects and crafts an individual design research brief. The work is underpinned by design research methodologies and frameworks revolving around three large axes: discourses, cases, and design.

In the discourses phase, students interrogate how extra-disciplinary contemporary discourses (on urbanization, ecology, material studies, etc.) are generative for architecture. Students gradually delimit a territory for their design research inquiry based on *problématiques* and debates within and beyond the disciplinary limits of architecture. Next, students compare and analyze existing case studies analogous to their own design research inquiry in approach or research topic. The design phase, lastly, provides the methods, frameworks, and representational techniques for design research projects to become interventions in the world. Like a palimpsest, this phase layers thermodynamic, material, ecological, metabolic, labor relations, and programmatic design drivers, each creatively superimposed and iterated.

Students' topics within the Directed Research path are varied but often underpinned by shared agendas. The work is generally circumscribed to a metabolic and transcalar agenda characterizing architecture as socio-natural bundles whose interdependencies cut across multiple scales and sites. It also shares a series of methodologies and frameworks aiming at systematizing tools with which specific research from design can be generated, for example: scenario-based projections, visually complex arrays of information, synthetic representations combining descriptions with projections, and time-based projections. Following these underpinnings and frameworks, three main topics prevail: 1) adaptive reuse, 2) revisiting infrastructures, and 3) new housing territories.

Adaptive reuse design research projects start from a preexisting building or built condition. They emphasize imagining alter-architectures, roads not taken, and futures that, while being new, can still be pinned down to spatially specific sites. This work relies heavily on scenario-based representations and system-oriented interventions. In other words, the underlying thesis is articulated and designed for more than one site, building, or condition. One project is not enough to "prove" the systemic nature of their design research propositions. Sung Hyun Hong's project (see pp. 35–38), for example, utilized three existing built projects, speculating on second-life scenarios that could be deconstructed and endlessly reassembled in new creative ways. Ece Cetin's work (see pp. 27–30), interrogates the role of the façade as a commodified space of capital reproduction by imagining alternative interfaces for three existing contemporary towers. Taylor McCabe (see pp. 43–46) offers struggling neighborhoods in Baltimore a systems-based design strategy to reactivate four different types of sites through the re-orchestration of reclaimed materials, reuse of vacant buildings, and meaningful community programs. Diyi Zhang's work (see pp. 55–58) revisits four decaying Italian villas through a creative palette of locally informed adaptive reuse strategies designed to reactivate the increasingly depopulated European hinterland.

Another group of students focused on expanding design's agency in infrastructural conditions. Starting from existing infrastructures—large-scale "machines" originally conceived as regulators of natural flows (water, oil, etc.)—they aimed to illuminate potential beyond techno-functionality, socializing and humanizing the infrastructures as opportunity sites for socioecologically meaningful interventions. The projects wove across multiple scales and sites, geographies and flows. Min Jin (MJ) Kook's work (see pp. 39–42) used multi-scale animations and scenario-based projections to creatively reimagine the fluxing conditions of urban risk-mitigation infrastructures when hybridized with a public program. Yangchuan (Niko) Tian's work (see pp. 51–54) revisited non-urban infrastructures in a not-so-distant future where obsolete oil rigs are repurposed as a transcalar network of ecological hubs.

The last group tackled the difficult and contested topic of housing. In the context of a global pandemic, an unprecedented ecological crisis, and an extended qualitative (and quantitative) deficit of housing, they investigated alternative forms of collective housing, revisiting historical typologies or sites. For instance, Elizabeth Parker's work (see pp. 47–50) recalls the almost forgotten typology of the "single residency occupancy" (SRO) as a starting point, providing a new typology of mixed-income housing that prevents the marginalization of any resident. Using the Cabrini-Green housing development in Chicago as a test site, Anya Drozd's work (see pp. 31–34) visualizes and spatializes, at multiple scales, how a new urban model of autonomous consumption, less dependent on far-flung resources, can inform prescriptive public policies and decision-makers to foster alternative ecological housing developments.

Together, the work in the Directed Research path presents architecture's role in engaging meaningfully with urgent socio-ecological problems. It demonstrates that every design is an opportunity to create mutually reinforcing feedback loops across scales—between the object of design and the broader territories that support them

Ece Cetin (B.Arch)

Critically Reimagining the Overt: Mediating Architectural Relationships

Mediating spatial, material, and programmatic relationships creates cohesion between the interior and exterior of large-scale development towers.

Continuous strands of commodification: One Times Square, New York City

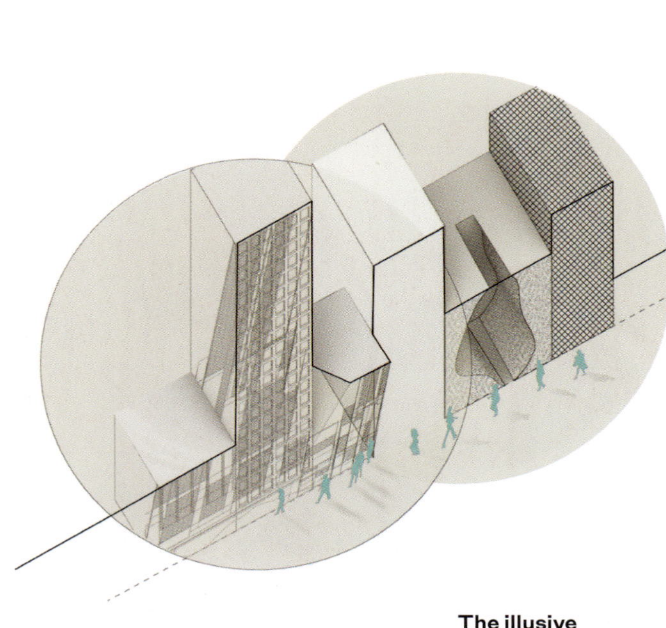

The illusive urban spectacle of diversity, axonometric

Farshid Moussavi argues for the multiplicity of architecture as an expression of diversity, showcasing through her material and formal operations a building's plurality and mutability.[1] Where Moussavi confronts the physical form of architecture, sociologist Richard Sennett connects the form to its social and economic implications. Recalling what critic Ada Louise Huxtable called "skin architecture"—slick urban façades covering neutral, standardized, and banal innards—Sennett sees a manifestation of "flexible capitalism" that is superficial, short-term, and disengaged from the city and the workplace.[2] My project engages Moussavi's material complexities while countering Sennett's noted

1 See Douglas Spencer, *The Architecture of Neoliberalism: How Contemporary Architecture Became an Instrument of Control and Compliance* (London: Bloomsbury Academic, 2018), 141–43.

2 Richard Sennett, "Capitalism and the City," in Stephen Read, et al., *Future City* (London: Routledge, 2005), 119–23.

ng: the Overt: Mediati

It is not as if the false facades are "hiding" anything or acting as a screen to prevent us from seeing that there is nothing behind them. We know inside is different from outside; it announces that in a very straightforward manner.

Vinegar, Aaron. Ducks, Decorated Sheds and Other Minds 85

Aron Vinegar

Architecture can no longer afford to structure itself as an instrument that either reaffirms or resists a single, static idea of culture.

Moussavi Farshid. Function of Form

Farshid Moussavi

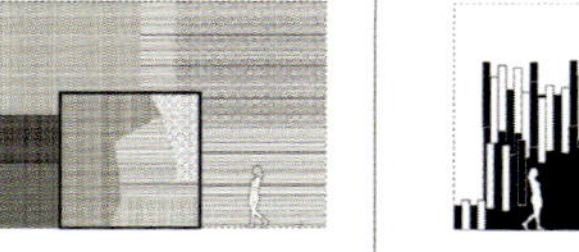

(...)And the larger the envelope becomes, the more sophisticated the interface has to be to guarantee an appropriate level of mix in the population of the envelope.

Polo, Alejandro Zaera. Politics of the Envelope pg 76-105

Alejandro Zaera-Polo

In western architecture there has been a humanistic assumption that it is desirable to establish a moral relationship between interior and exterior(..) The honest facade speaks about the activities it conceals. The humanist expectation of honesty is doomed and the interior and exterior architectures become separate projects.

Koolhaas, Rem. S,M,L,XL 1995, 501.

Rem Koolhaas

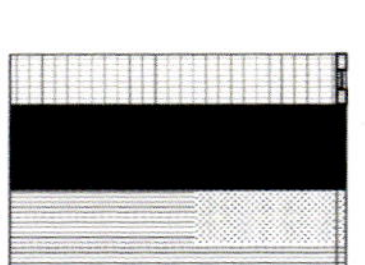

This is why the style elements of new-economy buildings become what US architectural critic Ada Louise Huxtable calls "skin architecture": the surface of the building dolled-up with design, its innards ever more neutral, standard, and capable of instant refiguration. (...)standardisation breeds indifference.

Sennett, Richard. Skin Architecture

Richard Sennett

There is always a struggle to be overcome or smoothed over in the implementation of neoliberalism, an antagonism to be supressed or turned into fuel for systemic optimization. The architecture of neoliberalism cannot openly acknowledge (...) Its rhetoric denounces the very thought of them and its appearance is bent on their dissolution within its smooth surfaces and fluid forms.

Spencer, Douglas. the Architecture of Neoliberalism 162.

Douglas Spencer

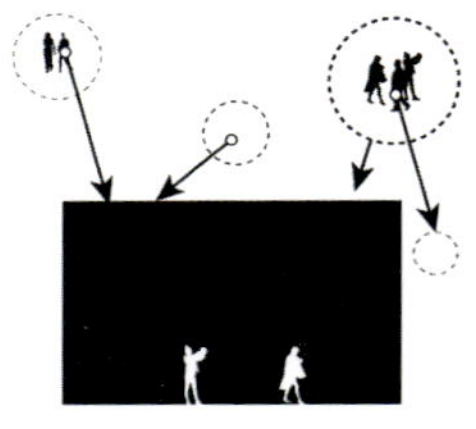

Translucent mesh as conceptualized transparency: Federal Building, San Francisco

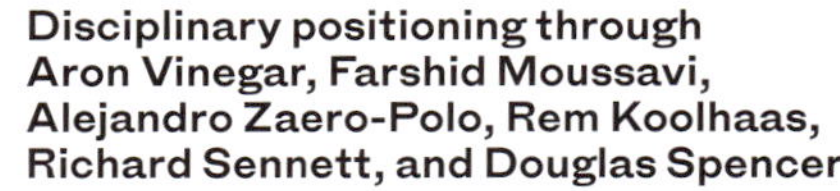

Disciplinary positioning through Aron Vinegar, Farshid Moussavi, Alejandro Zaero-Polo, Rem Koolhaas, Richard Sennett, and Douglas Spencer

A response to capital homogeneity in New York City, plan oblique

Response to green commodification at Maslak No. 1 Office Tower

sterility, merging the interior experience with the exterior presence.

Istanbul's Maslak No. 1 Office Tower by Emre Arolat Architecture explicates the inverted ethos of designers: much of the budget was allocated to its iconic façade while minimized assets were spent on the interior. Its exaggerated exteriority expresses notions of greenness, without actualized sustainability, whereas the office interiors are standardized and routine, lacking any greenery. In my design response, I added a new focal garden, accentuated by a shear wall, as a performative green space, and realigned the project by interweaving greenspace between exterior and interior, composing the entirety of the site as a greenhouse.

Salesforce Tower, designed by Pelli Clarke Pelli Architects in San Francisco, argues for openness and transparency. Yet its curtain wall simply wraps the office buildings with a homogenous layer, becoming generic and standardized on the interior. My response implements a perpendicular axis, cutting through the singular volume to provide programmatic overlap and views while enhancing daylight and more idiosyncratic spatial conditions.

The American Copper Buildings, designed by SHoP in New York City, reflect the capitalist homogeneity of materiality in the over-developed metropolis. It overwhelms a waterfront

Response to staged openness at Salesforce Tower

Interior rendering: American Copper Buildings

Reimagined communal space in the American Copper Buildings; redesign (top), existing (bottom)

Layers of design in New York: American Copper Buildings; existing (top), redesign (bottom)

Layers of design in Istanbul: Maslak No. 1 Office Tower; existing (top), redesign (bottom)

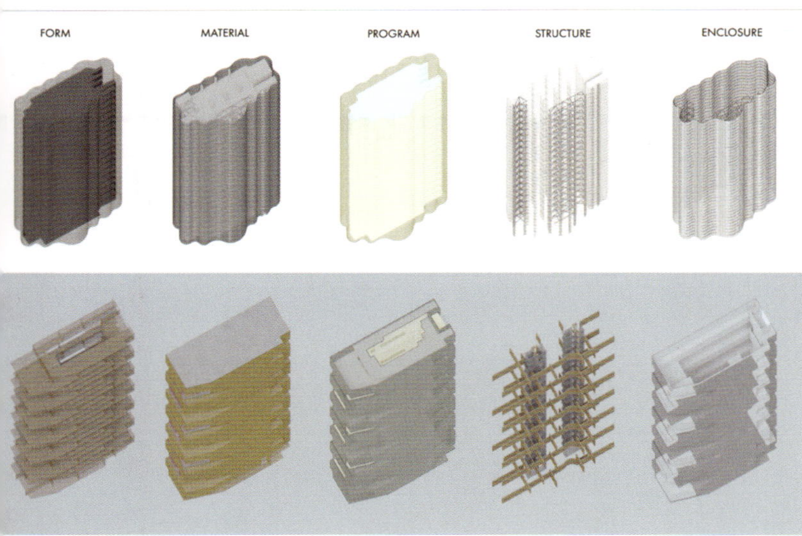

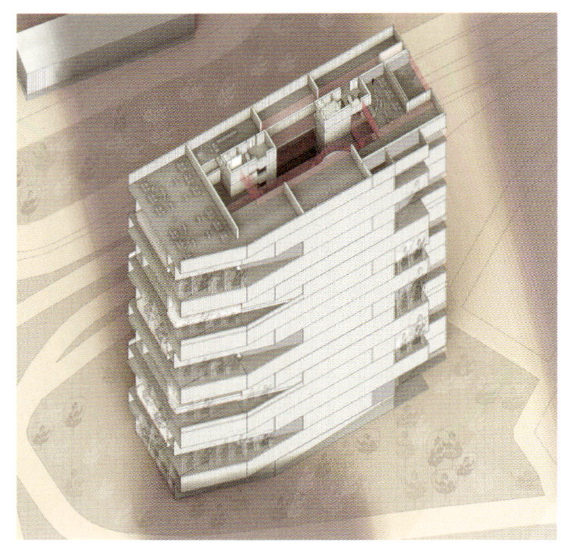

A response to green commodification in Istanbul, plan oblique

Reimagined workspace at Maslak No. 1 Office Tower: redesign (top), existing (bottom)

that is home to both the subsidized housing of Peter Cooper Village and the United Nations Headquarters. Rather than compete with the urban fabric of the city, I reengage the public in a privately owned tower, creating an elevated pedestrian street that interweaves the two buildings.

The commodification of greenspace in Istanbul, staged openness in San Francisco, and capital homogeneity in New York City sew a common thread through how architects prioritize exteriority. My thesis interrupts the cliché of image-making to reengage interiority as a platform for a design ethos. I expand the visual expression for each case study to integrate exterior arguments into interior spaces, inverting the contemporary culture in which image consumption has made the superficial "skin" of architecture all the more apparent.

Interior rendering: Maslak No. 1 Office Tower

ececetin.com

Interior rendering: Salesforce Tower

A response to staged openness in San Francisco, plan oblique

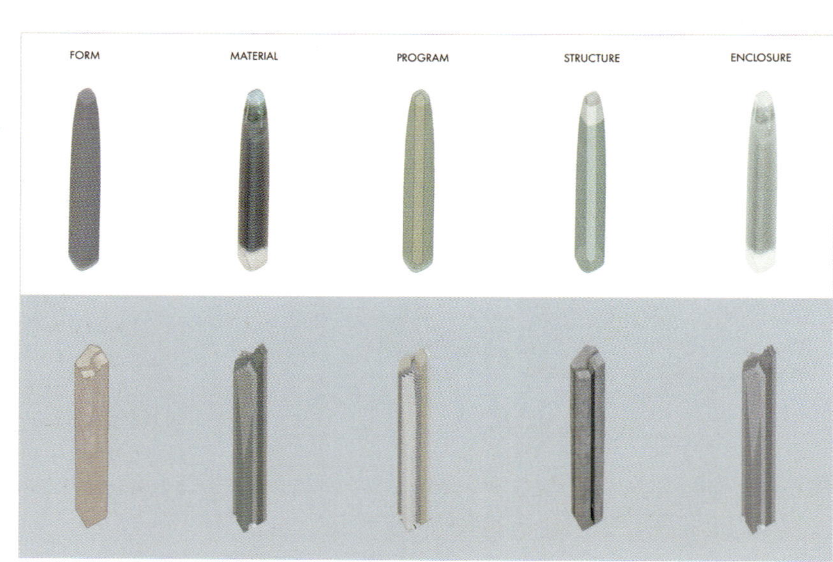

Layers of design in San Francisco: Salesforce Tower; existing (top), redesign (bottom)

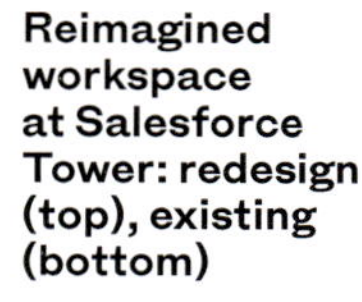

Reimagined workspace at Salesforce Tower: redesign (top), existing (bottom)

Anya Drozd (B.Arch)

Section of low-density housing

Sustainable Public Housing: Breaking the Barriers Between Consumption, Production, and Living

By reframing a model of consumption, a new public housing agenda creates a microcosm of autonomy and sustainability.

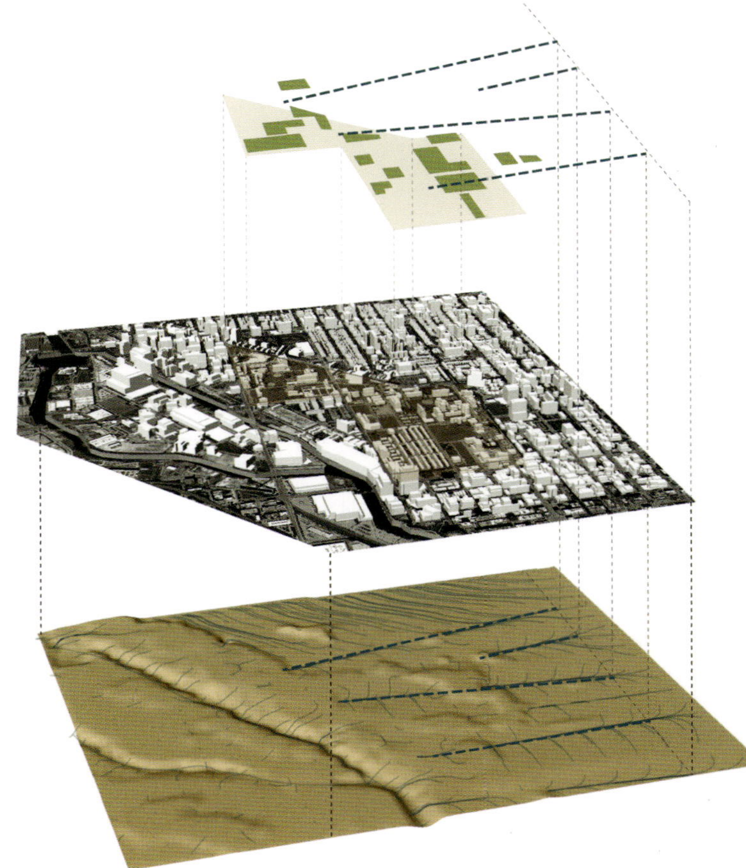

Hydrolysis analysis

Cities typically rely on black-boxed resource management systems that are relegated to the hinterlands, blinding us to cycles of production, consumption, and waste. My thesis tests an alternative model that uses public housing as a framework for redevelopment and for a new type of neighborhood that emphasizes autonomy and ownership among its residents.

Historically, public housing has failed in many ways. Consider Cabrini-Green in Chicago and Pruitt-Igoe in St. Louis, Missouri: large swaths of vacant land developed only to be beset by government neglect and public disdain. But we do not need to fall back on these antiquated models of public housing to deal with the ballooning housing crisis; there are myriad case studies pointing architects, developers, and governments to an ethos of sustainability and community-engaged housing. Projects like Alejandro Aravena's Quinta Monroy and Herold by Jakob + MacFarlane in France give residents

Exterior rendering of high-density housing and social aspect

Rendering of electricity hub in high-density housing

Section of high-density housing

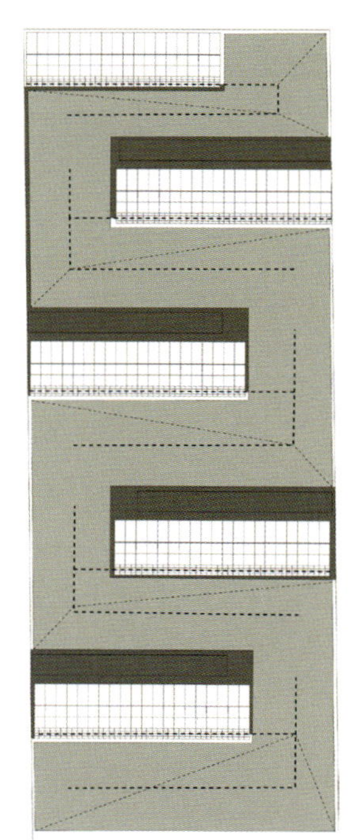

Diagram of low-density housing and agricultural fields

Rendering of agricultural fields

programmed greenspace and a sense of ownership. Copenhagen and many German cities use photovoltaic (PV) panels on their housing projects. Ontario and Seattle use natural topography to filter their rivers and rainwater runoff.

I chose the former site of Cabrini-Green as a space to reimagine large-scale public housing. The new Cabrini-Green collapses our complex living systems by producing and consuming resources on site. Eliminating the gap between production and consumption, each plot generates, stores, and provides energy. Every building collects, filters, and distributes clean water. Each resident grows, harvests, and shares food. With each scalar shift, every housing typology is tasked with a unique function to generate a resource for the community. At the macro scale, high-density housing uses a large collective greenhouse to pool resources for industrialized farming. Internally, each unit connects directly to this resource, with residents offering their labor to reduce rent, or apprenticing as an electrician, for example. The self-generating system creates jobs for community members.

A design for autonomy and economic and environmental sustainability, my project is not definitive or complete. It co-opts the preexisting housing system and rectifies its failures, showing one possible answer to the interwoven crises of our generation.

Site-specific systems diagram

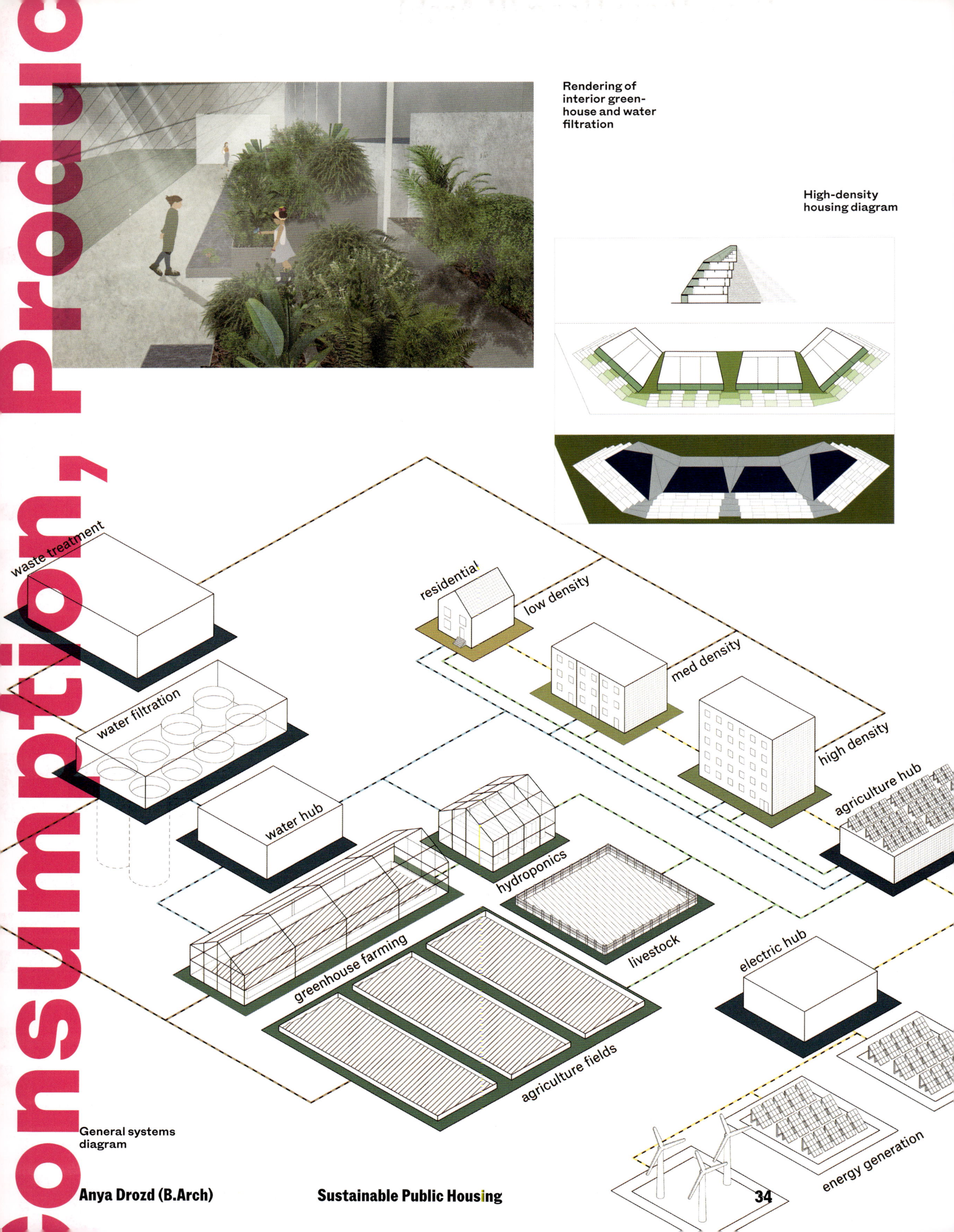

Rendering of interior green-house and water filtration

High-density housing diagram

General systems diagram

Sung Hyun Hong (B.Arch)

Subtractive Building

Illustration and color guide of precedents

Subtractive Building: Design for Deconstruction Redux

Subtractive Building: Design for Deconstruction Redux Subtractive Building responds to waste overload, employing a visual stratagem for new design methodologies that promote disassembly versus demolition.

Catalog of Subtractive Building

Buildings are commodities. Instant architecture favors economic gains over rigorous design, producing dull, repetitive forms. Efficiency provides certain economic gains but fails buildings in ways that live beyond their functional use. The failings of contemporary construction create strife for the undervalued architect, but more importantly, they negatively affect the environment. From renovations to demolitions, buildings will go through many life changes, generating and ultimately becoming debris. Construction debris pollutes the air, wastes energy, and is the largest contributor to landfills. While construction-disposal facilities and specialized landfills exist, they are rarely used due to the high expense. In an industry dominated by profits, this excess expense is worthless. Subtractive Building prevents this problem. Foreseeing the inevitable demolition of buildings, it designs for disassembly.

Subtractive Building draws from an existing method, Design for Deconstruction, otherwise known as DFD, which also bridges instant and conceptually rigorous architecture. Acknowledging the fact that buildings are impermanent, DFD principles design for disassembly and materials reuse. My research expands on DFD to further existing buildings' capacity for multiple lifelines. I identified three case studies: two using DFD principles through small, critical interventions, and one that expands beyond DFD to birth new life into the building over time. These three projects use various materials to establish the disciplinary advantage of each

Gordon Matta-Clark's ***Conical Intersect***

Gordon Matta-Clark's ***Splitting***

Subtractive Building in Hemeroscopium House

SUBTRACTIVE BUILDS

CATALOGUE OF CONFIGURATIONS
HEMEROSCOPIUM HOUSE 50%-100%

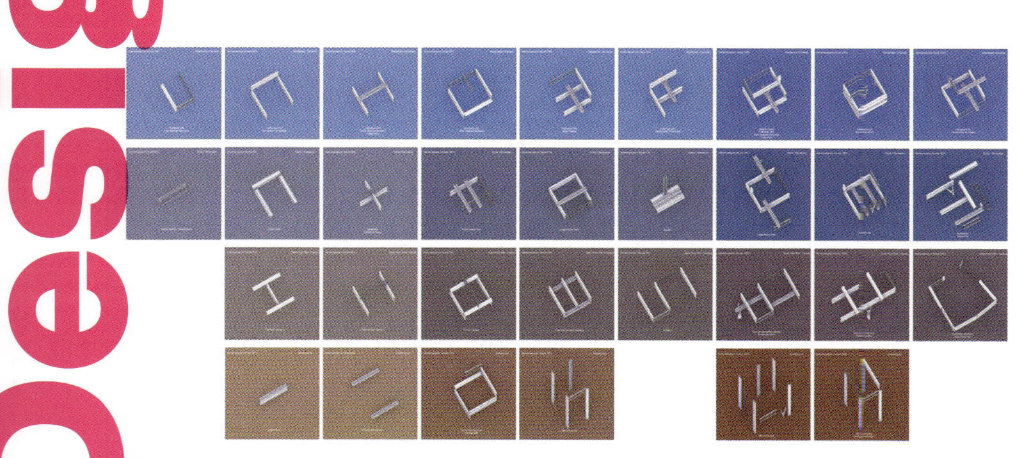

The Hemeroscopium house from 50% of its materials to 100% of its materials. Scenarios such as economic struggles or environmental hazards can account for material damages.and that ultimately can lead to material decrease over time.

SUBTRACTIVE BUILDS

CATALOGUE OF CONFIGURATIONS
HEMEROSCOPIUM HOUSE 200%-500%

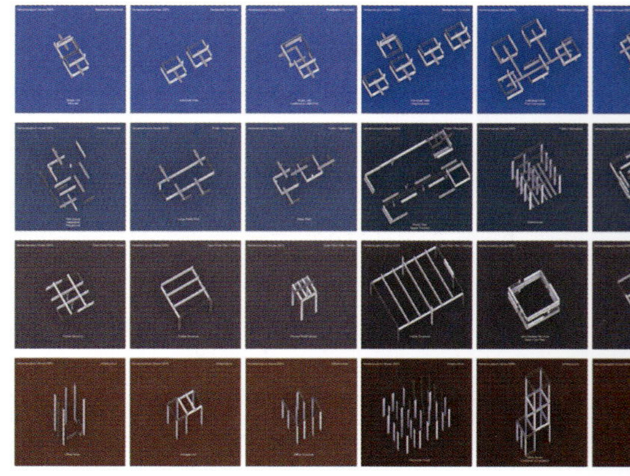

This set looks at a more positive trend towards growth, or the utopian future, with material gains of 200 and 500%. The become more community oriented as more materials become available that can be interchanged and reused among on

UBTRACTIVE BUILDS

CATALOGUE OF CONFIGURATIONS
FINAL WOODEN HOUSE 50%-100%

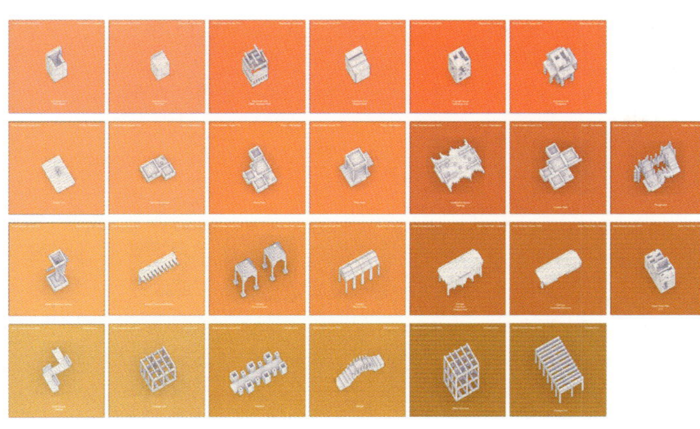

Final Wooden House from 50% to 100%. With the materials being much smaller, new possibilities for design is possible. For one thing, more detailed shear layers such as the furniture, or stuff, can be designed for.

SUBTRACTIVE BUILDS

CATALOGUE OF CONFIGURATIONS
FINAL WOODEN HOUSE 200%-500%

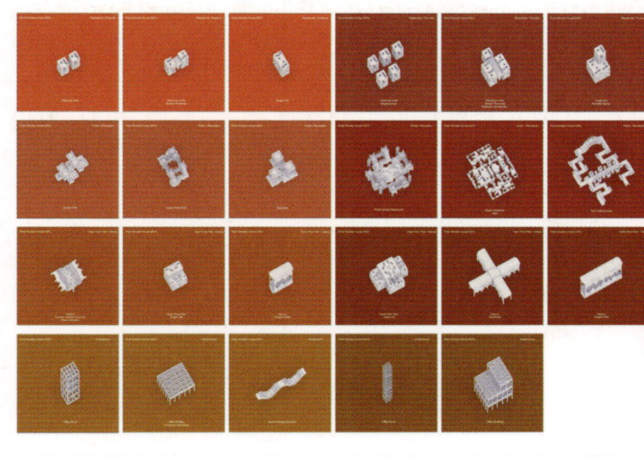

From 200 to 500%, the designs become much larger and zoomed out. The final wooden house is much more reliable in its ability to interchange, as they can be moved by manpower alone. As a result, easy and frequent interchangeability is much more sought out in these designs

Subtractive Building in Wooden House

BTRACTIVE BUILDS

CATALOGUE OF CONFIGURATIONS
LOBLOLLY HOUSE 50%-100%

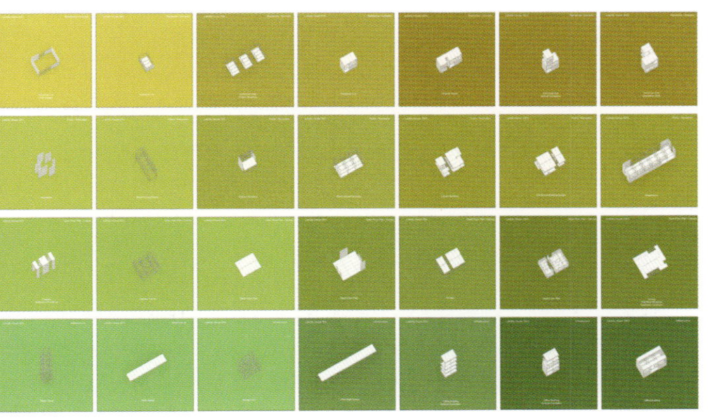

The Loblolly House designs were extremely limited due to the nature of prefabrication being very specific to the original house design. As a result, it was at 50% to 75% of materials, when certain pieces can be removed, that showed much more possible design choices.

SUBTRACTIVE BUILDS

CATALOGUE OF CONFIGURATIONS
LOBLOLLY HOUSE 200%-500%

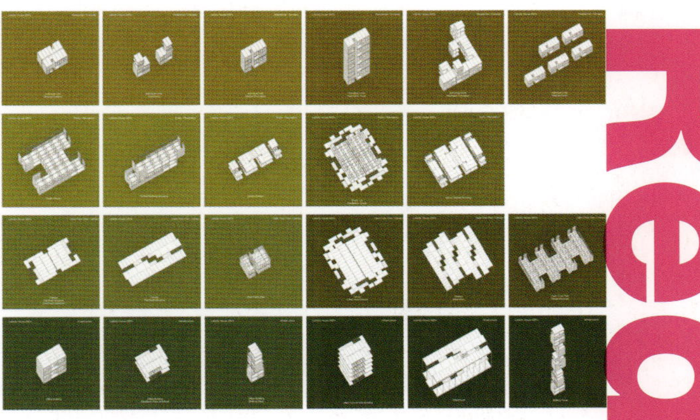

The large prefab pieces in the Loblolly and Hemeroscopium House instinctively seems to visually manifest itself for their original use, making it difficult to radically redesign for different general programs. As for the Loblolly House, it's pieces seems to orient itself towards being a building, rather than other structures.

Subtractive Building in Loblolly House

typology. Moreover, due to the transformative nature of DFD, construction and space allocation becomes especially flexible, allowing for scenario-based designs. This research developed into a catalog of transient moments for future building projects.

Subtractive Building reinforces that buildings are not static; they need to be in flux. Designed for disassembly, Subtractive Building activates material reconfiguration and redesign potential so that even external realities beyond the physical presence of the building can be accommodated. This scenario-based visual guide counters the generic and open floor plans of instant architecture. It offers a set of design principles that challenge disciplinary norms with a comprehensive approach to building for the future. Paradoxically, this approach advocates for building permanence through perpetual change.

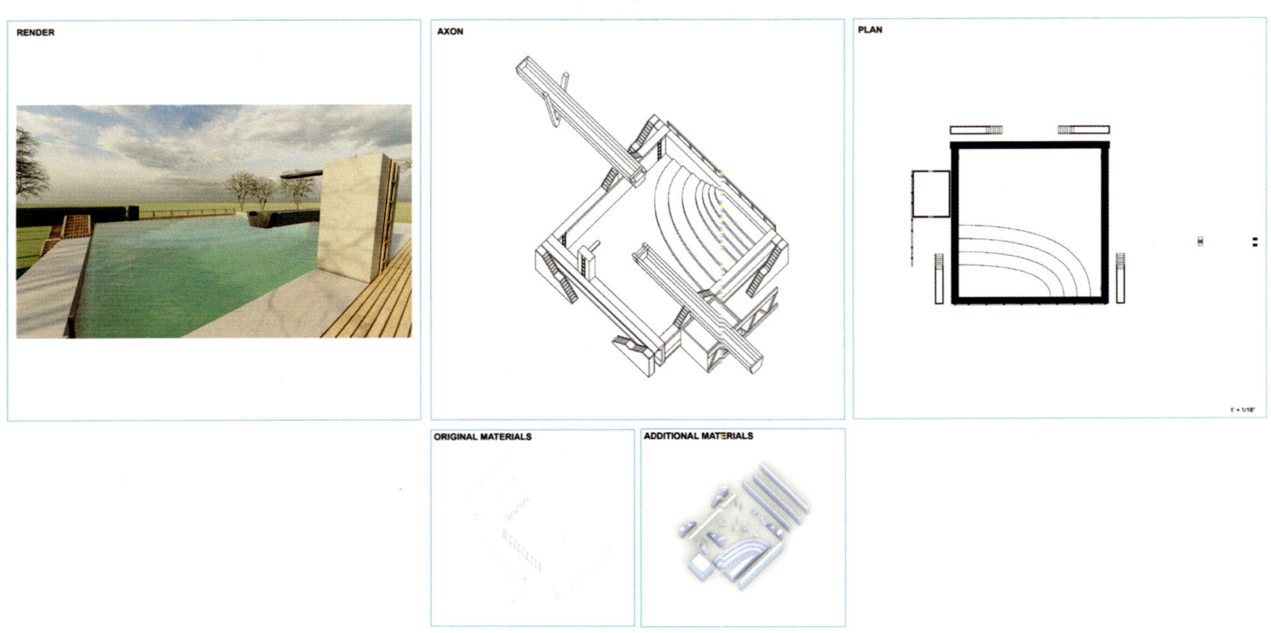

ORIGINAL MATERIALS

ADDITIONAL MATERIALS

Hemero-
scopium
House as a
public pool

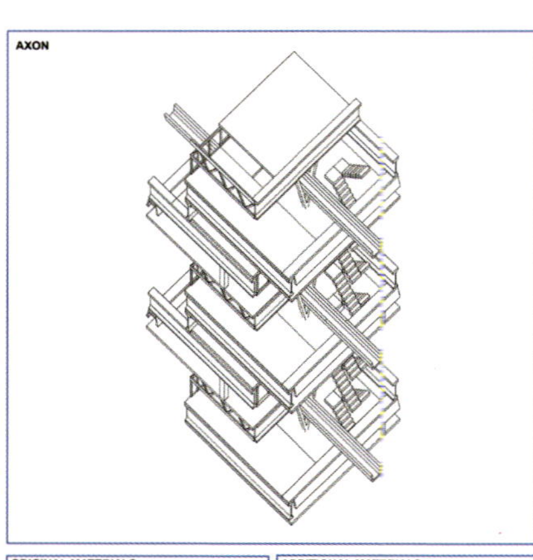

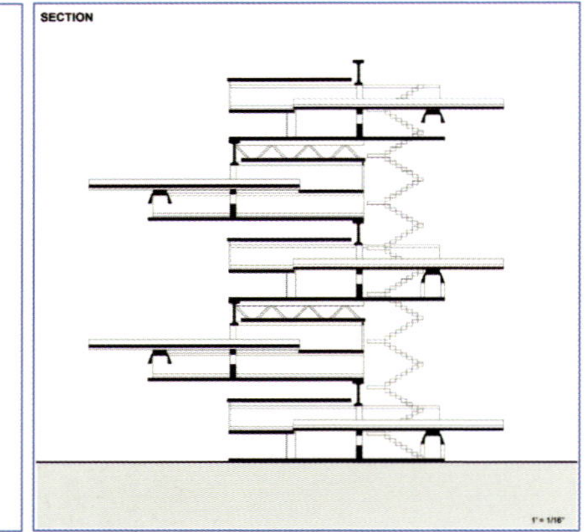

ORIGINAL MATERIALS

ADDITIONAL MATERIALS

= ORIGINAL MATERIALS x4

Hemero-
scopium
House as an
office tower

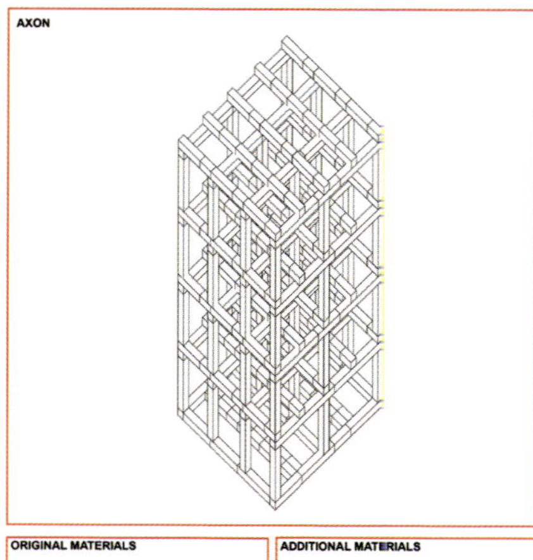

ORIGINAL MATERIALS

ADDITIONAL MATERIALS

= ORIGINAL MATERIALS

Wooden
House as a
wooden tower

Min Jin (MJ) Kook (M.Arch)

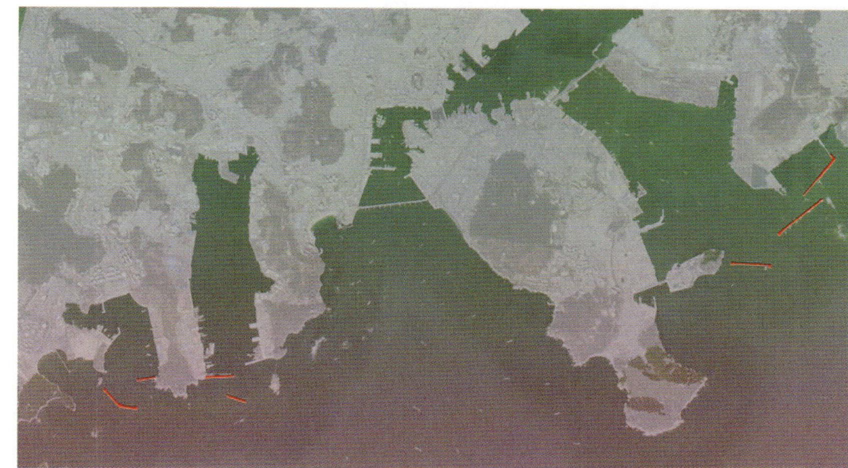

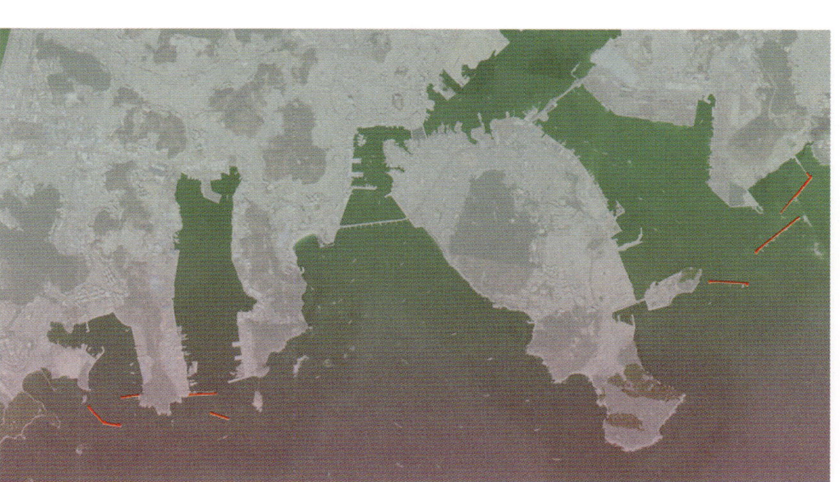

Busan, South Korea: Speculative flows of construction debris. Animation.

Un-Black Boxing Mitigation Infrastructures

Cities' urban mitigation infrastructures—so often invisible, monofunctional, and underutilized—are transformed via experiential animations into rejuvenating speculative designs.

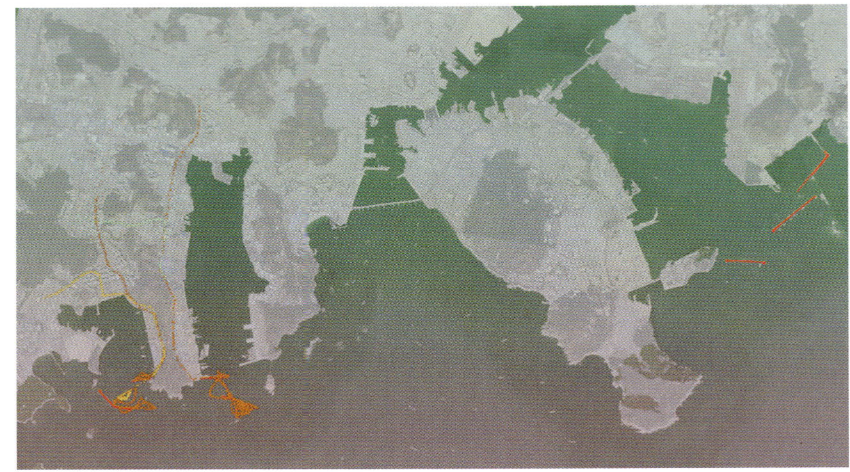

Modern architecture commonly minimizes the visibility of built systems. Utilitarian activities are black-boxed, hidden away in basements and corners, out of sight, sterile. At the urban scale, modern mitigation systems—underground retention tanks, seawalls, and hurricane barriers, for example—are mostly monofunctional, overlooked, or abandoned.

Andrés Jaque's 2012–13 exhibition *PHANTOM. Mies as Rendered Society* exposes the hidden, ordinary systems in Mies van der Rohe's Barcelona Pavilion, where cleaning and other necessary activities of architectural maintenance are hidden in the basement, away from visitors' views.[1] Inspired by this model, I investigated three geographically distinct case studies in sequestering water mitigation structures: the Barcelona underground retention tank in Spain; the LA River channel in the U.S.; and the Busan wave barriers in South Korea. Each operates at the sublime scale of the city, and each has the potential to expand further into systemic, accessible, multifunctional infrastructures.

Using alternative representational techniques—animations, experiential vignettes,

1 Andrés Jaque, *PHANTOM. Mies as Rendered Society*, https://officeforpoliticalinnovation.com/work/phantom-mies-as-rendered-society/, accessed June 24, 2020.

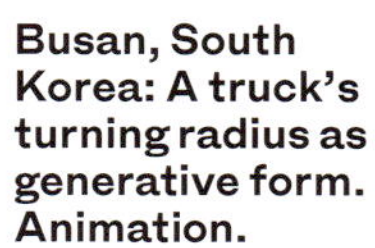

Busan, South Korea: A truck's turning radius as generative form. Animation.

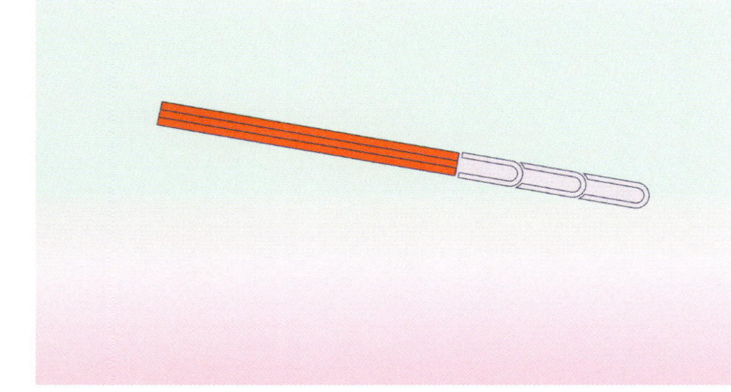

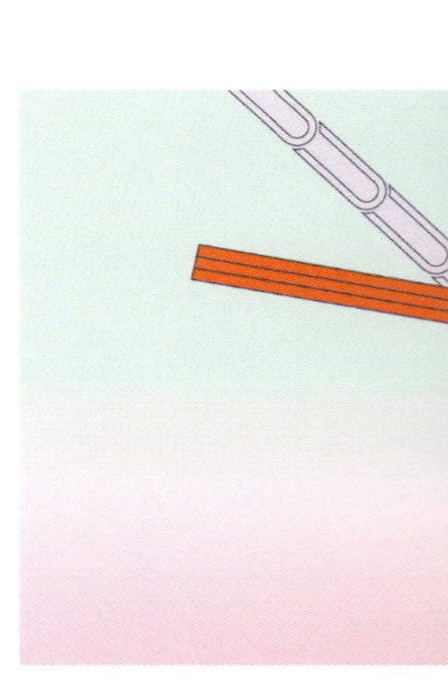

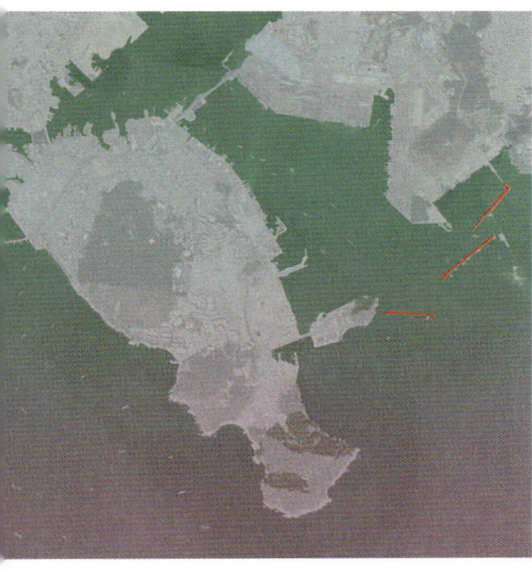

2 Busan Animation A: Metabolic Flows of Construction Debris

Busan Animation B: Turning Radius of Construction Trucks

Busan Animation A: New Debris Landscape

and catalogs—my work bridges contemporary disciplinary frameworks with architectural representation, bearing witness to an urban metabolism that compounds change and renewal. For the Busan case study, for example, I created a series of animations depicting a design solution for the city, in which seven million tons of construction debris are deposited on the coast to showcase a latent system of the city.[2] Animations A show metabolic flows of construction debris at the urban scale; Animation B presents the turning radius of construction trucks. Instead of depositing the construction debris in a landfill, the trucks deposit it on the coastline of Busan for a new ecological park. The experiential vignette shows the visual frames that embody the reimagined life cycle of the city's construction debris, from construction to demolition to reuse.

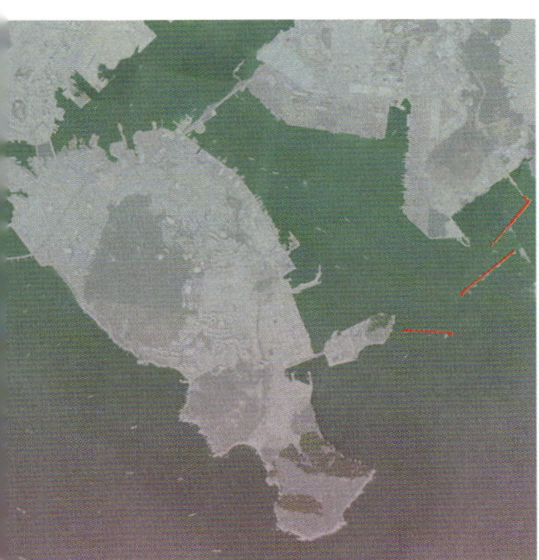

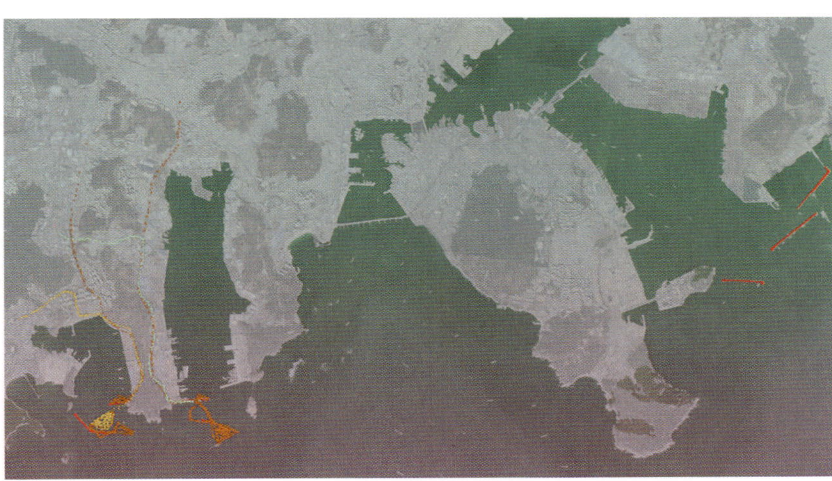

Busan, South Korea: Speculative flows of construction debris. Animation.

Los Angeles Urban Flow Condenser

Barcelona Metabolic Machine:

Los Angeles Phase Diagram

My experimental representational techniques helped me identify speculative design interventions to reveal existing infrastructures, and to understand the urban metabolism as the orchestration of continuous urban interventions. Upending the modernist zeal for concealment, the disciplinary contribution of each visualization more broadly emphasizes architecture as scenario building translated into multiple scales.

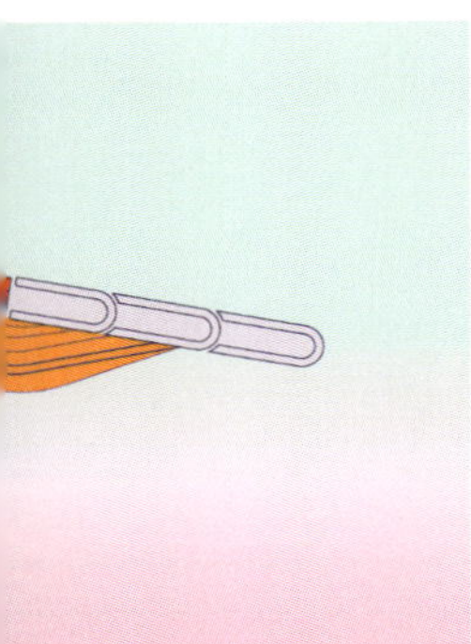

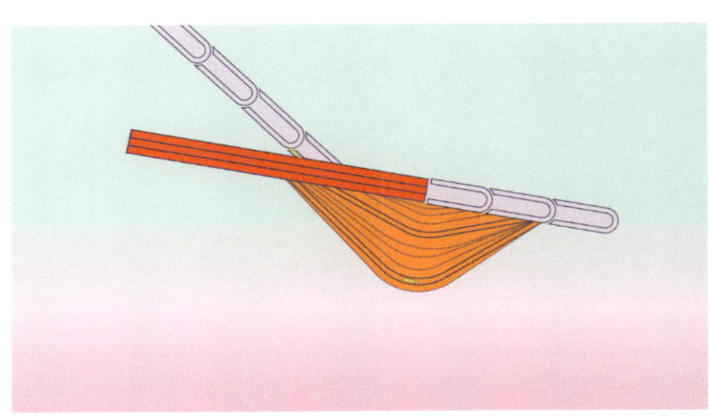

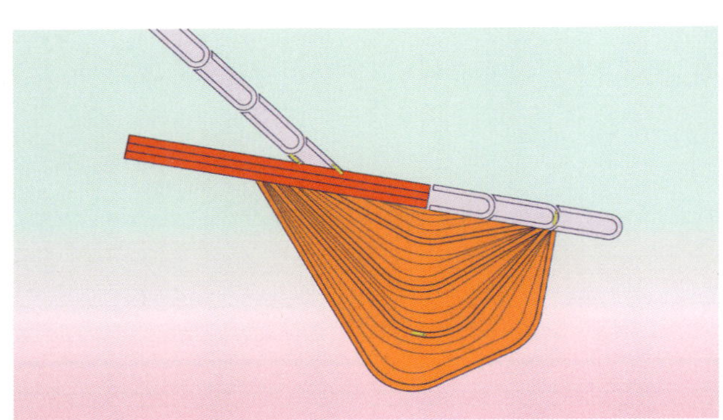

Busan, South Korea: The life cycle of construction debris. Experiential vignette.

Busan, South Korea: Extensions of the city. Experiential vignette.

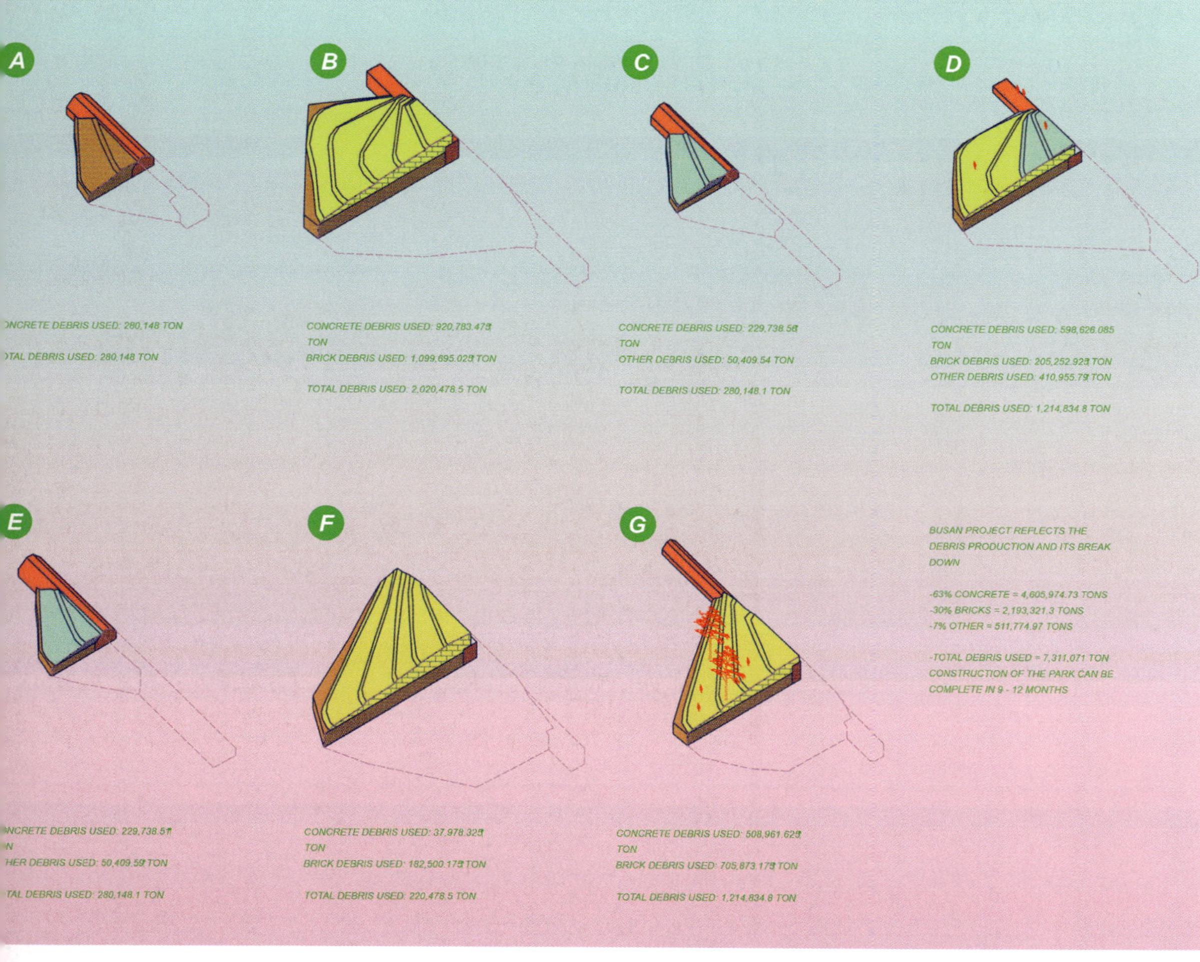

Busan, South Korea: Construction debris collection. Catalog.

Infill sites: market, perspective

Infill sites: market, isometric

Adaptive Reuse: A Pattern Book A new pattern book emphasizes rebuilding, reuse, and community reeducation as solutions to the problem of vacancy in Baltimore's rowhouses.

Architectural pattern books are historically used as a tool for disseminating building practices. They typically inform new construction projects, neglecting the potential for adaptive reuse and working with existing conditions. My research provides a new type of pattern book: a tool for repurposing buildings and challenging the tropes of capitalism associated with construction.

Baltimore, like many postindustrial cities, is filled with vacant lots. Its blocks of rowhouses speak to a history of development and misuse, symptoms of systemic racism, white flight, and a decline in manufacturing jobs due to globalization. Inherent to rowhouses are shared walls and continuous façades, which when subject to decay compromise the

1100 N. Carrollton Ave., Baltimore, MD, from Google Maps

Façade sites: material library, perspective

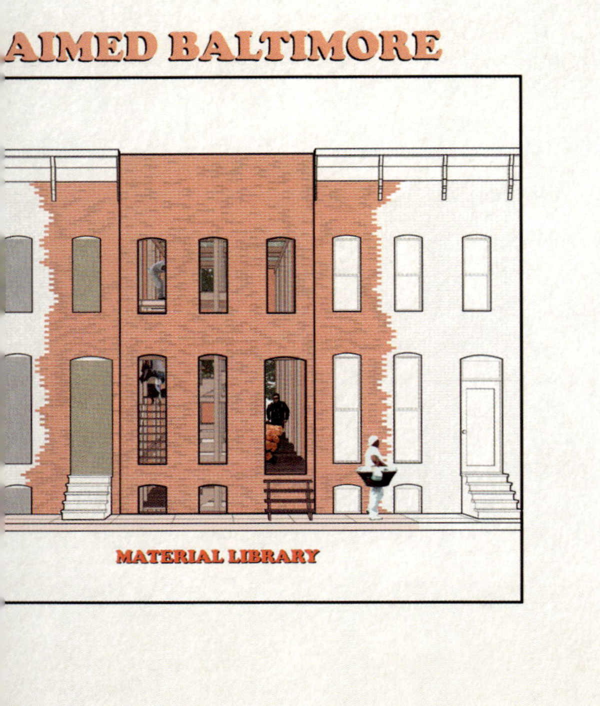

continuity of adjoining properties. When a form is repeated at such a large scale, the gaps in façades, fallen roofs, and plywood doors drastically shift the perception of the built environment. With about 16,000 vacant properties (mostly rowhouses), Baltimore presents an opportunity to reverse this decline and instead reconcile its neglected, decaying architecture.[1]

My pattern book democratizes redevelopment and focuses on reclaiming space for the existing community through strategies intended to create circular economies that resist gentrification. In vacant lots, a residential space becomes a greenhouse for plant production. Infill lots between two rowhouses become local markets selling produce and community-made goods. Sites with only a façade remaining are rebuilt as a simple shed-like material library. The library collects building materials from abandoned houses and stores them for future renovation and repair projects. When the rowhouse is just a shell, it provides a space for community workshops on how to preserve materials instead of demolishing and building anew. Each intervention relies on the existing spatial capital of the community and aims to support economic growth and a sustainable future. It inverts the logic of capitalism to subvert a system of oppression.

1 Baltimore City Open Data (2019), *Open Baltimore, Vacant Buildings Data Lens*. Accessed October 1, 2019, https://data.baltimorecity.gov/Housing-Development/Vacant-Buildings/cext-wn76.

Vacancy pattern

attern Book

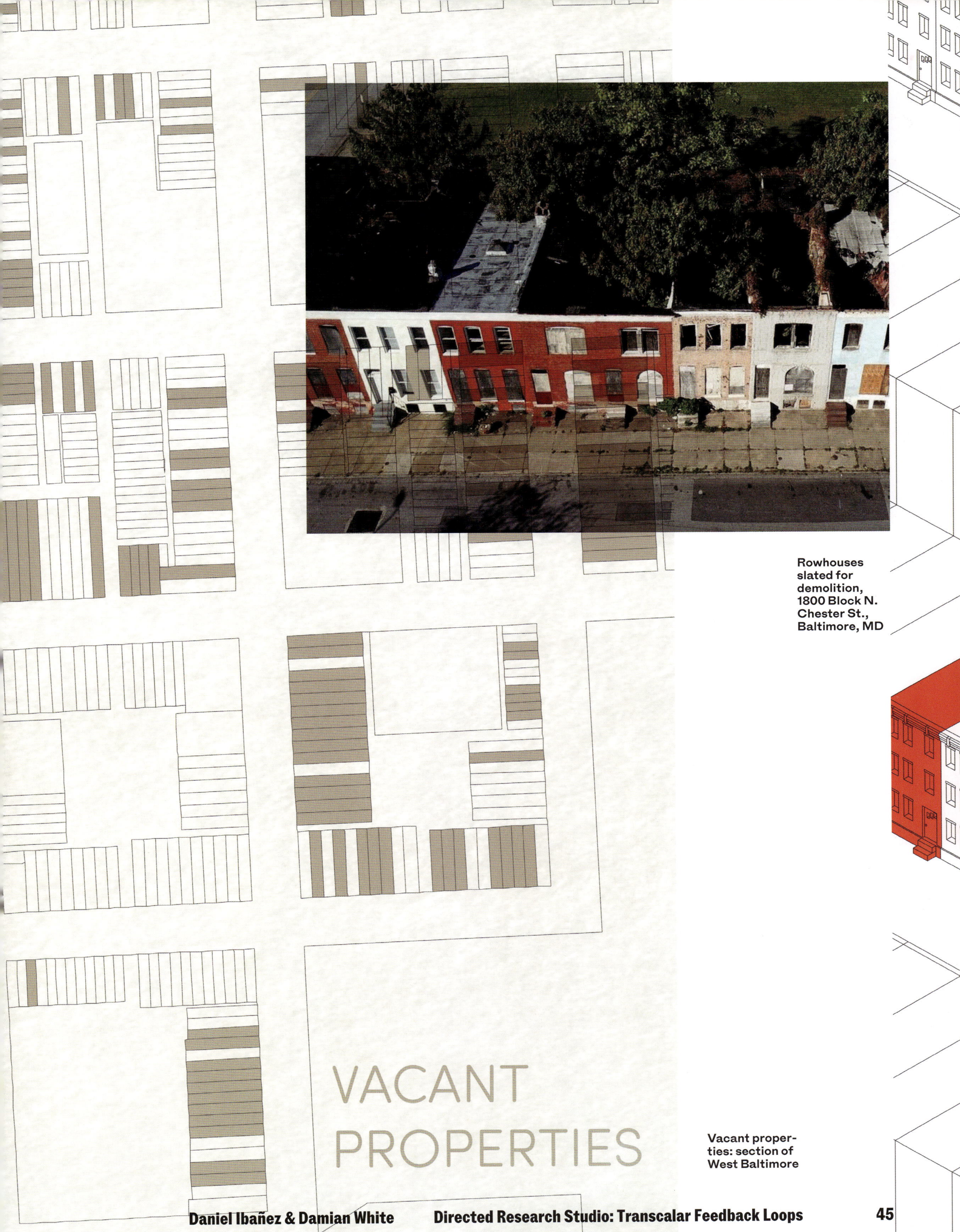

Rowhouses slated for demolition, 1800 Block N. Chester St., Baltimore, MD

VACANT PROPERTIES

Vacant properties: section of West Baltimore

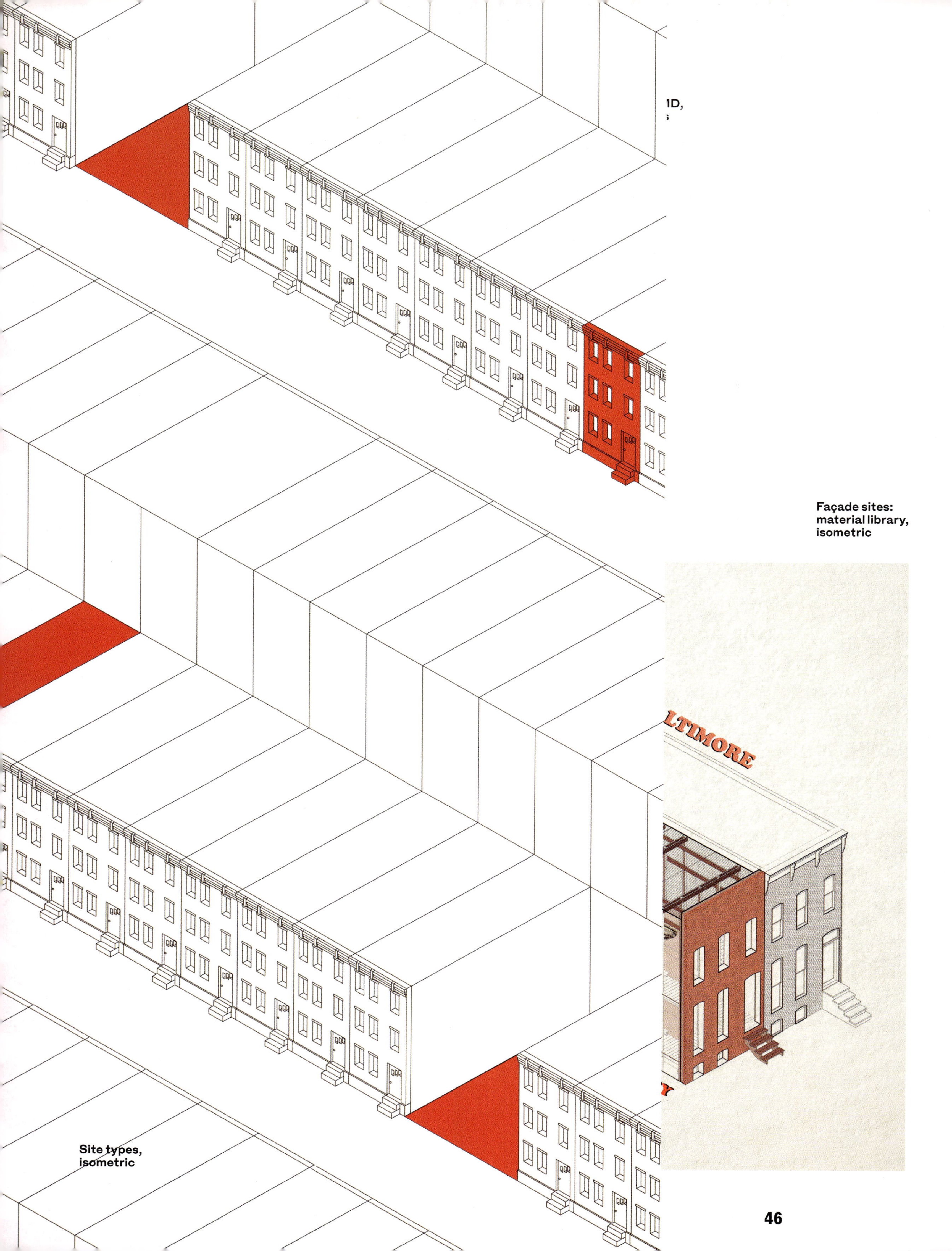

Site types, isometric

Façade sites: material library, isometric

Elizabeth Parker (M.Arch)

Revisiting the SRO: New Forms of Collectivity

An adaptable proto-typology emphasizes a compact, collective design ethos to revitalize Single Room Occupancy (SRO) housing.

View of the community rooftop garden and communal space, plan oblique

The affordable housing crisis is at a boiling point; home prices are increasing at double the rate of wage gains and nearly half of all renters in the U.S. are considered cost-burdened. We cannot keep up with the increasing demand for affordable housing as people are priced out and displaced. Reversing this harmful trend is vital to maintaining the diversity of our cities. My project approaches this issue by reimagining the Single Room Occupancy (SRO) hotel as a housing typology that blends efficiency and minimalism with aspects of collective living to create a new, inclusive model for community and affordability, privileging tenants over developers.

The recent 80/20 mixed-income housing program introduced in New York City offers incentives to developers in exchange for making 20 percent of units in new projects affordable (or below market rate). While this effort to reintroduce affordable housing in urban environments provides some hope, it does not effectively address the overwhelming issues of our cities. My project seeks to decommodify housing by inverting this model, pushing for 20 percent of market-rate units to subsidize the remaining 80 percent of affordable units.

View of the amphitheater and communal outdoor spaces, plan oblique

Flexible and adaptable, this new affordable housing model can be implemented in any city, responding to the nature of the place while maintaining the core principles of smallness and togetherness. Selecting Providence, Rhode Island, as a testing ground allowed me to investigate the spatial and social implications of a hybrid housing project in a post-industrial city. Providence's downtown, an area fraught with vacancy, provides an urban condition that lends itself perfectly to this experiment in micro-urbanism.

This new proto-typology aggregates a mixture of programs, uses, and people. Divided into four bands (two residential and two public), the programs weave together a larger circulatory system and strategically located communal spaces. Rather than mixing at random, I privilege each category's innate spatial needs to function independently, while tying them into the symbiotic system. The first public band invites foot traffic into the site while acting as a screen for the more private spaces beyond. The centrally located SROs allow for increased access to all resources, as these units are minimal and need amenities. The second band of public space serves as a landscaped buffer between the two residential bands—a generous backyard rarely found in urban housing. Finally, the larger rowhouse units face the opposite street, a familiar and unassuming typology, with a lower building height to allow southern light to permeate through the site. A series of bridges, or elevated streets, links the bands together to provide a sense of an interconnected community.

My thesis leverages spatial research and design to create a system that provides degrees of development without over-specification. By engaging local specificity and social, political, and ecological consciousness, I create a systematic approach to addressing the broader global issue of affordable housing.

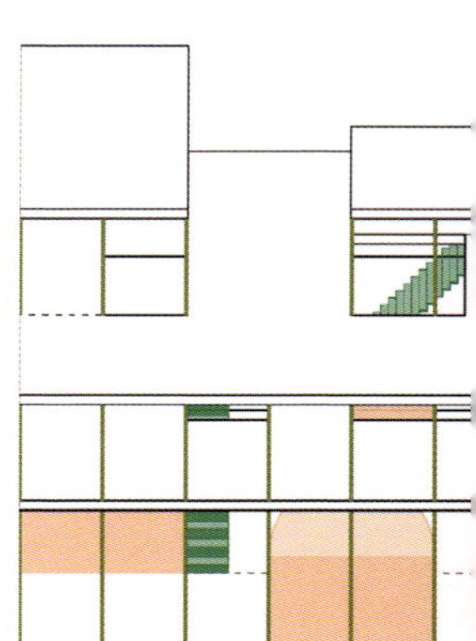

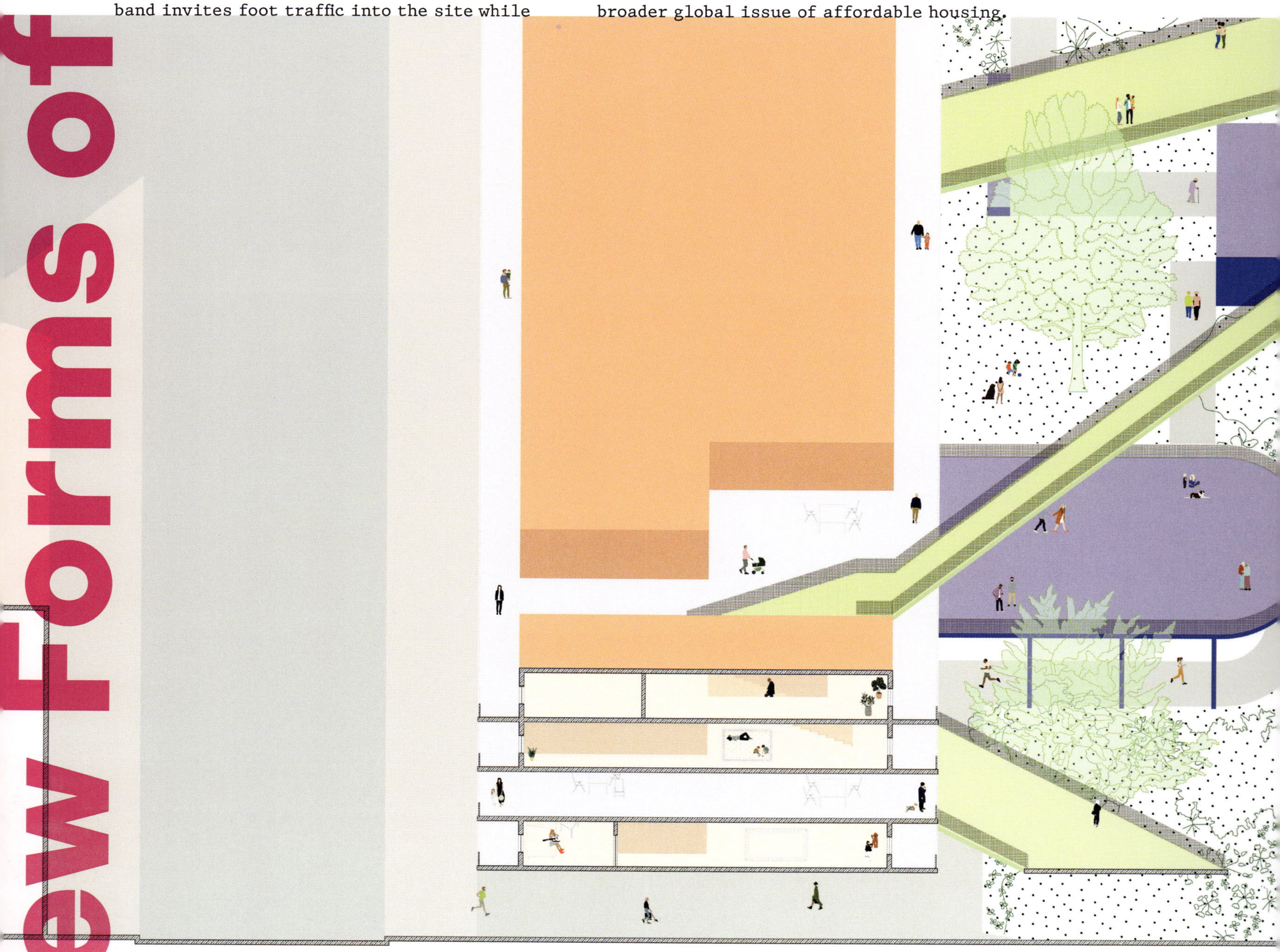

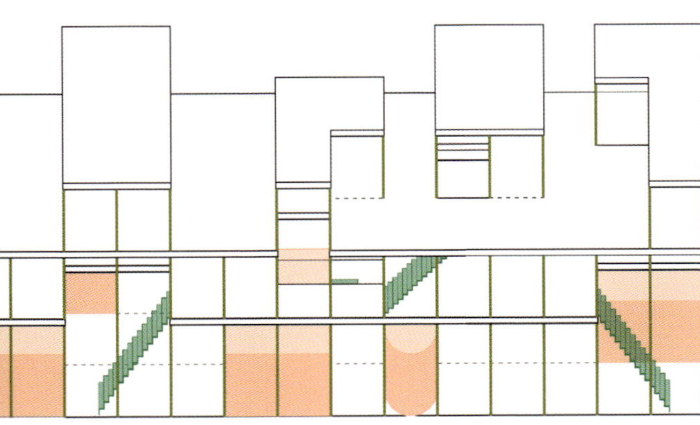

Public band: sectionally striated programming invites pedestrian foot traffic, plan oblique

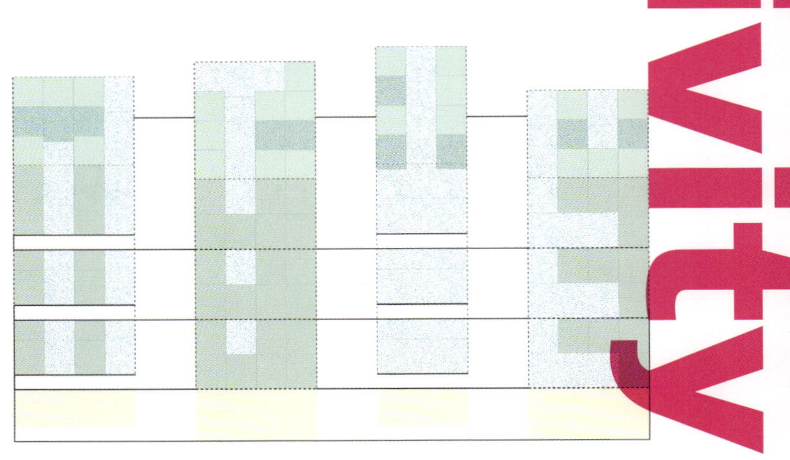

SRO band: individual units cluster together around communal spaces, creating dynamic "micro-communities," plan oblique

The mix of activity collapsed into a single moment, section oblique

Landscape band: a pathway divides variously sized parcels for residents' use, plan oblique

Rowhouse band: the larger, strategically porous residential units allow for communal outdoor use, plan oblique

Banded programs, Providence, plan oblique

Yangchuan (Niko) Tian (M.Arch)

Living on a Rig Island

Living on a Rig Island Decommissioned oil rigs are repurposed for domestic living at sea, saving funds and revitalizing the ocean environment, returning a “dead zone” to life.

The Gulf of Mexico is home to an especially dense field of oil rigs. Built in the 1980s with a 30-year lifespan, almost 60 percent of the rigs will fall out of commission by 2025. This infrastructural obsolescence is accompanied by some of the world’s worst eutrophication, a process by which excessive nutrients contaminate the seawater. The Gulf’s eutrophied “dead zone,” which fills with sewage from inland agriculture running south from Lake Michigan, has become an ecological ruin.

The postindustrial landscape has overrun urban areas, creating a need for a new type of industrial typology. My design proposes converting decommissioned oil rigs into livable spaces—transforming them from oil-extracting structures that increase greenhouse gas emissions into green infrastructures that harvest and filter the ocean using carbon sequestration organisms like kelp forests and oyster reefs. In addition to its environmental focus, my project is informed by progressive political, social, and economic agendas such as the Green New Deal. It envisions a new socio-spatial arrangement for communities, merging landscapes of production (hinterlands) and landscapes of consumption (cities) that are typically separate. By 2025, 400 billion dollars in oil drilling subsidies will be eliminated, and with them the enormous labor, energy, and cost of dismantling these massive structures will grow. This reuse project avoids all of these demolition expenses, ultimately repurposing oil rigs as vital bridges between land and ocean. Every rig platform adapts to a living community itself, yet remains connected to broader economic and environmental networks.

Detailed plan

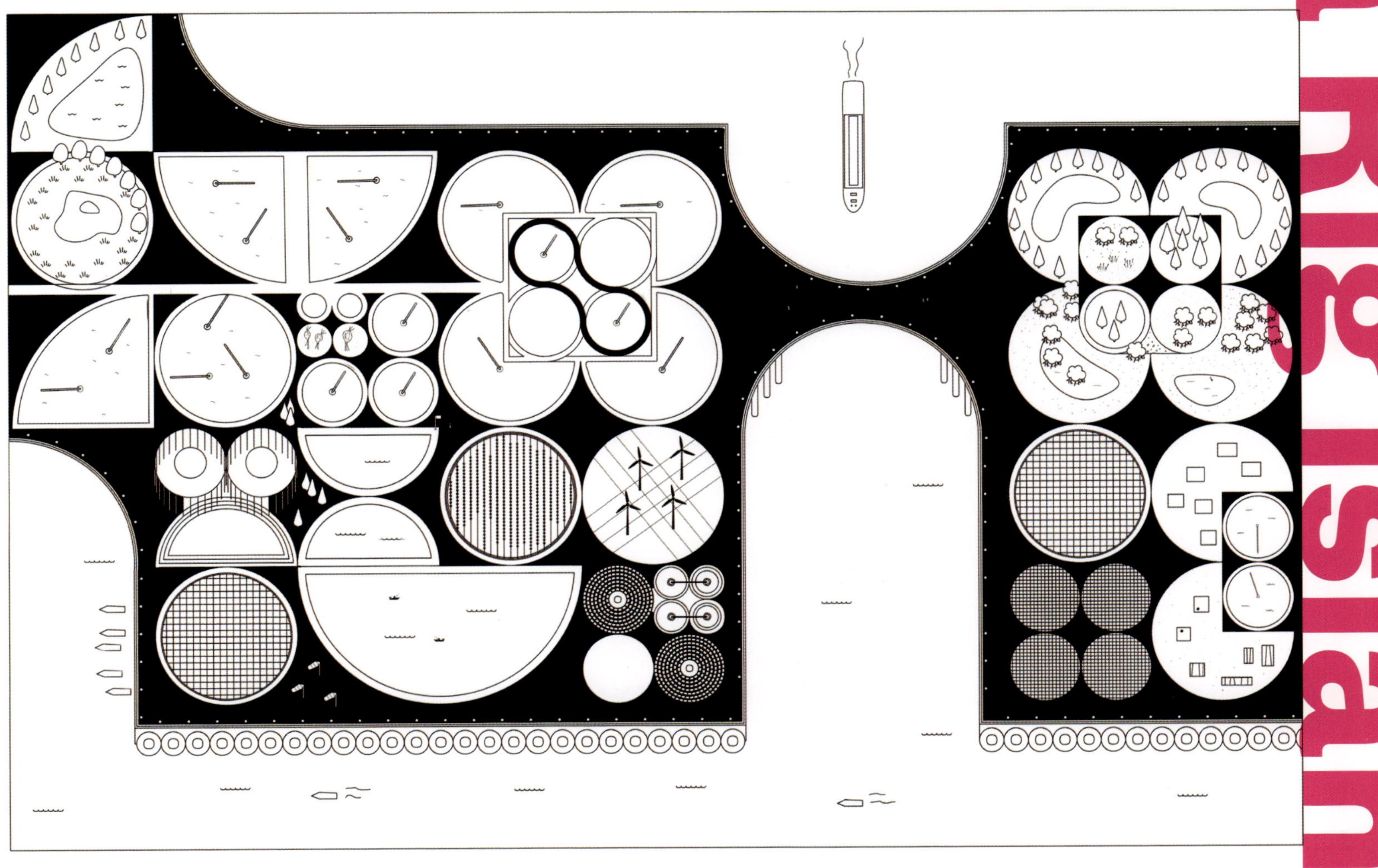

Detailed plan

Landscape water flow

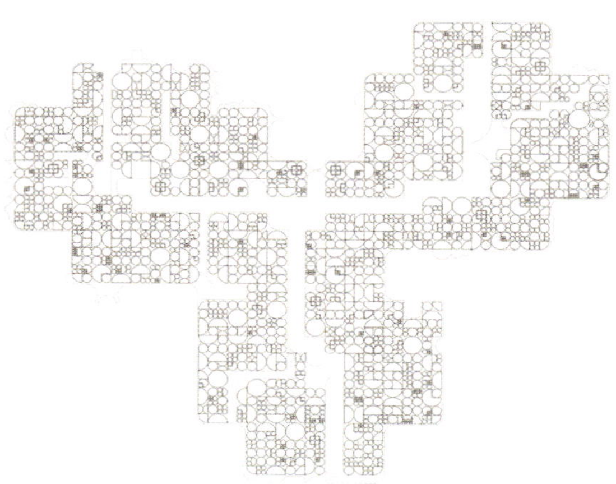

Landscape water programs

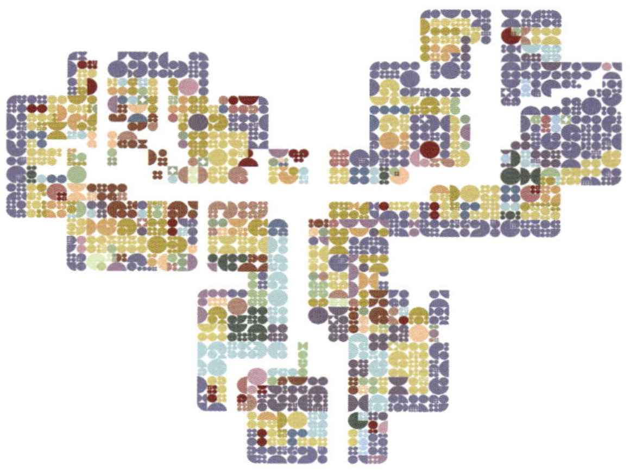

Master plan

Landscape water filtration

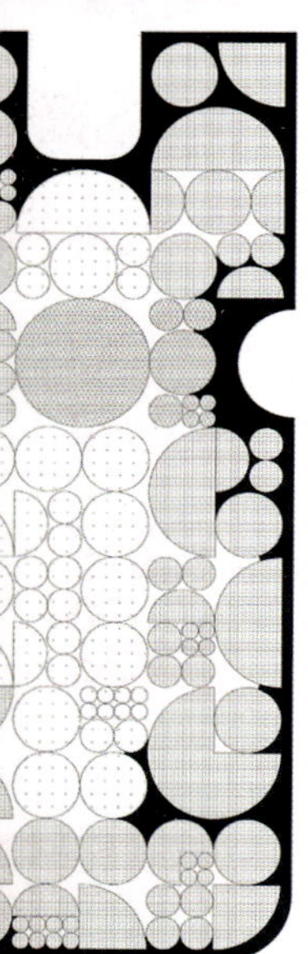

Living Rig Island: perspectives

Diyi [illegible]hang (B.Arch)

Borgo Schiro intervention: view from the east

The New Italian Domestic Landscape Through adaptive reuse, latent programs reinvigorate abandoned villages in rural Italy.

Borgo Schiro entryway

In the past several decades, Italy's population in rural areas has waned as people move to big cities for work and contemporary amenities. As a result, houses in rustic villages are being abandoned. Some projects have sprung up that sell homes for just one Euro in an effort to repopulate; others encourage adaptive reuse to breathe new life, economic opportunities, and sustainable development into urban rejuvenation in accordance with the European Union's guidelines. Yet there is still a downside: in Italy's rural exodus, citizens are losing their connection to their own production and consumption cycles.

My thesis scales up the daily domestic rituals of cooking, working, resting, and cleansing to reshape the rural landscape across the country. Focusing on villages with fewer than twenty buildings, I identified a gap in existing initiatives, a means to reinvigorate the economy and the towns while highlighting the embedded, rich history. I focused on four villages in the Italian landscape, each with a special focus: Leri Cavour (power/energy), Monteruga (industry/production), Roscigno Vecchia (resting/

Semi-public zone of Borgo Schiro

New Borgo Schiro, axonometric

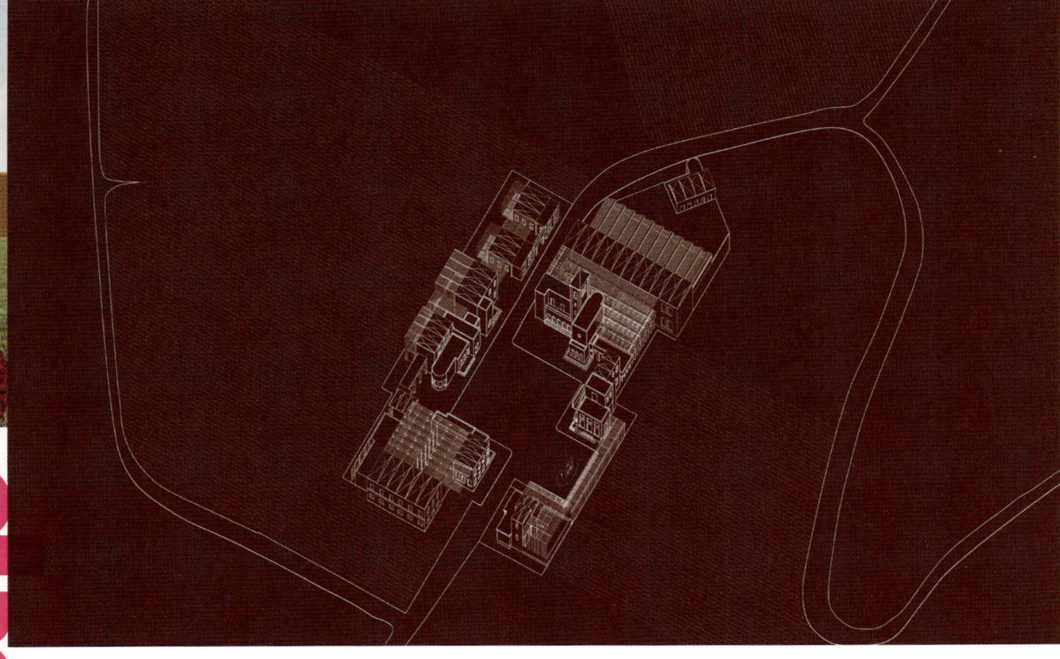

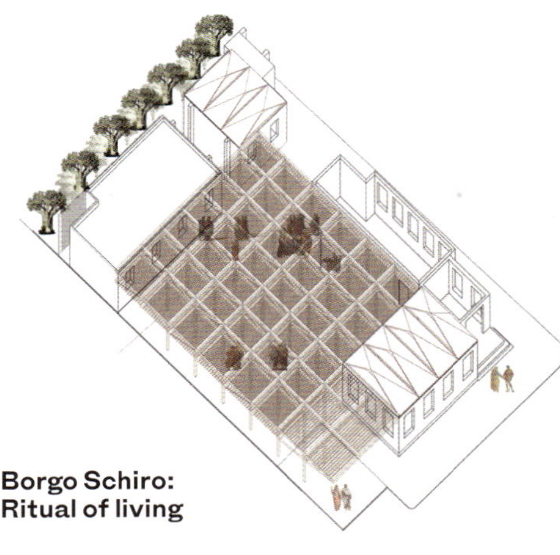

Borgo Schiro: Ritual of living

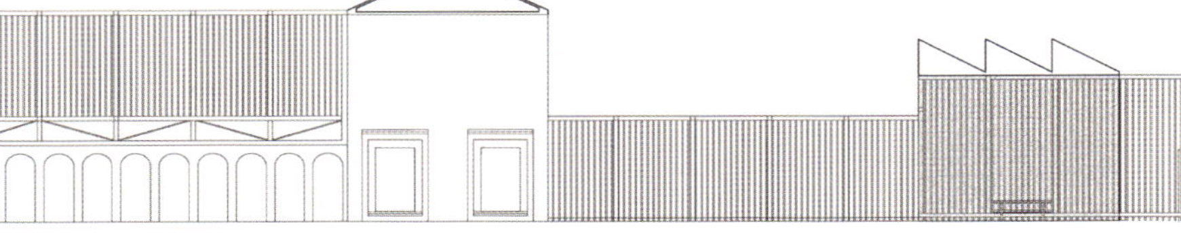

Adaptive reuse interventions at Borgo Schiro

Borgo Schiro: Ritual of working

self-cleansing), and Borgo Schiro (farming/ cooking). Leri Cavour sits near an abandoned power plant and now generates reusable energy through shaded corridors, single-axle wind turbines, passive cooling roofs, and solar panels. Monteruga is close to the Porsche Engineering Technical Center, offering a latent space to reactivate necessary capital and employment. Roscigno Vecchia, built solely for a nearby Benedictine Monastery, becomes a symbol of the ritual of resting as a retreat for self-cleansing. Borgo Schiro, which produced Marsala wine, recalls the ritual of cooking by holding workshops for harvesting grapes for wine, and using it in traditional meals. Each town is a latent shell, waiting to be reactivated culturally and economically, simply by relying on the site's inherent value and history.

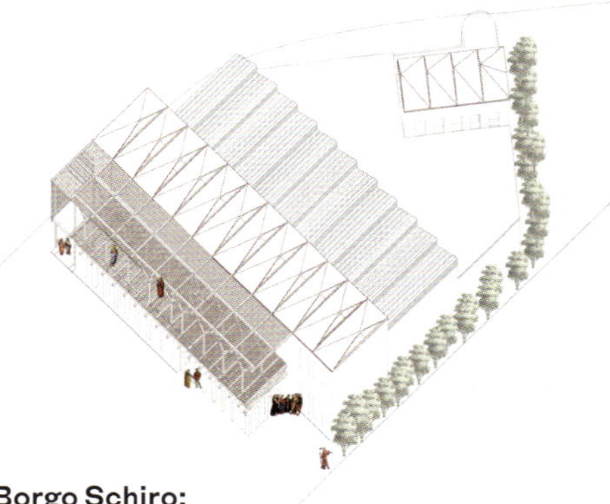

Borgo Schiro: Ritual of working

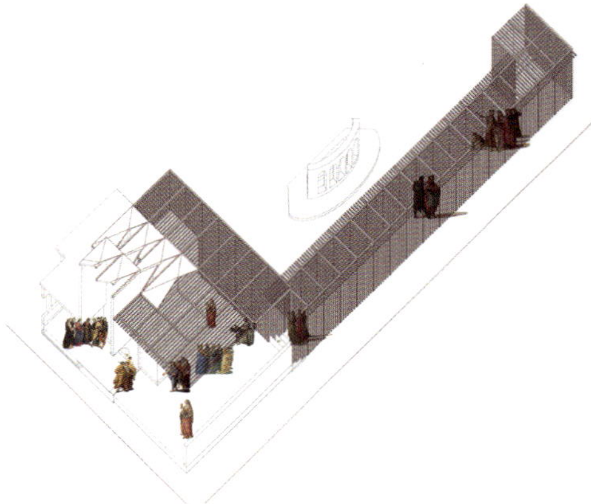

Borgo Schiro: Ritual of celebrating

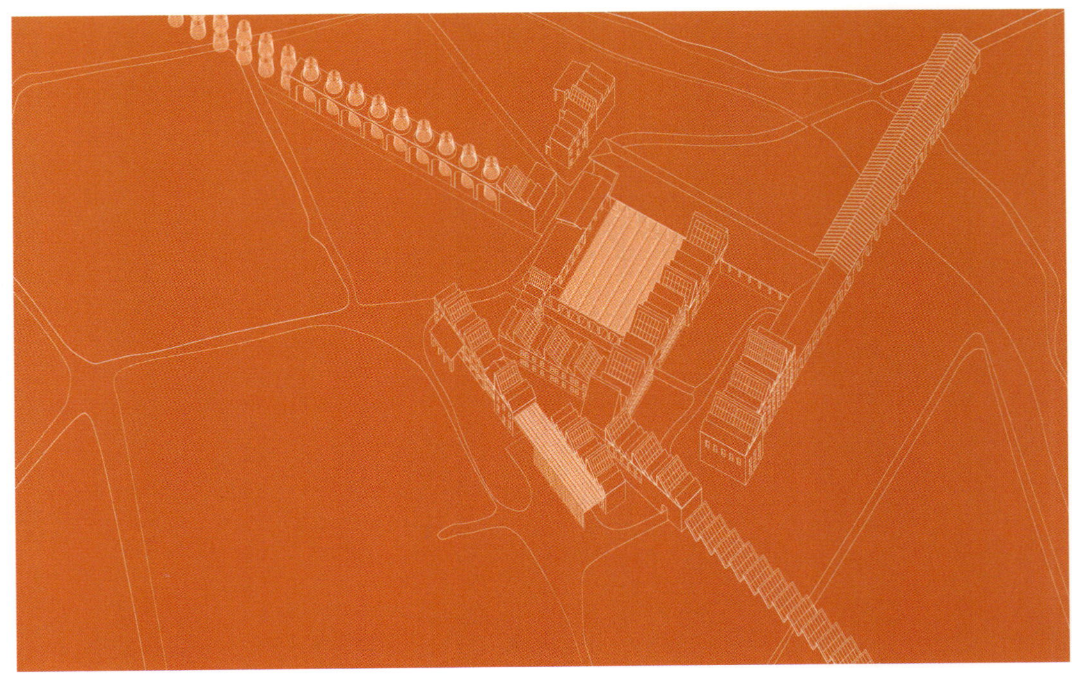

New Leri Cavour, axonometric

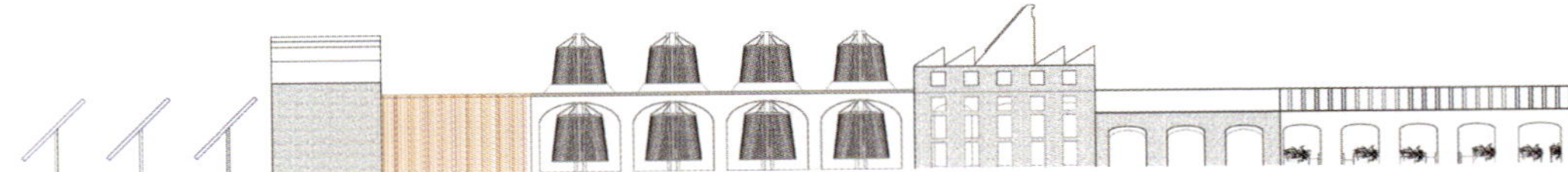

Adaptive reuse interventions at Leri Cavour

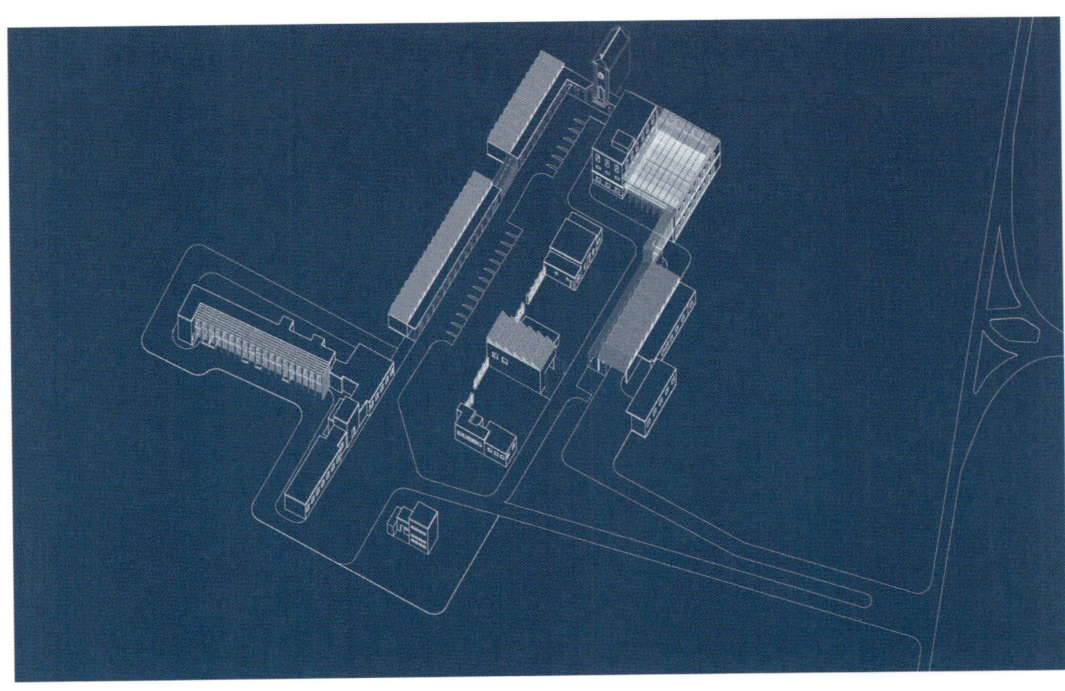

New Monteruga, axonometric

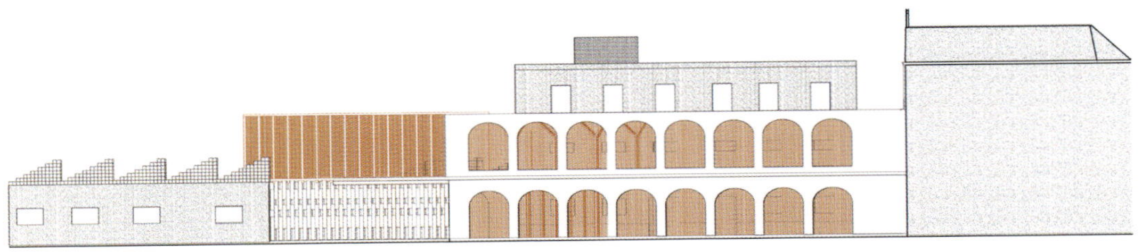

Adaptive reuse interventions at Monteruga

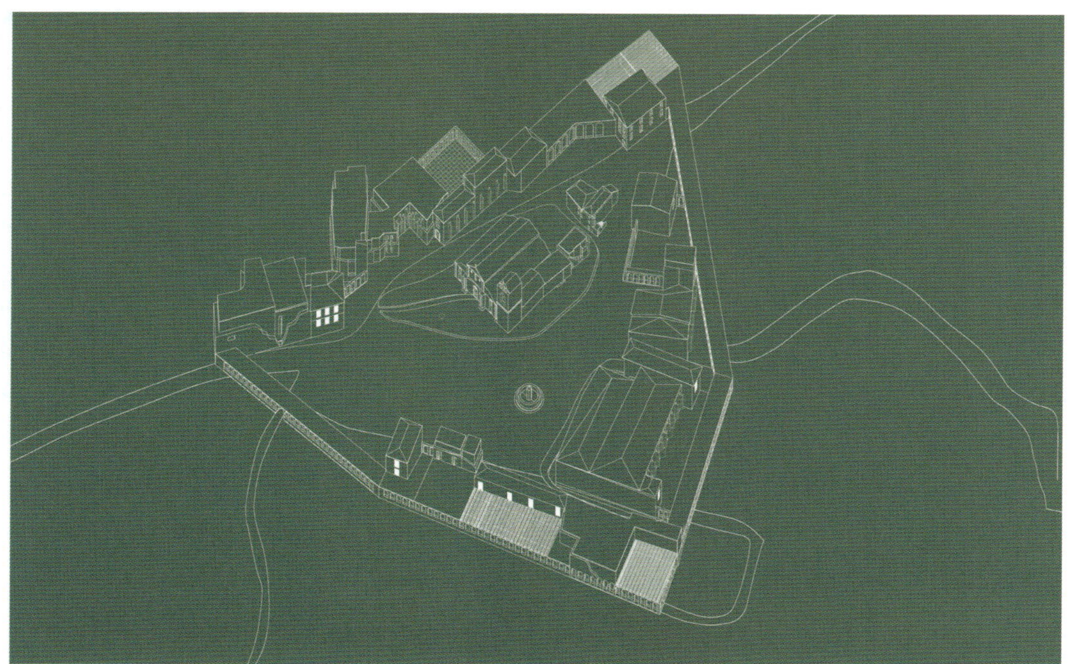

New Roscigno Vecchia, axonometric

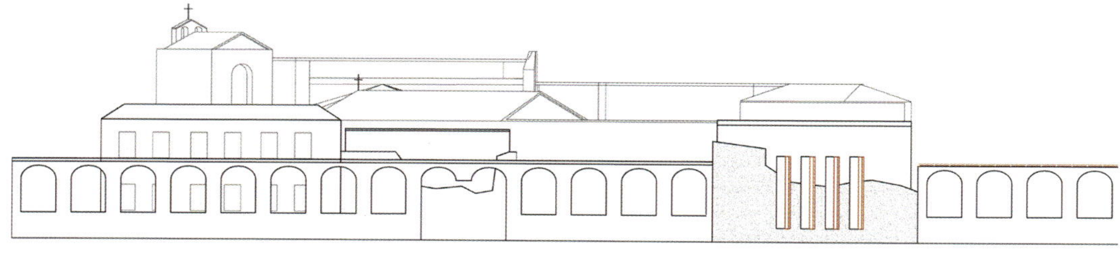

Adaptive reuse interventions at Roscigno Vecchia

Image 3.009

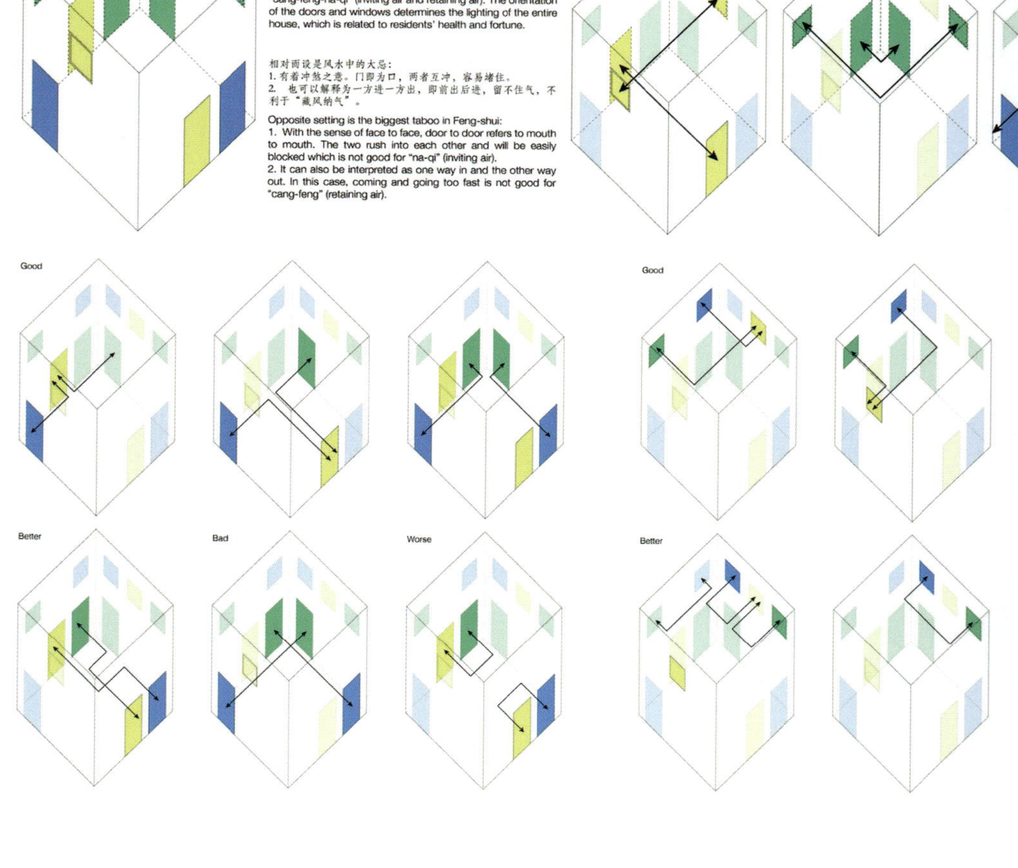

Hansy Better Barraza

Architecture Is Political
Introduction

Primary Advisor **Hansy Better Barraza, Professor, Department of Architecture, RISD**
Secondary Advisor **Silvia Acosta, Professor, Department of Architecture, RISD**

Students **Jae Hoon (Jason) Jang (B.Arch), Ka Hyun (Sarah) Kim (B.Arch), Jake Lefeber (B.Arch), Reishan McIntosh (B.Arch), Katie Chizuko Solien (B.Arch), Alexa Thorne (B.Arch), Cherry Yang (B.Arch), Wei Xiao (B.Arch)**

In this studio we embraced that the world is complex and acknowledged that in navigating this world through an architectural thesis investigation we would inevitably encounter all forms of prejudice and bias, both implicit and explicit. We recognized the abundance of intolerance, racism, misogyny, nepotism, sexism, xenophobia, and other extremely offensive, oppressive, and unjust behaviors that reinforce the power systems of a dominant group, most often at the expense of underserved communities and the environment. In framing a thesis, we challenged ourselves to contemplate these issues and to sew connections into the torn fabric of humanity to bring about a more just existence on our planet.

The thesis asks students to identify, frame, and develop individual responses and architectural tools to engage with complex social issues and environmental systems. We began with the following commitments:

- We draw from our social and political identities (gender, race, ethnicity, class, sexuality, ability) to combat racism, misogyny, nepotism, sexism, xenophobia, climate change, food insecurities, water scarcity, and mass displacement/relocation of the poor.

- We criticize architecture's general complacency. We understand that architecture can be used as an instrument of power to exert power and that the architect has agency and must learn how to exercise that agency for the betterment of society.

- We examine authorship. As architects, individually and collectively, we must use the authority entrusted to us to promote new power dynamics.

My pedagogical framing of the thesis is structured around three main tenets:

- **Diversity of thought and of formal expressions.** The thesis seminar is a means for producing knowledge about architecture as a practice and as a discipline. We go beyond surface representations into design as research. I welcome students with diverse thesis subjects and those who are still searching and defining their thesis. As a collective, our different points of view challenge us to form convincing arguments, building a discourse among peers and empowering each other in the process. We practice "grounded theory" in the way that researcher and author Brené Brown defines it—attending to lived experience rather than theory. Brown quotes the poet Antonio Machado in describing her own approach to research: "Caminante, no hay camino; / se hace camino al andar." (Traveler, there is no path; / you make your own path as you walk.) The idea is simple: we must establish our own positions and be brave enough to follow them through. We must, as Brown states, "trust in emergence." Faculty and critics must also have courage—the courage to allow students to find their own problems and develop their own responses in their own voice. This is how we release preconceived ideas, release what architecture is supposed to be, and focus on what it can do.

- **Taking risks and identifying and taking a stance on a problem.**
  In our world, specifically in the U.S., we have become increasingly desensitized to the political forces that enable institutional and systematic racism, misogyny, sexism, nepotism, xenophobia, educational disparity between white and poor, Black, and brown children and resulting loss of opportunity, gun violence, climate change denial, and the growing authoritarianism evidenced in U.S. migrant detention facilities at the southern border. If we don't take a position on these problems, we accept passivity and defeat. In the thesis studio, I help students identify and engage with such problems by asking: What do you value? How can you participate through architecture? With empathy as a guide, we ground our responses critically and strive to deepen our understanding with optimism. If we have the will, we can reimagine this society and architecture's role within it.

- **Testing ideas in an iterative process.**
  Thesis is about discovering, framing, and telling stories through things and the spaces they inhabit. We write and draw from things, and things inspire drawings and writings. The continuous process of making, writing, and reading guides the architectural pedagogy and ways of learning toward what I call the public discussion of architecture. We examine architecture as a social and cultural force, asking ourselves, What is architecture? What place does architecture have in the human condition? What is architecture's role in society? What is architecture's relationship to culture? And finally, Who does architecture serve? Who *should* architecture serve?

The Covid-19 pandemic forced students to confront and reimagine fundamental architectural topics—spatial relationships such as inside/outside and public life/private home, as well as access to health care, self-care, and education. Students' thesis projects bravely tackled issues including environmental racism, urban gentrification, spatial practices of the incarcerated, post-colonial narratives, environmental exploitations, reactivating public spaces, collective housing, and pandemic health structures. As we concluded the thesis year, I wondered whether the architectural profession had lost its relevancy as architects were not deemed "essential" to the health and welfare of the public. Then the brutal killing of George Floyd sparked national protests and further exposed racial disparities and the legacy of structural racial discrimination against Black people in the U.S. and global communities. We now see that the systems within architecture that contribute to and are complicit in systematic racism must be dismantled. The physical and social subjugation of Black people cannot be tolerated any longer. As a community of academics and students, we need to reframe the dominant imagination that has plagued our profession and work toward an equitable, just society and sustainable built environment for Black Americans and for the most vulnerable populations around the world.

Jae Hoon (Jason) Jang (B.Arch)

Homes inside a House: Rethinking Korean Collective Housing

A new typology for Korean housing blocks accommodates a wide range of Seoul's population, combining efficient, expressive living spaces with crossroads for communal engagement.

Homes inside a House

History of the Silim neighborhood

Since the 1953 Korean Armistice Agreement, South Korea's economy has been booming. The housing market has responded by building efficient and affordable urban housing, including Gosiwon, which translates to "exam room." Originally built to house students, the Gosiwon's efficient layout now accommodates low-cost, temporary housing that epitomizes the disconnected and efficiency-focused Korean residential typology. While the typology serves its quantitative purpose, its qualitative design is lacking. In the next fifteen years, Korea expects a rapidly aging population and a decline of birthrate and marriage. It needs a new residential culture responding to its fast-changing demographics. I propose a series of interventions that adapt and

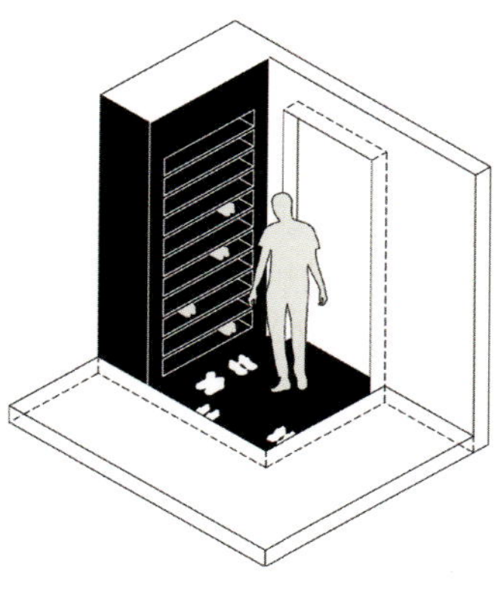

Entrance:
taking off shoes

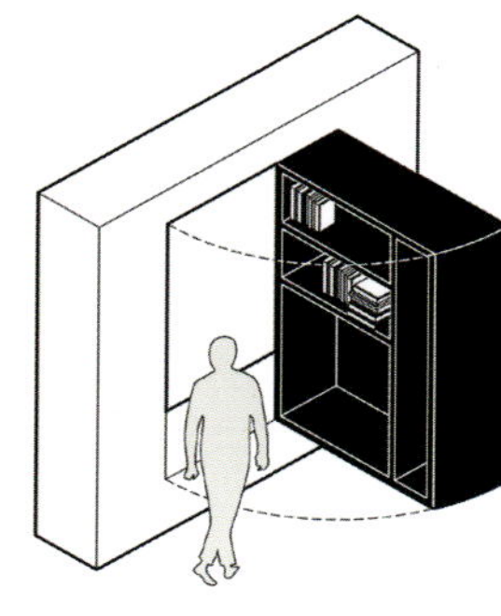

Storage:
expanding the boundary

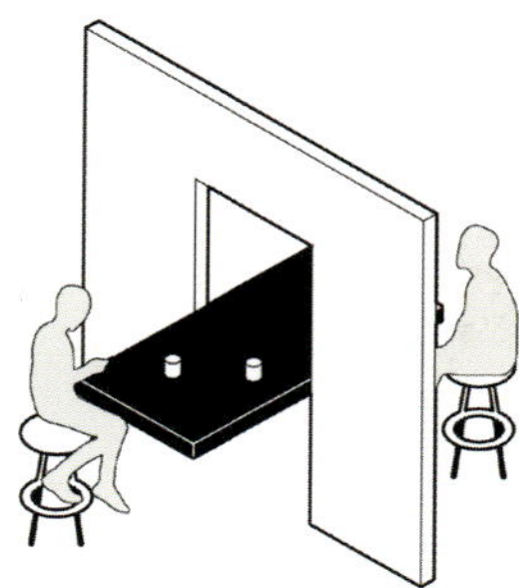

Connected Table:
semi-private interactions

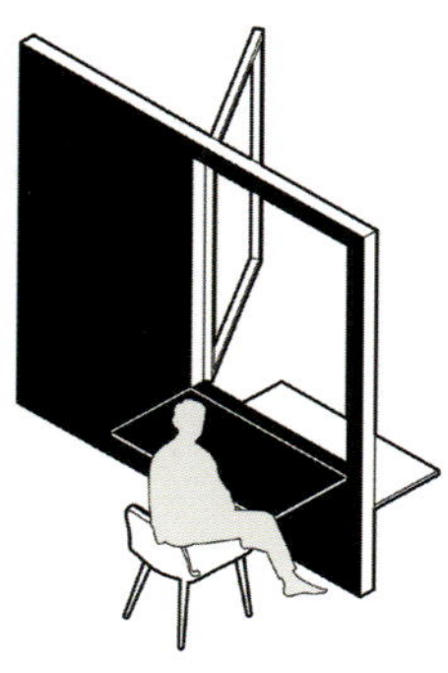

Meo-leum Desk:
interactions with outside

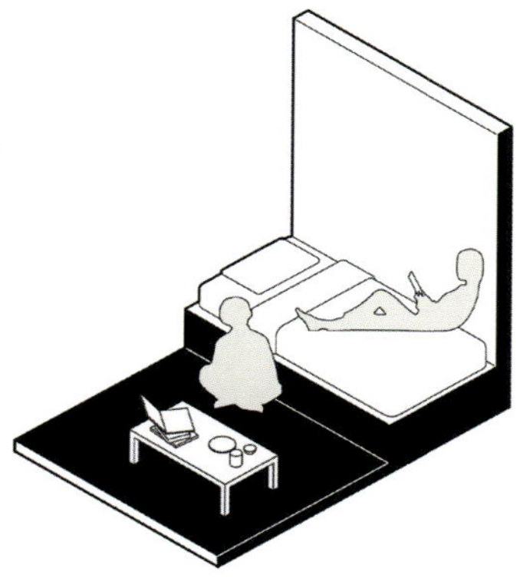

The Bed-Seating:
the living platform

Dae-Chung:
communal dining/living space

hybridize the single-occupant home to allow for more meaningful communal living.

My thesis rethinks housing as a collection of different "living stages"—a reference to the ritual spaces of Hanok architecture—as a means to highlight personal possessions as boundaries and props for idiosyncratic, and also deeply Korean, domestic rituals. The prototype also fosters a collective living environment, as intimate spaces begin to blur into a collage. Interior landings allow boundaries of privacy to fall, promoting interactions between the apartments and making visible the life inside. While the exterior façade presents a banal housing complex, the emphasis on interiority elevates each occupant's individuality and collectivity, making a case for people's agency in architecture while maintaining contextual frameworks around the history and culture of South Korea.

Revealing
social
interactions

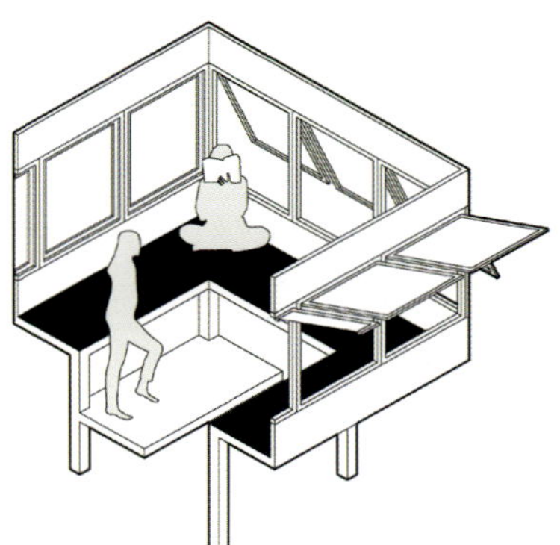

The Observatory:
private reading space

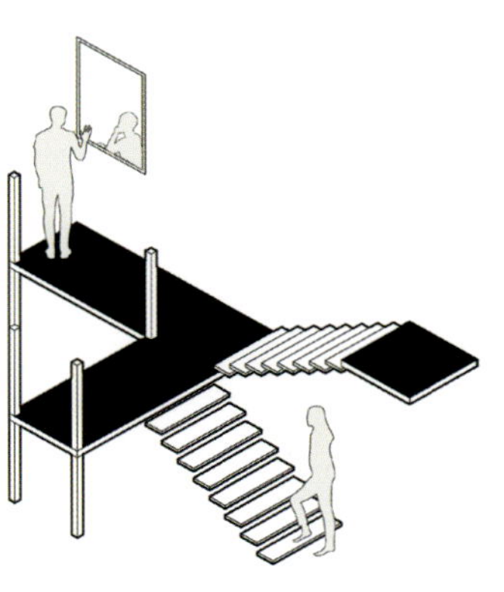

Maru Stairs:
corridors with interactions

Meo-leum Desk

n Collective Housing

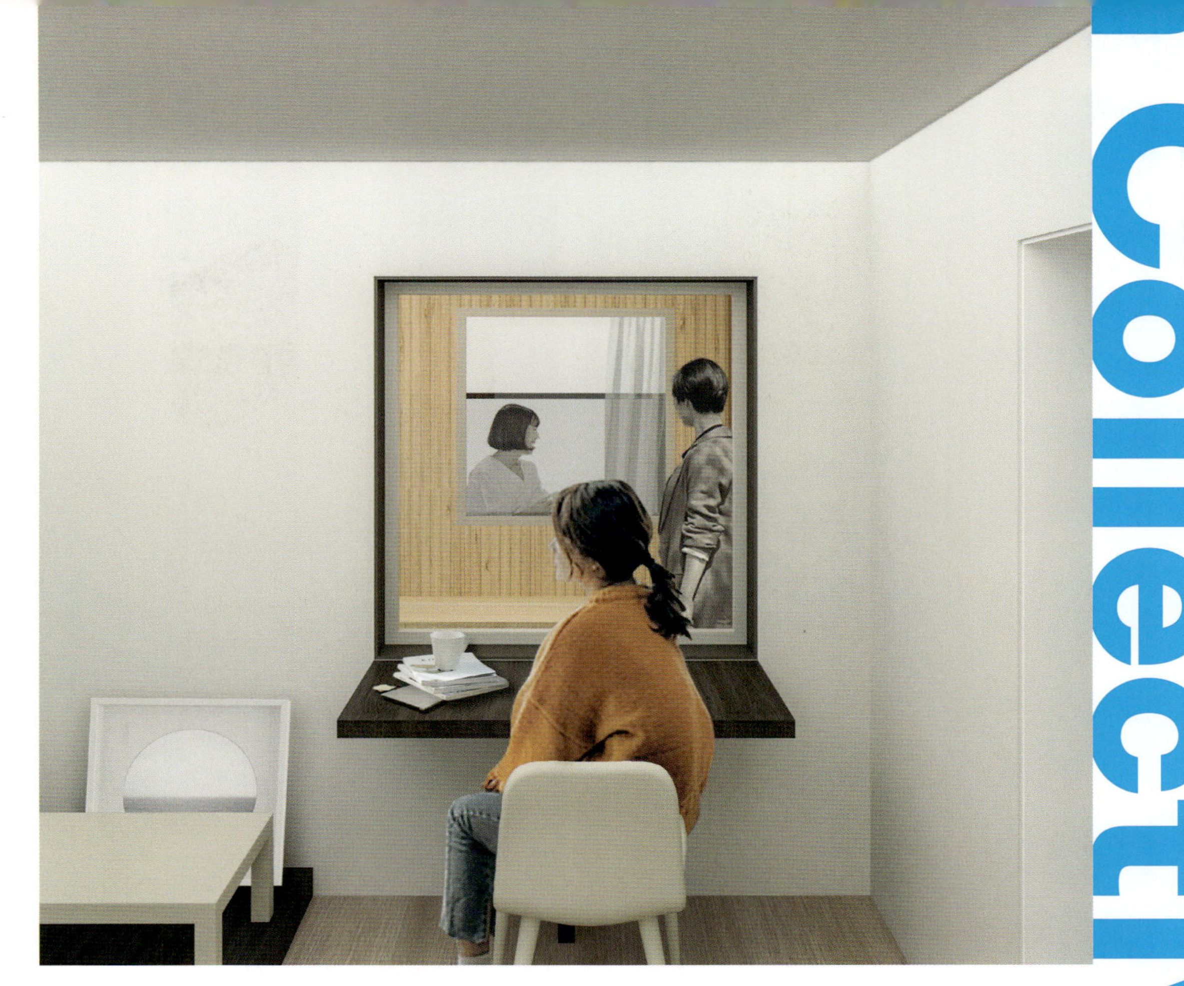

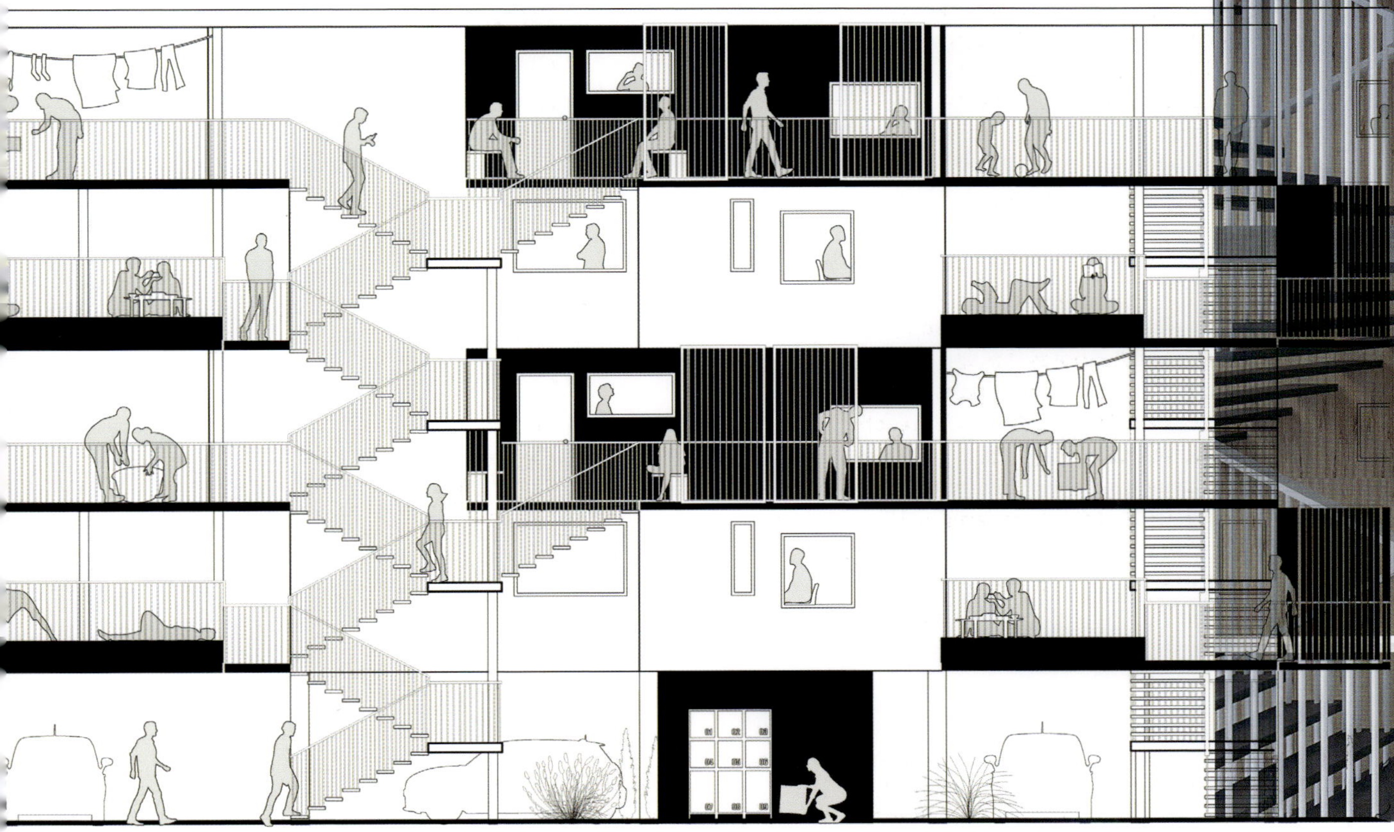

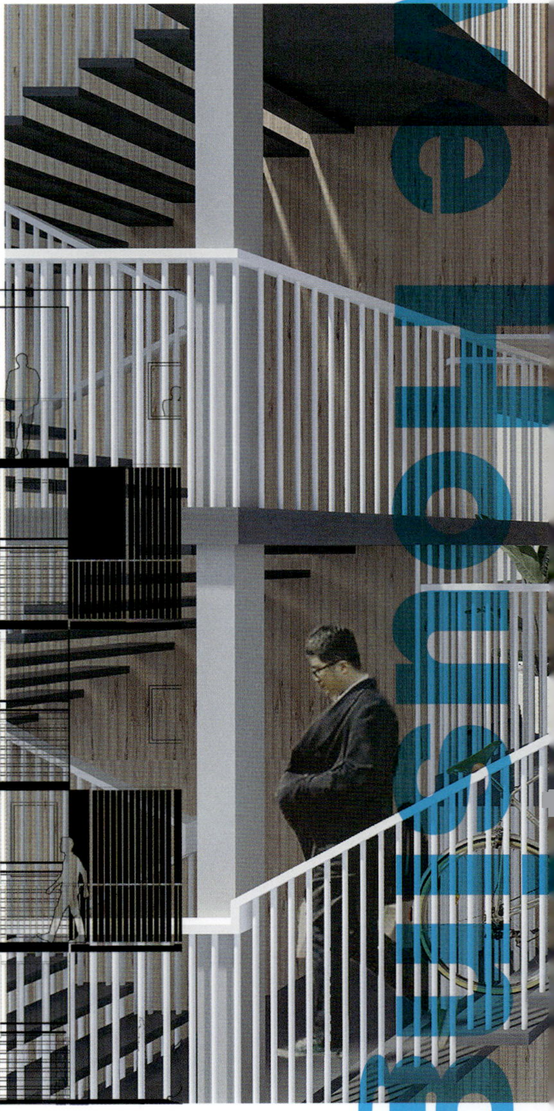

Things in control, wood

The Bed-Seating

Corridor of interactions

Ka Hyun (Sarah) Kim (B.Arch)

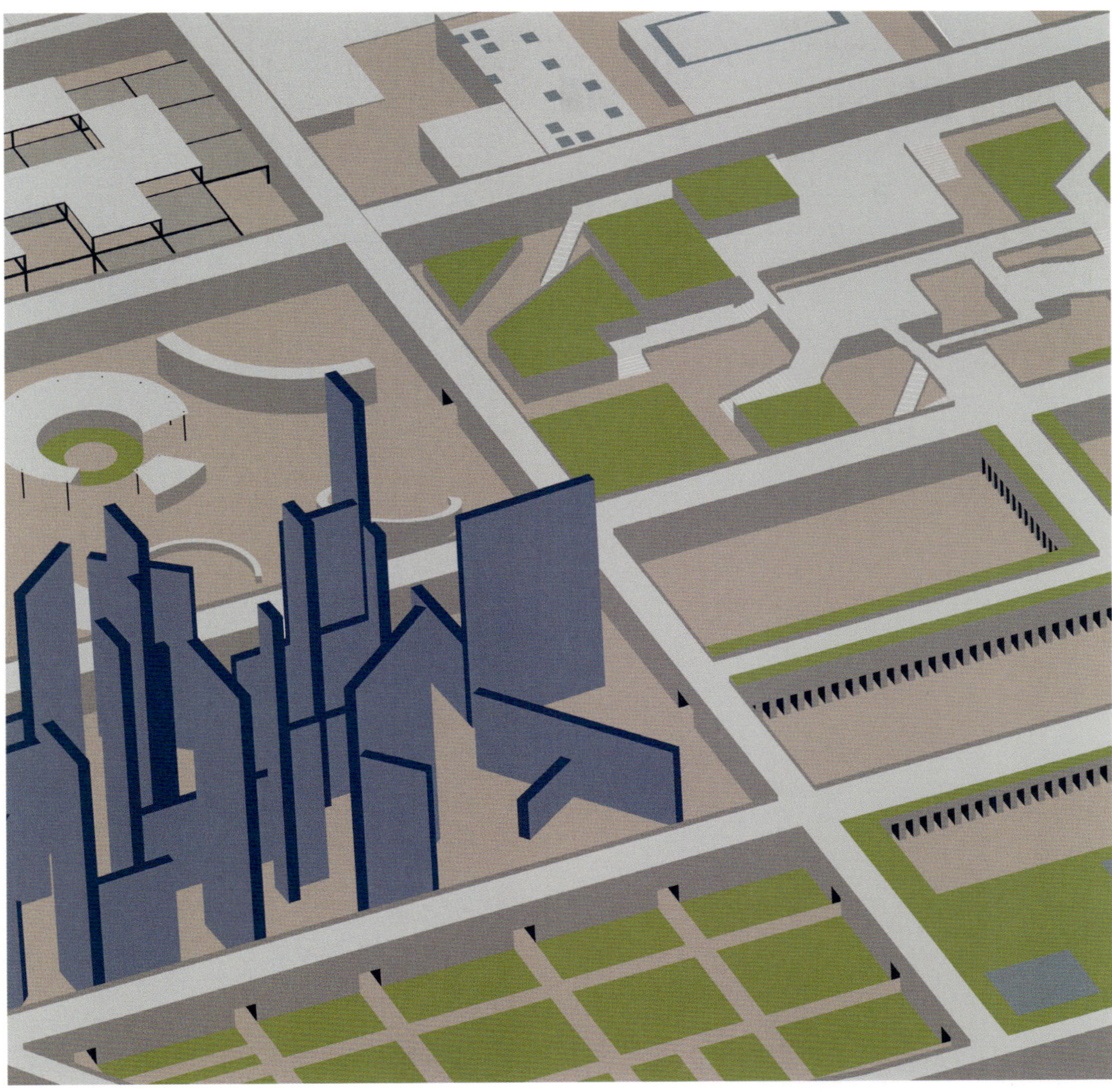

Aerial view of public parks

Data Crossing A design concept incorporates social media and the physical world to develop a new type of public space that revitalizes tactile interactions.

In today's technology- and media-based culture and society, we often lose our sense of physical reality. Our face-to-face interactions were already occurring primarily in cyberspace, even before the Covid era. We seem to prefer non-places, but dwelling in anonymous, abstract worlds, we lose the opportunity for meandering chance encounters. We need to develop new types of public spaces that emphasize haphazard interactions. Architecture's role in creating and providing such spaces can help us resist the isolation of virtual existence.

Hudson Yards in New York, home of the Vessel, the Edge, and the Shed, presents a hybrid environment between physical tourism

Park 1:
Connection

Park 2:
Circulation

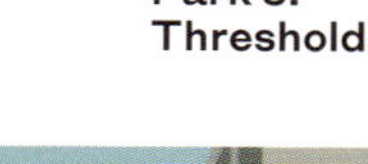

Park 3:
Thresholds

and media consumption. Situated near the High Line, a break in the city's grid, the site is a pinnacle of contemporary spectacle architecture. Extending the High Line and drawing from the city's grid without hierarchy, I created blocks within Hudson Yards to generate eight separate parks. Each park provides opportunities for a different type of physical interaction, a means to build relationships and exchange with the physical and virtual worlds. In response to Covid-19, my thesis leveraged social distancing as a way to subdivide public spaces and create visible boundaries on the ground plane. It projects toward a future soon to come, and initiates the architect's civic responsibility in a post-pandemic world.

Interpretation of social media platforms

Socially distanced parks

Socially distanced public

Park 4: Inside and outside

Park 7: Cover and expose

Public space in a pandemic

Jake Lefeber (B.Arch)

It’s Not a Sport: Understanding through Measuring

Inventive measurement tools interpret natural systems, instigate new knowledge, and activate consciousness of bodily presence in Newport, RI.

Constructed instruments: wind/waves/swell

A complex system of interwoven global phenomena, wave formation responds to the moon’s gravity, the resulting tides, and local wind trends. Waves are born far offshore but are mainly felt at the coast. Surfing relies on waves, which are fluid and without borders, and yet the surfer occupies physical space in a global experience and has a tectonic relationship with a place. Surfing thus serves as a microcosm of our intrinsically entwined world. I use the qualities of the wave as a scaffold for understanding the body in space. As the wave stretches beyond an individual occurrence, so does our idiosyncratic life. How do we physically interact with history? How do we introduce the body in an environment greater than ourselves?

Reading instruments: observing and recording gusts

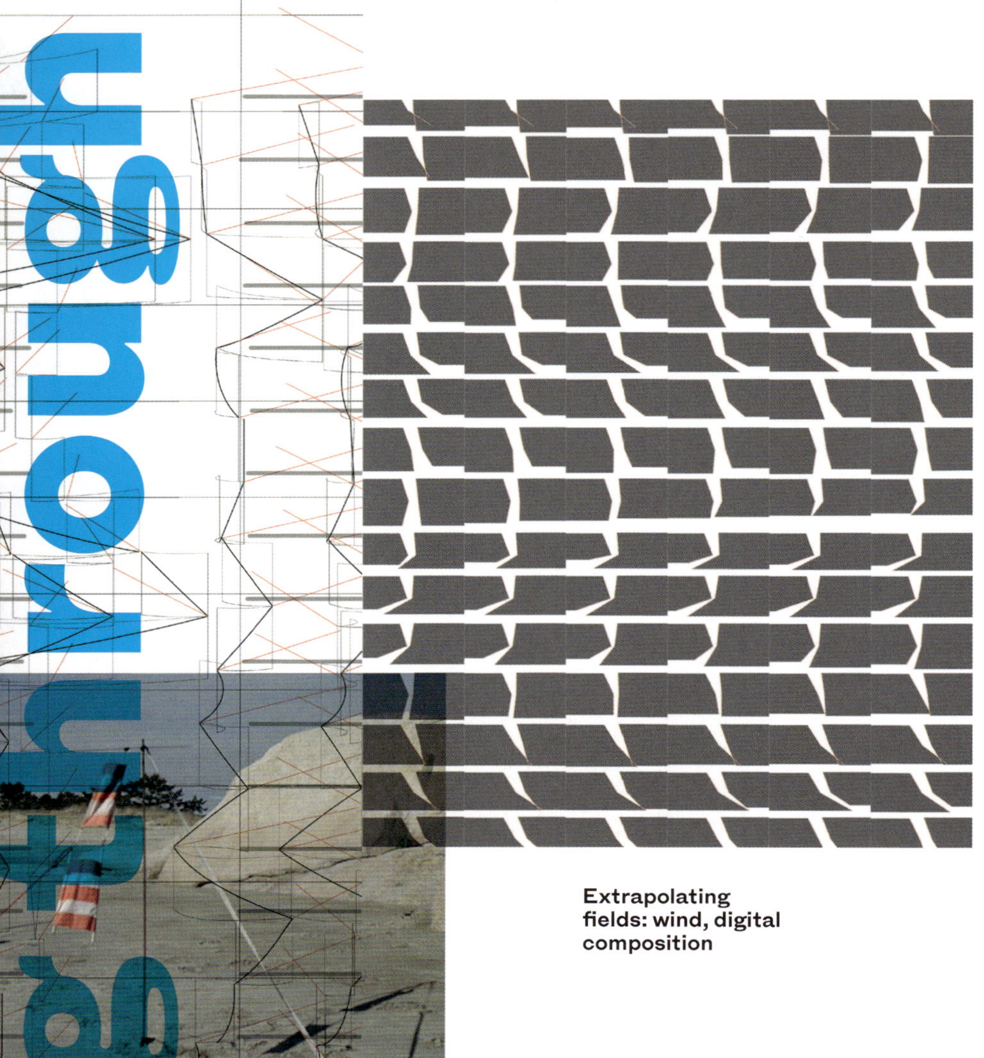

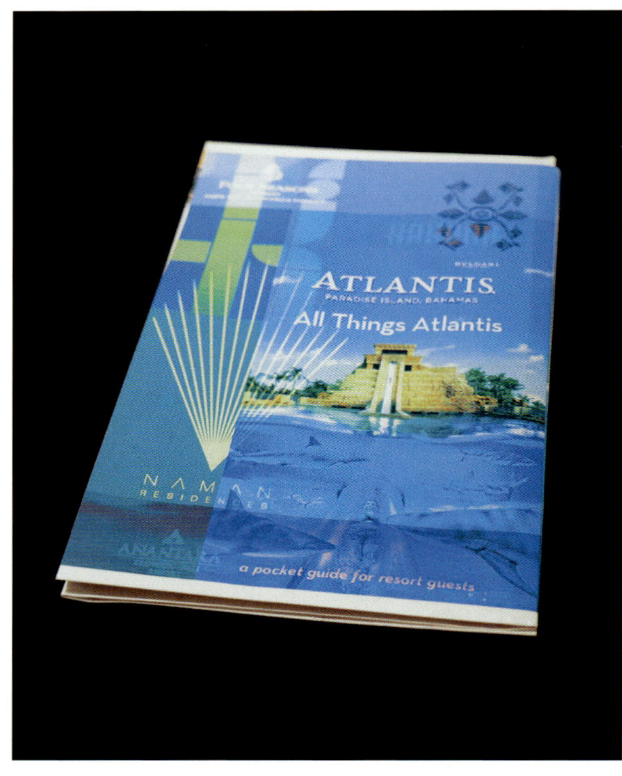

Extrapolating fields: wind, digital composition

Brochure of homogenous coasts, collage

Coastal regions, like the shores of Rhode Island, are notoriously contested. Property lines, land ownership, and restricted privatized waterfronts (public space) create fraught boundaries. Distinct lines and labeling create a complicated problem, asking, essentially: Where is the body allowed? When amenities take precedence over people in these often overdeveloped spaces, a location and its culture become a caricature, a set of simplistic, highly curated images.

I developed a series of ad-hoc instruments to document spatial experiences at three moments in Newport, RI: the land, ocean, and shore. These quasi-mechanical instruments were constructed to be both performative and utilitarian. While they move in ways that express

Decontextualized inhabitation, digital collage

Jake Lefeber (B.Arch)

It's Not a Sport

Wind turbine and device hub, animation

Wind turbine and device hub, animation

abstract phenomenological forces (waves, wind, swell), they also produced data sets of sea and land height, showing the relationships between these abstract forces. They became turbines, deep-water buoys, and cranes, which integrate as structures to facilitate inhabitation, as well as measurement. These tools of measurement became site conditions, providing a public easement for consistent access to the coast and disseminating its crucial information. Accumulated knowledge grants access to place and disseminates history and research, providing a highly trafficked tourist town access to spaces without overwhelming the nuanced forces at play.

My work respects our interconnected world but complicates it through individuality. Visitors are not the only inhabitants; fish farmers, marine biologists, oceanographers, and meteorologists also occupy the site. In encounter after encounter between visitor and researcher, people exchange stories and knowledge. With no prescribed path, with no explicit direction or sequence, the experience is at the discretion of the user.

Fish net and marine life research hub, animation

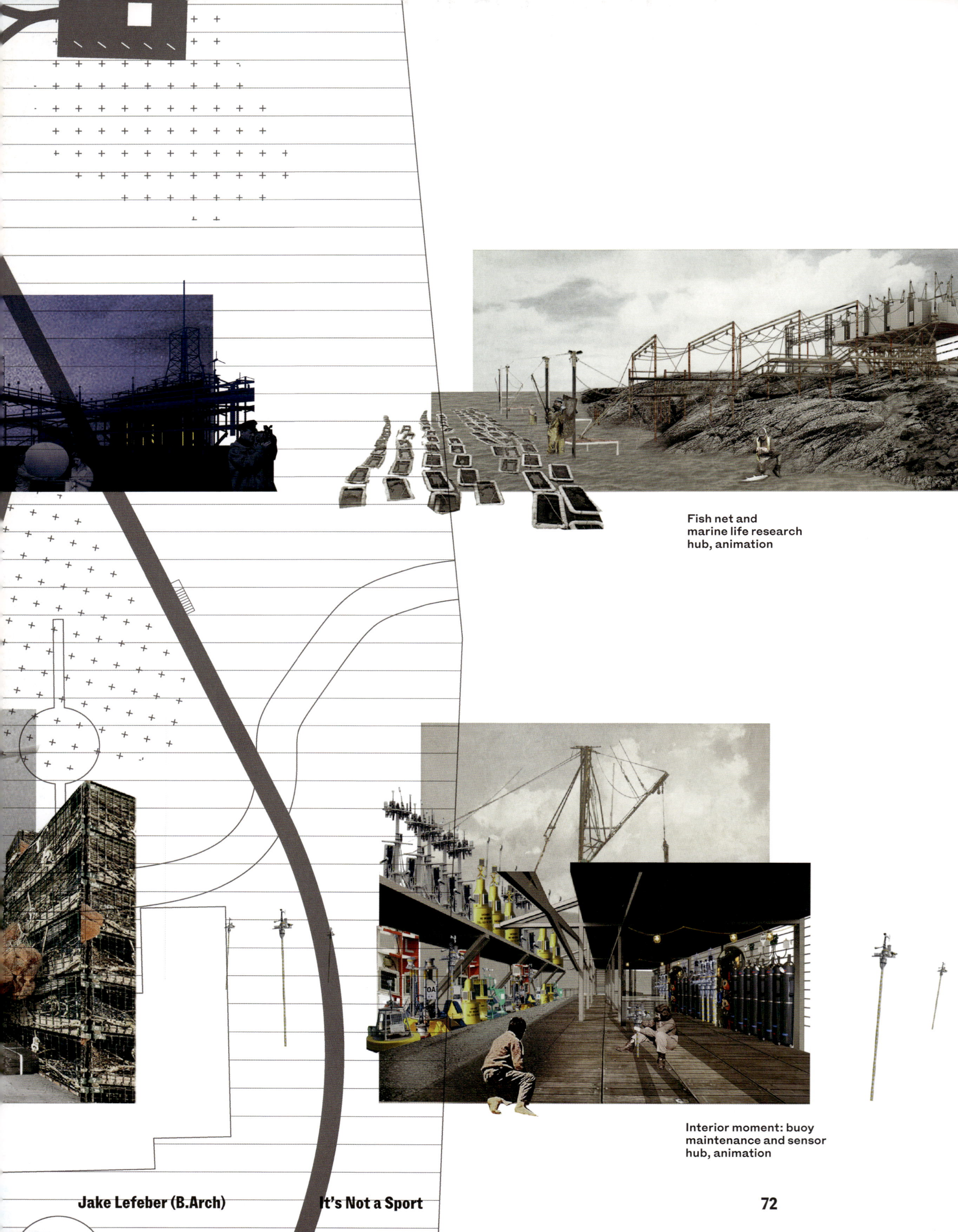

Fish net and marine life research hub, animation

Interior moment: buoy maintenance and sensor hub, animation

Reishan McIntosh (B.Arch)

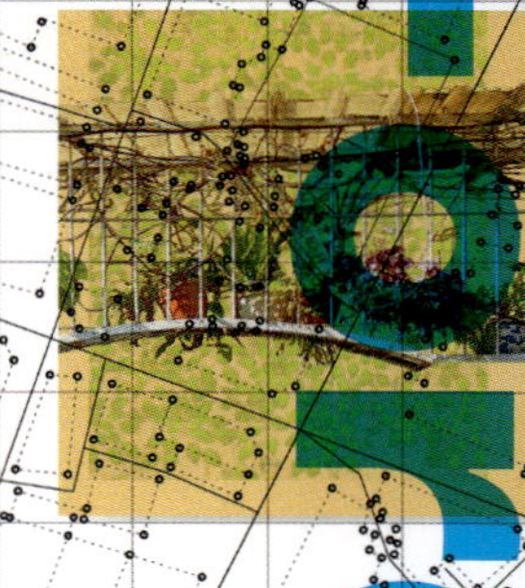

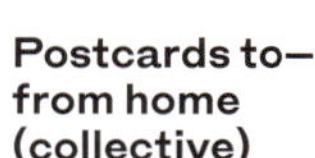

Postcards to—
from home
(collective)

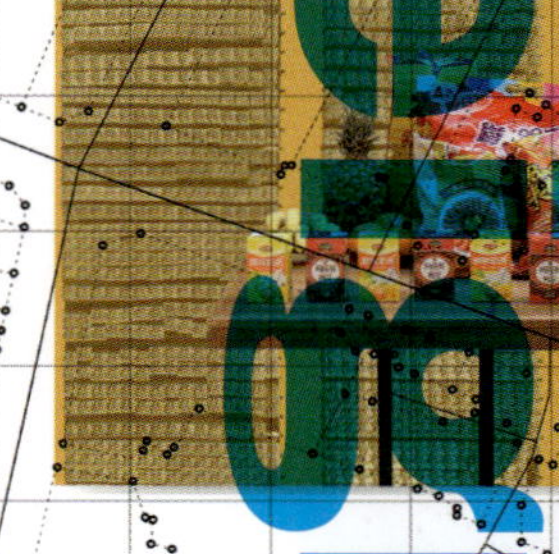

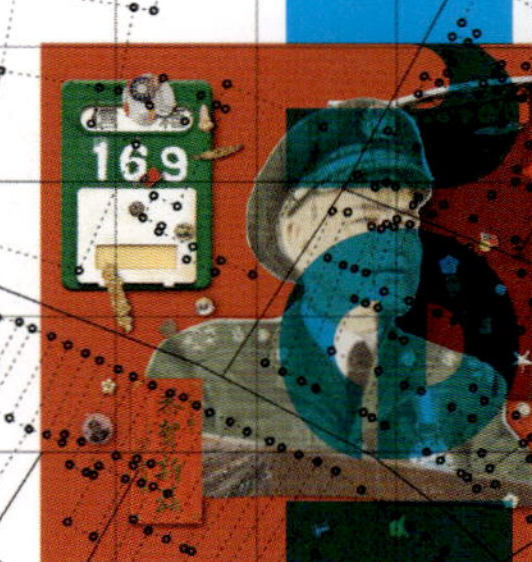

Foreigner at Home: Placemaking and Belonging in Postwar Taiwan

Modern architecture's cultural dominance tends to erase deep-seated histories of colonialism, yet the Taiwanese have overturned its history of rigid design hierarchies.

Thresholds blurred,
West Central District
中西區, Tainan

A country can be defined by its turbulent history. Japan colonized Taiwan for 50 years, then followed up with 37 years of martial law. Architecture became a tool to flaunt both modern building technologies and political agendas. Modern forms asserted their cultural dominance, ascribing a hierarchy to the buildings. Yet the people of Taiwan found ways to challenge modernism and blur architectural boundaries—public versus private, monumental versus ad hoc, inside versus outside—to ultimately subvert the imposed definitions of daily life and fit somewhere in between.

Taiwan's old capital, Tainan, is located far south on the island. Wide streets built during colonial rule run through the city but quickly divert to smaller roads, then alleyways. The edges of buildings do not denote an end, but rather a series of thresholds where inside and outside fluctuate. Boundaries of city life, cultural impositions, and space are blurred. Concepts of mixed-use and misuse demonstrate a practiced habit: citizens share a lot. In Taiwan the gods, saints, and citizens are all the same and so temples share walls with apartments, an unassuming table full of snacks sits in front of a business as an offering to the spirits.

My project appropriates and exaggerates material culture through two forms—the familiar (or contextual) and the unfamiliar (or the souvenir). Using familiar corrugated aluminum sheeting, tiles, and window grills, for example, I reframe housing in Taiwan through materiality. What is adverse can become customary, a compromise through which to approach a place as both an outsider and a local. In another experiment, I collage archival postcard images to capture unfamiliar narratives on a single page, removing context and combining new spaces so that each postcard frames a moment of materiality, environment, and actions. This reframing articulates the everyday experience, rather than the enforced political agendas of monumental buildings. Visually analyzing a collection of artifacts, I depict how the Taiwanese invert unfamiliarity: by making objects familiar in a process of re-creation through user adaptation.

Tiled façade: placed and distorted

Window grill: placed and distorted

Material:
tiled façades

Aluminum
roofing: placed
and distorted

Katie Chizuko So[illegible]ien (B.Arch)

Archive of Incarceration: Subverting Incarceral Containers through Domestic Spatial Practices

Spatial practice tactics create an archive centering the Japanese-Americans unconstitutionally incarcerated across the American West during World War II, providing spaces of healing, hiding, and solidarity.

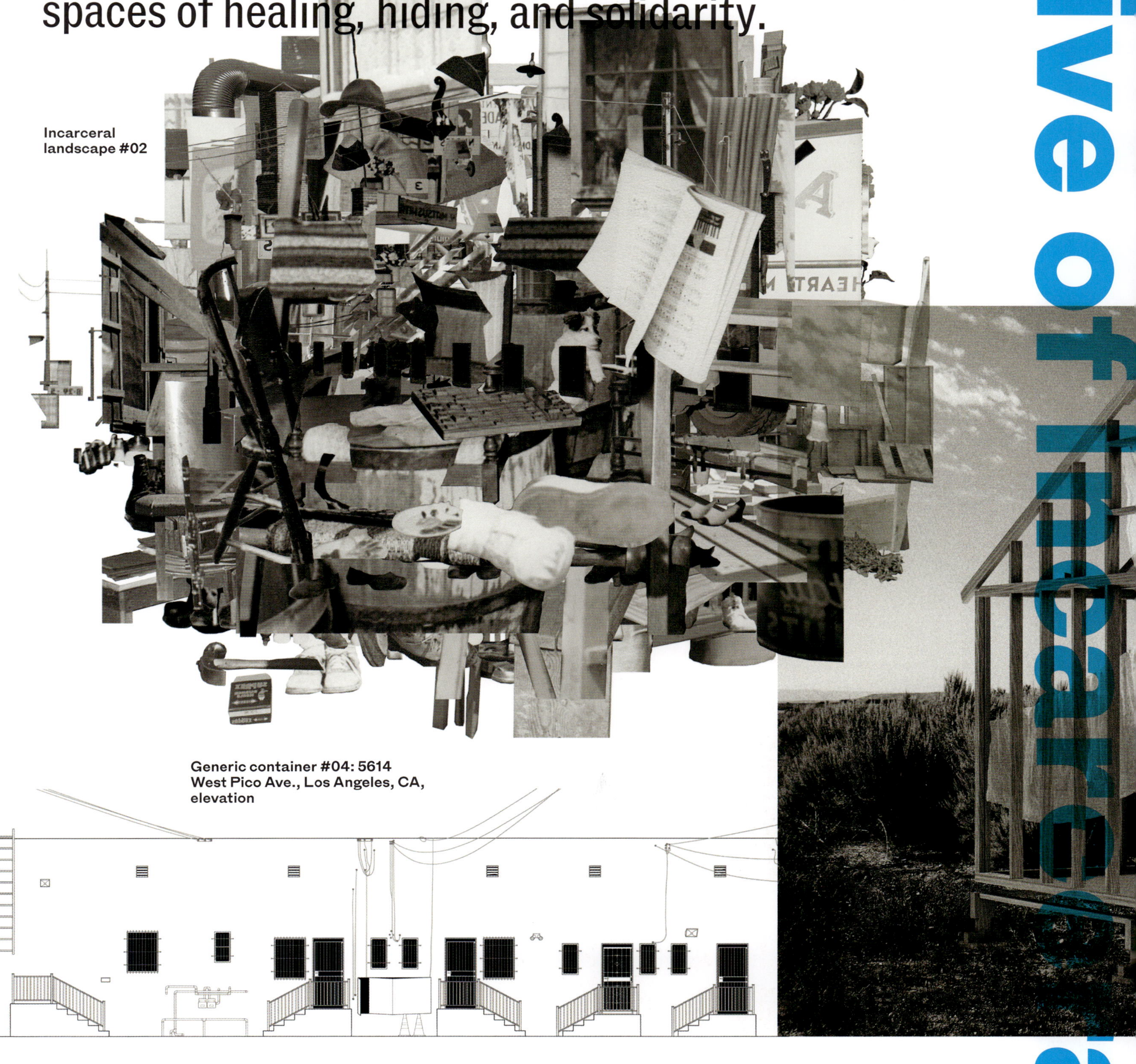

Incarceral landscape #02

Generic container #04: 5614 West Pico Ave., Los Angeles, CA, elevation

Uchi/Soto

Displacement is not a temporary condition for marginalized communities. Japanese-Americans forced into incarceration camps fueled multi-generational resiliency by subverting spaces to refute sociopolitical erasure. Within incarceral landscapes, generations of exclusion cultivated spatial interventions as a way to create semblances of place within containment. Photographs taken by the Japanese-Americans incarcerated in relocation camps during WWII provide an intimate look into the reality they were living in: they show the community's adamant refusal to accept their given landscape of confinement and neglect.

My thesis recognizes undervalued and seemingly banal spaces and their respective inhabitation, allowing us to reclaim and subvert the containers. It resists making new buildings, and instead elevates the domestic strategies developed through generations of displacement in a working archive of Japanese-American displacement. Through the use of collage techniques, I isolated the objects of resistance while retaining their position and scale within the photographs to expose new conceptions of life within incarceration. The incarceral space of relocation camps can no longer be considered as a landscape of neglect; the practices of daily life disobey and subvert such conceptions.

By measuring archival photos to build 1:1 scale structures, I created physical connections

Archive of incarceration

Out of place

Incarceral landscape #03: the Barrack

Generic container #06: Somewhere in Washington State, elevation

Archive of incarceration

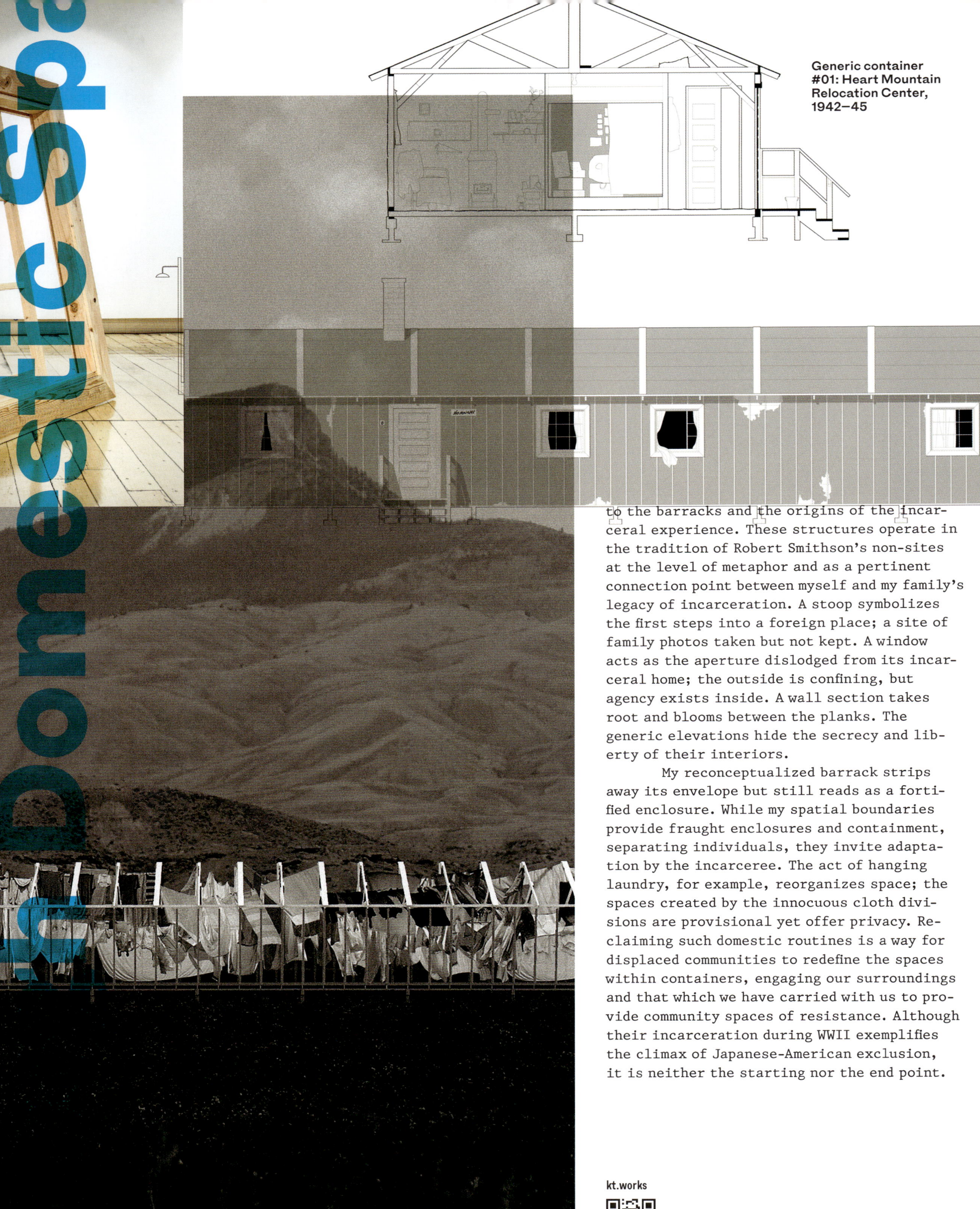

Generic container #01: Heart Mountain Relocation Center, 1942–45

to the barracks and the origins of the incarceral experience. These structures operate in the tradition of Robert Smithson's non-sites at the level of metaphor and as a pertinent connection point between myself and my family's legacy of incarceration. A stoop symbolizes the first steps into a foreign place; a site of family photos taken but not kept. A window acts as the aperture dislodged from its incarceral home; the outside is confining, but agency exists inside. A wall section takes root and blooms between the planks. The generic elevations hide the secrecy and liberty of their interiors.

My reconceptualized barrack strips away its envelope but still reads as a fortified enclosure. While my spatial boundaries provide fraught enclosures and containment, separating individuals, they invite adaptation by the incarceree. The act of hanging laundry, for example, reorganizes space; the spaces created by the innocuous cloth divisions are provisional yet offer privacy. Reclaiming such domestic routines is a way for displaced communities to redefine the spaces within containers, engaging our surroundings and that which we have carried with us to provide community spaces of resistance. Although their incarceration during WWII exemplifies the climax of Japanese-American exclusion, it is neither the starting nor the end point.

kt.works

Alexa Thorne (B.Arch)

Mended Fields: Appli

My project exposes architecture's connection to systems of environmental and infrastructural racism. As a designer, my role is to analyze these systemic and multilayered problems and, more broadly, the ways in which neglect of the environment parallels neglect of the descendants of slavery. Rather than perpetuate such negative conditions, my project seeks to remediate, repatriate, and enhance healing. The title *Mended Fields* is multifaceted. For example, literally mending the fields we work in can rehabilitate the ecosystem, helping us reenvision labor and employment. I have symbolically mended the site through experimentation with embroidered and patched maps of historically Black neighborhoods affected by redlining, natural disasters, or proximity to hazardous waste.

My repair efforts are sited in Badin, North Carolina, an area surrounding the Alcoa iron smelting plant. For nearly a century, energy moved from the dammed Yadkin River across the land into the center of town and then halted until its closure in 2008. Industrial waste was

Grandma's Tapestry: "If it's yellow let it mellow, if it's brown flush it down."

Mended Fields: Applied Systems of Oxygen and Sustenance

A shelter design activates site remediation and self-reliance in a town riddled with negligence and discrimination.

Badin, NC

This site choice was influenced by the movement of energy over the site. Badin is the home of the Alcoa iron smelting plant. Originally built by the French, the plant was preceded by a dam used for hydropower, now called the Cube Hydro Plant. The town of Badin was constructed by the power plant to draw labor to the site. As marked in pink on this map, Alcoa has dumped spent pot liner in various locations across the neighborhood, most of which are unidentified. These unlabeled patches of toxicity were pointed out on the residents' accounts.

Housing designated by the Alcoa smelting plant in 1915 includes housing design for segregated West Badin, referred to as the "Negro Village"

57 Quadruplexes
25 Duplexes (3 rooms toilets only)
4 Duplexes Henderson Ave. (7 rooms)

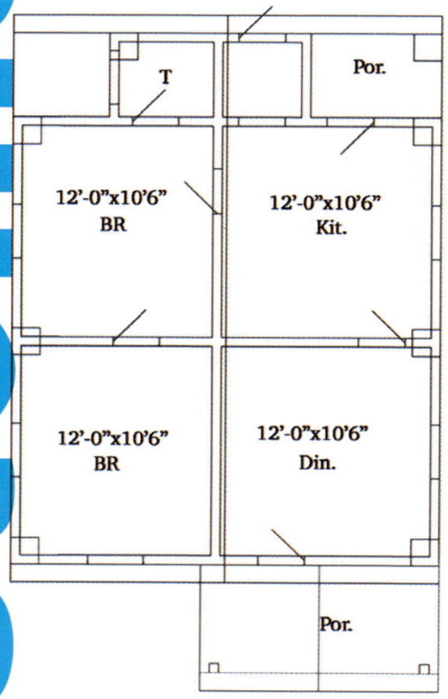

Type "G" house Negro Village

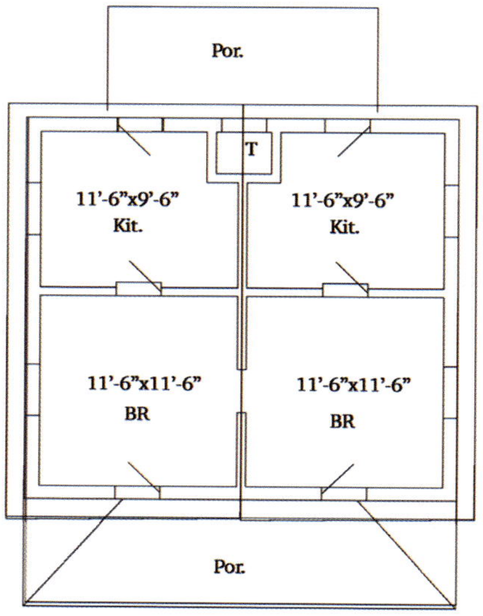

Type "L" family cottage Negro Village

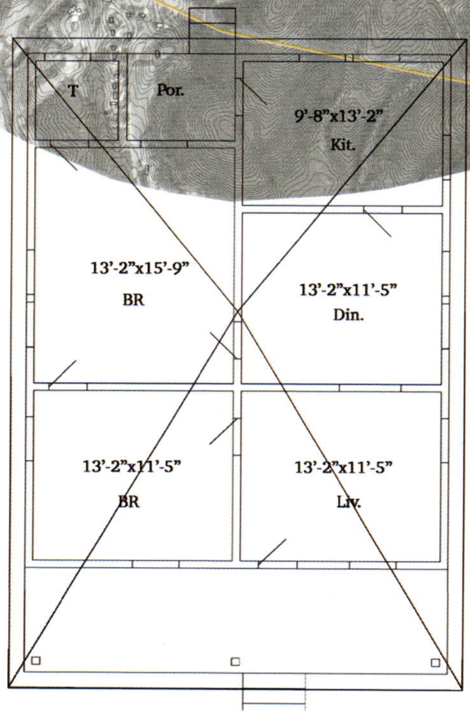

Type 5 room cottage, improved

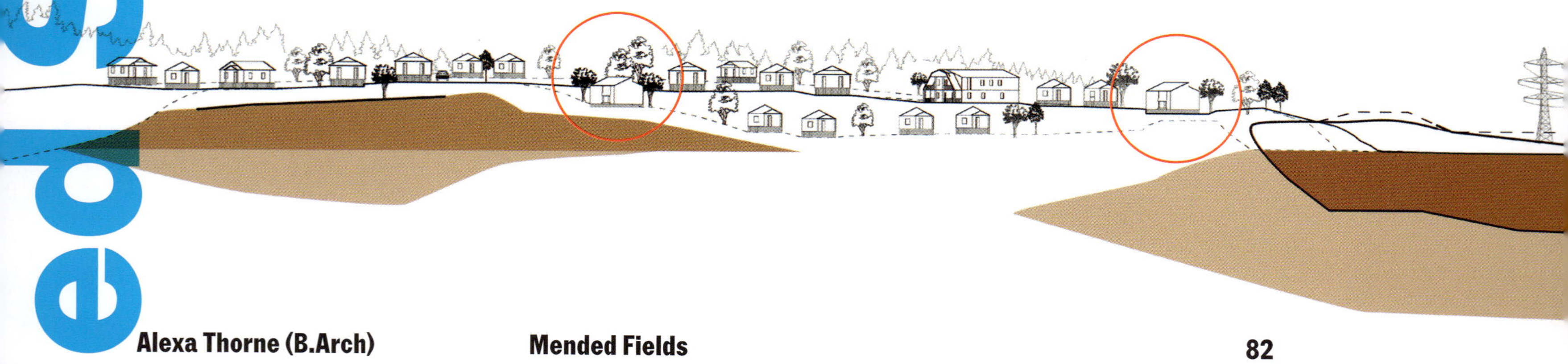

buried, submerged into the surrounding neighborhoods in unidentified dumping sites, mostly on the west side of Badin, the Black side of town. In 1915, Alcoa started building disproportionately small homes, often with only exterior bathrooms, to house its workers in what was known as the "Negro Village."

My design initiated the remediation of the sites where housing has been surrounded by contaminated sores leaking into the water supply and recreational spaces. My proposed homes, or "houses of care," root autonomy, self-reliance, and sustainability. They are based on my experience with "outdated" infrastructure. My grandparents spent their summers in a nineteenth-century Victorian cottage. There were no cavity walls or central air conditioning but the house's vernacular kept specific spaces cool during the day. I was inspired by their ability to alter the house to fit their needs. My design of the Badin houses embodies the same care and attention toward liberating occupants from relying on the infrastructure that neglects them.

Green New Deal principles also influenced my design intentions. I planned to rejuvenate the economy of the town, first by providing continuing education and a training center for its occupants after the Alcoa plant shutdown. The final intervention focused on Pink Collar Care Workers, specifically the underappreciated labor of family care. Not only does the passive housing infrastructure include perforated brick walls to let in oxygen and limit direct light, the walls, coated in a photocatalytic paint, also function as filters, creating healthier multigenerational homes.

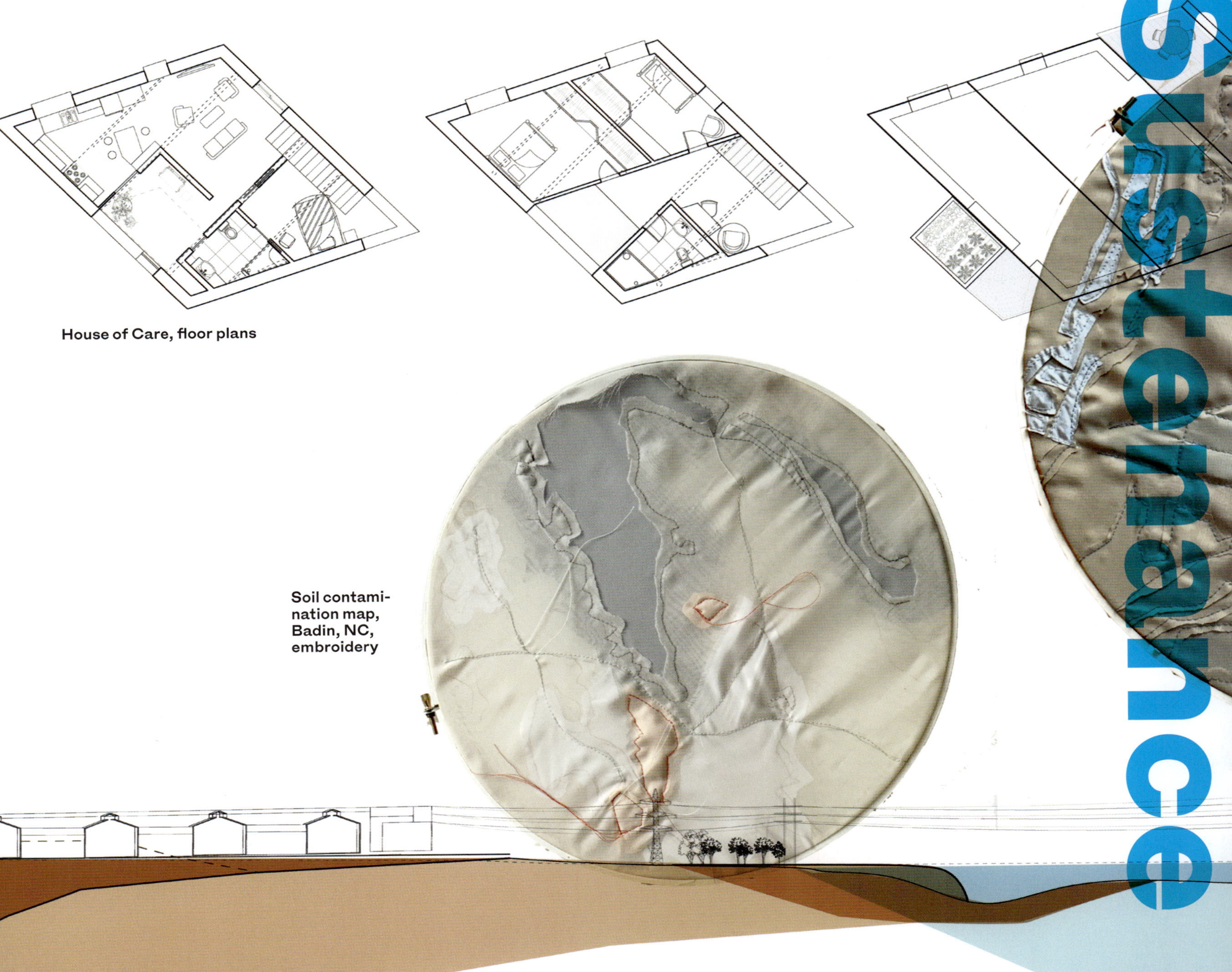

House of Care, floor plans

Soil contamination map, Badin, NC, embroidery

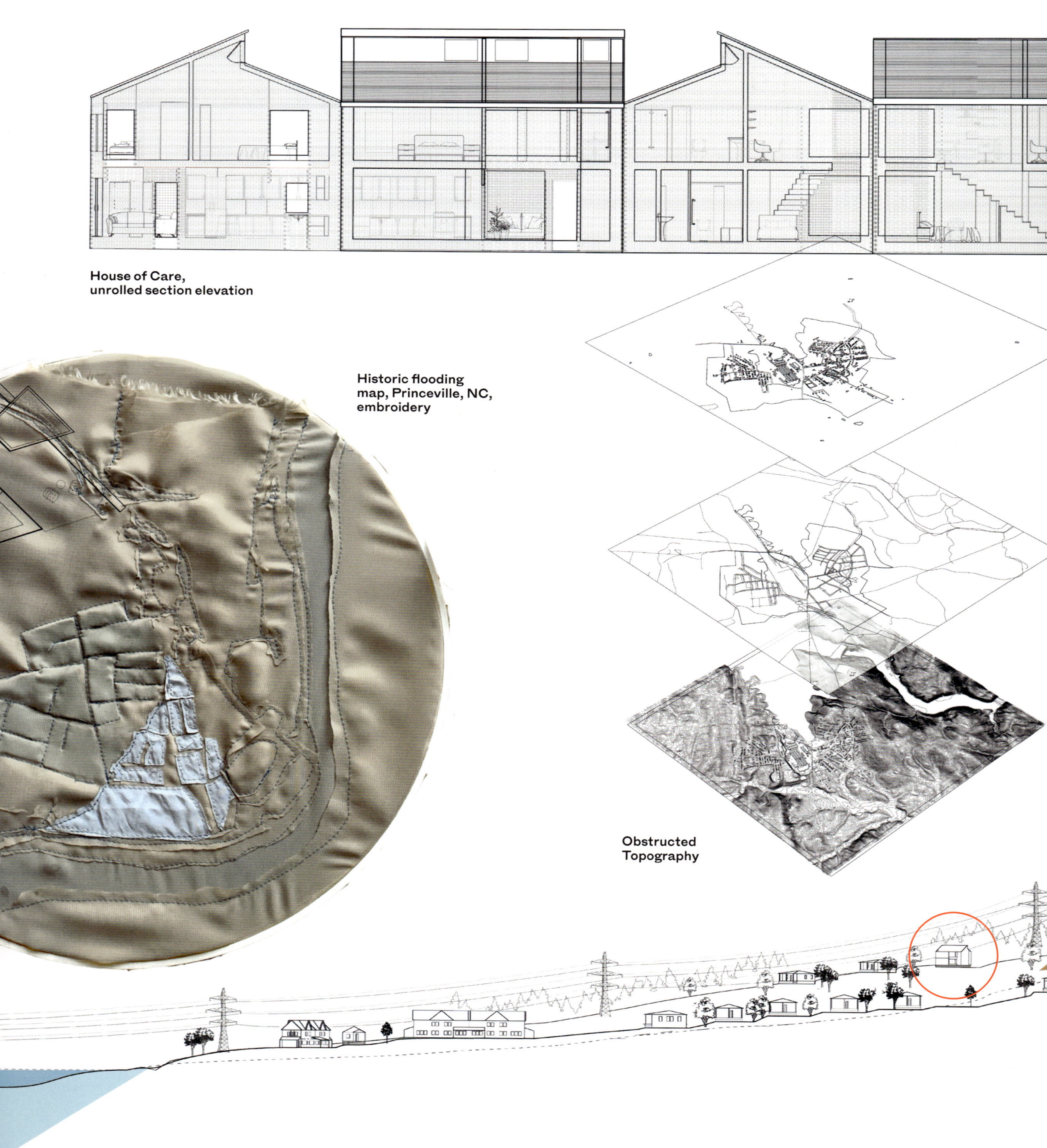

House of Care,
unrolled section elevation

Historic flooding
map, Princeville, NC,
embroidery

Obstructed
Topography

Cherry Yang (B.Arch)

Unforgetting: Re-Archiving the Spectator in Shanghai

Beneath the façades of consumption in Xintiandi hides a people's history, calling for exposure.

Remembering: the tourist's lens

Where China hid class signifiers in the past in order to sustain a perception of economic homogeneity, now it actively promotes capitalist gentrification as the exemplary Chinese identity. This is especially apparent in the rapidly commercialized zones of Xintiandi, Shanghai, where housing has been gutted and converted to high-end retail and restaurants catering to tourists. While this scene appears seamless, in reality, the government displaced thousands of people from residential areas to create this caricature of Shanghai. The result is a kind of architectural amnesia, in which state-sponsored narratives suppress the whispers of the people, replacing their histories of social unrest and trauma from the Cultural Revolution with a manicured image of a singular, dominating Chinese identity.

Memory reproduced, erased, and retained, plaster and clay slip

Demonumentalizing the brick wall, concrete

Xintiandi and the memory of alleyways, site plan

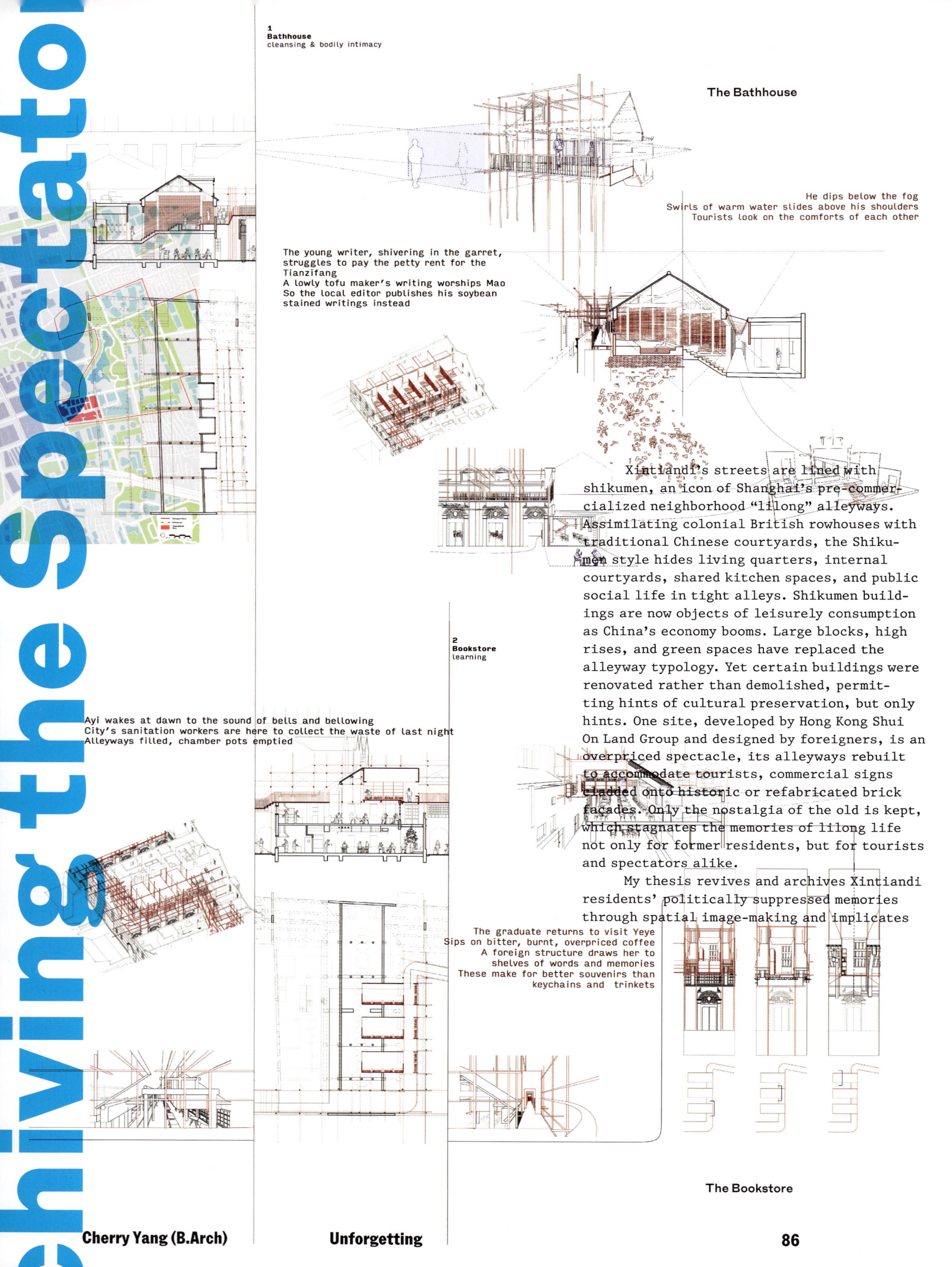

Xintiandi's streets are lined with shikumen, an icon of Shanghai's pre-commercialized neighborhood "lilong" alleyways. Assimilating colonial British rowhouses with traditional Chinese courtyards, the Shikumen style hides living quarters, internal courtyards, shared kitchen spaces, and public social life in tight alleys. Shikumen buildings are now objects of leisurely consumption as China's economy booms. Large blocks, high rises, and green spaces have replaced the alleyway typology. Yet certain buildings were renovated rather than demolished, permitting hints of cultural preservation, but only hints. One site, developed by Hong Kong Shui On Land Group and designed by foreigners, is an overpriced spectacle, its alleyways rebuilt to accommodate tourists, commercial signs cladded onto historic or refabricated brick façades. Only the nostalgia of the old is kept, which stagnates the memories of lilong life not only for former residents, but for tourists and spectators alike.

My thesis revives and archives Xintiandi residents' politically suppressed memories through spatial image-making and implicates

3
Darkroom
collecting & creating

Li Zhensheng's journalistic eyes
Shutters now capture a new era
Brushing past the bygone days
When Red Guards stripped his apartment for his films
Fresh film strips hang dripping in red light

rin Shanghai

The Darkroom

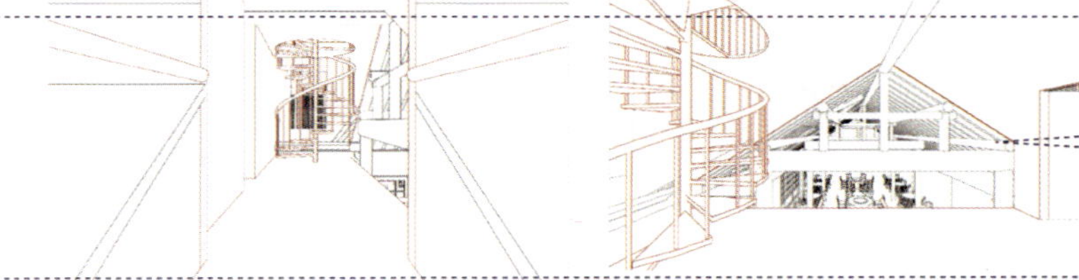

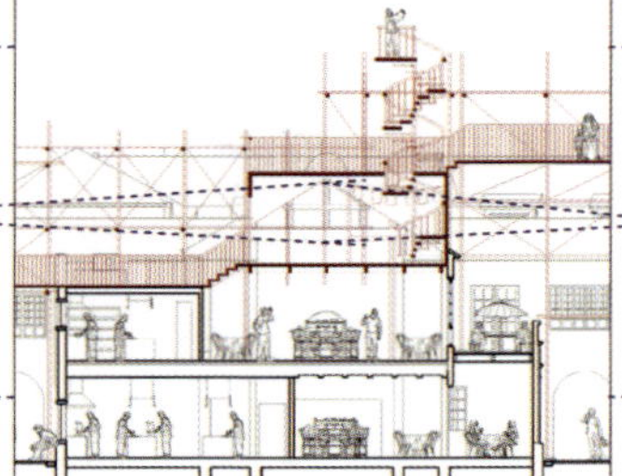

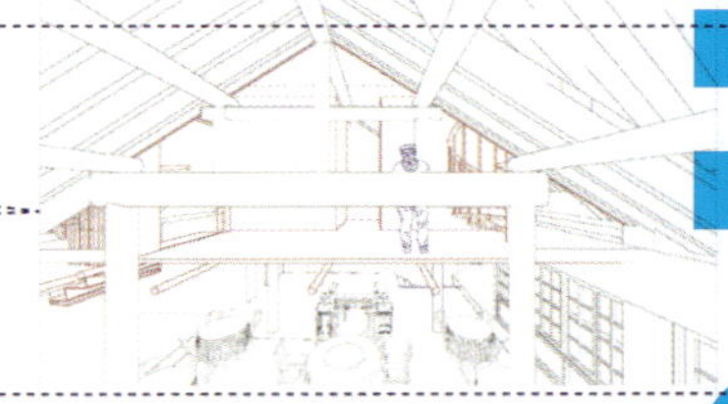

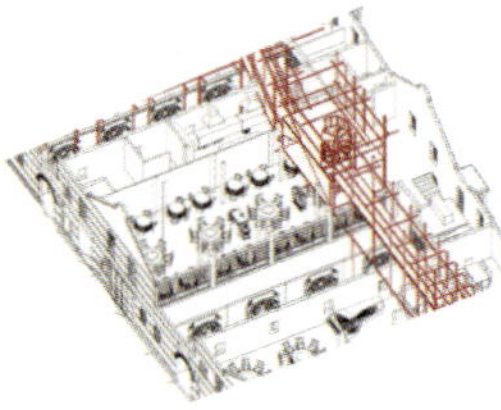

Jiejie folds the laundry for her
Mama, baba, didi, Xixi, nainai, waigong
Where Mao once had his rice
Writing for the first meeting

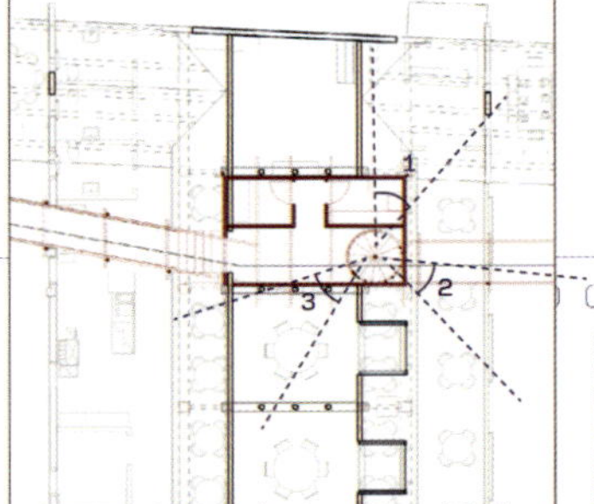

1

2

tourists as active players in the framework of the city's history, as agents for a forgotten history. Penetrating the Xintiandi site through a linear procession of scaffolding, the platforms and program bring visitors through four stages of "unforgetting," each keyed to a shikumen-sited space: cleansing (bathhouse), learning (bookstore), archiving (darkroom), and reflecting (gallery). The bathhouse, where visitors become aware of their bodily presence, is situated above a café, the clichéd tourist landing spot. The bookstore comprises three masses, simulating the layout of shikumen rooms; the visitor moves between the bookstore's interior and the platform's exterior, between displays of archived documents and the living archive of Xintiandi. The visitor then submerges into the darkroom, where photographers develop current scenes and insert them into the archive, and finally arrives in a gallery showcasing contemporary images set against the government's scriptures. Having encountered these staged events, visitors are spit back out into the city, now prepared to propagate the people's history as a counternarrative to the government's platitudes.

The Gallery

4
Gallery
archiving & reflecting

-inai wobbles up steep steps
-ards dipping from generations of torn soles
-lloused fingers slip hand washed laundry onto the bamboo poles
-terlacing the sky between the Gelou

In the moment of breaching lightness above the stairwell
The rails bring her to a box of memories on display
Images from another time and place
A guarded conspicuousness before returning to daily comforts

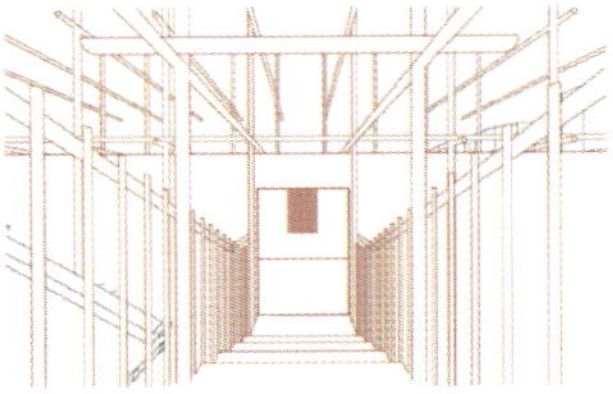

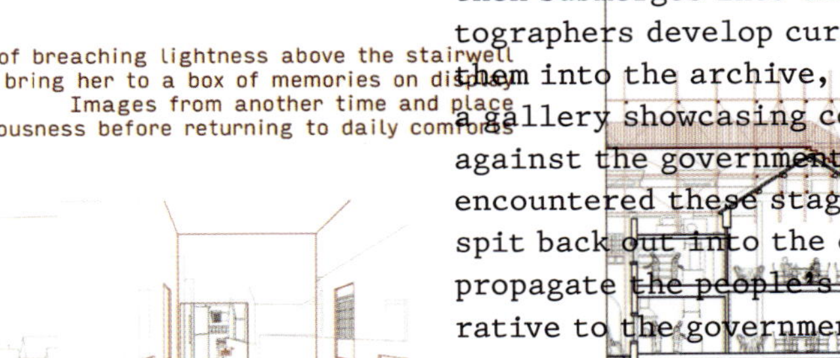

1 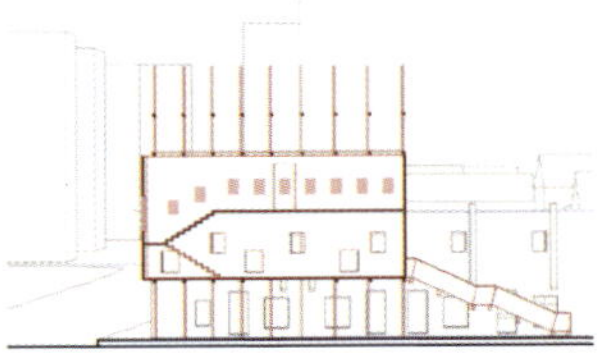 2 3

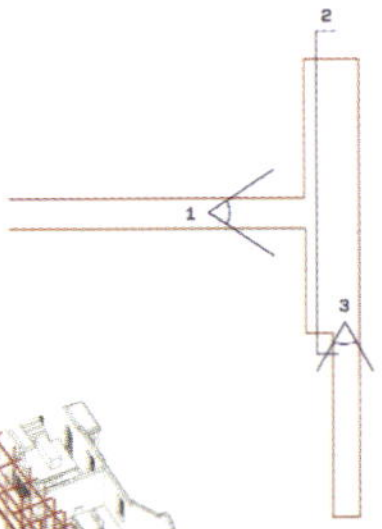

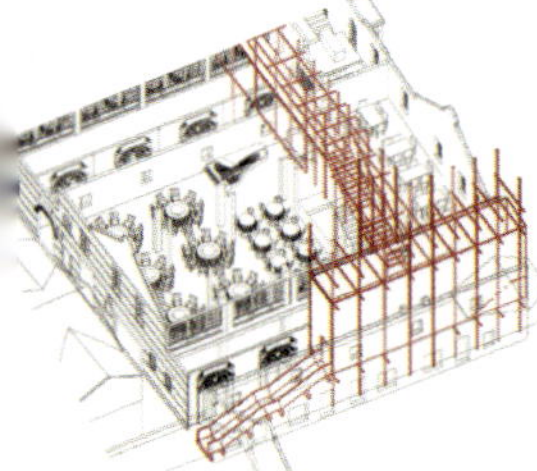

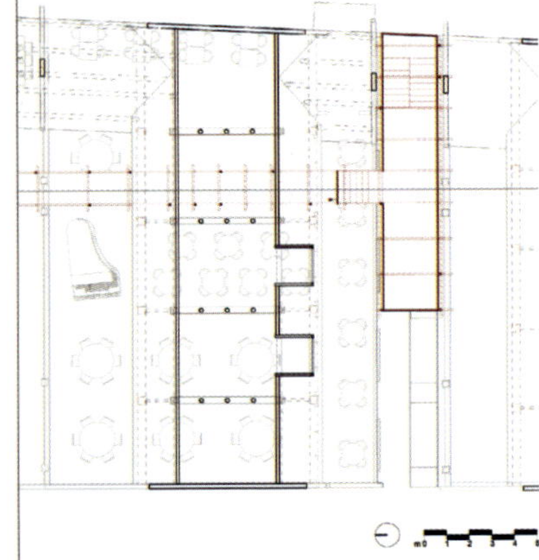

Narratives and image-making, section, plan
Site, axonometric
1
Bathhouse
to provoke consciousness of one's body's inhabitation of space and bring uncomfortable self-consciousness of one's use of a space
(entered through a cafe as a tourist camouflage)
2
Bookstore
to supplant the role of the souvenir shop, and allow for a way to take away knowledge rather than self-exotified images and products
3
Darkroom
for a film photographer for the collection and creation of constantly renewing content
4
Gallery
for the viewing of new archives / r
archives to place the viewer in the
present time and bring awareness t
the unending motion of time

Wei Xiao (B.Arch)

Urban villages—communities that maintain rural traditions within Chinese cities—have been an important part of China's urbanization planning since the beginning of the twenty-first century. Occupied by various types of residents and housing typologies, urban villages provide the last remnants of heterogeneity in an ever-expanding homogenous world. Recently, however, the government initiated a nationwide Urban Village Reconstruction Plan due to the villages' economic and relating social issues. In contemporary China, as gentrification outweighs diversity, urban villages are quickly disappearing.

I grew up in one of the urban villages in Haiyan, a third-tier city along the southeastern coast of China. Recently, I witnessed the government's urban renovation plan demolishing older structures and displacing residents to make way

安置城中村 Resettling Ur

安置城中村 Resettling Urban Villages: Toward an Inclusive and Heterogenous City

A critical evaluation of urban gentrification and pressing housing issues in contemporary China is seen through the lens of the urban village.

Artifacts

rban Villages: Towar

11: 30 AM

周末的时候天气不错，
我决定和其他的工友们一起做顿大餐。
我们就在厨房外头的水槽旁一边洗菜一边聊天。
休息的时候总是好的。
楼下单位的退休教师们今天也在外面聊天呢。

View toward cluster's outdoor platform

The weather is nice this weekend,
I decide to make a big meal with other workmates.
We wash vegebtables and chat with each other besides the outdoor working platform.
Resting with friends is always a good thing to do.
The retired teachers from Danwei below is chatting outdoor too.

7: 00 AM

View toward Danwei's shared reading space

我一般早上7点起床，
去公共阅览室看报读书。
还会和邻居聊聊家常。

I usually wake up at 7 am,
Then I go to the shared reading space to read newspapers and books.
Sometimes I would chat with my neighbours about daily stuff too.

6: 30 PM

晚上6点半下班了和工友一块走回家，
一起在共享厨房做了晚饭。
我们烧了两荤一素，
就着啤酒结束这一天。

View toward cluster's shared kitchen

At 6:30 pm I finish work and walk back home with workmate,
We cook dinner together in the shared kitchen.
We together make two kinds of meat and one vegetable,
And we end our day with a cup of beer.

9:00 AM

上午的时候我打扫了一下自家的小菜园子，
摘了些新鲜的蔬菜准备做中饭。
我的父母还会顺便一起侍弄一下他们在园子里养的花。
白天我们基本上都会呆在院子里。

Individual family's gardening experience

I clean up the little growing field that we have in our garden in the morning,
And I pick some fresh vegetables for our lunch.
My parents would also take care of the flowers in the garden.
We basically spend our morning working outdoor.

View toward Danwei's outdoor platform

2: 30 PM

吃完午饭我午休到了下午2点左右，
起来看看电视。
有的时候还会和楼里的其他住户在院子里聊天下棋。
到晚饭的时候就回家吃饭。

After lunch I rest until around 2 pm.
The I will wake up and watch a bit TV shows.
Sometimes I go chart or play chess with neighbours in the outdoor garden.
I head back home again during dinner time.

for the construction of new, uniform residential apartments and shopping malls. As a consequence, existing physical, urban textures and structures are disappearing simultaneously with the eradication of an embedded diversity in the urban identity.

In an attempt to support multiple publics through the representation of heterogeneity in places, my thesis utilizes preservation tactics to support this unique social group against the trending homogeneity of gentrification by preserving the notion of the urban village in the framework of high-rise buildings. By collaging a variety of lifestyles and housing typologies in vertical expansion, I elevate the urban village's daily rituals so that residents' diversity can propagate throughout the building. My project reclaims erased places, giving authorship back to people.

Exterior view from ground level

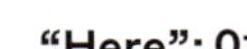

"Here": 01

"Here": 02

Front of proposed commercial flyer

Back of proposed commercial flyer

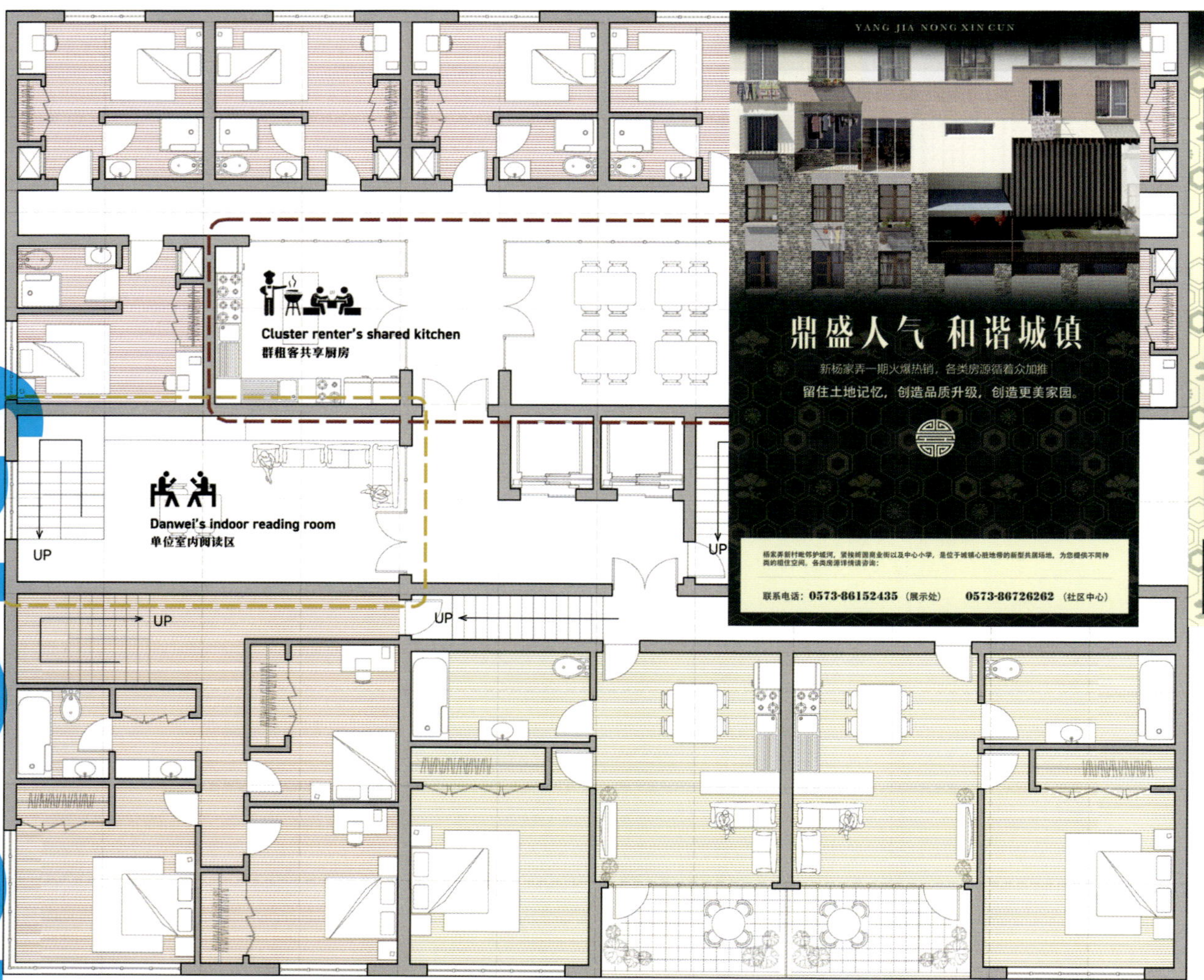

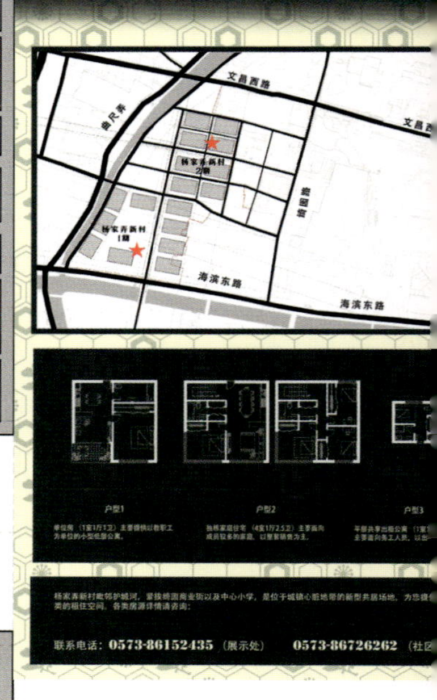

Typical floor plan ...

... and its inspiration

"Here": 03

"Here": 04

Second Natures
Introduction

Primary Critic **Rachely Rotem, Critic, Department of Architecture, RISD**
Secondary Critic **Ijlal Muzaffar, Associate Professor, Department of Theory + History of Art + Design, RISD**

Students **Marina Bibidakis (M.Arch), Hannah Langmuir (M.Arch), Brittany Knowlton (M.Arch), Loretta Quint (B.Arch), Bobby Zhao (B.Arch)**

This studio questioned our second natures by designing architecture for new spatial habits. It called into question the assumed separation between architecture and the natural world by redrawing the borders between nature and technology, indoor and outdoor, interior and urban. We explored two parallel interpretations of second nature, one based on repetitive behavior in society and the other on phenomena in the physical world. The first involves the everyday habits so deeply ingrained in our spatial memory that they appear automatic—as in opening a door, entering an elevator, or walking through a lobby. When these habits are repeated through collective action, they form a set of social relations that occur repeatedly in the built environment. In this way, an act as simple as walking through a lobby is different in Italy than in Japan, as is sitting in an urban plaza. The second challenges the previously held belief that nature is architecture's opposite. This ideology has reinforced many borders in the built environment, especially between the artificial and the natural. However, the notion of "natural" is constructed by human perception: the natural is, in fact, manmade. Nature, on the other hand, is the sum of phenomena that occurs regardless of human consciousness in both indoor and outdoor environments. Second Nature argues that architecture and nature are not in opposition but function as extensions of each other—with architecture as an extension of nature, and vice versa.

The Covid-19 public health crisis caught us midway into the thesis process and enhanced the initial premise of the studio, revealing an environmental paradox: as billions of people stayed indoors to "flatten the curve" and help our health workers, urban nature had a chance to recharge. As manmade habits changed abruptly, pollution receded, city air became cleaner, and nature softly began wilding our temporarily empty public spaces, showing the beauty of gentle life that manifests itself post-human occupation. At the same time, the more we stayed indoors, living and working in nonstop interiors, where virtual spaces enabled by technology have replaced the physical spaces of social interactions, the more we find ourselves feeling the need for daily, healthy connection with nature.

The framework of Second Natures was open enough for students to bring forward their own topics of interest and scales of operation. Marina Bibidakis, for example, celebrates the found ecosystem in abandoned buildings that were originally designed for machine occupation in the industrial age, repurposing them for the use of future machines (see pp. 95–98). Her project produces a hybrid of open buildings and their surrounding natures while designing for the machines (and humans) of the future. Brittany Knowlton connects the low voting rating in underprivileged neighborhoods in Chicago to a lack of communal gathering spaces, proposing a formal and informal design for performance spaces to encourage a sense of community and civic participation (see pp. 103–106). Hannah Langmuir brings the act of sport play into the emptying office typology, suggesting that connecting to the natural world should evolve into more than adding greenery; it should also include athletic activities that bring us closer to our primal selves and each other (see pp. 99–102). Loretta Quint explores how defensive architecture becomes offensive both to marginalized social groups and to the environment and instead proposes a network of infrastructure that can foster resilience in coastal cities and support informal activities by skaters and homeless people (see pp. 107–110). Bobby Zhao studies monuments in different cultures and develops strategies to transform them into anti-monuments for the benefit of the public. He uses the Hudson Yards development in New York City to test his theories by dismantling the architecture of privilege for the benefit of all New Yorkers (see pp. 111–114).

These thesis projects and others in the studio tied together the social and the environmental in unexpected ways and worked in opposing scales simultaneously, thus transforming architecture itself into the design of an ecology.

Marina Bibidakis (M.Arch)

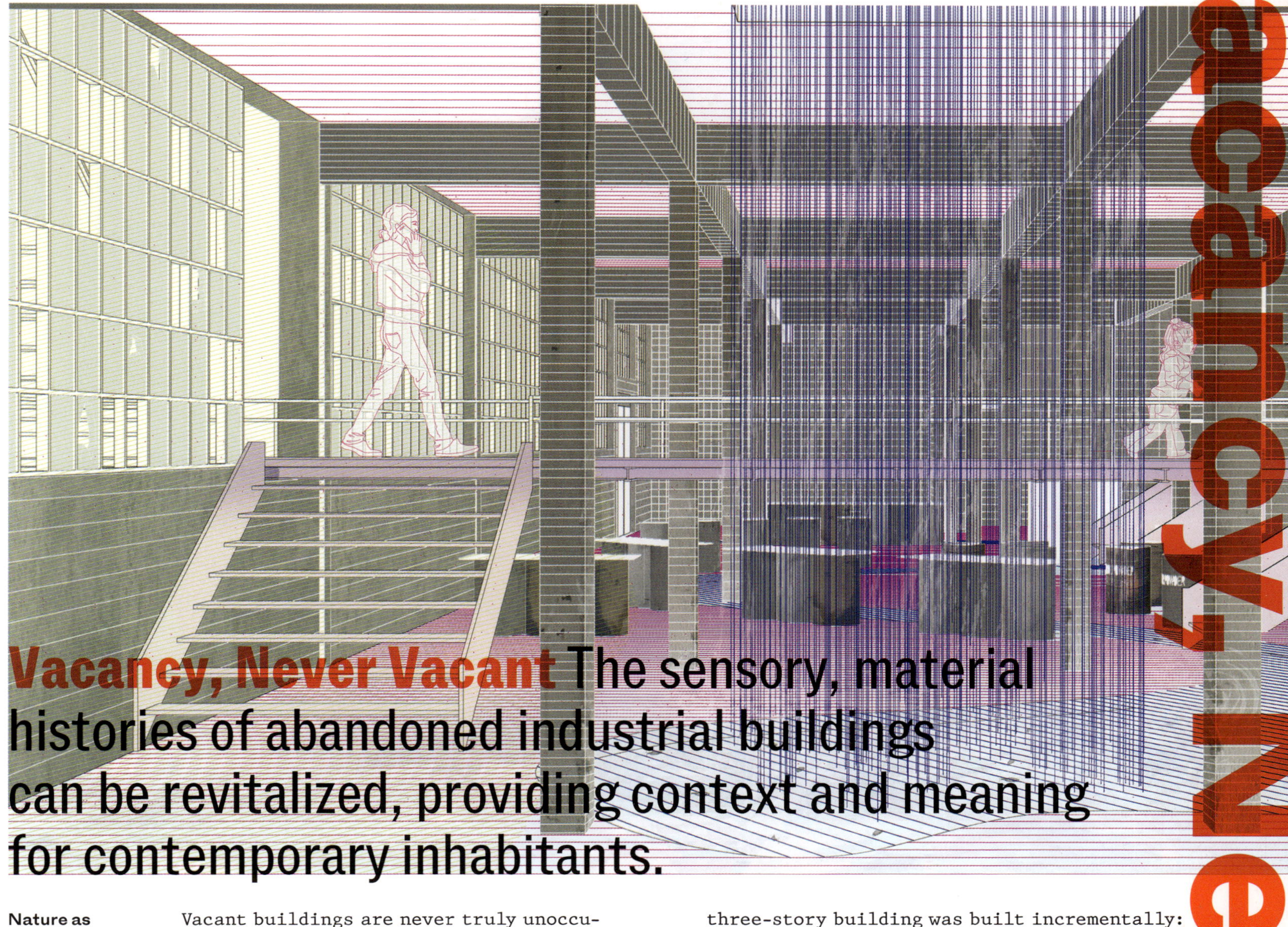

Vacancy, Never Vacant The sensory, material histories of abandoned industrial buildings can be revitalized, providing context and meaning for contemporary inhabitants.

Nature as cooling device, digital experiential rendering

Vacant buildings are never truly unoccupied. A building's program changes over time, and yet signals of its original use remain. Industrial buildings, for example, use massive columns to support heavy machinery and large, open spaces optimized for fabrication. Those features persist even when manufacturing has ceased. My thesis revisits the relics of an industrial building that was used as a highly optimized model for production in Athens, Greece.

Athens has a vacancy problem, especially after the recent financial crisis and current pandemic. My site is a button factory called NINA, located close to downtown in the Agios Eleutherios neighborhood, which is known for apparel production. The three-story building was built incrementally: the first floor in 1940, the second in 1951, and the third in 1956, then ultimately abandoned in 1980. Today the old button factory houses temporary occupants: squatters take over the ruins, while nature starts its work.

Critically engaging the future of building in Athens, my thesis chronicles what exists, emphasizing reuse and rejecting the modernist zeal for building anew. I embrace transitional moments: walls crumbling, waste left behind, cracking floors, and sprouting grass. Acknowledging the building's history by prioritizing its relationship to the landscape and social context, I focus on the polarized post-machine occupancy as it meets an anthropocentric program. Athens's warm

Vacancy, Never Vaca

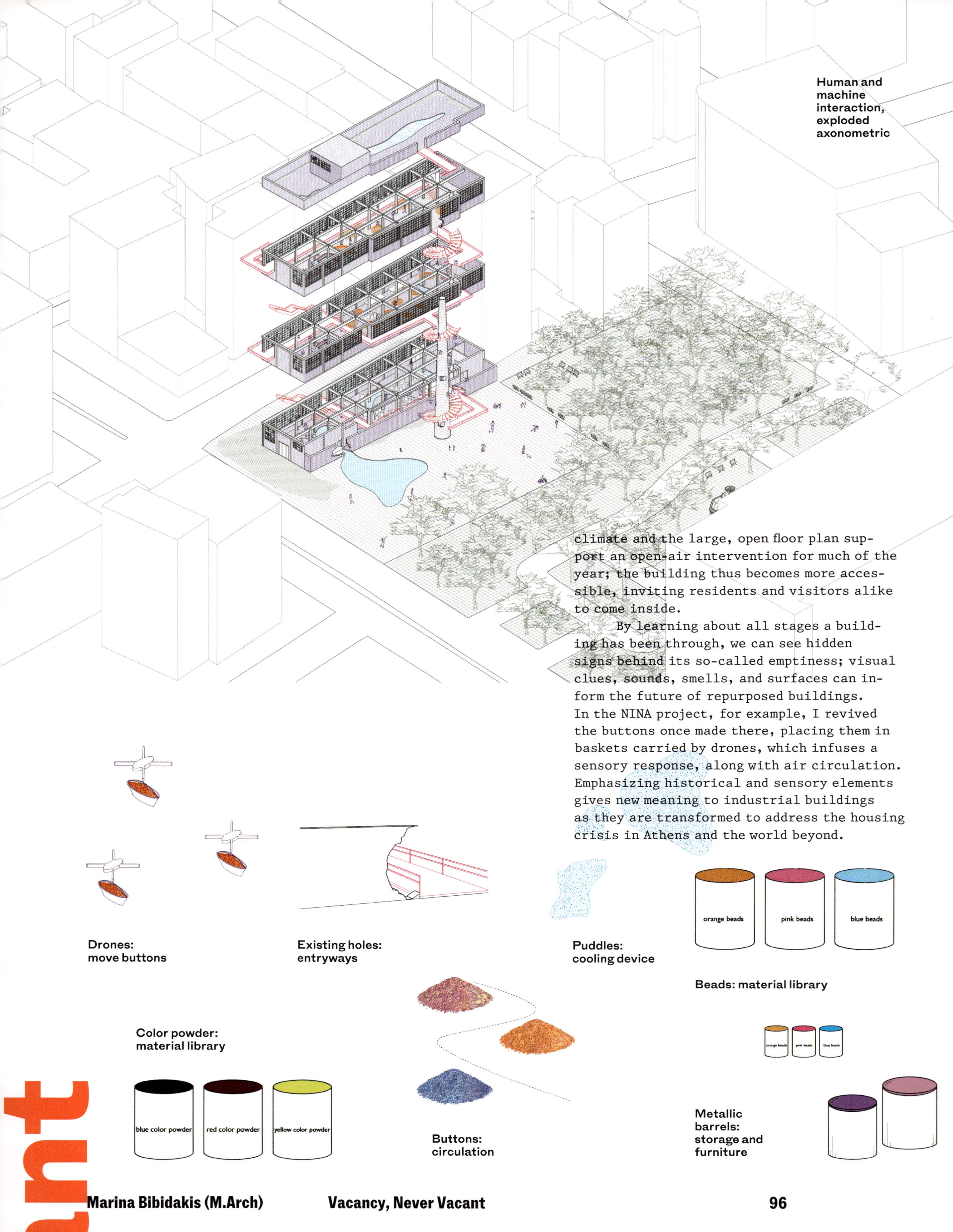

climate and the large, open floor plan support an open-air intervention for much of the year; the building thus becomes more accessible, inviting residents and visitors alike to come inside.

By learning about all stages a building has been through, we can see hidden signs behind its so-called emptiness; visual clues, sounds, smells, and surfaces can inform the future of repurposed buildings. In the NINA project, for example, I revived the buttons once made there, placing them in baskets carried by drones, which infuses a sensory response, along with air circulation. Emphasizing historical and sensory elements gives new meaning to industrial buildings as they are transformed to address the housing crisis in Athens and the world beyond.

Addition to existing conditions, digital experiential rendering

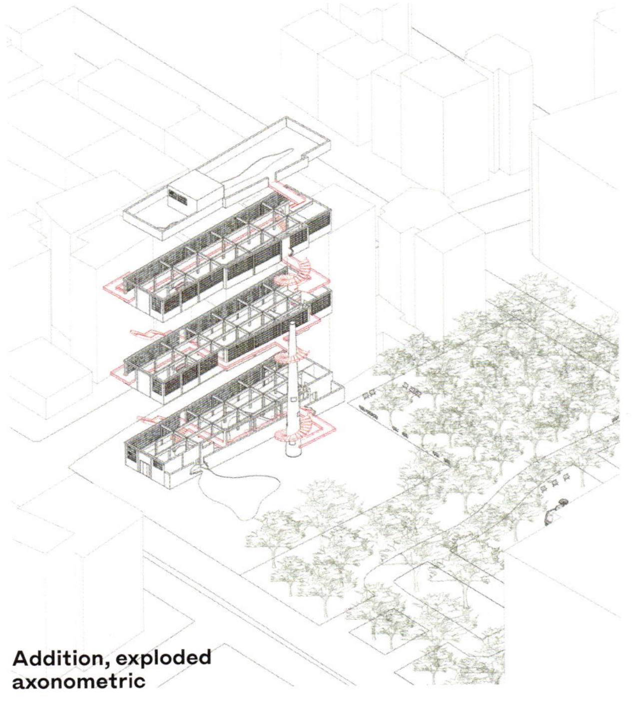

Addition, exploded axonometric

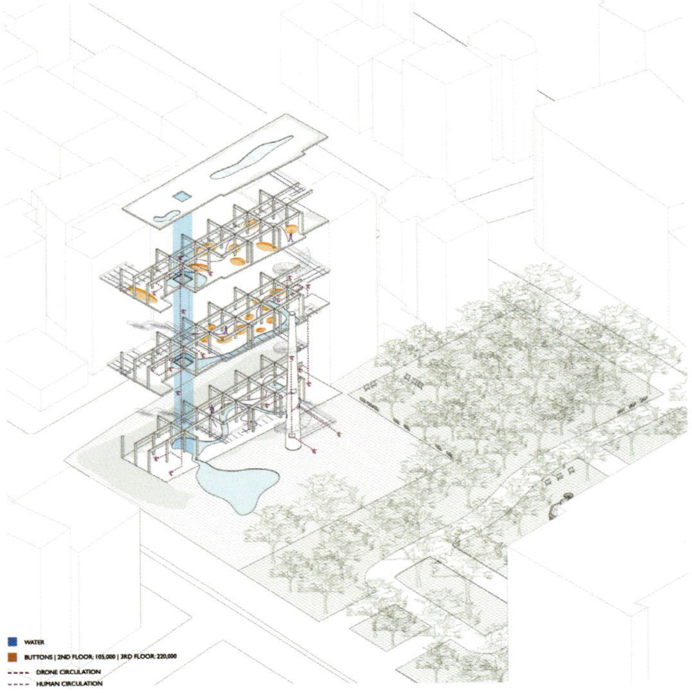

Water and circulation, exploded axonometric

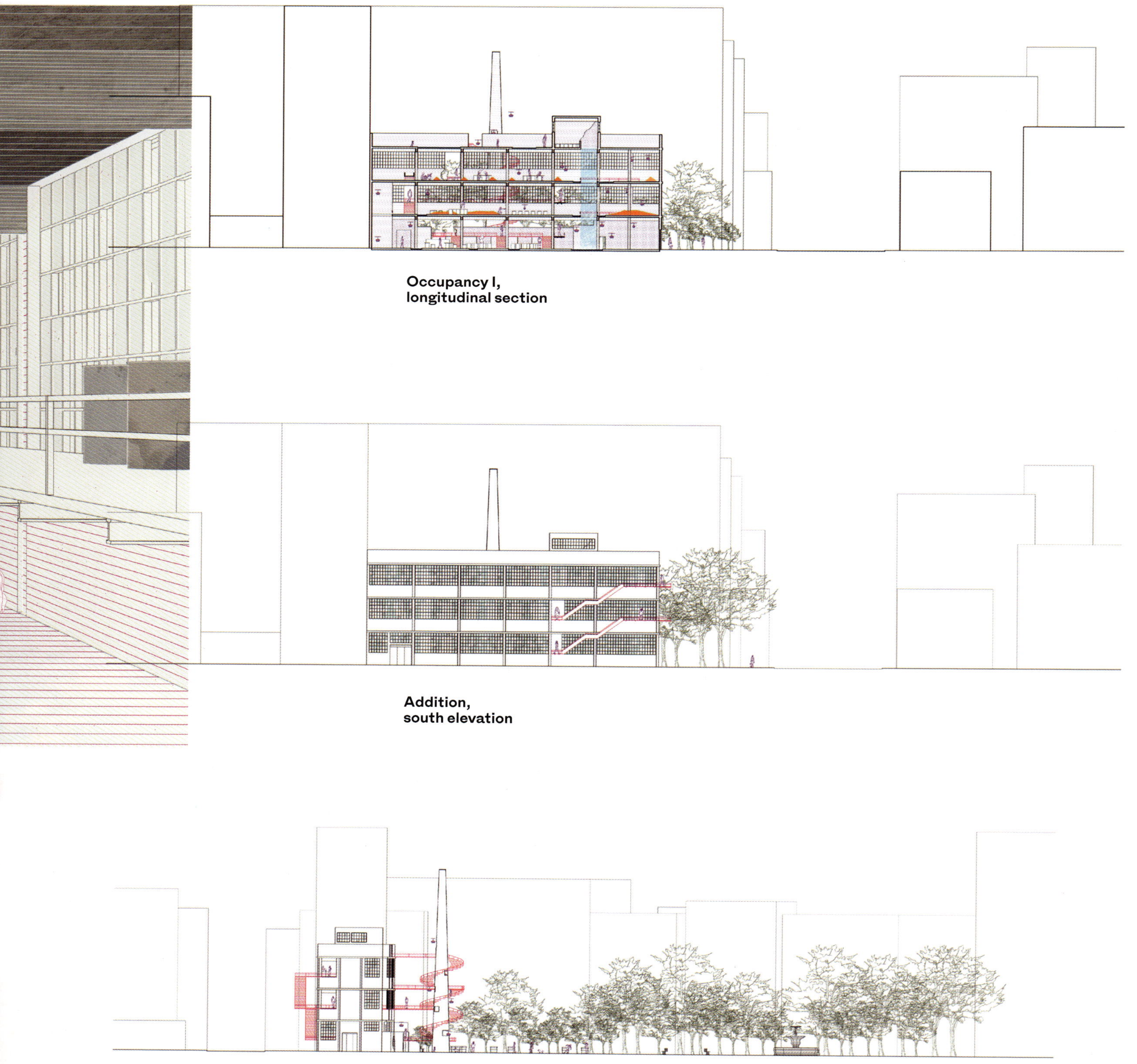

Occupancy I,
longitudinal section

Addition,
south elevation

Addition,
east elevation

Hannah Langmuir (M.Arch)

Play Grounds: Typological Interventions of Playing in Providence Play becomes a programmatic tool to create symbiotic relationships between humans, nature, and architecture.

As Western society began favoring technological development over the natural environment, we confined ourselves to limited states of being. Gridded cities, micro-apartments, and cubicles restrict our interactions and behaviors. Proponents of modular design promise adaptability, though once the designs are constructed, they are often never changed again. My thesis reintroduces the modular system as a means to activate our surroundings, encouraging playfulness and a symbiotic relationship between humans, nature, and the built environment. Using play as a programmatic tool to organize new built environments enables users to engage not only with external environments but with our most primal human natures as well.

Sensory Map, elevation

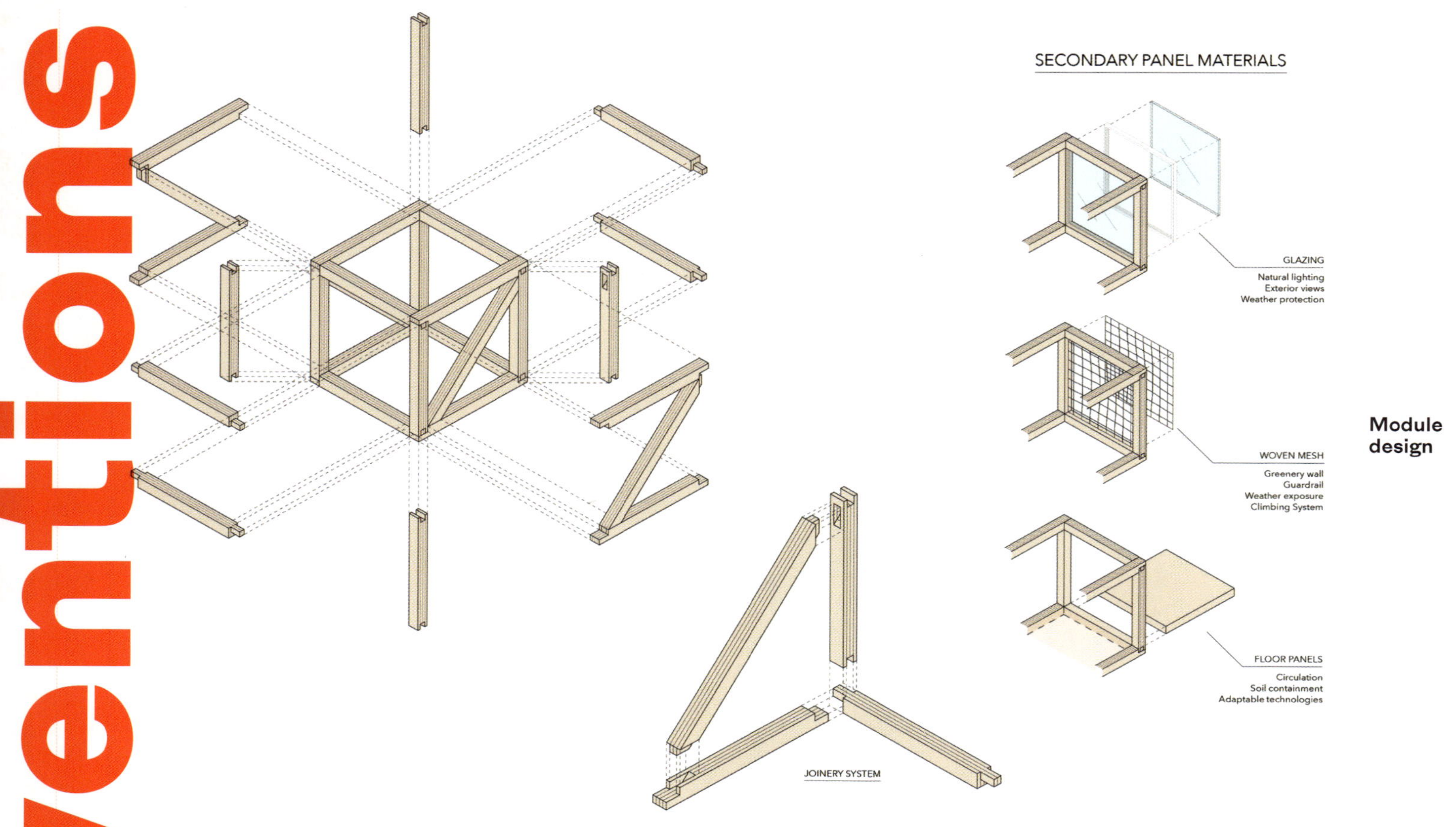

Module design

I selected three sites across existing office buildings in downtown Providence, Rhode Island: One Financial Plaza, Turk's Head, and the Old Stone Square. With three programmatic typologies tested in each building, the playing grounds highlight a series of spectrums: the amount of programmatic freedom, the integration of natural elements, and the degree of disruption to existing office space. In a city rife with vacancy, the proposed design interventions seek to revitalize not only their users, but the buildings they permeate and the natures they introduce as well.

In the Vertical typologies, the sheer height of One Financial Plaza became a guide for designing climbing walls, micro-forests, and trampoline rooms that ascend the façade and encourage occupants to do the same. This set of playing grounds is the most programmatically freeing, with little structure or formality applied to the new spaces. The second programmatic type, the Lateral, emphasizes horizontal circulation by integrating varying types of footpaths throughout the building. At Turk's Head, Lateral interventions interrupt formalized pathways to promote meandering,

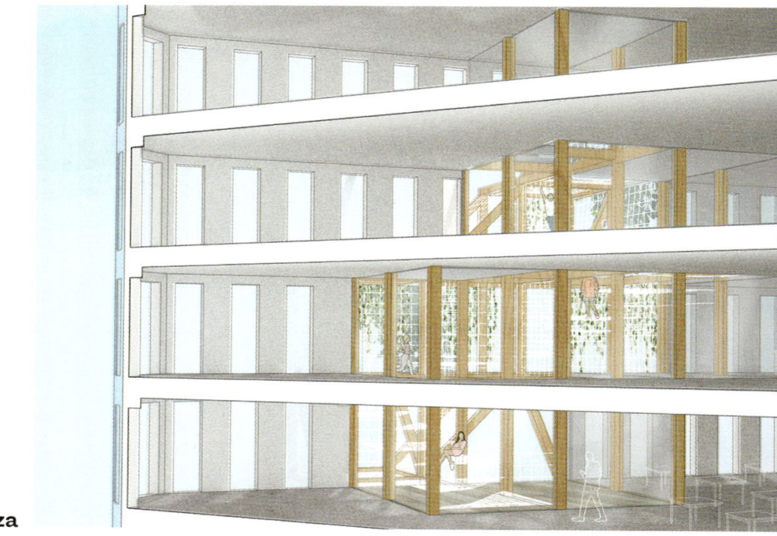

Trampolines at One Financial Plaza

Running track at Turk's Head Building

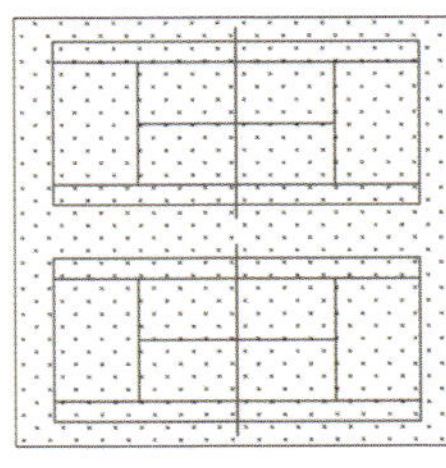

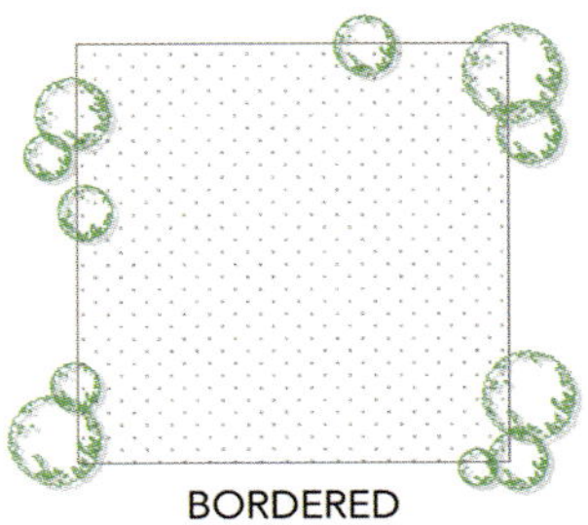

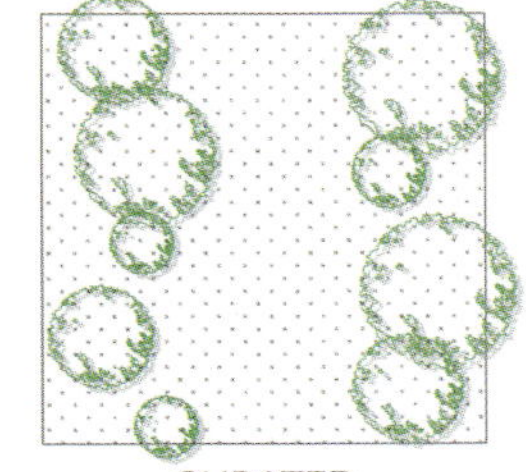

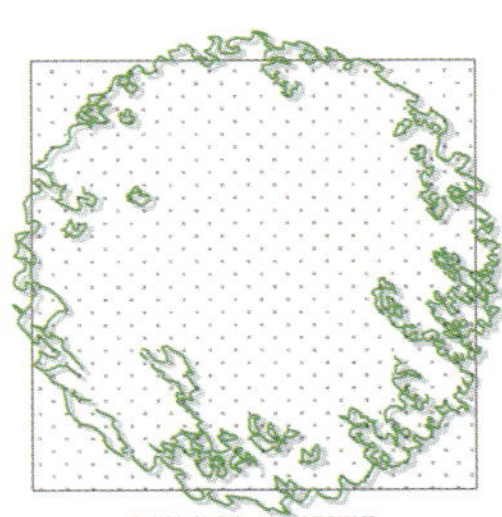

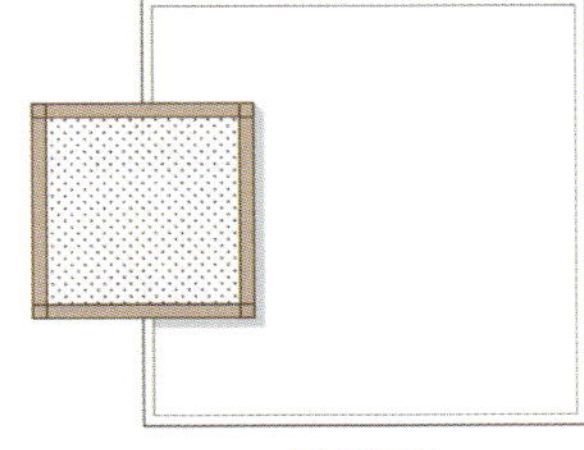

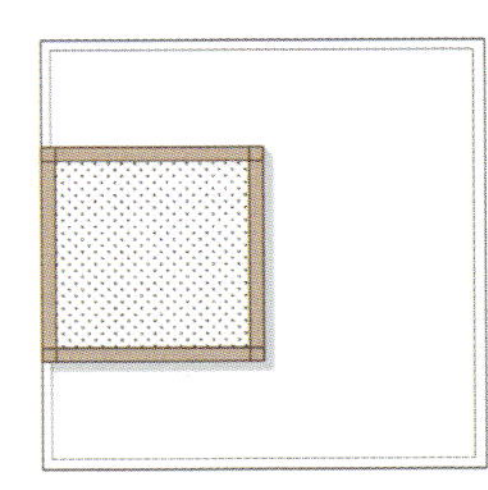

Spectrum of adaptations, plan diagram

providing a new means of interaction and egress by occupying the gap of the building's V-shaped form. Lastly, the Grid typologies adhere to the overall logic and order of the building, cleanly integrating new programs into the existing gridded office layout. Despite Old Stone Square's rigid organization, the playing grounds themselves encourage flexibility by employing LED floors and walls to create adaptable court spaces.

Climbing a tree and sitting beside one or gazing at a mountain range and hiking through it are very different acts. Connecting with nature demands more than a relative proximity; it requires an active engagement of the body and with its surrounding environment. Through a taxonomy of adaptations, my thesis reintroduces play spaces into banal gridded forms in an attempt to rescue a vitality long left behind.

Adaptable court at the Old Stone Square

Micro-forest at One Financial Plaza, plan detail

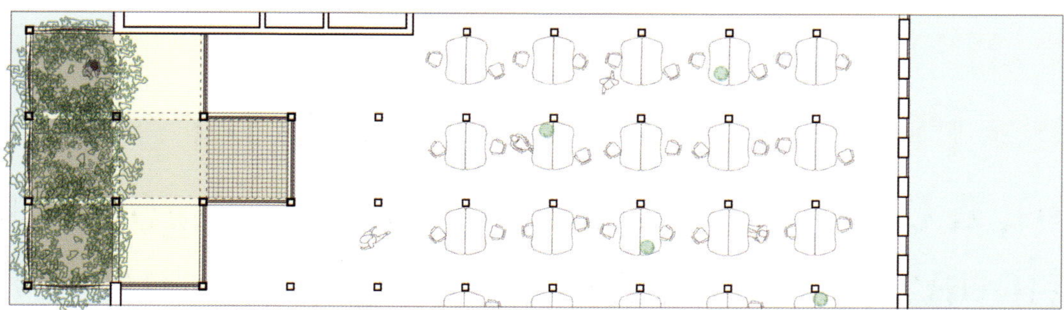

Micro-forest at One Financial Plaza, section detail

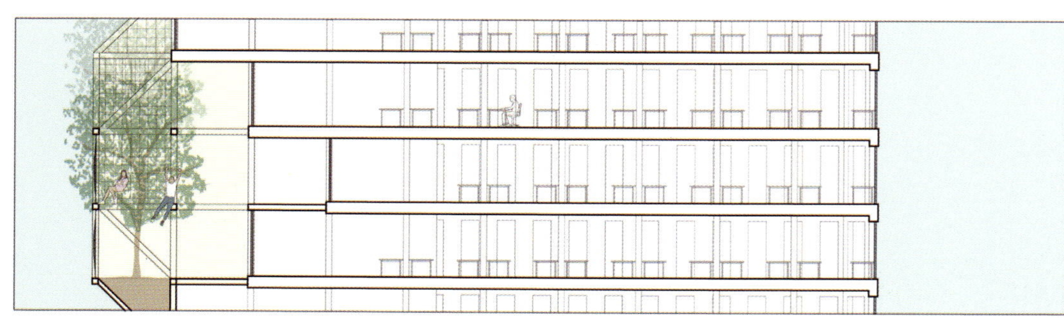

Terrain at Turk's Head Building, plan detail

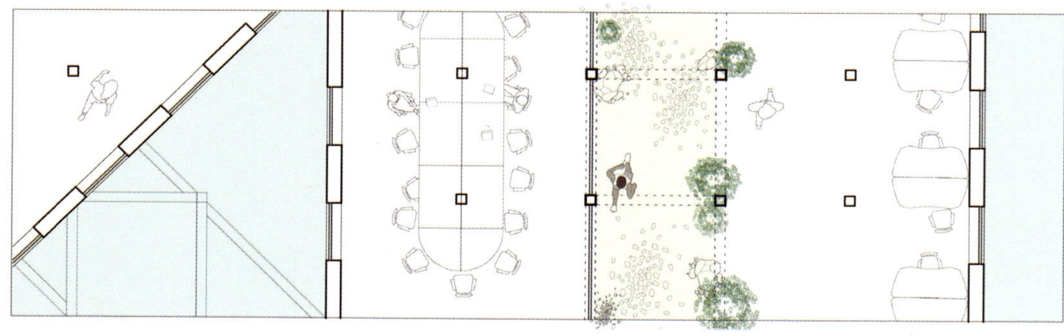

Terrain at Turk's Head Building, section detail

Terrace court at the Old Stone Square, plan detail

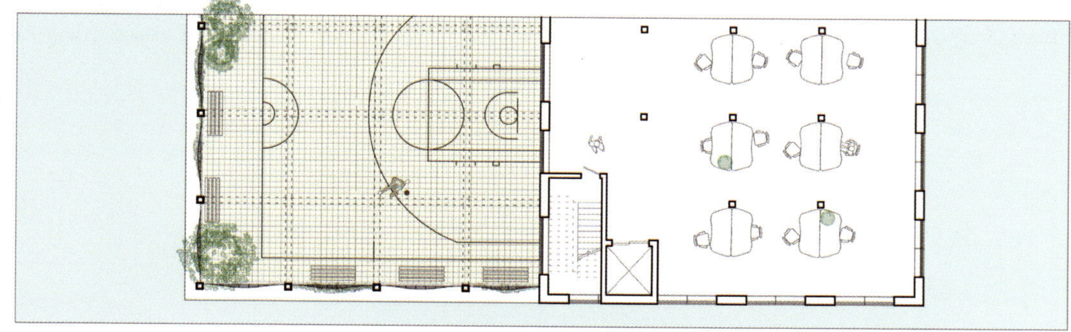

Brittany Knowlton (M.Arch)

Architecture as Performance: The Spectacle of a Conscious Public

By setting a stage for performance and education, a community center in Chicago provides multiple functional uses and manifold civic benefits.

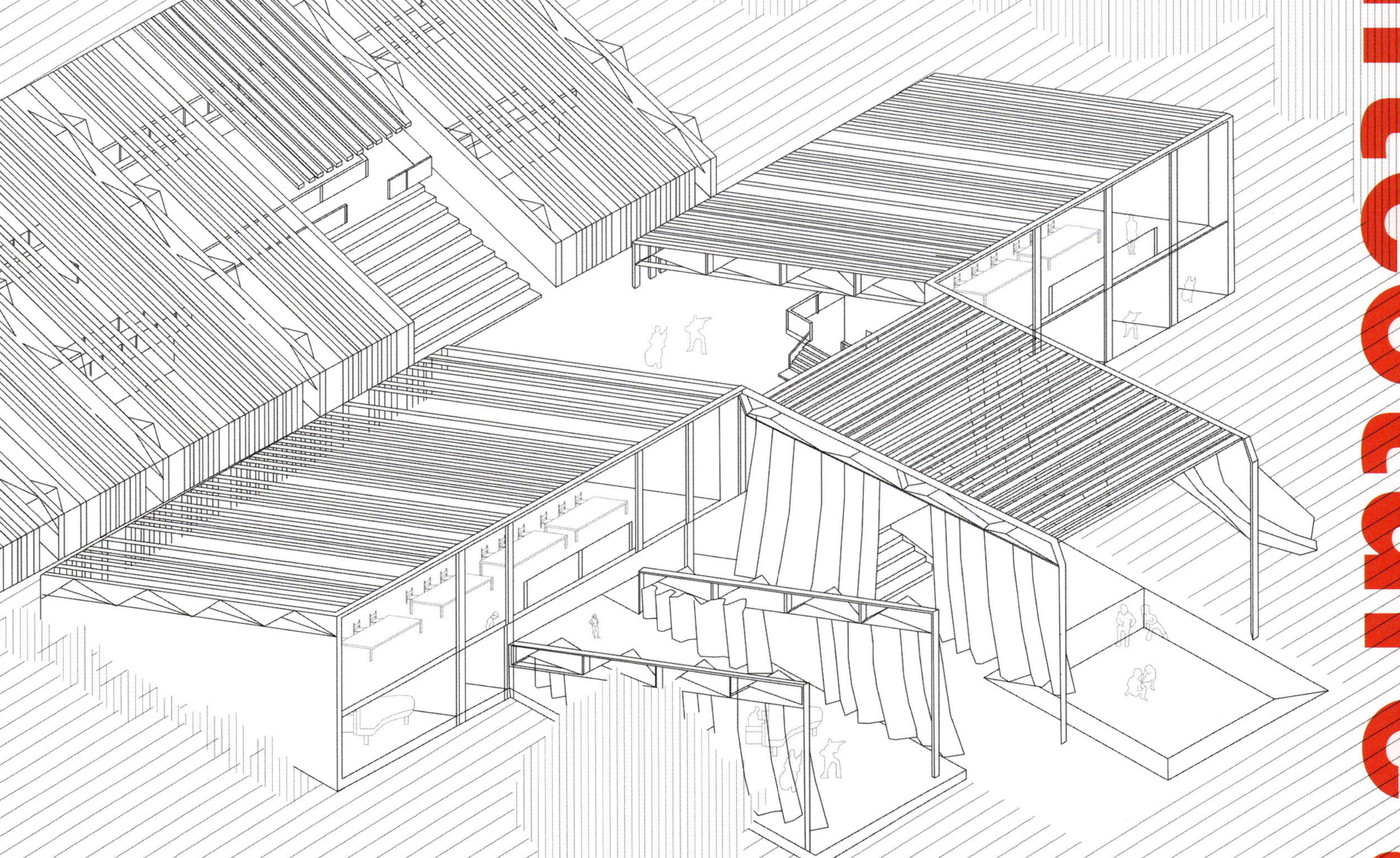

View of interior/exterior classrooms and individual practice spaces

Urban spatial organization has a performative nature, architecture has a capacity to create performance space, and citizens have an opportunity for conscientious involvement within that space. Can the relationship between the city and its citizens create a distinctive place of belonging while allowing its spatial order to shift? My thesis aims to catalyze action and pride of ownership by reversing Chicago's declining public policy, its social injustice, and its sensible architecture. Designing in response to existing structures in Chicago's urban environment to blur boundaries in public space, I provide the city's inhabitants with accessible public locations for daily tasks, expressive freedom, and democracy.

Emphasizing music and performance, my thesis positions a stage of continually transforming views as a community center. As both performers and spectators, participants become the spectacle as their engagement with the architecture creates moments of performance, enacting an exchange between watching, learning, and acting. Texts welcoming visitors appear at the intersection of interior and exterior walls. The dissected interstitial space positions a representational technique that drafts the visual intimacy of looking at or up at the performer. Each line resonates with the vibrations that connect performer and audience. The line between them blurs. The community center hosts various ways to educate the public. Classrooms provide continuing education alongside a central exhibit on the history and context of the community. Space is never one thing: a classroom is at once a space for practicing and learning while also a platform for performances; a closed auditorium can open up. The pop-up farmers' market sells local goods, providing business opportunities for community members. As you inhabit the structure, space becomes a part of you; sound moves through the building just as you do. This is a stage for speech, music, local trade, and, above all, the ability to express freely in an urban environment.

View of graffiti wall, outdoor/indoor auditorium, and farmers market

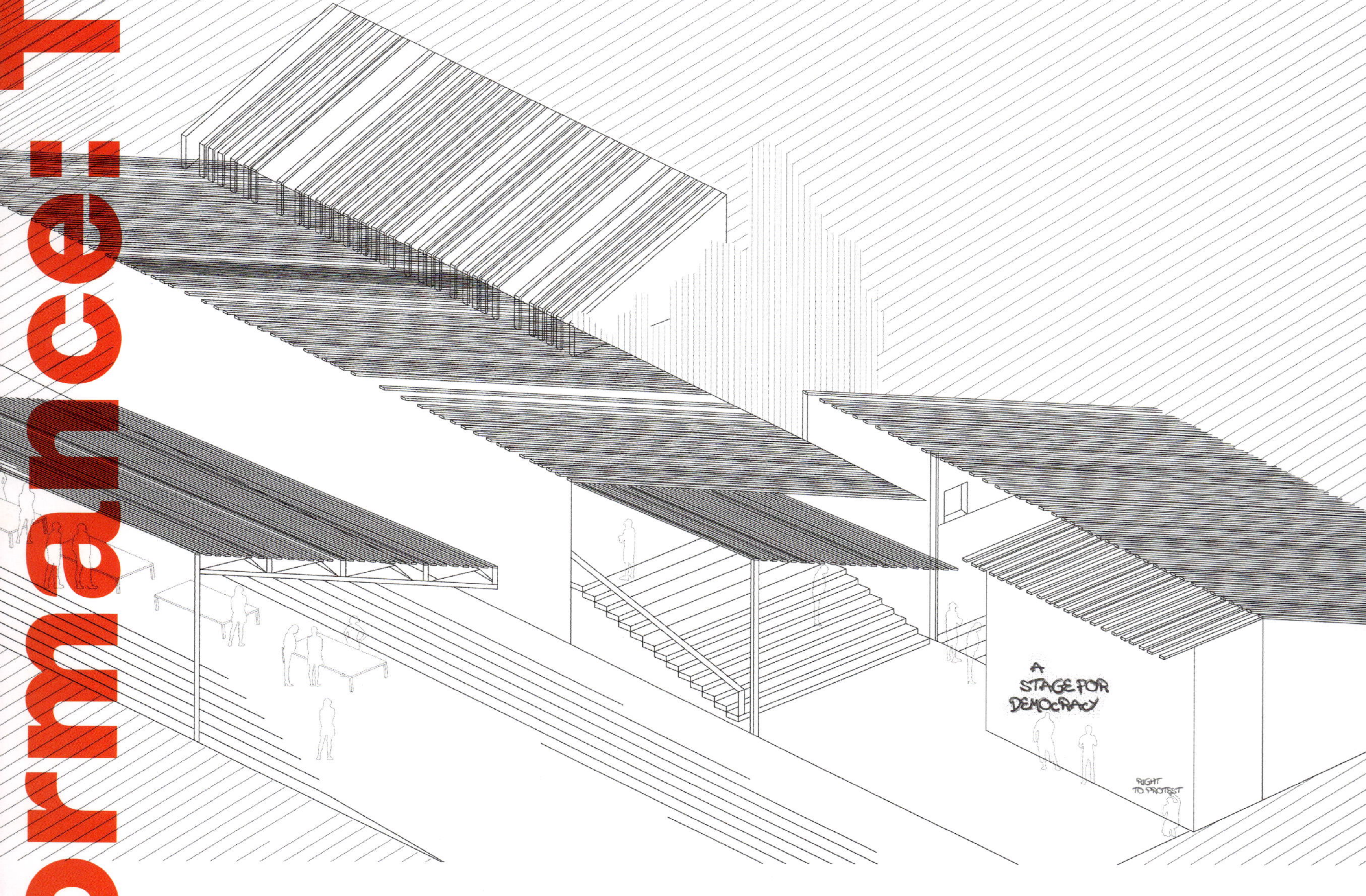

acle of a Conscious P

Blurring of audience and performer: a street performance

Blurring of audience and performer: everyday life as a choreographed event

SITE PLAN
1. URBAN FARMING
2.FARMERS MARKET
3. GALLERY
4. CLASSROOMS
5. AUDITORIUM
6. OUTDOOR PERFORMANCE/ CLASSROOMS
1
2
3
4
5
6

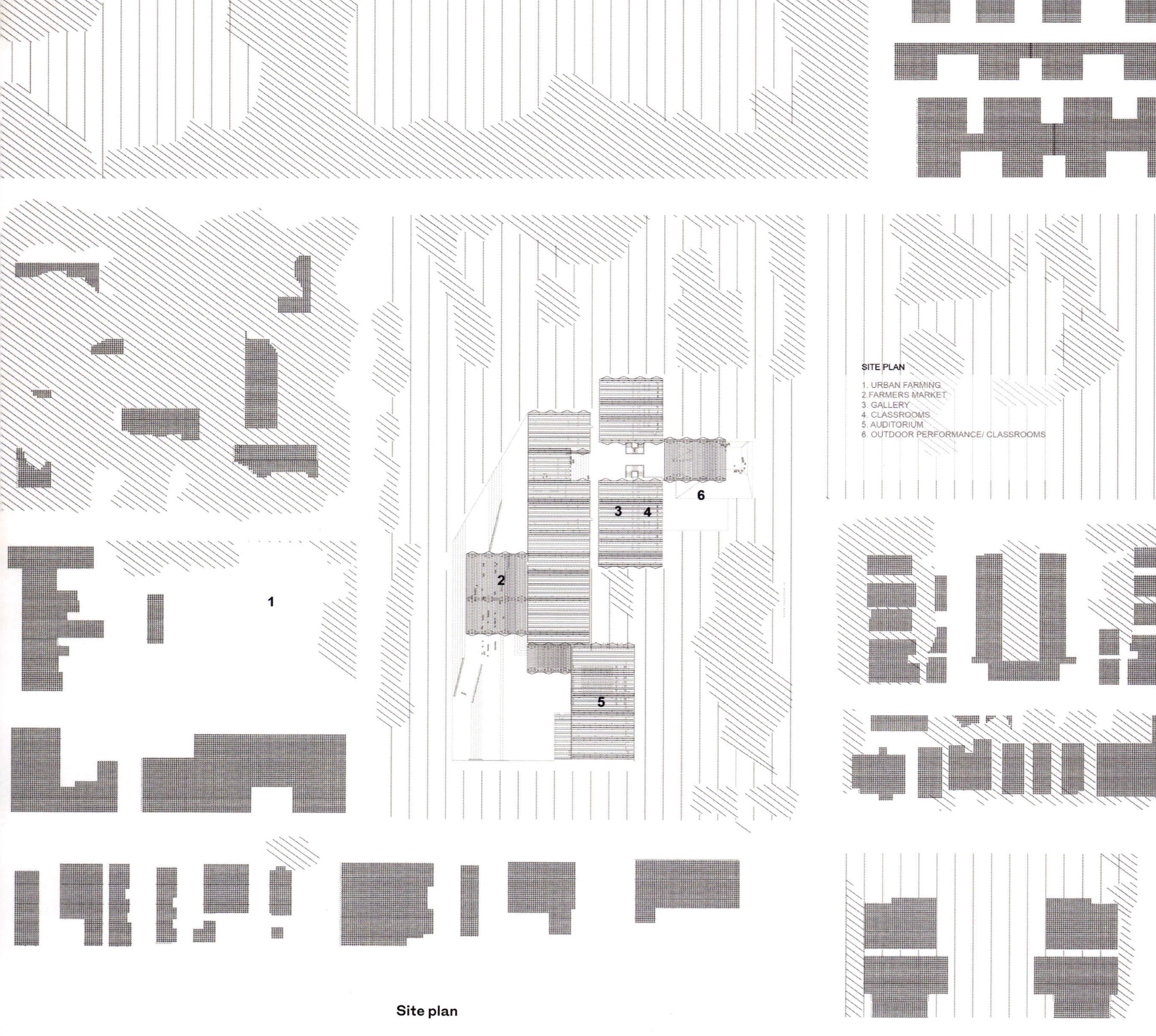

Site plan

Loretta Quint (B.Arch)

Hostile benches of New York City

Fourth Places: Legalize Loiter

Turning hostile design into hospitable design gives the city back to the people, alleviating infrastructural elitism and asserting everyone's right to spatial liberty.

Occupying hostile benches

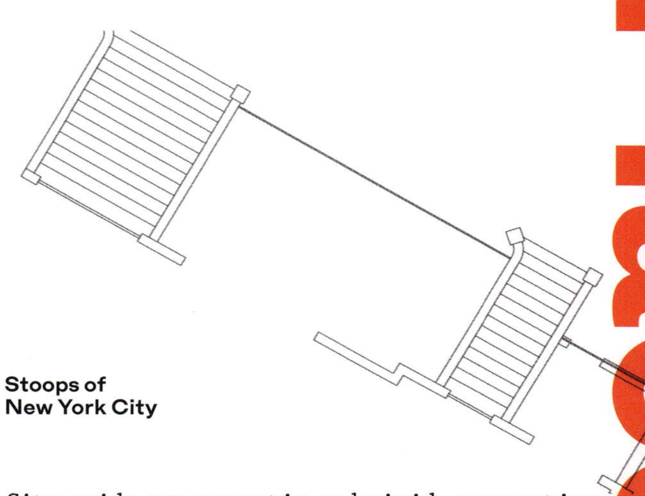

Stoops of New York City

Probe redux

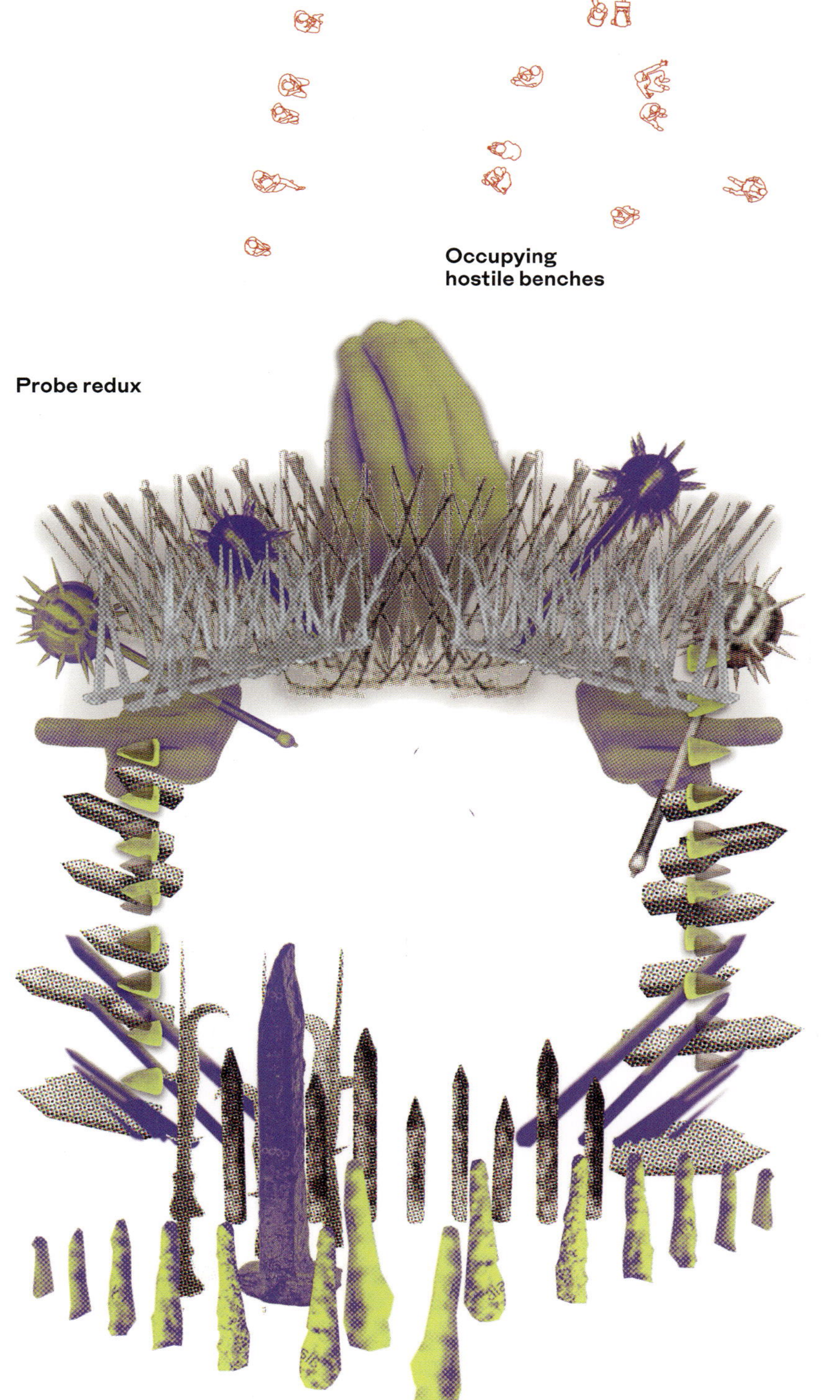

City grids are panoptic and rigid, augmenting ordered movement and visibility, overwhelming the spatial logic and the embodied experience of our urban environments. Within the grid, on the streets, and in the buildings, hostile design—a flawed system of control that proliferates at all scales of urbanity—takes over. Metal dividers split bench seats, preventing people from lying down comfortably; spikes are drilled into concrete windowsills to prevent sitting; a building's façade is cast at a slant to repel pedestrians who might otherwise lean on it. These urban design tactics fulfill a modernist obsession with control and perpetuate a fabricated, elitist otherness within our society. Boldly removing agency from the pedestrian, hostile design makes loitering a crime.

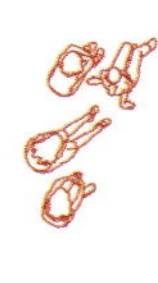

Occupying the stoop

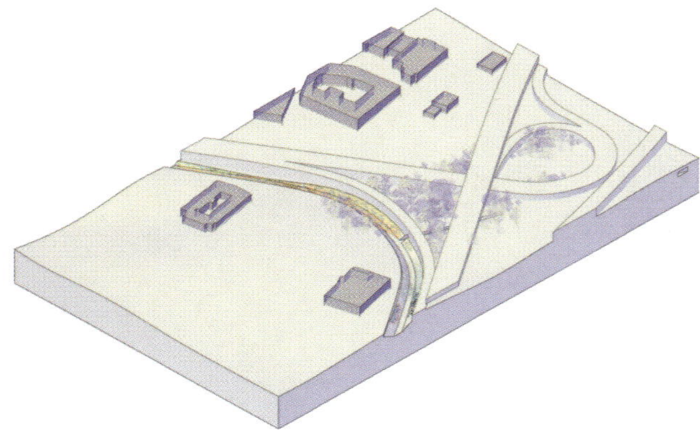

Highway drainage ditch in Philadelphia

Occupying the drainage ditch

The design strategies and rules that govern criminality in the public realm are obviously class-based and anti-homeless and overdue to be overturned. My thesis work—a series of tools that give the built environment back to the people in New York City—enables and calls for a radical shift in urban design. Identifying New York's taxonomy of hostile design, I commandeered its coercive tools to reframe loitering in the city. Stretching out across a bench suddenly becomes an act of defiance. The rectilinear grid becomes a fluidly moving curve, giving back the natural environment from which it was wrought. Metal bars curbing skateboarding are removed, and widened paths allow for intersecting modes of pedestrian traffic. Wherever there was dense, inaccessible public space, my design preemptively awards misuse, my interventions discover new urban forms, prevent alienation, and support spatial liberty. They make misuse a defiant act and point to a hopeful future.

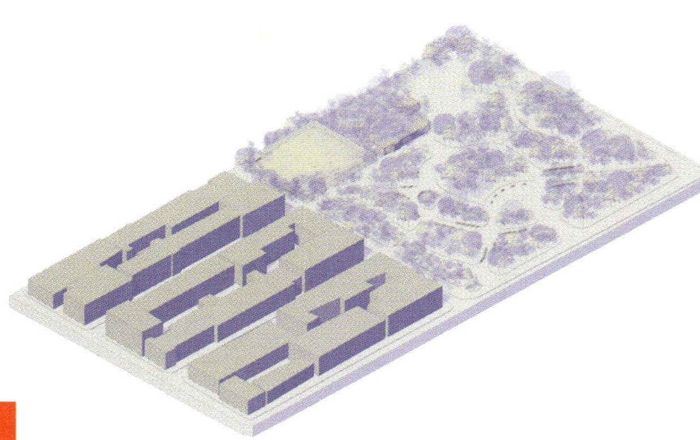

Tompkins Square Park, New York, NY

Callous objects fastened to windowsills to prevent pedestrians from sitting.

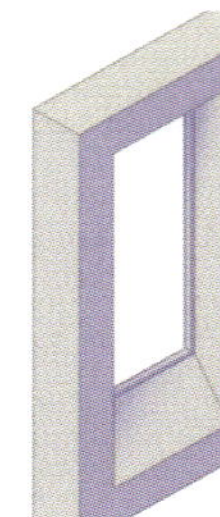

Slanted windowsills prevent comfortable sitting.

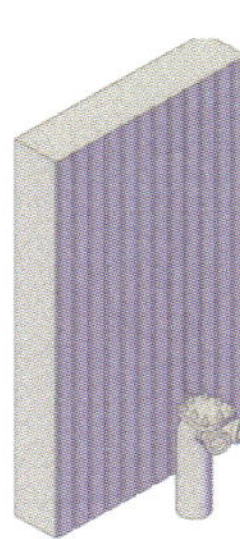

Spikes on a fire hydrant deter the use of what was already a very temporary seat.

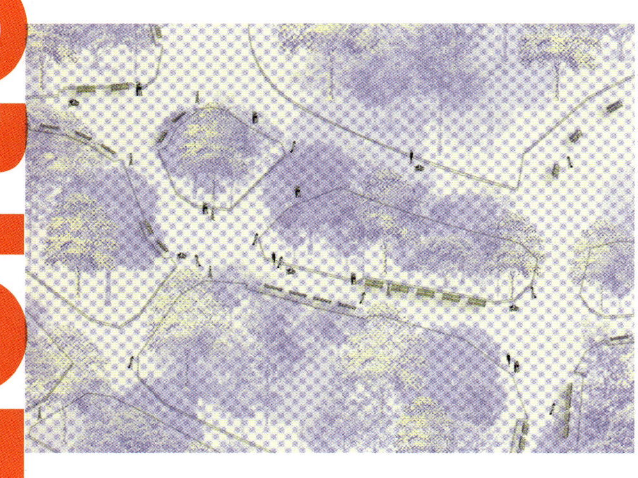

Aggressive landscaping of Tompkins Square Park

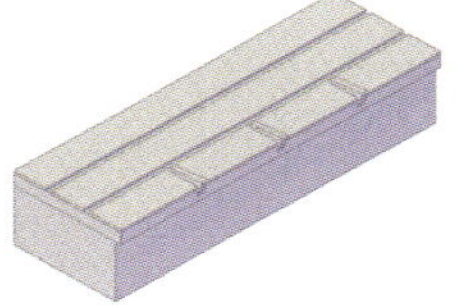

Metal stubs fastened to benches to deter skaters.

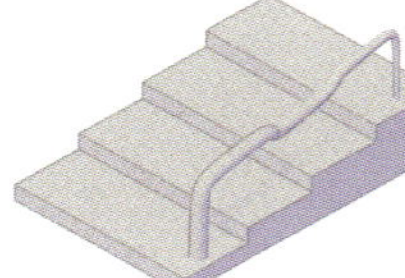

Custom railing on a public stairwell designed to deter grinding.

Benches designed to be less appealing to skaters through design inconsistencies.

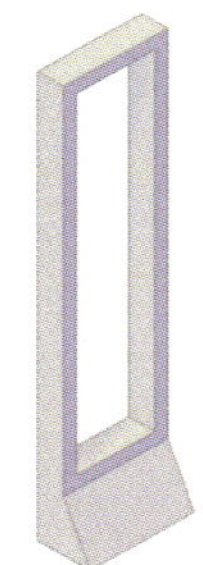

Anti-homeless slant incorporated into the façade of a building.

Spikes installed in the ground in front of a building to deter loitering.

Dividers on benches meant to prohibit people from laying out.

A taxonomy of hostility

ize Loiter

Site proposal for Lower Manhattan and the East River

Sidewalk extension proposal

Roofed housing for rainwater purification system

Rainwater collector

Public showers

Bench module proposal after decay

Pre-decay of the East River, Providence

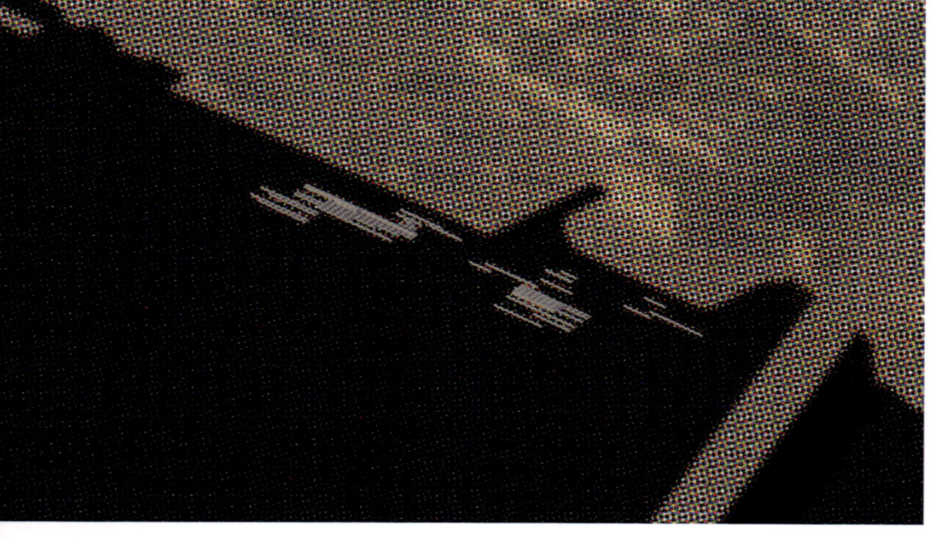

Bench assemblage

Phased rendering of the East River, Providence

Bobby Zhao (B.Arch)

Monument as Anti-Monument A reassembly of monumental buildings reexamines monumentality through a historically and socially inclusive lens.

My thesis examines monumentality in architecture, which is marked by both a distinctive physical appearance and heightened labor and costs. Confronting monumentality's duality of labor exploitation, commercialization, and projection of power and glory, I seek an alternative design solution for the post-modern commercial skyscraper typology—one that is more socially inclusive and programmatically diverse.

50 Hudson Yards: deconstruction

Skyscrapers sit on a podium, privatizing public space. Monuments rest on a pedestal, emphasizing social hierarchy. The Vessel (Hive) of Hudson Yards, a pseudo-public space, adds bureaucracy to a daily stroll, instantaneously creating an icon of Manhattan while also representing the problematic relationship between developers and public land. The Hive is part of a long history of building ideology; it joins the ranks of the unbuilt

The Monument:
people's vertical
marketplace

Hudson Yards Mall:
deconstruction

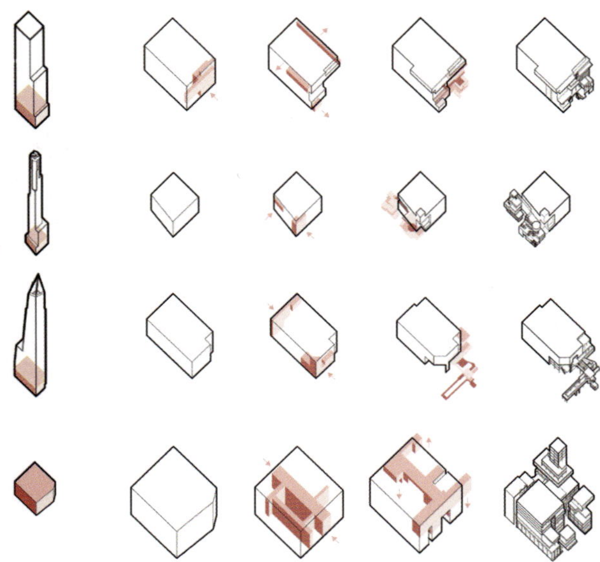

Hudson Yards:
deconstruction strategies

Palace of the Soviets in Moscow, Boston City Hall, New York's High Line, and the British/international festival known as Fun Palace.

I designed a kit of parts to deconstruct the pedestal or podium. Formally decentralizing monolithic structures, I generated various access points, creating a porous building. The dedensified anti-monument continually questions who or what we are praising. The muddied form opposes monolithic ideology and building. Visitors engage in historical representations of what the monument used to be, which integrates education into redesign.

35 Hudson Yards:
deconstruction section

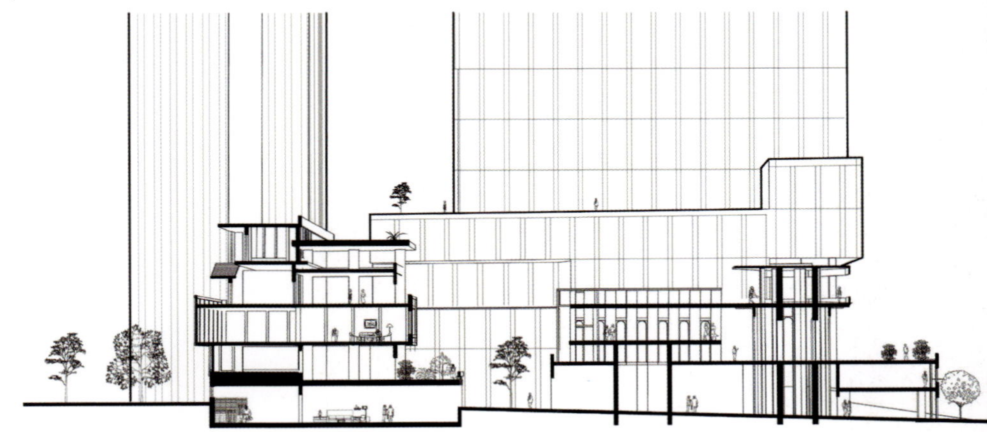

30 Hudson Yards:
circulation park section

Hudson Yards Mall: deconstruction

Hudson Yards Mall: deconstruction urban corridor

Masterplan

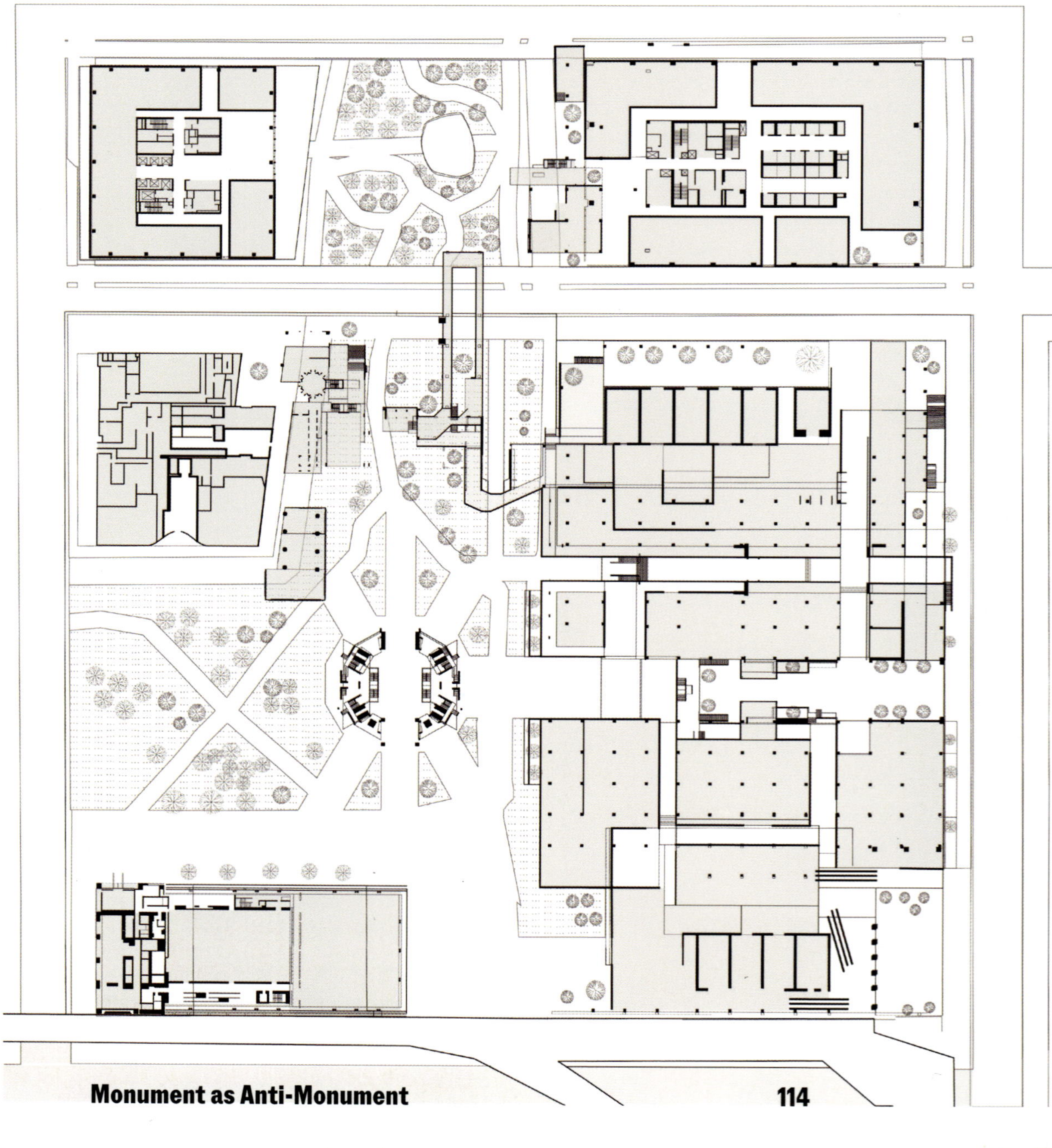

Ben Pell

The Problem Is …
Introduction

Primary Advisor **Ben Pell, Critic, Department of Architecture, RISD**
Secondary Advisor **Lauren Bordes, Critic, Department of Architecture, RISD**

Students **Peter Niels Heller (M.Arch), Yemo Koo (B.Arch), Patrick Spence (M.Arch), Fangyu Wei (M.Arch), Sam Wesselman (M.Arch), Zhan Zhang (M.Arch)**

Our studio was scaffolded by a series of questions that suggested both how to frame one's work through disciplinary reference points and how to construct problems. We began in the fall with three heuristic exercises, each asking the students to consider their thesis in a different context—historical, cross-disciplinary, and situational—as a form of strategic positioning.

Positioning a project relative to a constructed history and projected future

Acknowledging that our work as architects does not evolve in a vacuum, this opening exercise explored where one's preoccupations might sit relative to a history of events, phenomena, and experiences that have arguably led to the present moment. Where the historian might look for fixed coordinates and causation, students were encouraged to think more speculatively, selectively identifying historical data points that correlate and synthesize into a unique view of the world. That is, to think of history as being, in a word, autobiographical. Extending this speculation into the future, students were also asked to imagine how their work might participate in and contribute to what comes next. If history provides the corollaries to prove the inevitability of our work, we must also speculate on the events that will lock in its continued relevance.

For Zhan Zhang (see pp. 137–140), whose thesis explored the policies behind China's mass relocation program, this exercise outlined both the key events that contributed to today's problematic practices and speculated on ways to strategically disrupt these practices through new policies that would alter the future course of development. Patrick Spence (see pp. 125–128) adopted the various periods of construction and renovation of Providence's Market House as a medium to explore the role of memory in architecture.

Positioning a project relative to existing artifacts across disciplines

Setting aside the cult of the original for a moment, we focused on how one's work develops in conversation with artifacts in the world around us. This exercise asked students to curate an exhibition of conventionally unrelated objects and observations, which together could begin to identify the parameters of a disciplinary field for their research—a kind of *Wunderkammer* into and against which their thesis could be situated.

Positioning a project in, on, or of a site

With a cultural and discursive framework emerging around each project, the third exercise asked students to locate a site where their work would be made visible. Students were given latitude in how they interpreted their site—perhaps as a fixed, physical place with geographic coordinates or a provisional relationship between body and space—and were also reminded that a site is never neutral. While a site receives one's intentions, assertions, and impositions, it also pushes back. Students identified the characteristic pressures of their site, exploring how they might influence the physical manifestation of their theses.

Fangyu Wei's thesis (see pp. 129–132), which examined the balconies and other envelope appendages of mid-block alleys in Taipei, appropriated these provisional architectures to create a new kind of liminal public space in the dense city fabric. Similarly, Yemo Koo (see pp. 121–124) situated his thesis in Seoul's defunct Sewoon Sangga megastructure, reorganizing the building around spatialized lifestyle differences and overlaps for a new model of intergenerational housing.

Through these three exercises, the students identified a discursive field in which their thesis could reside, making that field more visible to themselves and to others. The focus on shared methodologies of constructing problems that were nevertheless unique to each student underscored the need to address a common question in their respective arguments: What's at stake for architecture as a discipline and/or a practice? As they moved into the spring semester, students were asked to think about their position relative to this question in three parts: observation (this is what I've noticed about a particular phenomenon or condition in the world), reflection (this is how I think architecture can address or otherwise engage this condition), and declaration (this is what I specifically intend to do to explore architecture's role in this situation).

For Peter Niels Heller (see pp. 117–120), whose thesis examined the impact of climate change on building practices, this question pointed to both the social and material implications for architecture as a place of refuge when all else fails. In his exploration of the urban periphery, Sam Wesselman (see pp. 133–136), challenged the conventional oppositions of urban/suburban and architecture/landscape, proposing a new order of materials and techniques of placemaking more relevant to the vague in-between spaces that surround us. Such in-between spaces both clarified and muddled in late spring as we all dispersed to our individual homes and met collectively on our virtual screens.

Peter Niels Heller (M.Arch)

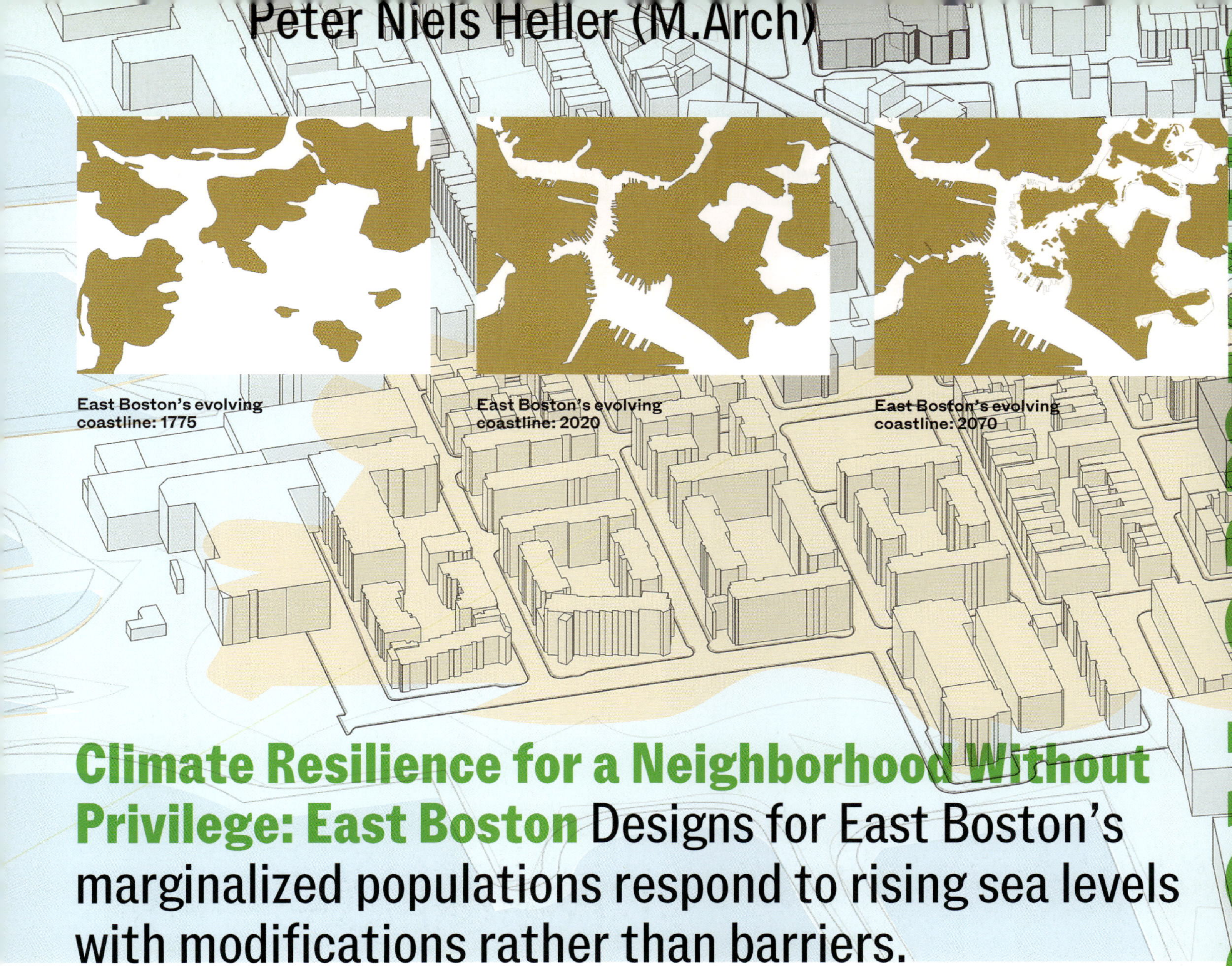

East Boston's evolving coastline: 1775

East Boston's evolving coastline: 2020

East Boston's evolving coastline: 2070

Climate Resilience for a Neighborhood Without Privilege: East Boston Designs for East Boston's marginalized populations respond to rising sea levels with modifications rather than barriers.

East Boston buildings and 2050 flood levels

The burdens of climate stress have often fallen disproportionately on marginal populations.[1,2] Rather than relocate, people typically prefer to adapt to rising sea levels. These adaptations, like the levees of New Orleans, work until they fail disastrously, as they did during Hurricane Katrina. Instead of barriers that attempt and sometimes fail to hold back flooding, we need soft modifications that help moderate water levels. Infrastructure must be made resilient for public assets, housing, and neighborhoods in the heart of flood zones to survive.

The project site is East Boston. Once an archipelago, the area is now connected to the mainland via landfill. Best known as the site of Logan International Airport, it is

1 See Wolfgang Behringer, "Cultural Consequences of the Little Ice Age," in *A Cultural History of Climate* (New York: Wiley, 2009), 121–67.

2 See John M. Barry, *Rising Tide: The Great Mississippi Flood of 1927 and How It Changed America* (New York: Simon and Schuster, 1998).

Mississippi flood refugees at Hamburg, LA, 1927

Climate Resilience fo

or a Neighborhood W

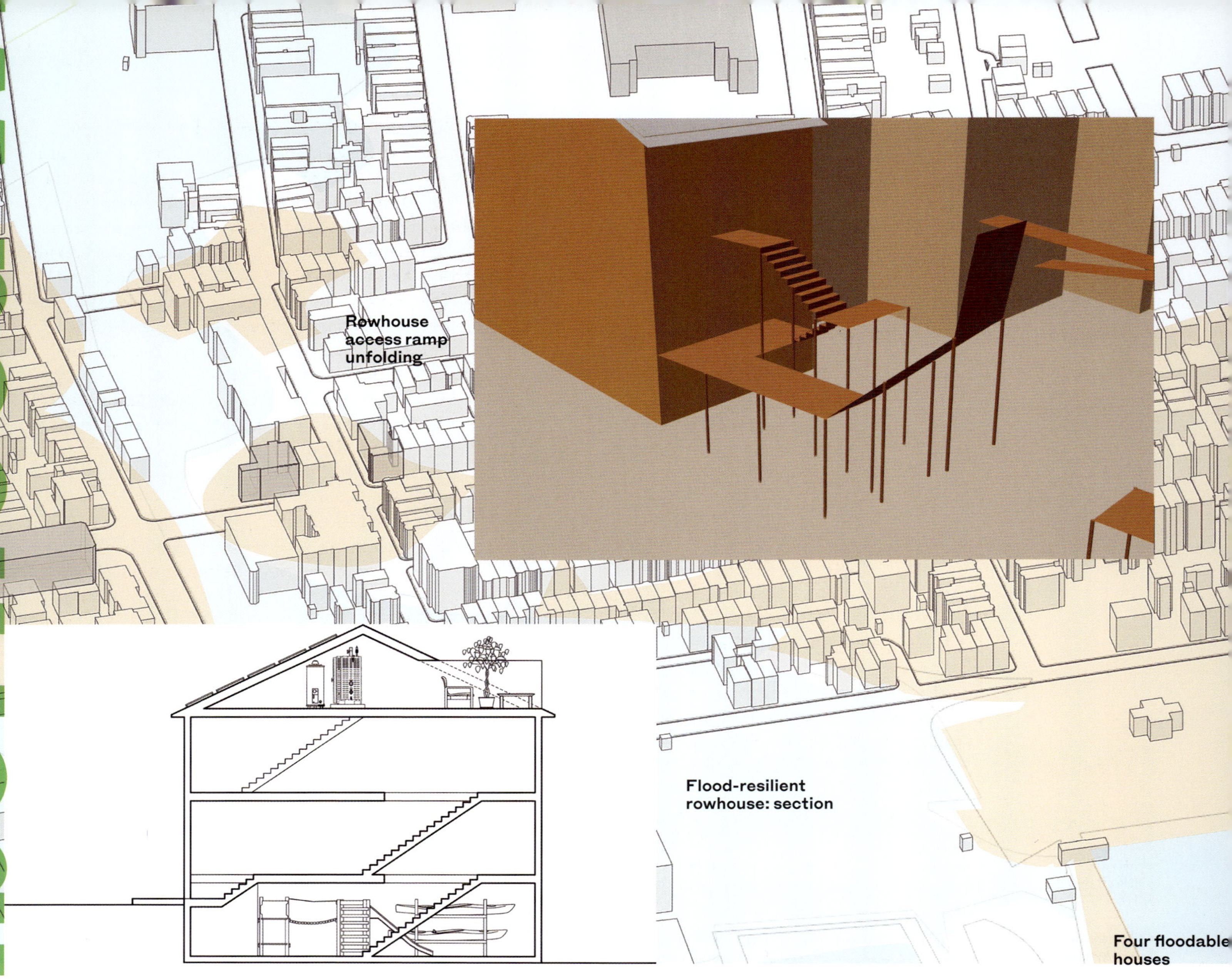

Rowhouse access ramp unfolding

Flood-resilient rowhouse: section

Four floodable houses

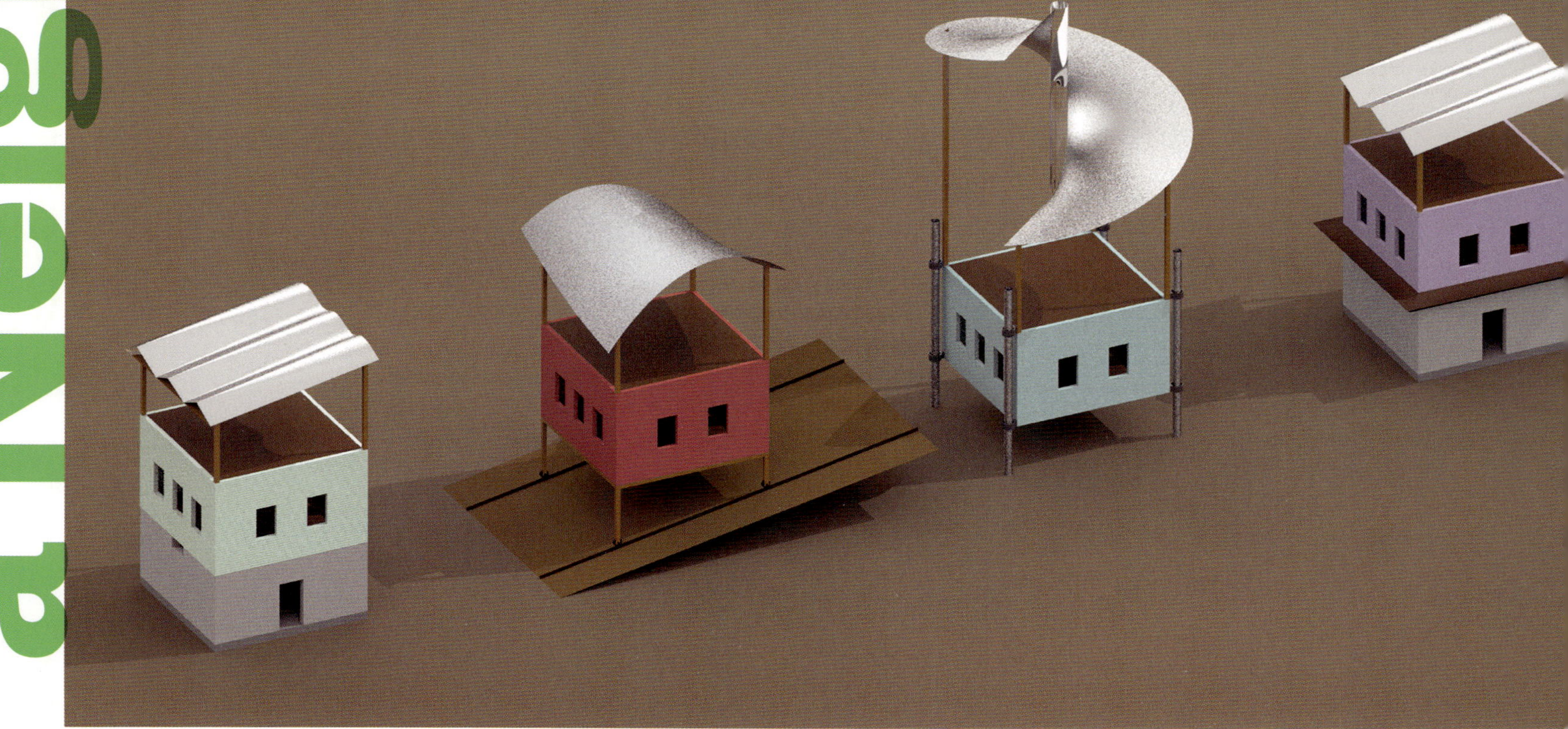

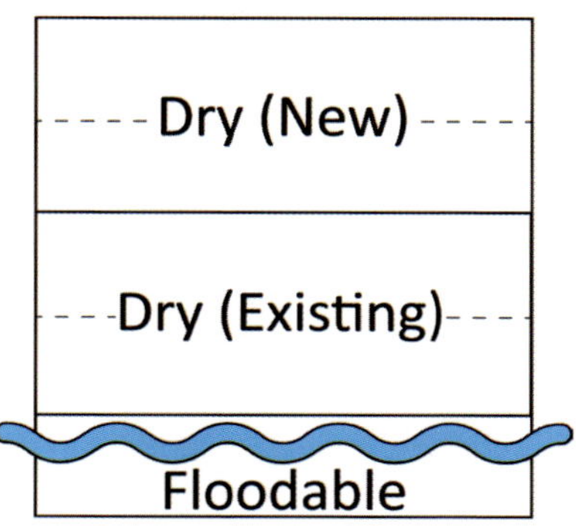

Health center partition: flooding

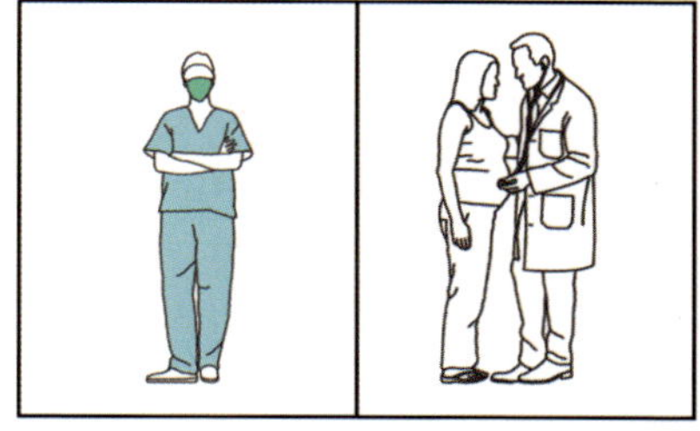

Health center partition: infectious disease

also home to 40,000 people—more than half of whom are Hispanic immigrants—and a century's worth of health and community centers, churches, and schools. The human-modified coastline poses significant and persistent flooding risks for East Boston and leaves a coast of low-income, non-native English speaking populations constantly at risk.

The project pulls from a lineage of projective architecture: Gordon Matta-Clark surgically altered existing structures to interact differently with their surroundings; Lebbeus Woods speculated how buildings might respond to trauma; and O. M. Ungers modeled partial abandonment and intensification in changing urban conditions.[3,4,5] My design reacts to the sociopolitical agents of climate change through adaptable systems and reformulated building typologies. My floodable rowhouses have a first floor that responds to floodwaters, while the middle level embodies existing tropes and remains dry. The upper floor is open to the sky and future growth. The outdoor, private space naturally extends to the roof while the backyard floods. In this flooded East Boston, public movement is elevated to a spine of raised walkways down back alleys, with each homeowner controlling their degree of access.

Beyond the dwellings, the East Boston Neighborhood Health Center's medical headquarters exemplifies how a public asset might adapt to sea-level rise. I treat each level differently, moving critical and capital-intensive programs out of the floodable first floor, safe from rising waters. The ground plane becomes a drive-up pandemic testing center. The entire medical building is split in half to separate treatment of infectious diseases and non-infectious conditions, creating a lobed plan referencing East Boston's geographic origins as a set of islands. Circulation operates flexibly, with ramps and mezzanine floor levels that change their function as flood levels vary. As with the rowhouses, the roof becomes an active site, including a heliport for patient transport. Together, these design explorations form a kit of parts for modifying built elements of the neighborhood to help its fabric adapt and persist in the face of rising sea levels as well as the current pandemic.

3 A. S. Bessa and Jessamyn Fiore, *Gordon Matta-Clark: Anarchitect* (New York: Bronx Museum of the Arts/Yale University Press, 2017).

4 Lebbeus Woods, *Pamphlet Architecture 15: War and Architecture* (Hudson, NY: Princeton Architectural Press, 1993).

5 O. M. Ungers and Rem Koolhaas, *The City in the City—Berlin: A Green Archipelago* (Zurich: Lars Müller Publishers, 2013; orig. 1977).

Health center combined partition

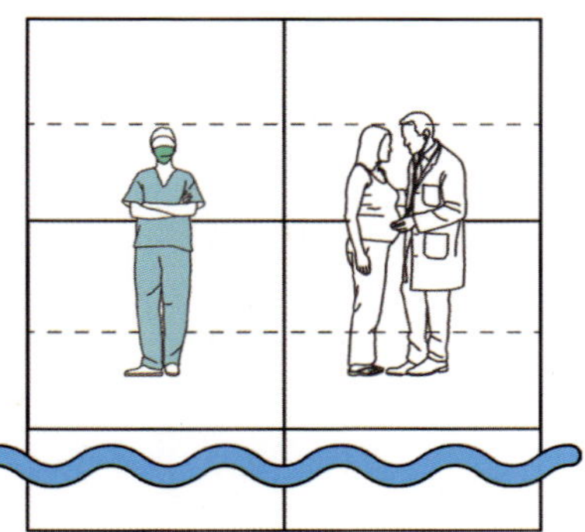

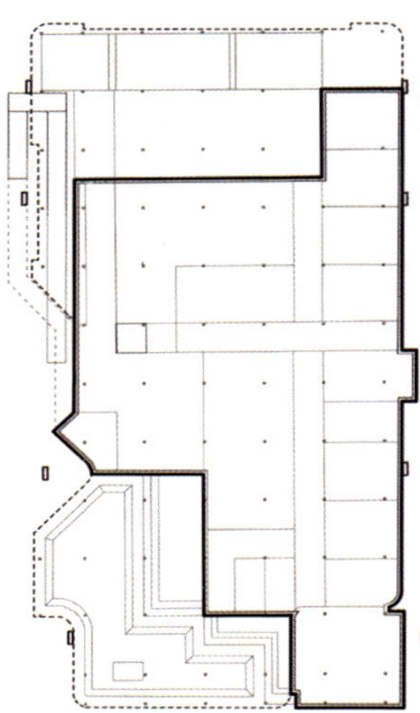

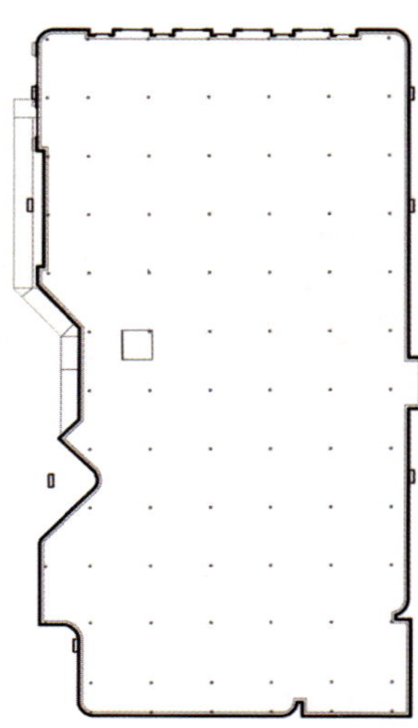

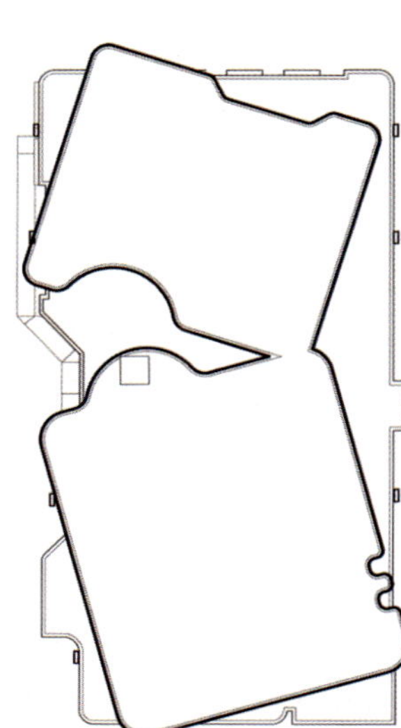

Resilient health center, plans

Health center: heavy flood condition, section

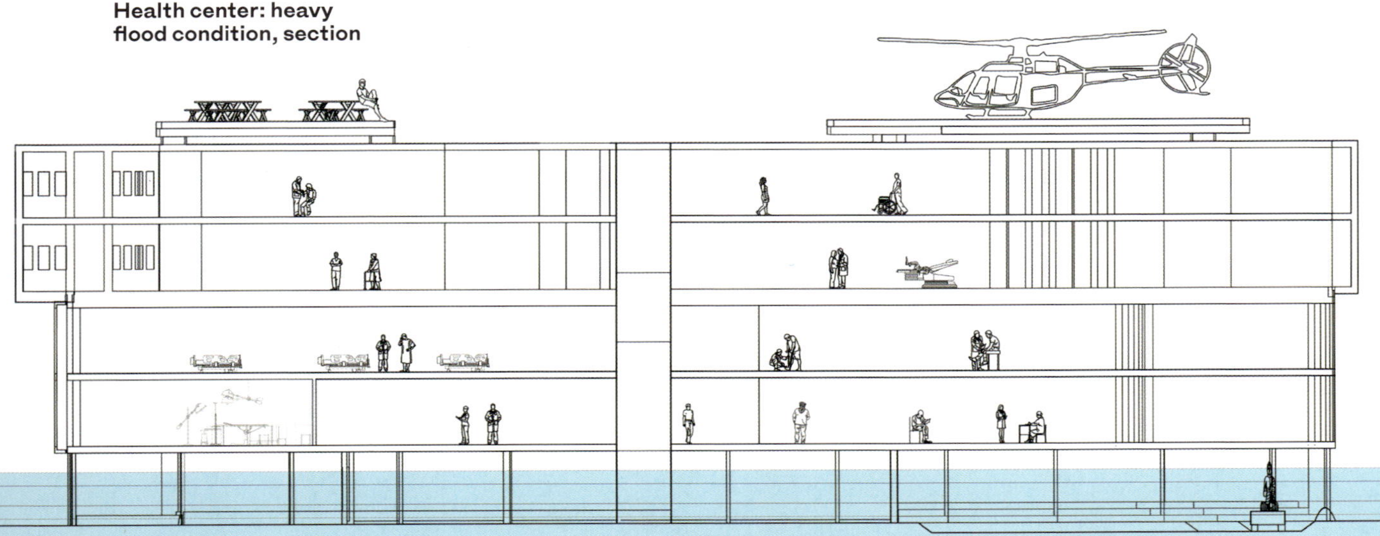

Heavy Flood (SLR-DFE, 7 ft above ground)

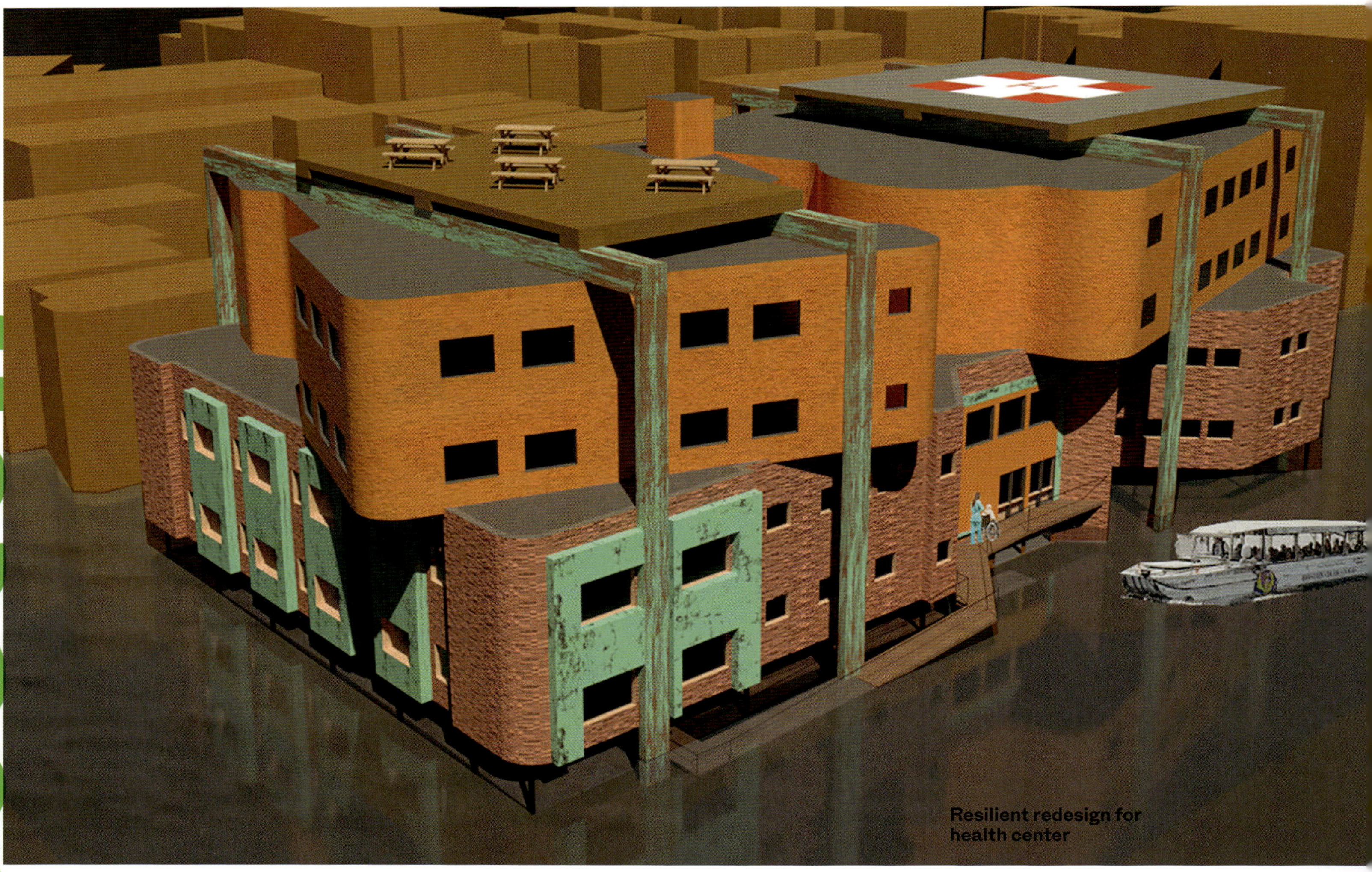

Resilient redesign for health center

Yemo Koo (B.Arch)

Cross-Life: A Cross-Generational Co-Living Development

A nearly abandoned high-rise in Seoul is transformed into a multifaceted living space for young and old.

Isometric rendering

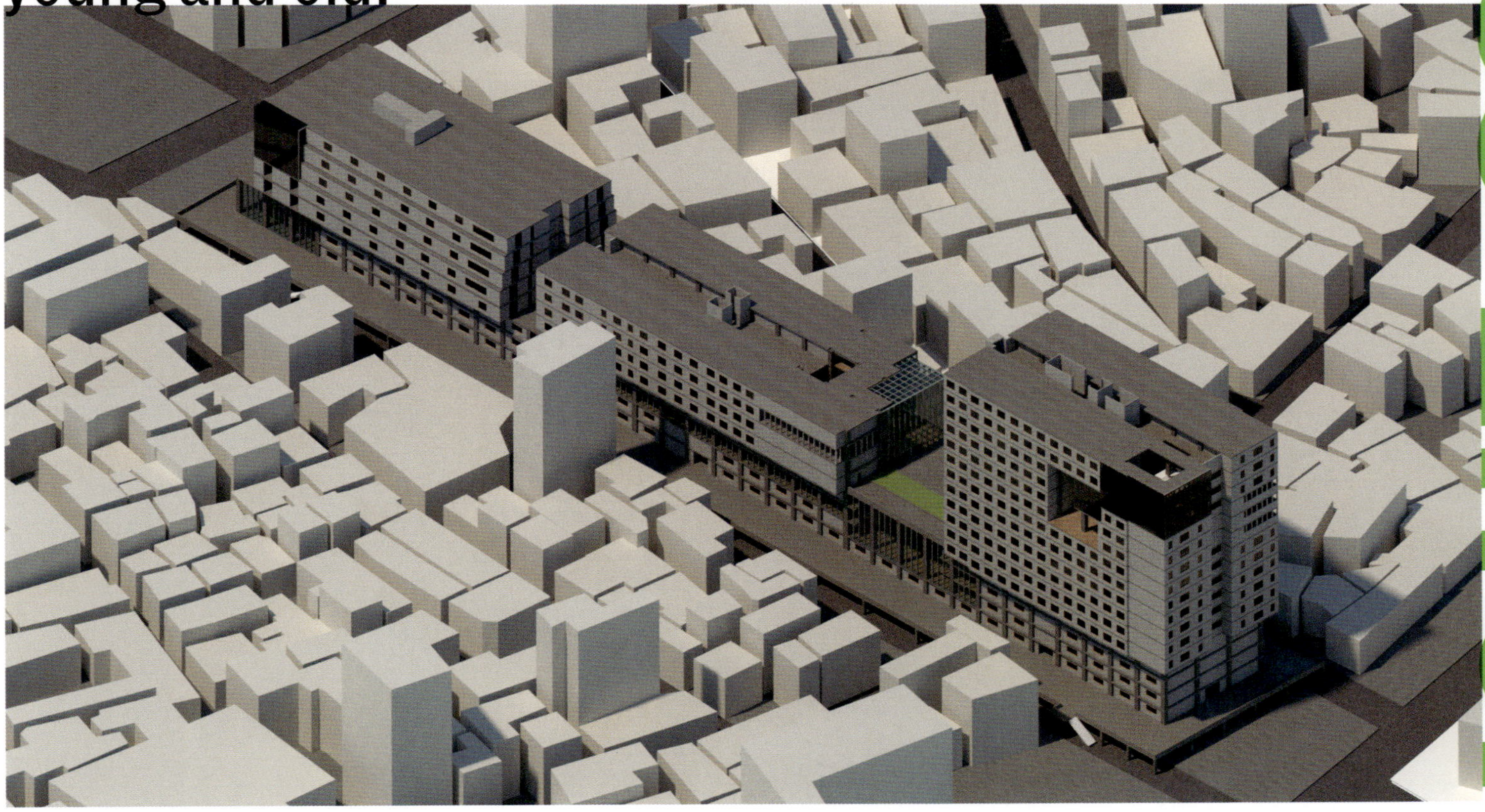

In the near future, senior citizens will overwhelm the population of South Korea, businesses will face recruiting problems due to rampant retirements, and affordable housing will be in high demand. We are at a critical junction at which to create a system for the older generation to cohabitate with the younger one. Cross-generational co-living addresses the future housing crisis with cohabitation facilities and programmatic overlays between young and old.

Jinyang Sangga was the first multifunctional high-rise of its kind in Seoul. Built in the 1960s, it was an incubator for both business and residential living. During the 1980s, however, the business tenants began to move out, leaving much of the megastructure unused.

Isometric diagram 1

Isometric diagram 2

Isometric diagram 3

Soon after, residents began to move out as well. Jinyang Sangga was left to become outdated and poorly maintained. This typology proliferated throughout the city.

In designing a program for the Jinyang Sangga site, I identified vital amenities that support a compromise between the young and the old. The program, however, critically emphasizes differences between these generations, providing unique spaces delegated for their own use. Echoing OMA's Seattle Public Library, I created a word diagram that presents formal arrangements across the site. Complicating this diagram further, I added a daily schedule that respects each generation's routine. This daily timeline became a critical tool to provide functional programming that avoided naïve optimism for merging the communities.

The sectional diagram for the redesigned Jinyang Sangga features a series of interconnected circulation routes throughout the megastructure. Using the building's existing massing, I removed parts of the building entirely, while adding passageways to link specific spaces and provide direct access between the programs. The Boolean command in Rhino emerged as a discursive tool to create unions and voids.

My work aims for a compromise not only between young and old but between the optimistic designer and the pragmatic developer. The design is hopeful that a new relationship between the young and the old can be fostered, a critical demand as Seoul's population ages. But, it also provides functional living spaces and a multifaceted program for anyone's use, young or old, thus extending its purpose for any social conditions that might emerge.

Moment section 1

Moment section 2

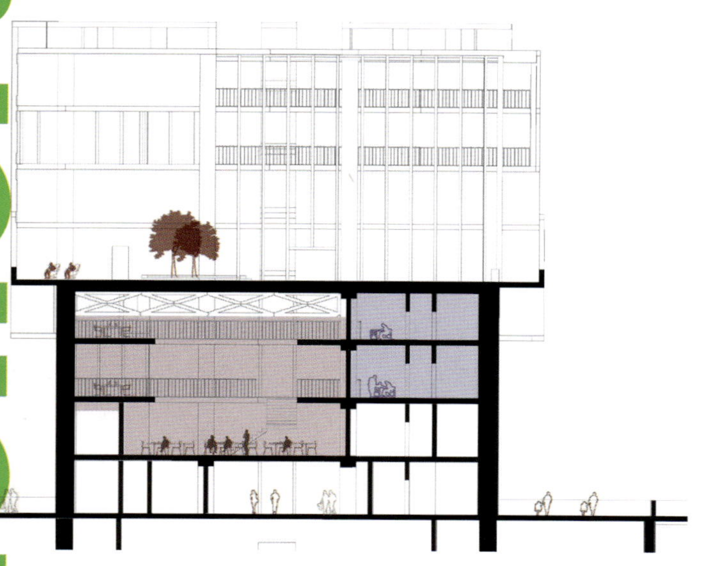

Moment plan 1

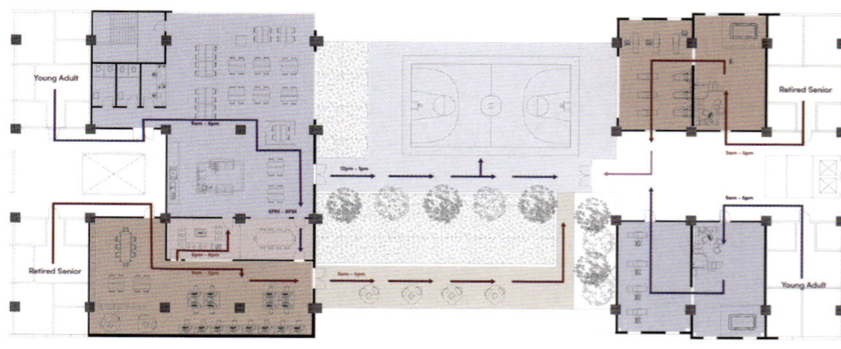

Reinterpreted Jinyang Sangga, front

Moment plan 2

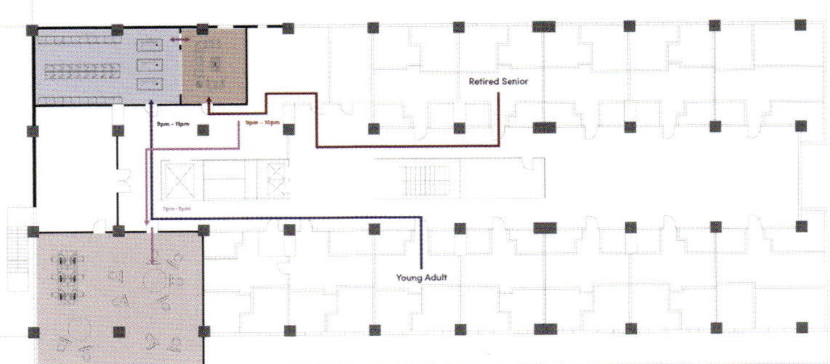

Moment plan 3

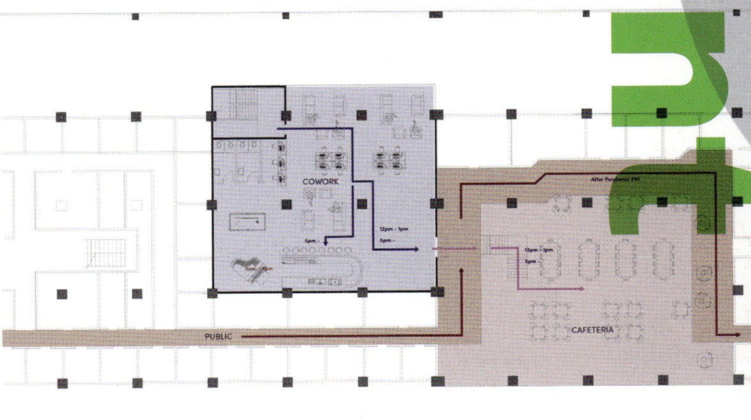

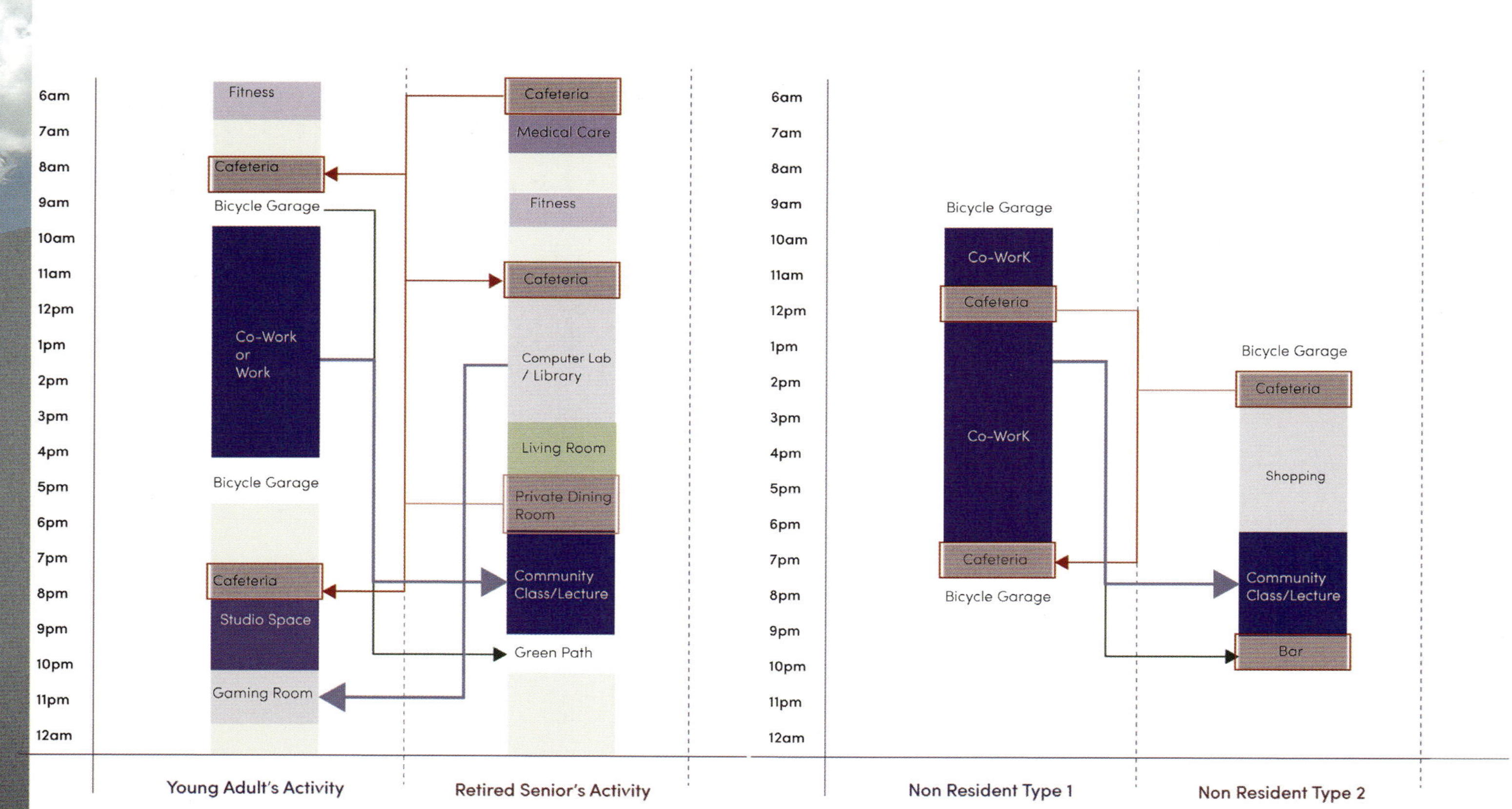

Amenities program scenario

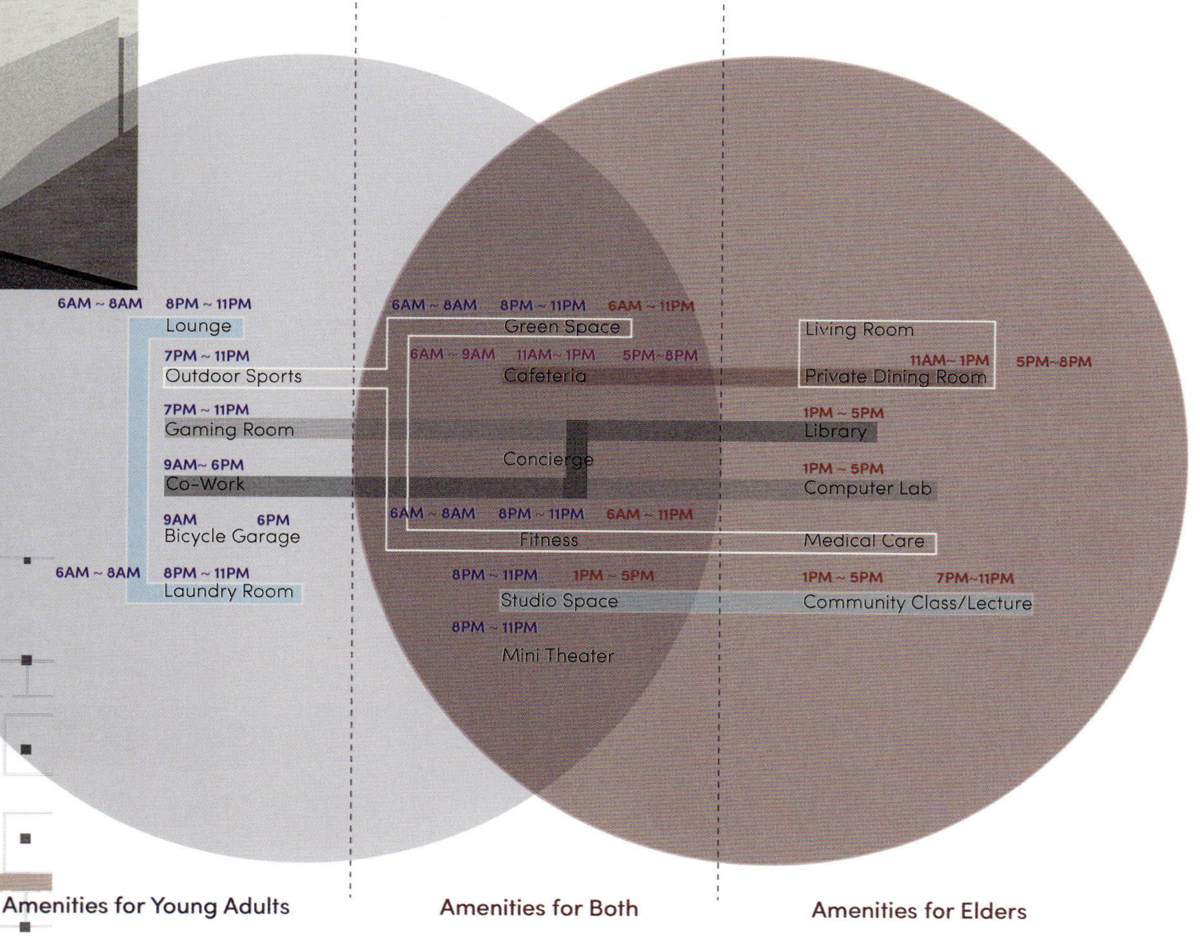

Amenities program diagram

Patrick Spence (M.Arch)

The Story of Market House

The Story of Market House In this intervention, the untold story of slave-trading unearths a historically preserved site, bridging the way to truth and healing for future generations.

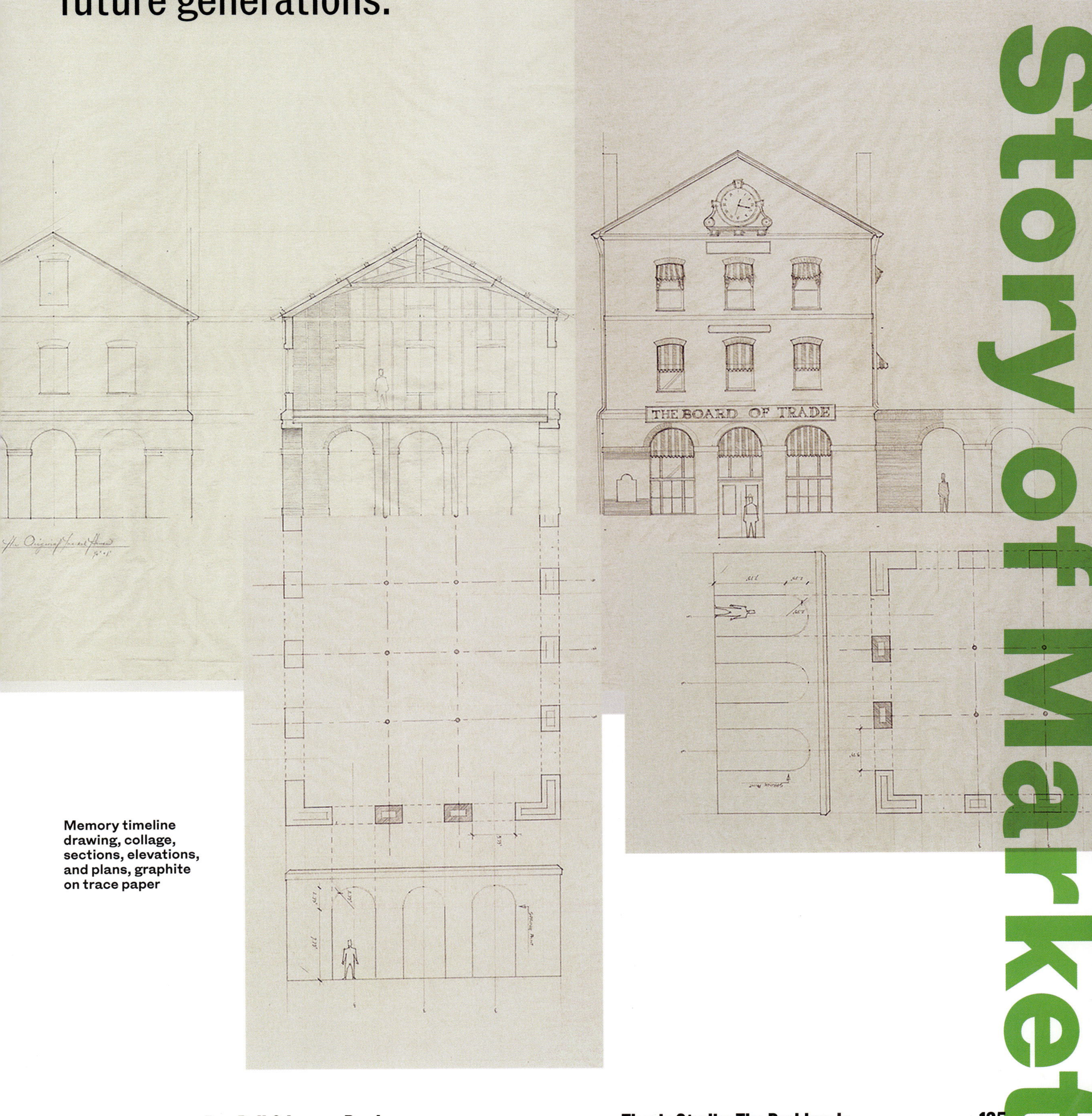

Memory timeline drawing, collage, sections, elevations, and plans, graphite on trace paper

By exploring the memory of place and learning fraught contextual histories, architects have the capacity to shed light on the racial injustices of the built environment. The discipline needs to acknowledge the pain of the past to work toward healing. My thesis is a work in progress. I absorb lessons from the Black Lives Matter movement, emphasizing the much-needed work in recognizing the pervasive racial injustice in our society. As Assistant Professor of Historic Preservation at Columbia University Erica Avrami writes, "The built environment itself can serve as a conduit for inequality. The persistence of certain structures or sites and the effects of decisions made over time can perpetuate patterns of segregation and injustice."[1] Observing history through this lens enables us to view the built environment as layered memories, telling us stories and defining who we are, our values, and our identity. My thesis asks, whose stories are told and whose are forgotten? Understanding our past will help us as designers plan for a better and more informed future.

Like other sites enmeshed in the history of slavery, Providence's Market House tells a dark story of oppression and suppression. Market House, which sits on Market Square next to the Providence River, was built in 1775 as a market and meeting house, but it served as a slave trade market during the nineteenth century. The site currently obscures this history, its historic plaques cherry-picking events like protesting tea taxation in 1775 and the Great Storm of 1815. These selective narratives intentionally hide the site's role in the history of slavery.

By documenting and exposing the building's many alterations and hidden past, my thesis aims to remember and tell an unbiased, amalgamated story, true to the comprehensive and forgotten histories, projecting a new chapter of Market House that will serve generations to come. Market House sits at the divide between Providence's east and west sides, which are divided not only by a river but by socioeconomics. My design recognizes both the memory of Market House and the city's present inequities by building a bridge, Market Bridge, as a passage and connector. Market Bridge amplifies underrepresented voices in the Providence community, specifically BIPOC and historically disenfranchised voices. Engaging RISD's community of artists to bring the Bridge to life, I envision a flexible space that can tell the site's history and host meetings, reflection, programming, an exhibition hall, and a farmer's market, offering healthy food options to the locals. On any given day, Market Bridge strengthens the existing community, elevating the voices of its diverse people, and paving the way for future generations. Looking ahead, I view *The Story of Market House* as the beginning of my role as an architect who recognizes the injustice sewn into the built fabric of our communities, and who is working to unravel and reconstruct authentic narratives.

1 Erica Avrami, *Issues in Preservation Policy: Preservation and Social Inclusion* (New York: Columbia University Press, 2020), 10.

patrickjspence.com

House

Market Bridge becomes an open-air exhibition space during summer, historical collage

Market Square becomes a healing garden for students and visitors to retreat and reflect, historical collage

Market Bridge as a viewport, historical collage

Fangyu Wei (M.Arch)

Void spaces

The Possibilities of the Void Void spaces break contracts, occupy the tension between two surfaces, and show how people interact between interior and exterior spaces, between formal and informal occupancy.

Desire for green space in the private sphere

Architectural surfaces and urban environments are in constant tension. The transient boundary between an inner, domestic core and the external, urban environment demarcates how we experience urban form. My project engages the varied definitions of voids—void of context; void of culture; contractual voids—and uses these definitions to counter unused potential. Peering into individual action, ideas, and criticality, urban voids have become catalysts for social interaction and creative spatial experimentation. Void spaces encompass this architectural phenomenon of spatial tension between two surfaces. You might say we live in the poché.

From Anthony Vidler to Pier Vittorio Aureli, architectural discourse has incorporated occupying the poché, the wall, the space

Void spaces within two surfaces, plaster model

The generational shift shown on the building's surface

between things for decades; it is an innate feature of building. The emerging debate centers on vacant lots as a new place between walls, utilizing the temporality of voids to program empty spaces. Abundant urban void spaces invite informal appropriation as a strategy to reclaim unused land. This at once provides agency for occupants and reconsiders the terms of contractual ownership, offering a new approach to community-driven urban redevelopment. Activating void space offers a much-needed shift in an age of civil unrest.

In Taipei, people are already appropriating, inhabiting, and building informal structures in vacant sites. Residents utilize voids as shared urban space either vertically or horizontally, essentially voiding the government's land ownership contract. Alleyways are especially critical sites. Occupants of alleys in Taipei's Wanhua District are in constant tension with legitimized buildings. This fragile spatial condition delicately balances permanence and temporality; it is an inherently unstable built form connecting space and people. How do we understand this instability and tension in the alleyways of Taipei? Void spaces become platforms and incubators for diversity and engagement—for void residents and formalized residents alike.

Existing conditions, elevation

he Void

Perspective from first level

Perspective from second level

Section perspective

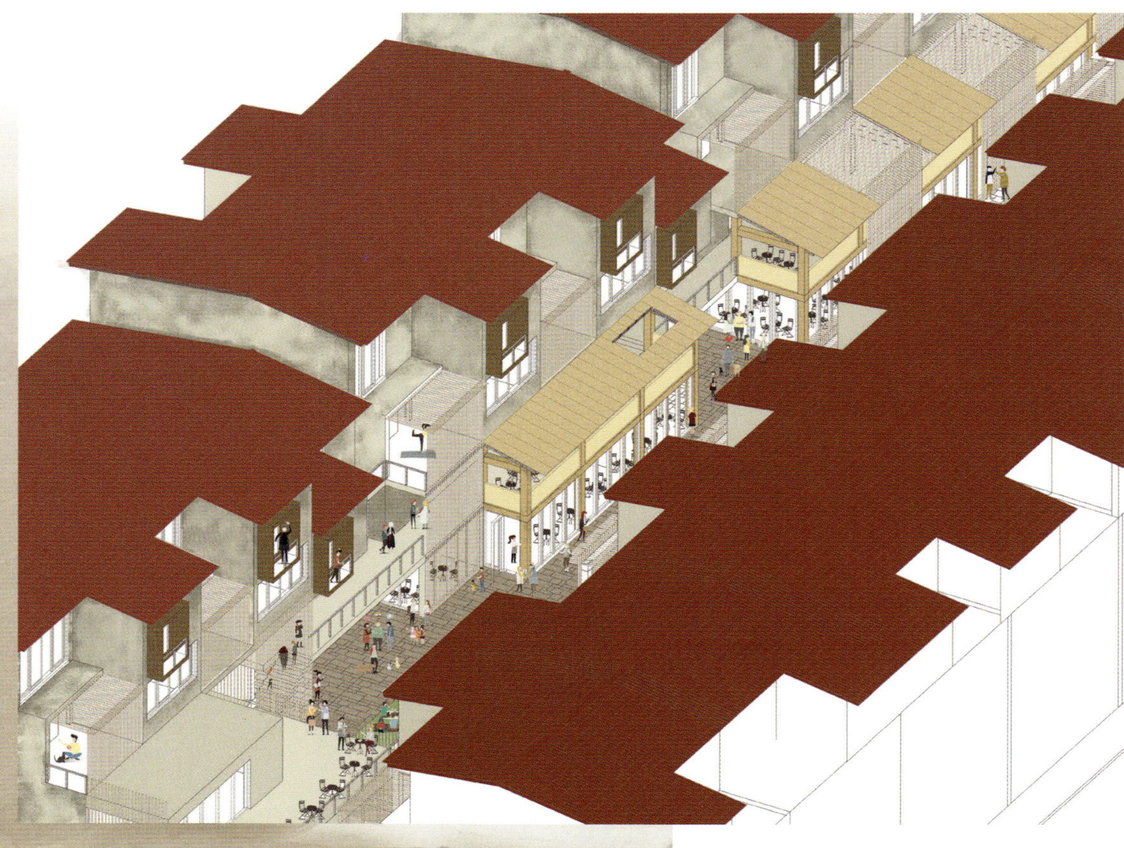

Alleyway, axonometric

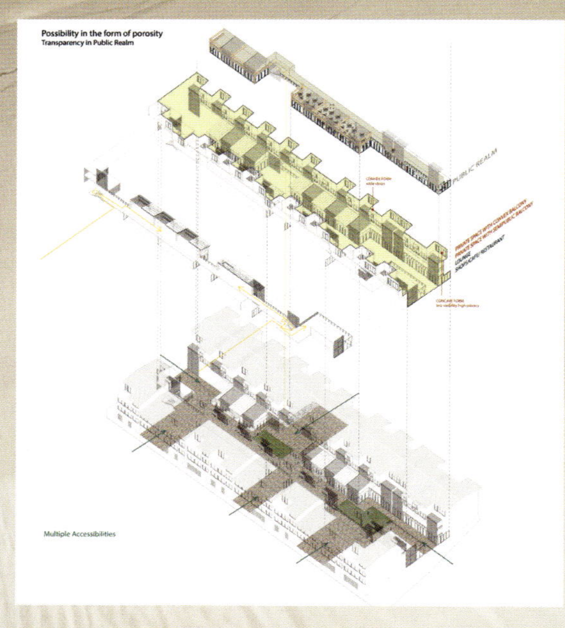

The possibility of porosity: transparency in the public realm, axonometric

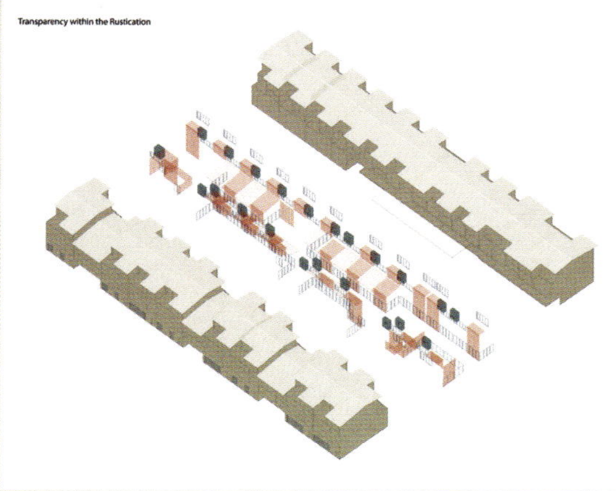

Transparency within oxidation, axonometric

The role of semipublic spaces, axonometric

Sam Wesselman (M.Arch)

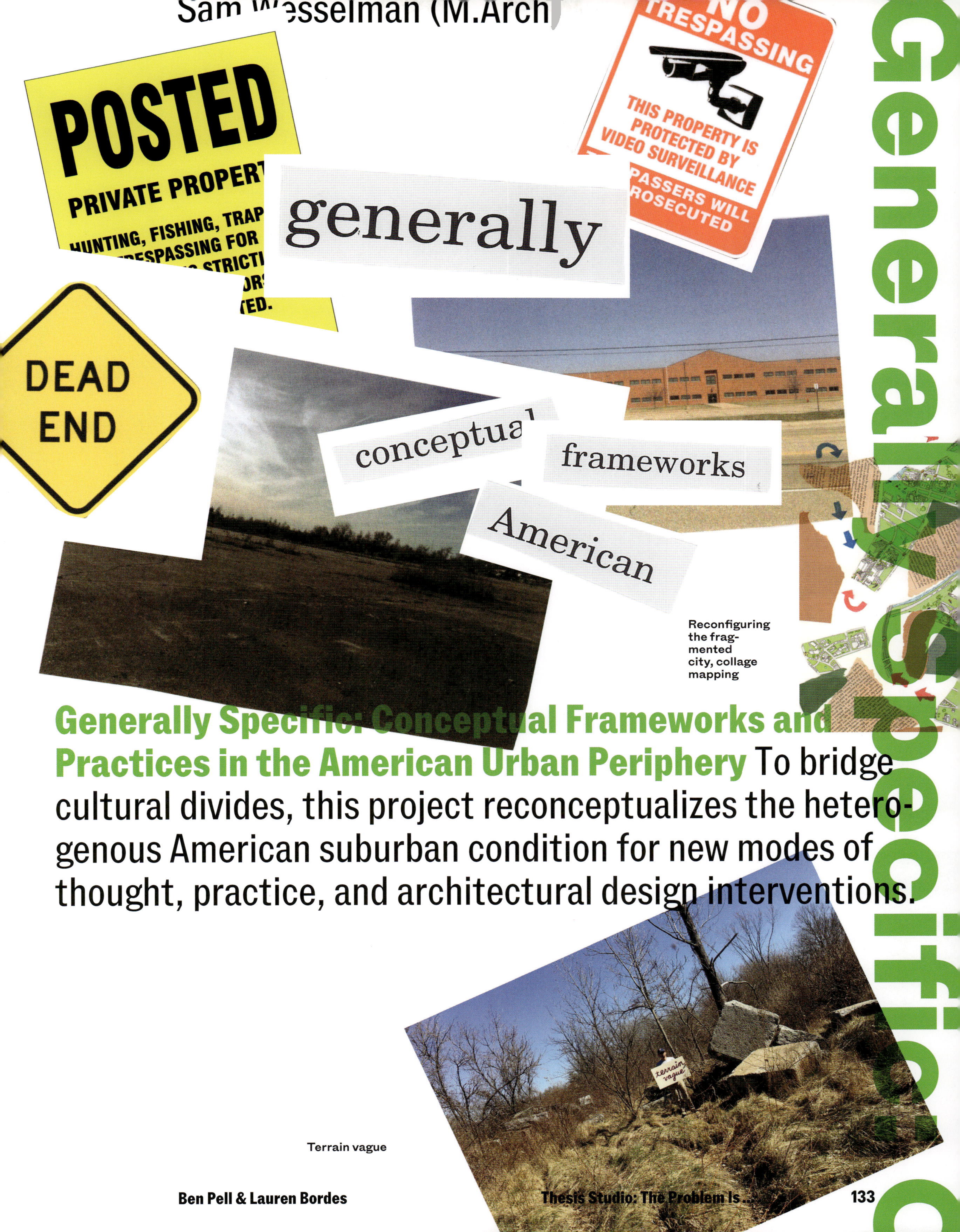

Reconfiguring the fragmented city, collage mapping

Generally Specific: Conceptual Frameworks and Practices in the American Urban Periphery To bridge cultural divides, this project reconceptualizes the heterogenous American suburban condition for new modes of thought, practice, and architectural design interventions.

Terrain vague

Henderson Expressway, collaged site map

Polarized politics draw hard lines in the U.S., typically dividing generalized urban and rural identities, which reinforces an outdated reading of the population as an abstraction in simplified terms. The suburb is a mode of peripherality—a space defined by its adjacency and fluidity. It offers de-centered, heterogenous practices that defy divisive logics and ideologies of dogmatism and purity. If the suburb is neither urban nor rural, what can it teach us about bridging cultural gaps?

Built in the 1960s, the Henderson Bridge was intended to replace an older steel truss bridge that followed the line of Waterman Street, crossing the Seekonk River from Providence to East Providence. It was proposed as part of a larger freeway, extending Interstate-195 to the Massachusetts state line in East Providence. Despite all the surrounding land being acquired and cleared, only one segment was built adjacent to the bridge in East Providence. The land cuts across the entire city, abutting residential areas, big-box commercial stores, half-occupied industrial land, as well as the river, and additional nature preserves and parks on the eastern edge of East Providence. To this day, this interstitial land remains vacant and fenced off, which has had the unintended benefit of allowing unique urban plant ecosystems to grow.

My thesis uses this indeterminant *terrain vague* landscape as a site to test the potential of suburban peripherality. The design activates a range of nearly invisible interventions, thereby maintaining the novel ecosystems, and leverages highway structures as explorative architectural forms. The expressway remains as an infrastructural relic, opened up for use by pedestrians, cyclists, and roller bladers, making it part of the landscape and the terrain vague ecosystem itself, a once latent site that now stitches the city back together.

Inspired by the haphazard and commonplace spaces of the Midwest, where factories and farms and quiet homes coexist in a non-rural, non-urban matrix, my thesis promotes interstitial, fragmented, and decentered modes of practice and ways of living. Architecture in the periphery acts in between and in collaboration with other disciplines. In the suburban condition, the discipline can site new practices, creating physical nodes for experimental forms of heterogeneous activity, ownership, and collaboration.

Mapping terrain vague: Boston/ Providence region

Concept collage

Expressway intervention, isometric detail

Shared workshop, isometric detail

Open architecture, isometric detail

Forest intervention, isometric detail

"Architecture can suggest what is, in my view, essentially a fallacy: that a city is a kind of work of art, that it is to be understood as beautiful – or it can find a way to embrace the disorder and chaos of a living city, and through that, try to find the means of understanding and predicting their behavior. Architecture is ready to embrace both utopian and dystopian ideas about the nature of the city." (2014)

Pieces of periphery

Technical Center: perpetual construction

Terrain vague architecture, construction

Outside architecture/outside nature:
peripheral scene 1

industry

"…that the modern ideal of a workman seems a boy, without the knowledge of any handicra industry he or she is employed in, who is only whole life the same infinitesimal part of some

naturally such a school would be called an art s interpreters of fine art would not only be allied t serve, but would stand there at the center of an i is inspiration and influence to younger talent in desirable mass production." (1932)

"By the same token, rural occupations once isolate level of the city could have the advantages of scien animated activities, originally a big city monopoly; between urban and rural, between industrial work too." (1961)

see **city, countryside, urban, rural, ag**

landscape

"Learning from the existing landscape is a wa (1972)

"To move through this landscape is to move o commercial landscape." (1972)

"By forming the institution within a directed a space is left for the tactical improvisations and enclosing envelope." (1999)

"And conversely, the remaining scraps of landsc even though these landscapes have already bee

"Under capitalism there is, then, a perpetual appropriate to its own condition at a particula the course of a crisis, at a subsequent point in

see **countryside, ground**

rban co
qualiti
etween
ity and

Outside architecture/outside nature:
peripheral scene 2

Technical Center:
perpetual construction

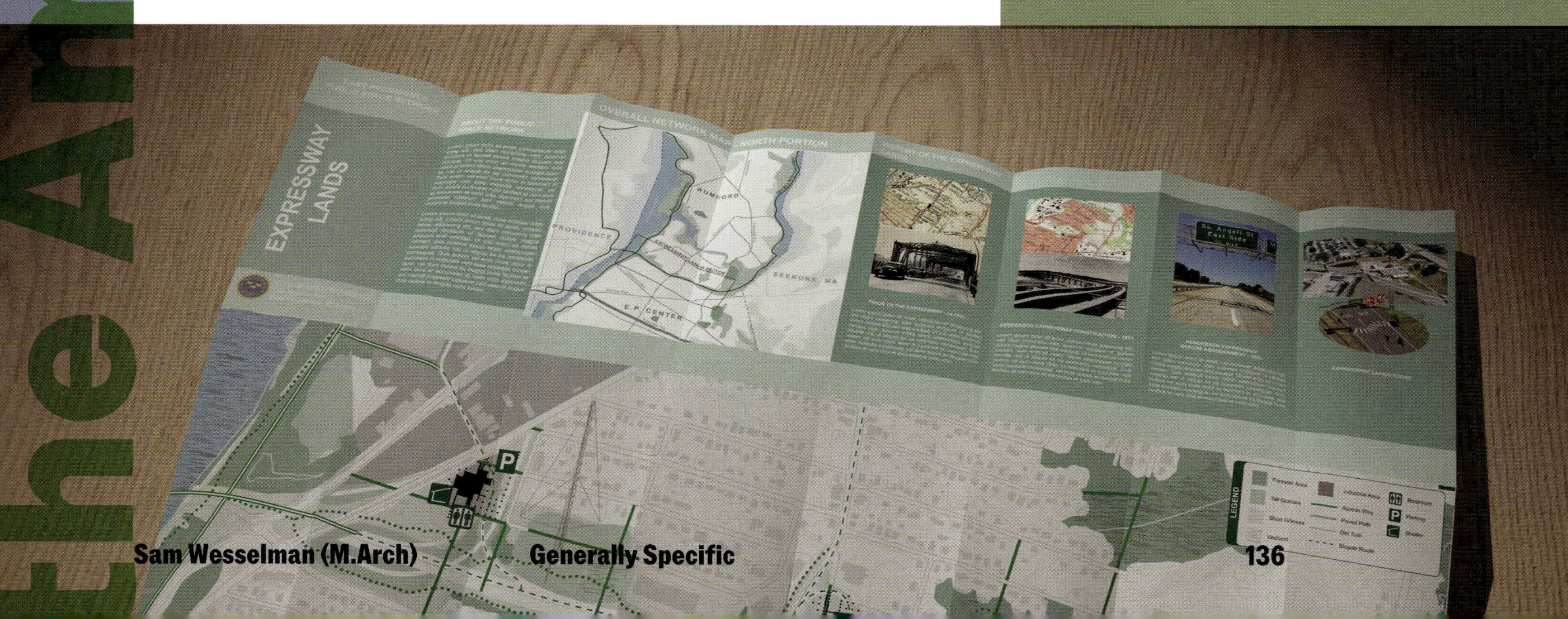

Zhan Zhang (M.Arch)

Taming the Monster:

Rooftop structure redeveloped

Taming the Monster: Relocation Community's Revival In Jiangsu, the pain of China's rapid urbanization and forced relocation is offset by putting the material remains of past structures to use in and around the new.

Ancestral shrine embedded in the main structure, elevation

Library and bar, elevation

Southeast façade of the community

Relocation Commun

There are few joyous occasions while living in the middle of rapid urbanization in Jiangsu, China. I know firsthand what forced relocation feels like. We leave behind homes, fields, land, and people when we relocate to government-ordered urban spaces. We don't have a choice; we must move, and the loss is dire.

There is no way to reverse China's forced urbanization. As grim as that is, it does not mean we must sit back passively. One way to mitigate the stark contrast between residents' old and new living conditions is by normalizing transition in building practices and allowing residents to engage with the building process. Specifically, during demolition, residents can hold onto the tradition of their old building and invest in their new community by harvesting materials for new purposes.

My thesis formalizes this process to challenge the monster of Chinese urbanization. Rather than rely only on the existing energy of resurgent communities (Jiangsu residents have already reclaimed the sidewalks and streets as an extension of their domestic spaces), I designed a conscious and consistent method for rural dwellers to move into their new homes. Latent spaces, like rooftops and walkways, are new public domains, where residents have agency to use materials found during demolition. Planks taken from demolished homes become the supporting structure for enclosed gathering spaces on rooftops. Rubble becomes the bedding for urban farms. These interventions act as tokens of the past, keeping hold of an unfortunate loss while putting it to new use.

Eatery and public kitchen, elevation

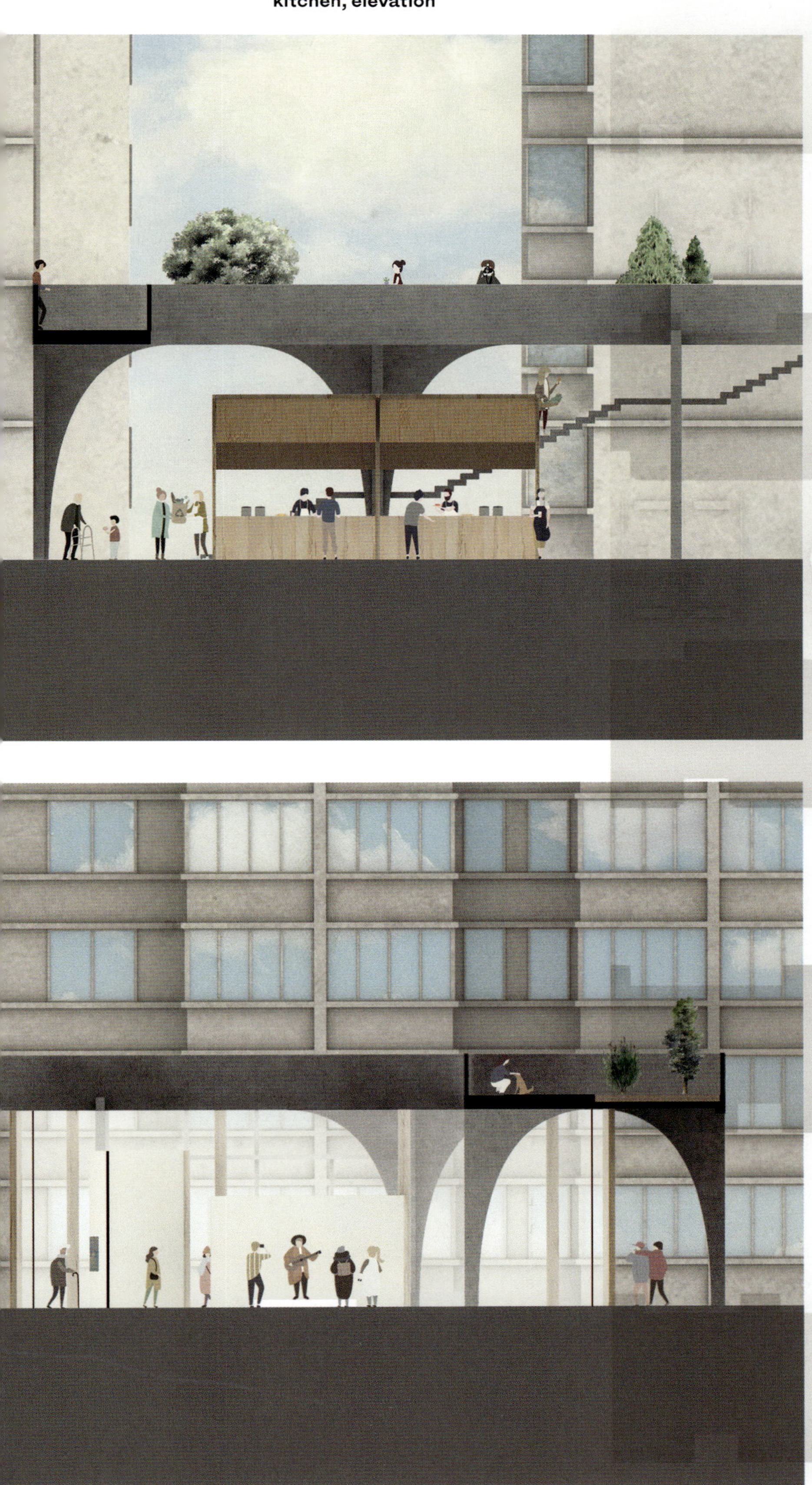

Gallery and indoor gathering space, elevation

nity's Revival

Jiangsu redesigned, plan

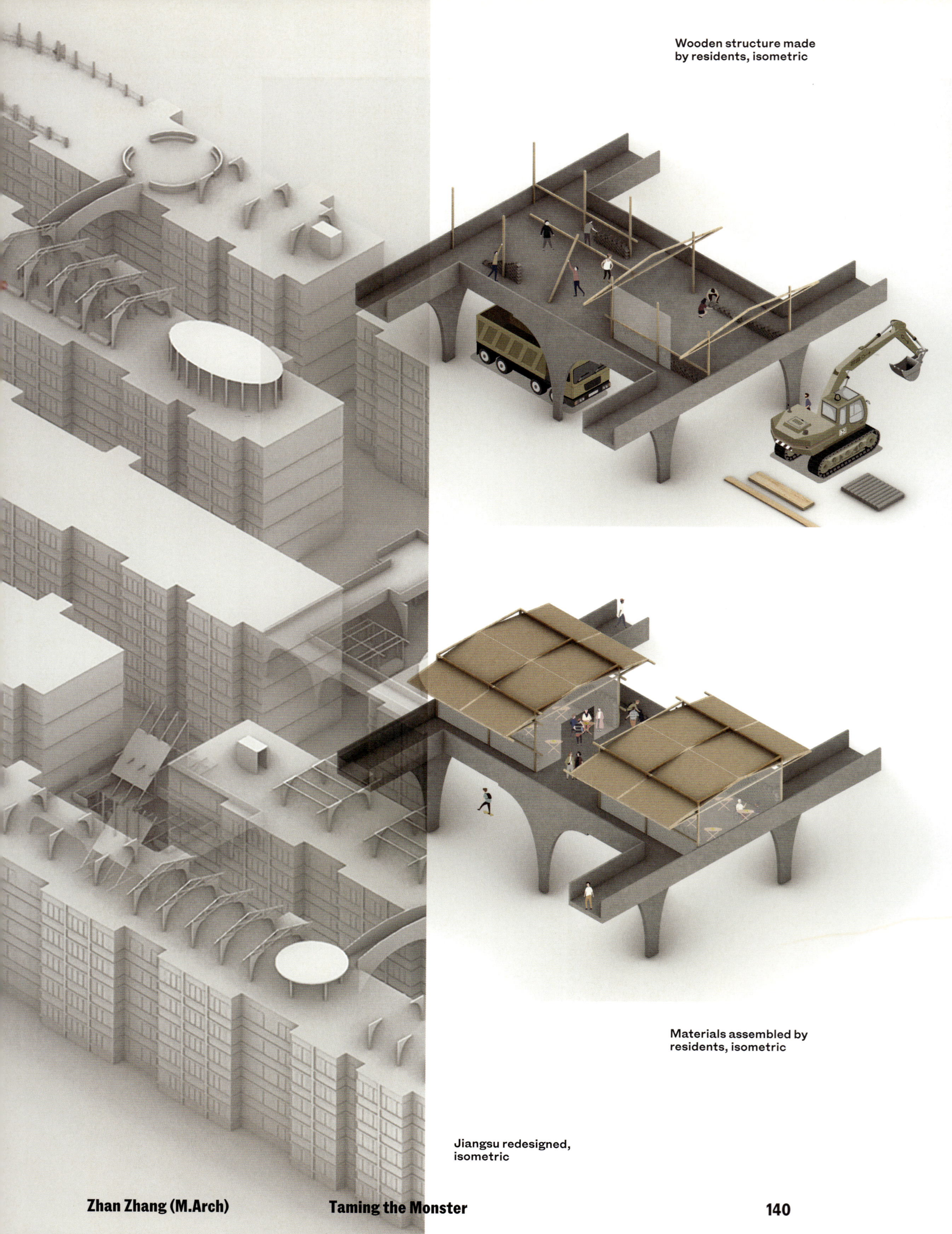

Wooden structure made by residents, isometric

Materials assembled by residents, isometric

Jiangsu redesigned, isometric

Pause, Voice, and Revolution
Introduction

Primary Advisor **David Gersten, Senior Critic, Department of Architecture, RISD**

Students **Sina Erol (B.Arch), Joyce MinKyung Kim (B.Arch), Jiamin Lin (M.Arch), Lilly Zhang (B.Arch)**

We will not go back to normal. Normal never was. Our pre-corona existence was not normal other than we normalized greed, inequity, exhaustion, depletion, extraction, disconnection, confusion, rage, hoarding, hate, and lack. We should not long to return, my friends. We are being given the opportunity to stitch a new garment. One that fits all of humanity and nature.
Sonya Renee Taylor

Poets, prophets, and reformers are all picture makers and this ability is the secret of their power and of their achievements. They see what ought to be by the reflection of what is, and endeavor to remove the contradiction.
Frederick Douglass

This publication presents an extraordinary group of works created by a rare group of people, each voicing intelligence, depth, and vision, each capturing and embodying with great nuance a rare period in all of our lives. The precision and emotive power of the works documented here are gifts of hope and despair, inviting thoughtful reflection on life, loss, and memory within this pause/rupture. I would offer that deep within their depths, between the words, between the stones, between the spaces, between the lines, we hear the early murmurs of revolution.

When the first wave of the pandemic hit our studio and we woke up in a Zoom Space, a Zoom State, and a Zoom State of Mind, as a group we immediately recognized the new spatial inhabitation. It was as if we woke up in the Wim Wenders film *Paris, Texas*. In one way or another we were now all Travis and Jane, trapped in the images of ourselves we had become. This was of course destabilizing, disorienting, unsettling; we felt trapped. As a group, we decided that casting these feelings aside and pushing on, heroically pursuing our projects, was probably *not* a very good idea. We decided to stop, to pause, to in fact embrace the odd, unsettling spaces and emotions of the experience and attempt to share them, to voice them to ourselves and each other. Rather than encourage the students to push forward through the storm and continue their "work" against the challenges, I asked them to stop, to put their projects down, to sit down in the cold snow of this rupture and just allow themselves to be quiet, to be still, to feel the embodied sense of all that was happening. I asked them to trust that these experiences contained the seeds of a new architecture and simply attempting to share, to express what we were living could bring us toward a new social political vision. We did this; we began to slowly create conversations around what people sensed was happening, and together we realized that something extraordinary was happening, that it simply would not make sense to carry the baggage of the prerupture works into the storm, that we had the opportunity to "stitch a new garment" and that we had to embrace this, regardless of how far we got in the short weeks we had left in the semester. In one way or another each work shared here embraced this moment, and the fact that the spatial/material imagination is a dimension of human life. We introduced a politics of slowing down, of resisting our current accelerating violence; of searching for new modes of concern for the other, new promises for distributing risk and resources, new spaces of empathy and ethics, new words for rebinding freedom. This is a pragmatism of creative urgency that emerged from our studio.

Architecture and humanity share the same predicament. When space breaks down into barbarism, this does not remain external. The porosity of being offers no such shelter; the plane of collective tyranny becomes a line penetrating the individual, manifesting an inner disregard for another's humanity. Architecture can repel violence and be violent, perhaps, at the same time. Our poetic imaginations are the most precise and therefore pragmatic means of addressing our social and political lives. They produce oxygen within the fibers of our social contract, pockets of space within the collapsed structure of capital's hegemonic language. The poetic imagination is a dimension of human life, a mode of insurgency, a language of empathy and difference that includes our nuanced fragilities, in our shared stories. Perhaps, unbeknownst to itself, architecture too is a mode of insurgency, opening pockets of space within the collapsed structures of capital's hegemonic *time*.

I am moved by the precision and emotive depth of the works in this publication, each emerging from a deep commitment to exploration, to space and voice. Each person slowed down, entered their space, and asked their questions. Their works are gifts of spirit, precision, care, and courage. They responded to the challenges of our time, not with known forms of "crises management" but with a depth personal exploration, of excavation and existential hope. These are exploratory, independent, uncontainable works, sparking from the pragmatics of the poetic imagination in search of the ethical dimensions of life. Heard in their own proper beat and measure, each work offers a deeply human sonnet, empathetically calling us close, whispering in gentle overtones: revolution. They are announcing that we cannot go back, and there is more to come, and it will come, from *you*, from your questions, your voices, your creative urgencies. The urgent need for social political movements, for civic engagement and exploratory works of empathy and ethics is as present as it has ever been, and it is for all of us to find the works and movements of our time, to listen to the unheard voices, to search for the unknown linkages, to ask the questions that have not yet been imagined, and to create the transformations that embody our best hopes and aspirations. It's time.

Sina Ero (B.Arch

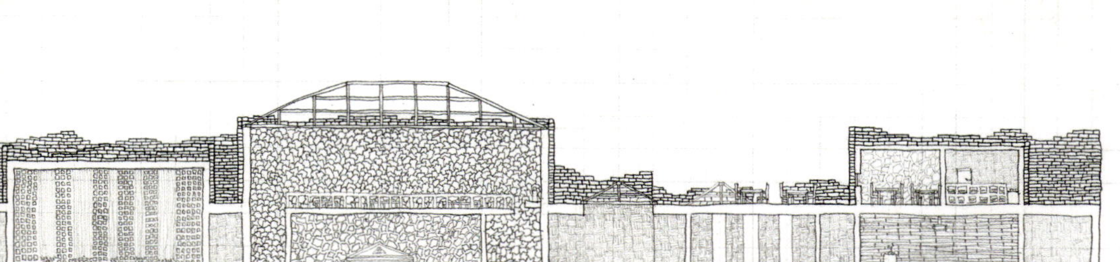

Building sections, graphite on paper, 18 × 24 in.

Reciprocal Space: Poetic Archeology in Assos

A poetic, hand-drawn exhibition design illuminates storytelling and honors our essential ephemerality.

The Assos Archeology Museum in Assos, Turkey, is designed to manifest experience as poetic imagination. Working with a team of archeologists who are unearthing the ancient village of Assos, I interpreted their stories of discovered artifacts to imagine new spaces for housing and exhibiting the excavated work. My interwoven narratives of the history and identity of the site are displayed alongside the artifacts. My design thus responds to surgeon and author Richard Selzer's elegiac awareness when he asks, "Where is the architect who, from the moment he begins his design, will be aware that in each room of his finished hospital someone will die?"[1]

Each gallery reflects a specific historical, contextual, or archeological condition. Upon entrance, the façade of each room, constructed

1 Richard Selzer, "Down from Troy, Part 1," in *The Exact Location of the Soul: New and Selected Essays* (New York: Picador, 2002).

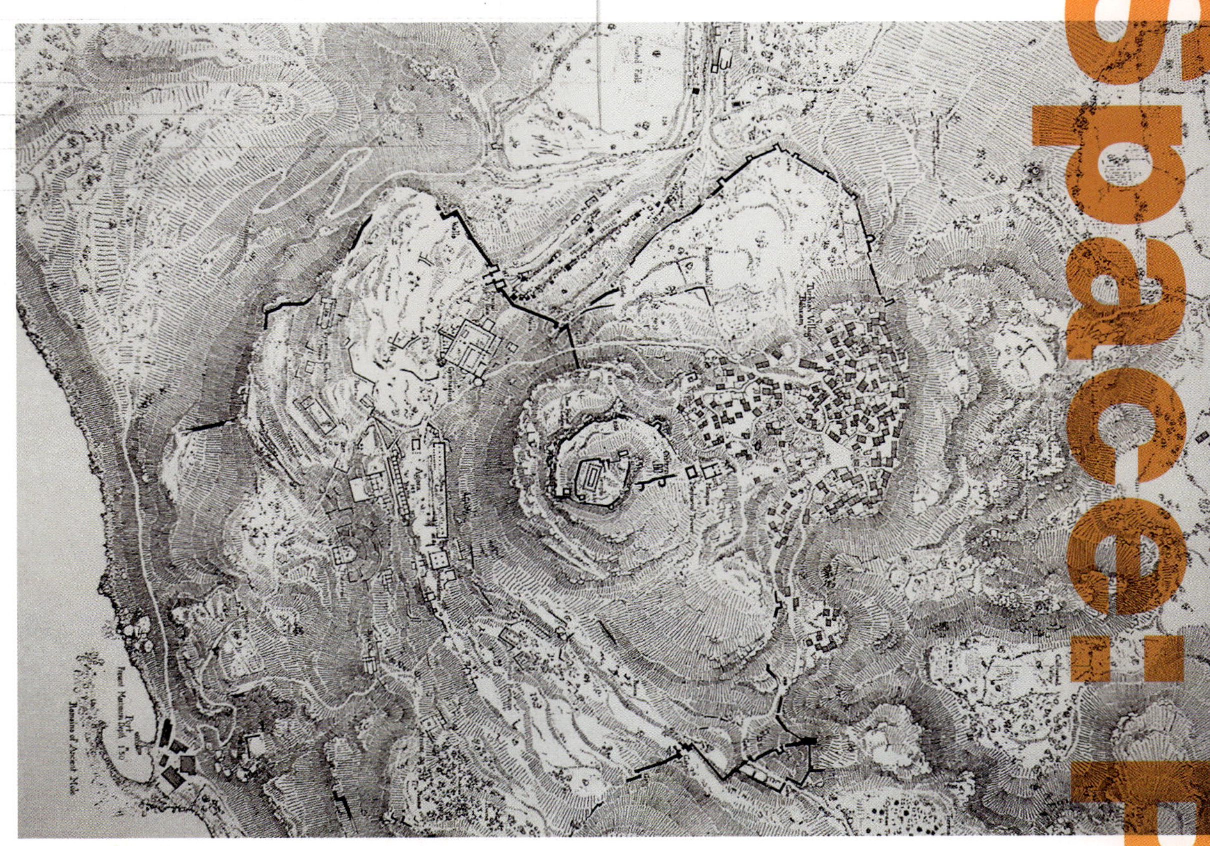

Assos: site plan, digital drawing, 28 × 42 in.

Underground oblique floor plan, graphite on paper, 42 × 42 in.

Assos: site plan, digital drawing, 28 × 42 in.

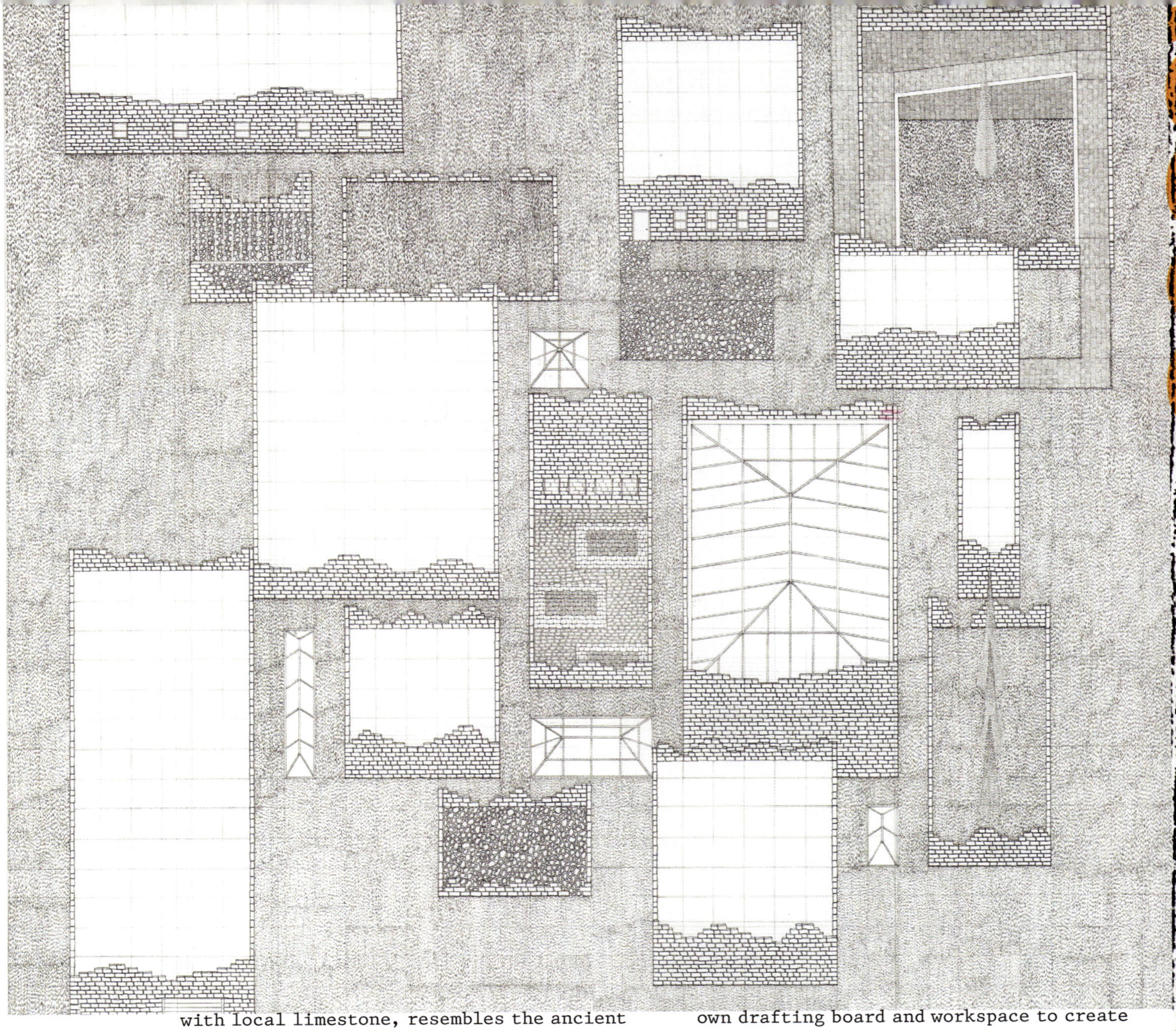

Oblique roof plan, graphite on paper, 42 × 42 in.

with local limestone, resembles the ancient fortress walls that circumscribe the historic city. Embedded into the ruins, the circulation path tours visitors underground. This burying allows the building to claim its place within the ruins of its surroundings, concealing its diversity of programs and spatial experiences. The scattered galleries recall a chain of islands, creating hubs that underscore the value of the stories and artifacts.

My design process starts and ends with hand drafting. Working by hand has a tectonic quality that does not translate into the digital realm. While working from home, it may have been easier to switch to drafting on the computer, but the pandemic only strengthened my urge to draw by hand. I constructed my own drafting board and workspace to create large-scale drawings, which again recalls Selzer, when he asks, "Who, while seated at his drawing board, will pause to feel upon his naked forearms the chill wind of his mortality?"[2] Hand drafting reflects a disciplinary core of values that extends beyond art and architecture; our constraints are an impetus for innovation.

2 Selzer, "Down from Troy."

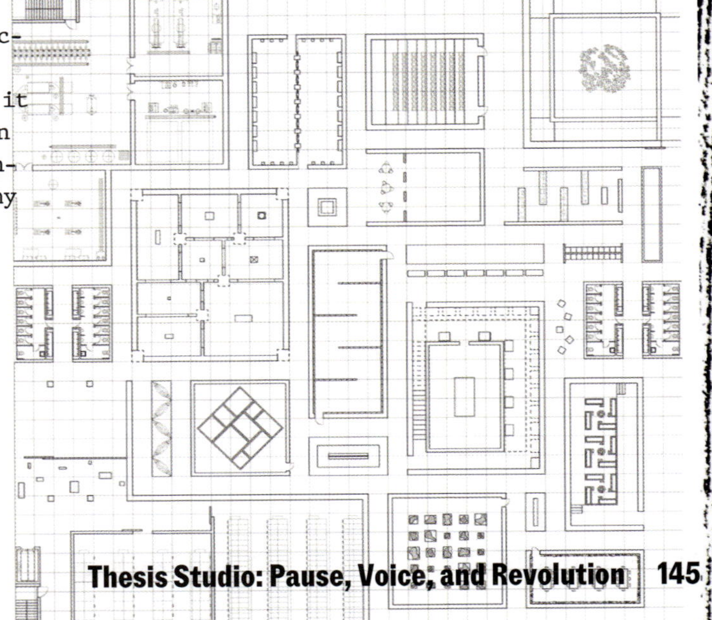

Floor plan diagram, digital drawing, 42 × 42 in.

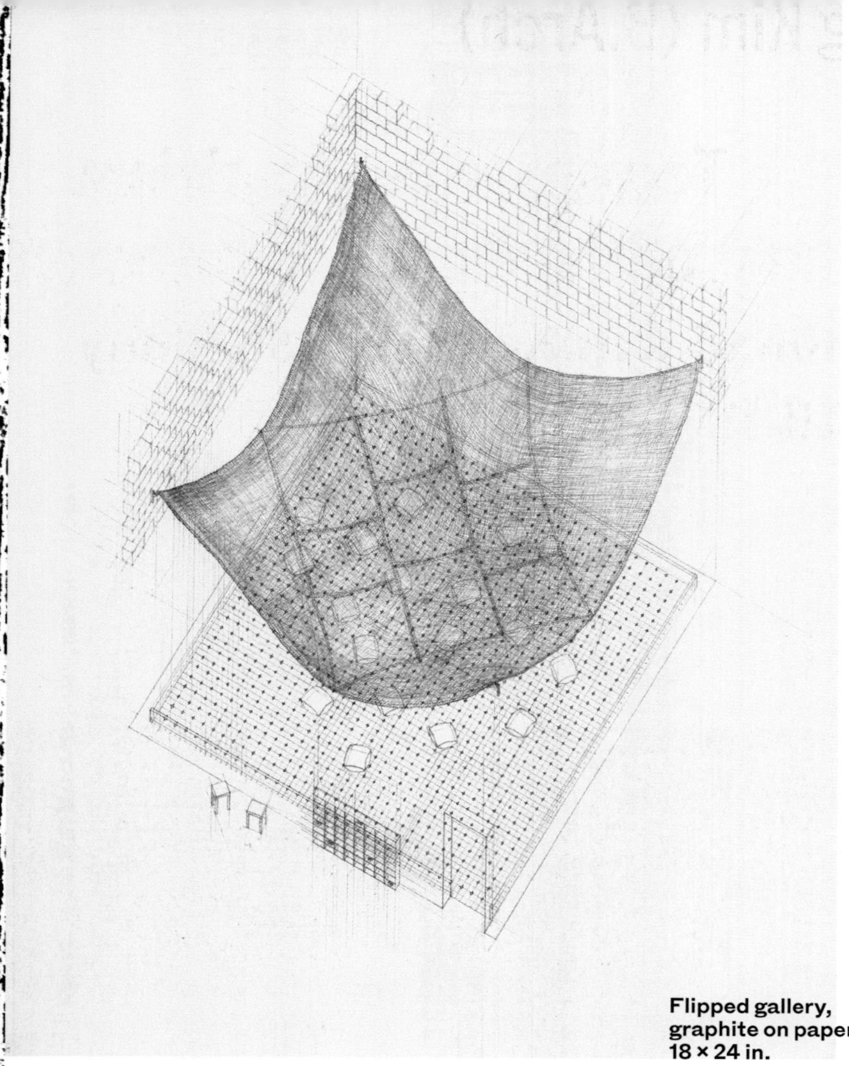

Flipped gallery,
graphite on paper,
18 × 24 in.

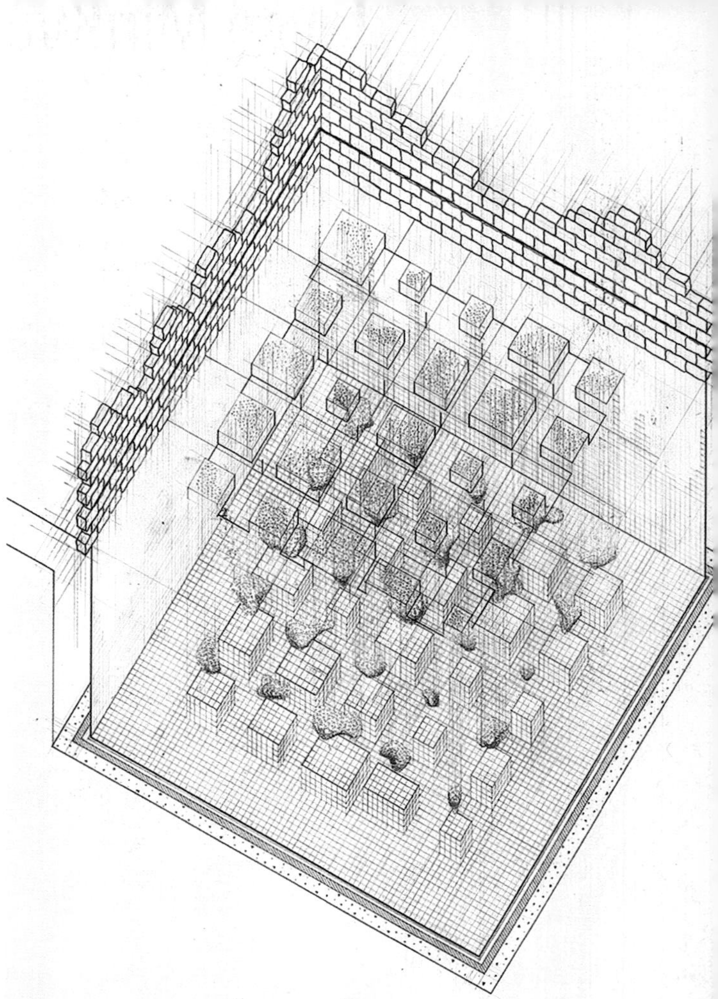

Cosmos gallery,
graphite on paper,
18 × 24 in.

Decay gallery,
graphite on paper,
18 × 24 in.

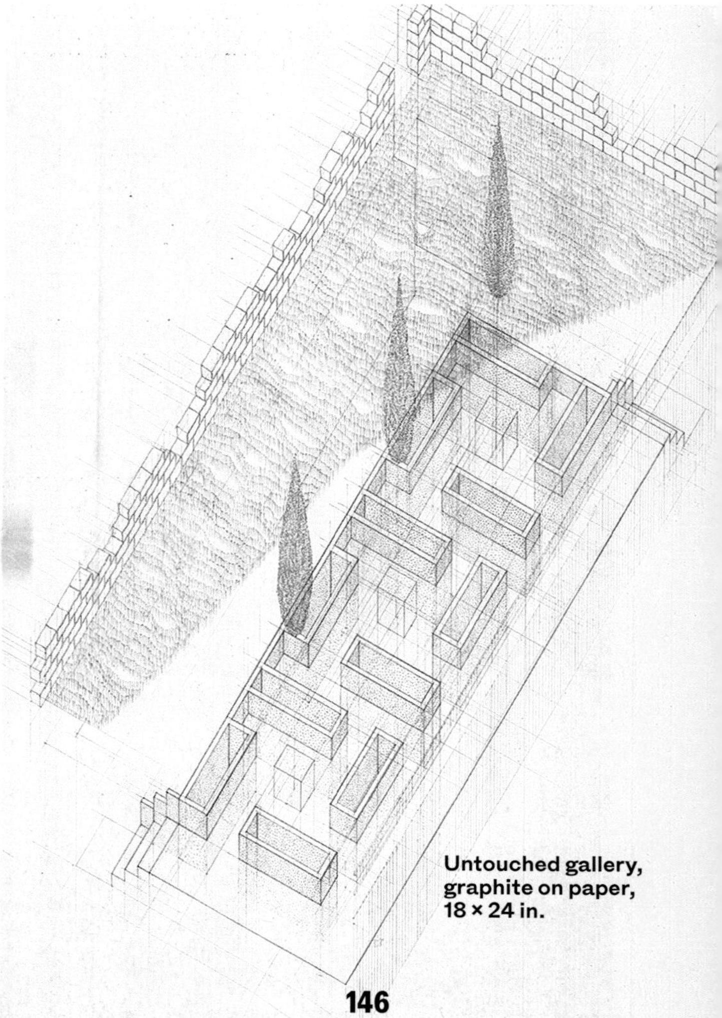

Untouched gallery,
graphite on paper,
18 × 24 in.

Joyce MinKyung Kim (B.Arch)

DESIRE+: Reclaiming Eros Transgressive eroticism counters the disembodiment of the digital architectural image, inverting repression and imagining a sexually progressive disciplinary turn.

Double body, clay in a mirrored Plexi case

Architectural representations frame a vision that reveals our inner desires and fantasies. In the twenty-first century, they depict a life of becoming digital images. As I spend more time living outside my body and in the over-sexed, over-saturated world of images, I lose my physical sense of what it means to be human. I exist between living my life as an "image" and living my life, less and less often, as a body. Calling up the opposing forces of Eros (love) and Thanatos (death), I constructed a narrative tool to play out the consumption of images:

> **Eros, you are in great danger. Your existence is denied in every fabric of our capitalist history. We live in a world of hyper-stimulation and physical isolation, invested in living in the hairless surfaces of the digital image. This virtual suppression is threatening the body, both the commonality and the true individual. You are dying, displaced by Thanatos, by the dead no-place of virtual (un)reality. I can feel your death across all human and non-human beings as we try to connect with each other across screens, images. We lost our voice, the bodily voice, where we communicate through our eyes and understand each other through our bodies. I think I am dying ... fearful of your disappearance and desperate to speak your language.**

I use this narrative as a heuristic device in sculpting myself as the Crouching Venus by

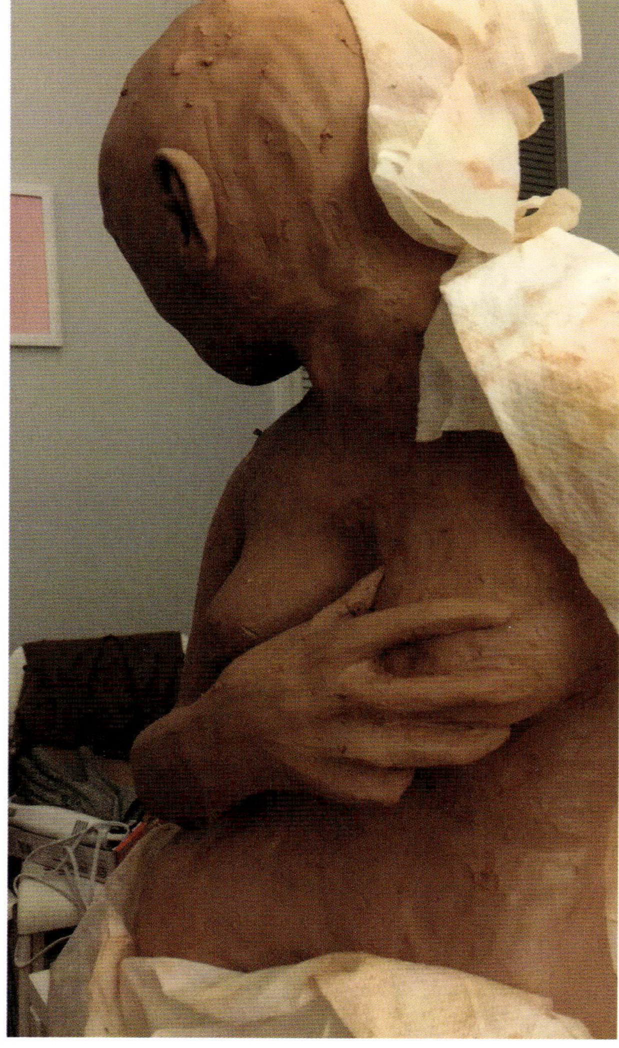

Double body, sculpture process in clay

Double body, clay in a mirrored Plexi case

Eros

Double body, clay in a mirrored Plexi case

Diodalsa. Venus—Roman goddess of love, desire, beauty, and prosperity—celebrates a chaste, orderly, superior, divine form, while the lower, corporeal Venus is cast as the root of all evil. Through the duality of Venus, I explore the concept of the double body. Working from reference photos of myself taken from every angle in front of the mirror, naked, I created a figurative sculpture from a 75-pound block of clay. The figure is placed in a display case with three surfaces constructed of mirrored Plexiglas; she faces away from the viewer, her back turned, existing as multiple images, reflected and reproduced. To look at her, to meet her gaze, the viewer must navigate the boundaries of the space, move around her material, three-dimensional body. Peering around the chamber, viewers may even see themselves as their eyes touch the cracks of her body. It is this constructed image, rough and complex, replicated in the mirror, that forms an architectural space of embodiment and sexual progressivism. As we reflect on the physical form, we also see ourselves.

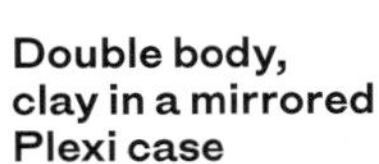

Double body, clay in a mirrored Plexi case

David Gersten

Double body,
clay in a mirrored
Plexi case

Jiamin Lin (M.Arch)

About Intimacy: Monastery with Swings and Theaters

Definition of space and scales of intimacy are explored through film and theater as an iteration of monastic life.

Chairs in the wild

Imagine a person who goes everywhere carrying a chair. From the moment she places her chair on the ground, she defines an invisible space around her, a kind of enclosure. My thesis started from this moment, with an attempt to define this spatial intimacy.

My exploration began with filming the interaction between bodies and larger entities, translating time into measures of movement and occupancy of space. Film and architecture both mobilize spatial and temporal modes of perception. Film produces virtual spatial experiences and an automated linear structure, while soundscapes function autonomously from images, describing the scale and texture of space and filtering perception by joining all of the senses.

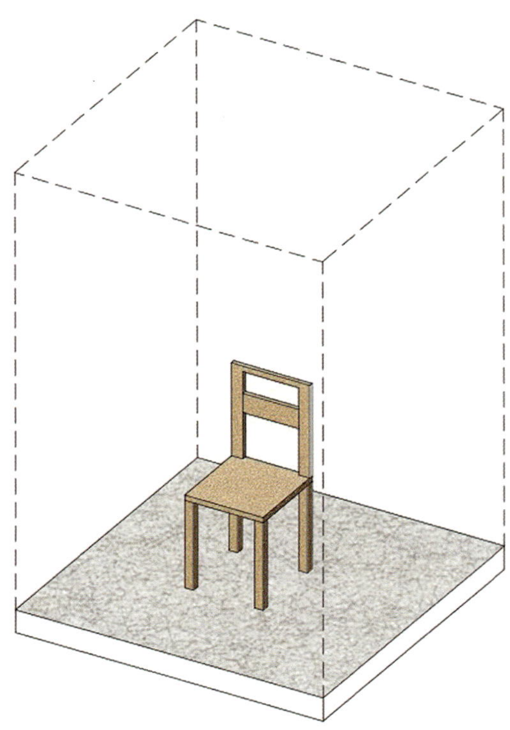

Chair(s)

The word “monastery” comes from the Greek “to live alone,” and “a place for doing something.” It represents both individual and spiritual space. Life inside a monastery is usually socially separated from the surrounding populace. Isolation supports idealized contemplation. Some religious traditions mandate ascetic lifestyles that forgo engagement even with other monks. I wondered: What if the monastery sits quietly in the city, behind a wall that permits no sign of its existence, but at the same time allows for more social interaction with the local communities? Imagining a space for living and a space to rethink intimacy, I rewrite the monastery’s program. It’s no longer a lifelong commitment; people may enter the monastic community in phases.

Theater was my second spatial reference. How does it feel when you are living inside a theater set? Is it real or still life? The theater’s “fourth wall” creates an intimate space. Similarly, the floor, the fifth façade or elevation of architecture, can definitively communicate and interact with people. Thus I rethought the floor as a designable interface in architecture. I also considered materiality, focusing less on visual signals like color and weight and more on tactile signals, which make us rethink the relationship between our body, its skin, and space.

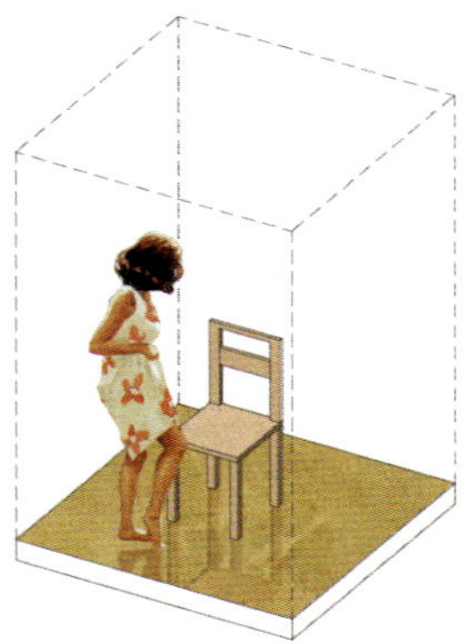

Materiality: metal

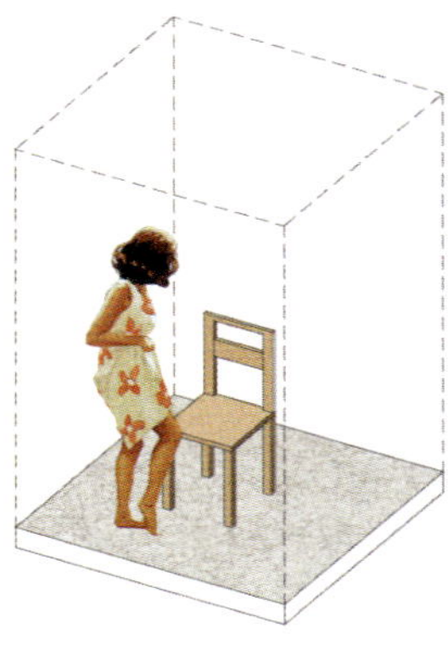

Materiality: concrete

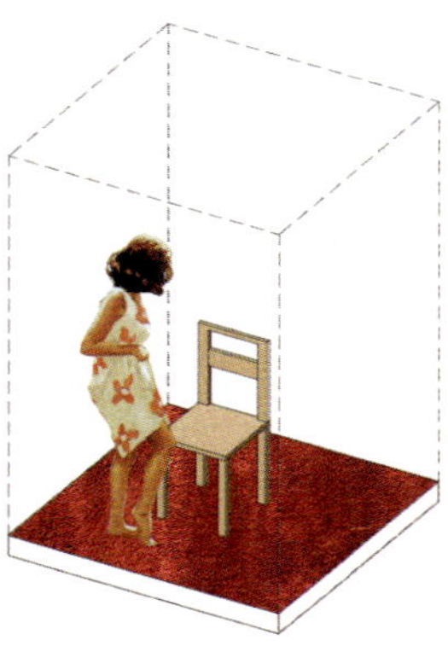

Materiality: velvet

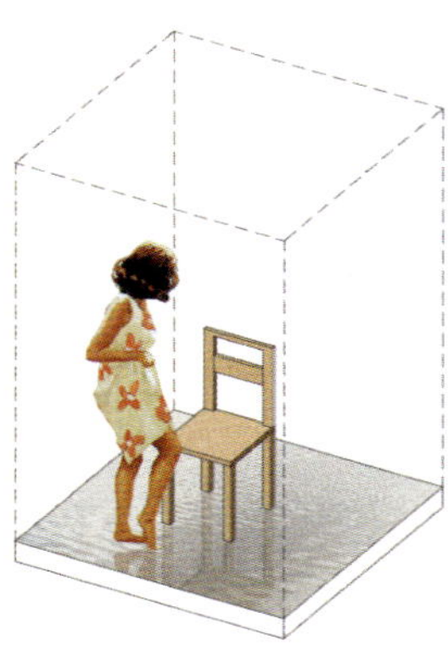

Materiality: liquid

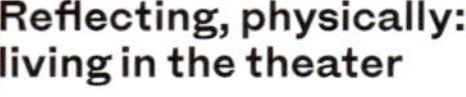

Reflecting, physically: living in the theater

Materiality: marble

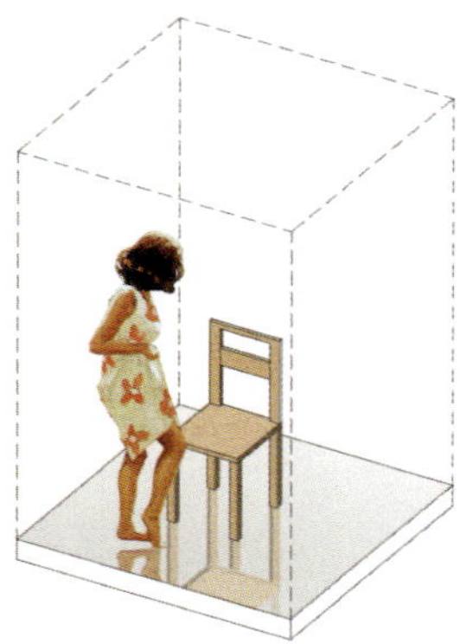

Materiality: mirror

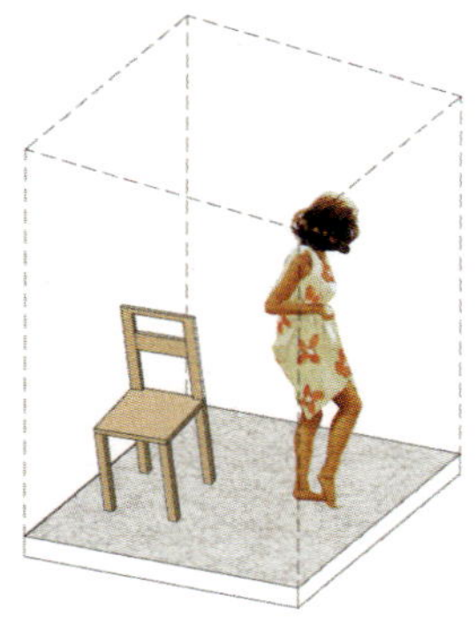

Tendency of movement of …

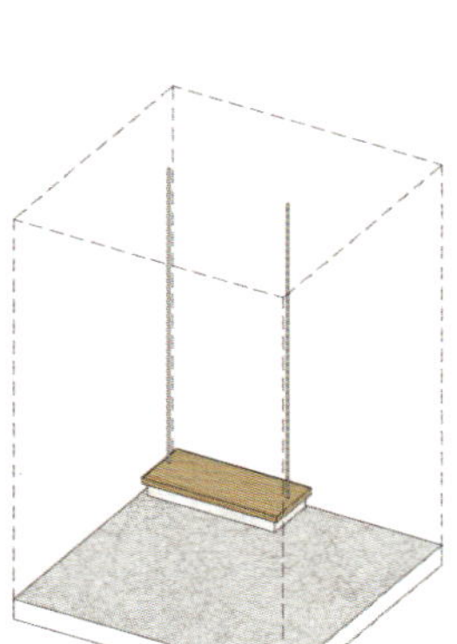

Chairs: swing

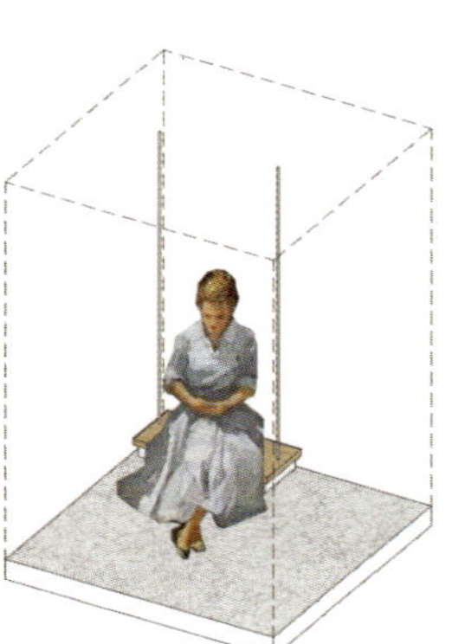

I swing, and I see myself on the ground defining space itself

Fixed chairs in place, the exact location of the soul

Finally, I thought about different parts of the human body, our feet, for example. It is hard for human beings to put our whole body weight on our hands, but easier on the feet. Feet have an intricate relationship with gravity. They require more delicate sensors, functioning as a powerful communicating medium between the body and the architecture. They are a conduit, their soles a fabric through which to experience spatial intimacy.

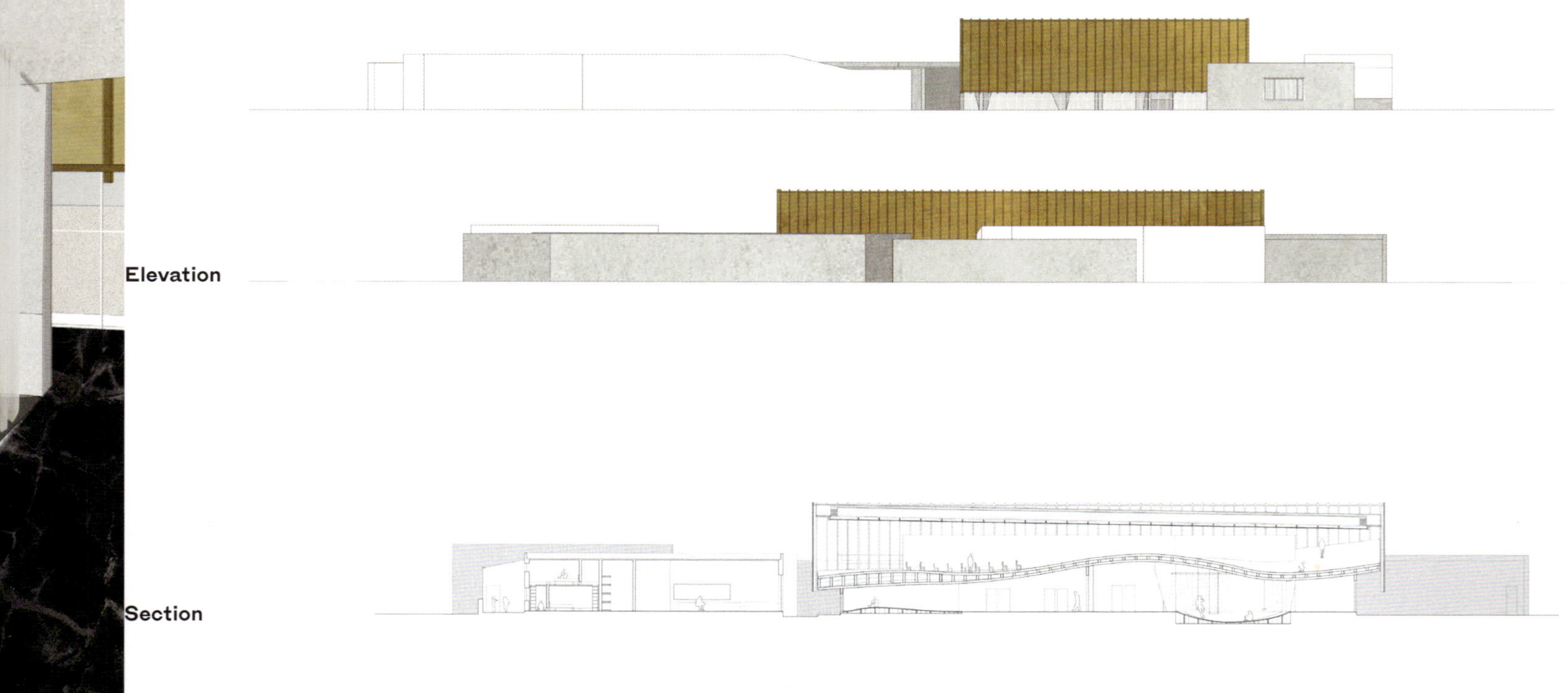

Elevation

Section

Lilly Zhang (B.Arch)

Living in Harmony Feng shui, a practice of balancing oneself with one's surroundings, is incorporated into design to create equilibrium between our senses and ourselves.

Living in Harmony

Modernity introduced a homogenous and mechanical form of existence, infiltrating both work and domestic life and making us oblivious to the psychological elements of our built surroundings. Our individual bubble and the world we live in are imbalanced. Yet advancing technologies offer opportunities for a never-before-seen connection between life and the environment.

Architecture has responded to these cultural phenomena by focusing on programmatic needs and economic gains; it has become a tool. Kitchen renovations, building extensions, and other small-scale projects dominate the practice. We need to create changes to buildings that are meaningful to the individual and considerate of the building's spirituality. Design is more than just the practical and aesthetically pleasing; it is an art.

Emotional Balance I–IV, burn marks on watercolor paper

My thesis incorporates the balancing act of feng shui design with attention to the senses, as described in texts such as Juhani Pallasmaa's *The Eyes of the Skin*. Feng shui is a traditional Chinese practice that uses energy to harmonize individuals with the environment around them. When traditional practice and the senses meet today's demands, an experiential architecture and theory emerges—one that reconsiders an individual user's needs to help them achieve inner equilibrium. Life is in direct relationship with built form, which has a significant effect on our state of mind.

Quarantine mood, negative, burn marks on acrylic

Representation of experiential sensation, carving on MDF

Quarantine mood, positive, burn marks on acrylic

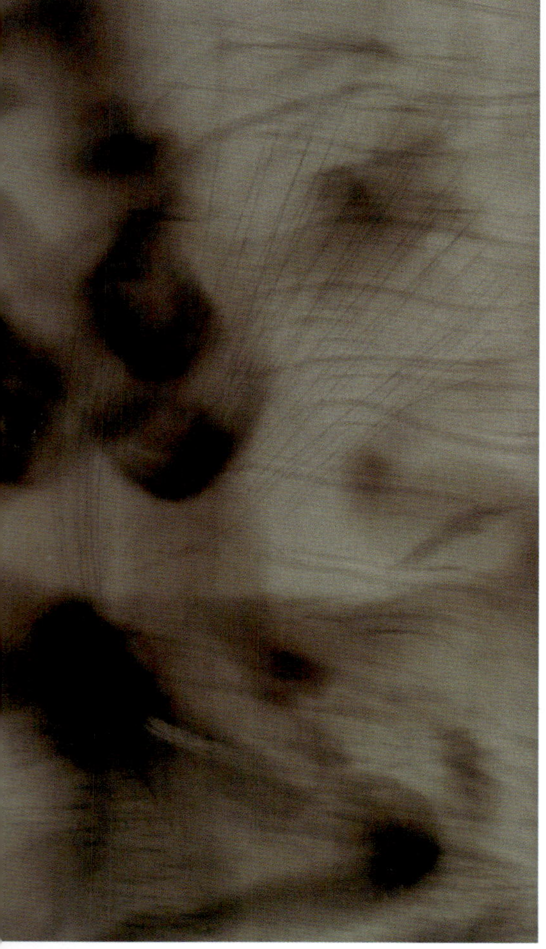

Image 3.003

Image 3.004

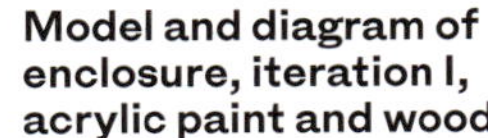

Model and diagram of enclosure, iteration I, acrylic paint and wood

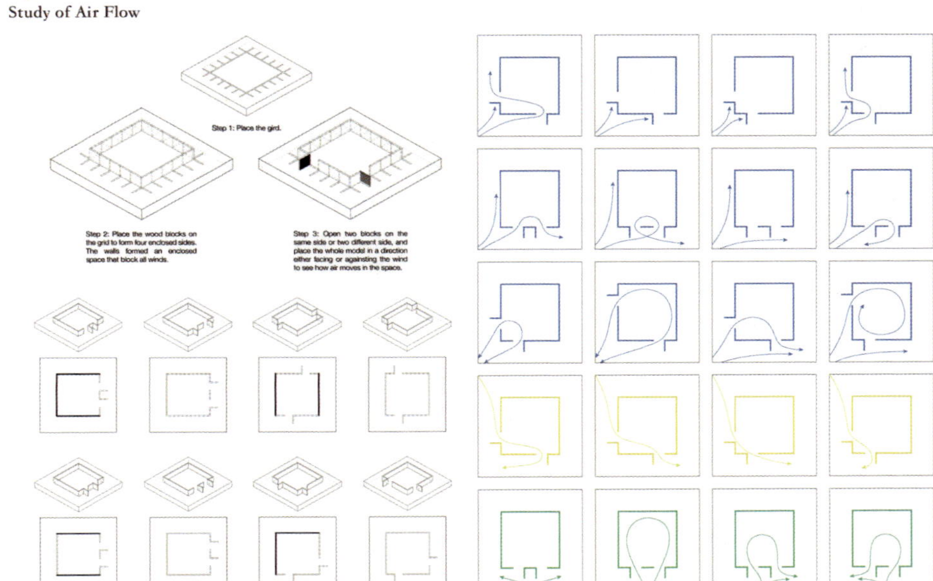

Image 3.005

Image 3.006

Image 3.007

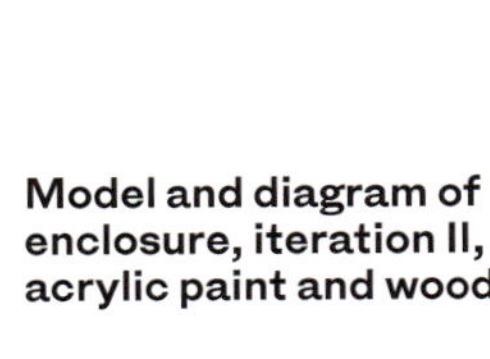

Model and diagram of enclosure, iteration II, acrylic paint and wood

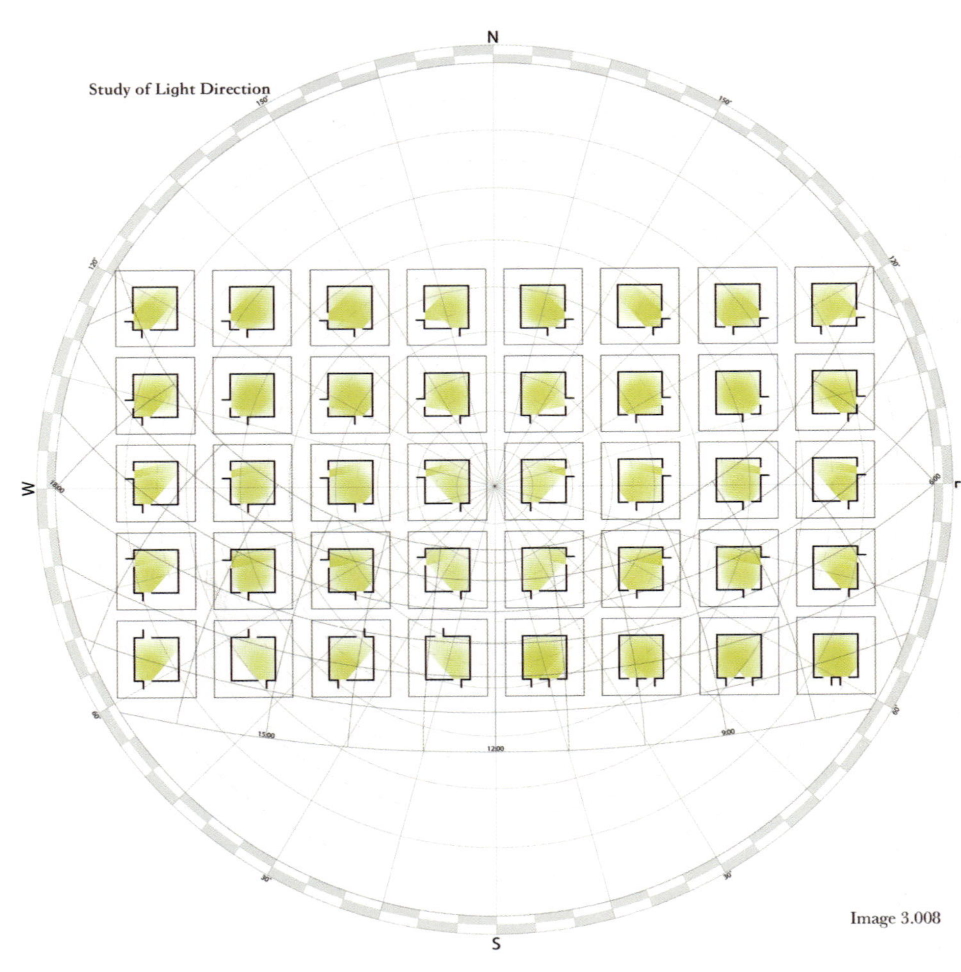

Image 3.008

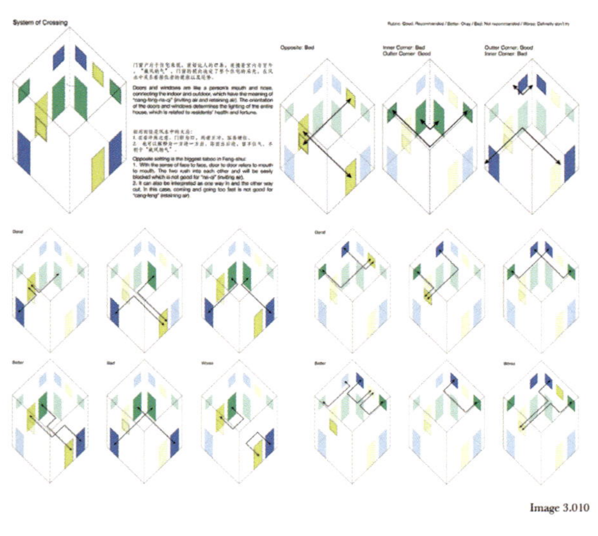

Model and diagram of accessibility for system of crossing, acrylic

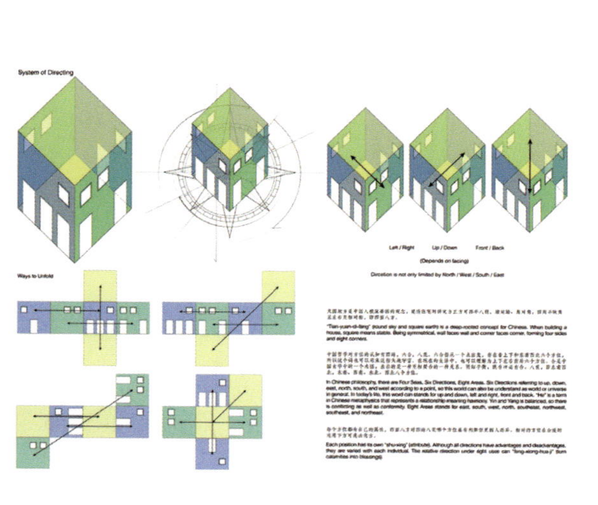

Model and diagram of accessibility for system of directing, colored acrylic

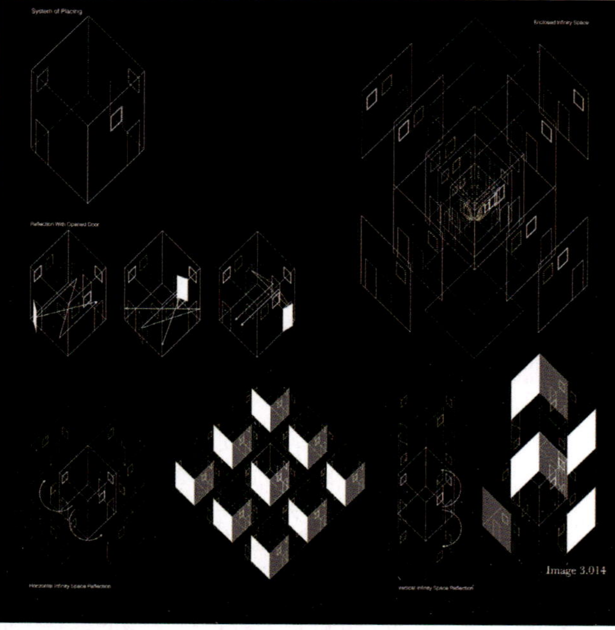

Model and diagram of accessibility for system of placing, mirror and acrylic

Regional Building Group
Introduction

Primary Advisor **Ryan McCaffrey, Critic, Department of Architecture, RISD**
Secondary Advisor **Jacqueline Shaw, Assistant Professor, Department of Architecture, RISD**

Students **Rashi Lalaji (M.Arch), Yunchao (Derek) Le (B.Arch), Dong Eun Lim (B.Arch), Laurence von Lignau (B.Arch), Yi (Eva) Lu (M.Arch), Mikéla Sumner (M.Arch), Avril Teo (B.Arch), Christopher Pak Villalta (M.Arch)**

In the context of an increasingly globalized society and homogenized built environment, Regional Building Group investigated the production of buildings that are specific to regional conditions. Today, the production of the built environment is governed by building codes, standardized products, and the opportunistic imperatives of financial flows. In contemporary construction worldwide, the relation between architecture and environment is most often value engineered to the bare minimum. Rem Koolhaas argues that this oft-derided generic nature is not a flaw, but a feature of the process of liberating ourselves from classical forms and outmoded ways of living. Architects should embrace the generic, he argues, because "People can inhabit anything. And they can be miserable or ecstatic in anything."[1]

Yet our planet and our places remain vast and variable. Geography, climate, sociology, politics, and economics inform locally specific dynamics relevant to the production of buildings. For architects these limits are as varied as material availability, historically relevant building systems, building types, and heating and cooling systems. By working directly with these limits, Vincent Canizaro argues that the promise of architectural regionalism is both practical and existential: "to foster connectedness to place and respond to local needs, not in spite of global concerns and possibilities, but in order to take better advantage of them."[2]

If the discipline of architecture today seems in a subaltern position with respect to the complex realities that govern building, that is so because it has failed to confront the transformations that have emptied out its categories and concepts. Regional Building Group takes these contingent realities of construction and locality seriously—studies them—as the basis for effective action. Effective action (the content of design) is here understood as being able to contribute substantially to a real condition, rather than superficially comment on or make metaphors of the lived reality of people. This attitude is opposed to the abstract, the general, and the universal; it understands each community's needs and conditions as different, and does not assume that there is a singular way of practicing architecture.

Each project here describes a complex, heterogenous world. These regional stories contradict the assumptions of places reduced to soundbites and catchphrases: is Mumbai (Rashi Lalaji; see pp. 161–164) ruled by corruption, and Seoul (Dong Eun Lim; see pp. 169–172) a well-mannered metropolis? Is Vermont (Mikéla Sumner; see pp. 181–184) an idyllic resort, or Hangzhou (Yi (Eva) Lu; see pp. 177–180) an ancient city stuck in the past? Each place presented here is all of these things and significantly more. Our status as a "group" suggests that while the conditions of each place are different, our methods are related in taking the facts of daily life and experience seriously. The work of secondary advisor Jacqueline

1 Rem Koolhaas, "From Bauhaus to Koolhaas," *Wired* magazine, 1996, https://www.wired.com/1996/07/koolhaas/.

2 Vincent Canizaro, *Architectural Regionalism: Collected Writings on Place, Identity, Modernity, and Tradition* (Princeton Architectural Press, 2007), 12.

Shaw was integral in holding each project accountable not only to the reality and specificity of these lived conditions, but also to each person's initial impetus to work on a certain topic. When remote learning altered our group's methods, we found new forms of collectivity as the new and improved Regional Building Online Community (RBOC), in the inaugural "People's Choice Lecture" (TikTok Culture), and in a collaborative playlist made by our group members.

In the end we aim to have projects that can match and contribute to the heterogenous, uncertain, and exciting conditions of the environments we live in. In some ways, our intention remains best described by the introductory lines of our communal playlist, written by our very own Laurence von Lignau: "RBOC presents the spiciest, most thought-provoking, and absolutely international playlist! Can you be specific in your work while listening to this transnational playlist? Let's find out on RBOC, where the groove is central. All languages and all regions are welcome."

Rashi Balaji (M.Arch)

Tenement/corridor/ courtyard relationship

Two-Gather—Collective Living: Housing and Recreational Facilities in Suburban Mumbai

Chawls, a collective, affordable form of living, offer a preexisting platform for modular communes to challenge the housing crisis within the broader urban context of Mumbai.

The densely populated city of Mumbai has suffered from lack of infrastructure and affordable development strategies. For years the government and developers have exploited the city's real estate market and violated land-use policies, developing the urban edges of Mumbai haphazardly, quickly overwhelming any open, ecological space and robbing the public of healthy living.

Chawls are a form of residential housing built in Mumbai during the industrial boom of the 1900s for industrial workers in the textile factories. Affordably constructed, they rely on shared spaces for communal living. My thesis work argues that this successful, existing typology can be redeveloped within the existing urban framework and provide a plausible

Site strategy and massing

solution to affordable housing issues. By adding large, open spaces within the housing, chawls can be adapted to Mumbai's continuous economic disparities, re-development schemes, and rent policies. The original chawls' built structure remains unchanged, but its inner fabric varies in its architectural articulation and tenement sizes, facilitating cultures for communal living.

My design creates non-barricaded, non-exclusive, non-elitist spaces through affordable housing and recreational facilities. I frame twelve entryways into the housing, offering various access points to the interior space. The courtyard, corridor, and individual home play an essential role in healthy community living. The courtyard provides space for public interaction and activities; the corridor is a semiprivate space that visually bridges the communal courtyard to individual tenements. Variously sized courtyards dictate different purposes, serving as anything from a small, private yard to a large cricket field, and create a healthy relationship between volume, scale, and the ecological edge of the site. With this simple modification to the existing chawl structures, my project provides access to all people and defines community living and open spaces that go beyond gardens and recreational grounds to include vast, diverse assets for the city.

Site strategy and massing

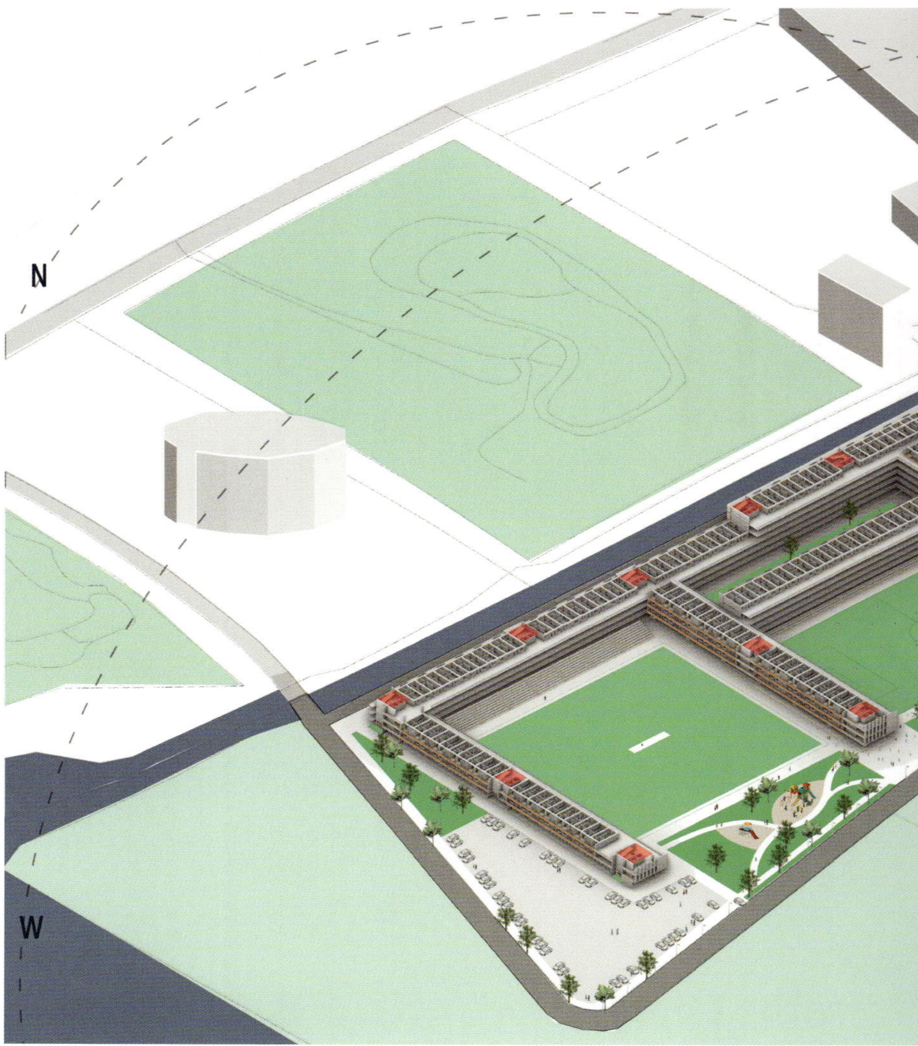

Existing Slums

Program Relations

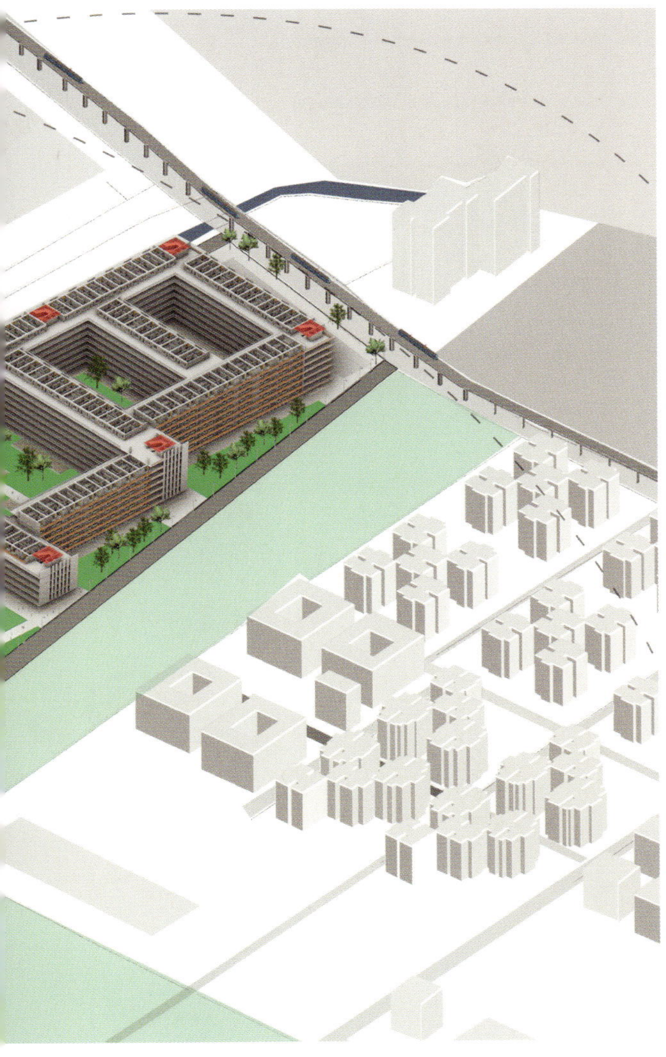

Volumetric relation between the housing and cricket field

Typical entrance

Volumetric relationship between courtyard and housing, section through the soccer field

Private courtyard
and housing, section

Cricket field
courtyard, plan

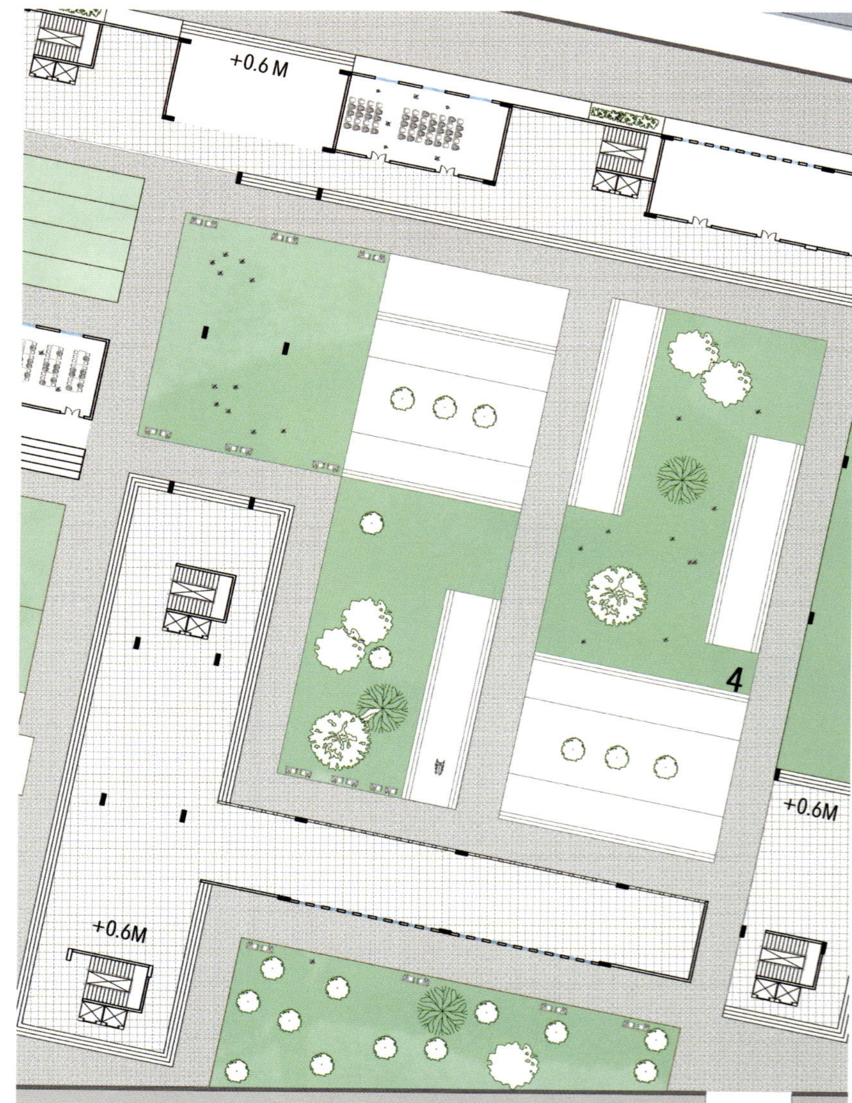

Semiprivate
courtyard, plan

Shanghai Prototype: Living Between Markets and Data Center How do you compromise state-controlled infrastructure and colonial building types? Through the Hybrid.

Masterplan: ground level

Shanghai Prototype examines Shanghai's contemporary built environment through three lenses: the Common, the Large, and the Hybrid. The Common focuses on the shikumen style, a regional building type using brick and timber. Built by imperial colonizers in the nineteenth century, shikumen compounds were first constructed by native Chinese craftsmen and sold to wealthy merchants, but their function later changed. After the Communist government gained full control of China in 1949, Shanghai was designated the economic center of the state. A population mobilized by economic opportunities, demand

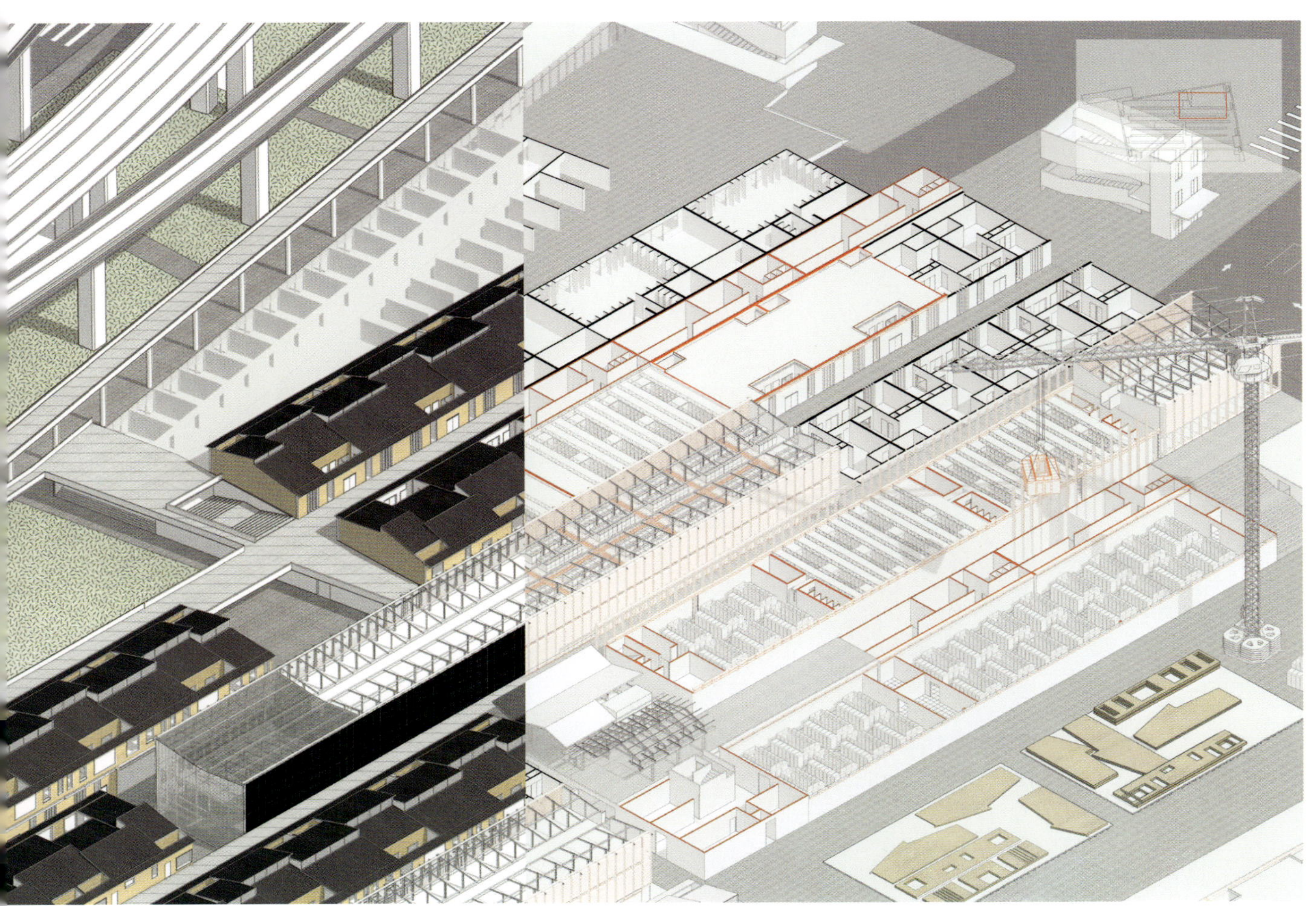

Axonometric: construction

View of the Hybrid from a metro window

View of streetscape

for labor, and a chance to participate in modernization rapidly densified the city. Single-family homes were soon subdivided to accommodate multiple families, with hallways becoming a space for daily chores and social interactions. By increasing occupancy load, the common shikumen type home was effectively turned into social housing by the state.

In the last five decades, Shanghai's legacy of imperial and internal colonization has perpetuated the urbanization of an economic center with a residential and infrastructural periphery. The metro system has accelerated consumerism by amplifying connectivity. Now, colonial shikumen-style housing has become either a skeleton for globalized retail or entirely replaced by new, massive commercial buildings, i.e., the Large. Zoning laws permit dense, large-scale structures, such as shopping centers and residential towers, to be built directly adjacent to the shikumen buildings, dwarfing the culturally significant Common, if it is not razed entirely. The commercialization and eradication of shikumen buildings submerge both Shanghai's colonial history and contemporary oppression.

My thesis challenges this trend by introducing a new paradigm: the Hybrid. Sited on a 15-acre zone attached to the No. 4 line's Baoshan Road station, the Hybrid approach symbiotically merges critical infrastructure systems (the metro system and data center) with low-density residential dwellings and markets. Integrating the data center brings an invisible service powered by the state into view. I propose large data center blocks across the grain of public thoroughfares, interrupted by housing units and intersected by parks. The large patch of

View of a bedroom

kets and Data Center

View of courtyard above office space

View from lane

low-rise structures connects to an elevated walkway feeding into the metro station. The Hybrid also imagines a new, regionally specific building type, one not reminiscent of its colonial past, but as a viable way to compress the distance between the state and the people. The two-story dwellings are organized around entry courtyards, providing communal outdoor space as an opportunity for social exchange, daily chores, and recreational activities. The collective footprint of the Hybrid programs dictates circulation paths, which embody resistance to internal colonization as they ring back to the Common as a space for the people.

View from lane

Section perspective: unit and service

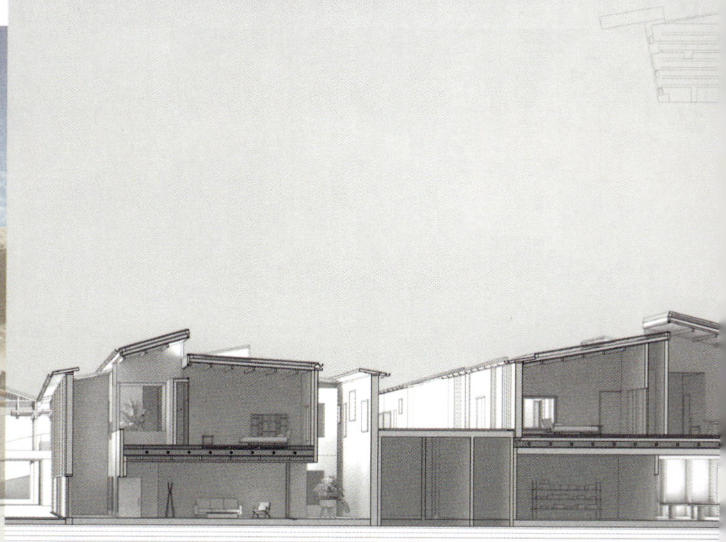

Mikela Sumner (M.Arch)

Adapting Home: Residential Development and Domestic Comfort in Vermont

A plan for homes in a Vermont town emphasizes comfort as an economic, social, and physical construct and allows for adapting the dwelling over time.

Speculative development, site plan

Looking south through the arterial path

Levels of shelter, light, and climate control define physical comfort. Social comfort is defined by degrees of privacy or cohabitation, more space or an open layout. Social insulation—a form of social comfort favoring privacy—distances people; in architecture, the design of the home, placement of the front door, and size of the site can all contribute to social comfort. While social insulation offers gradients of privacy, social isolation wholly disconnects occupants from the surrounding environment. The National House, a typical suburban house with superficial customization, favors social isolation and a pre-packaged idea of comfort. National Houses are constructed to appear as if they were adapted over time, but they were in fact

Adapting Home: Resi

The Courtyard, fully developed second-floor plan

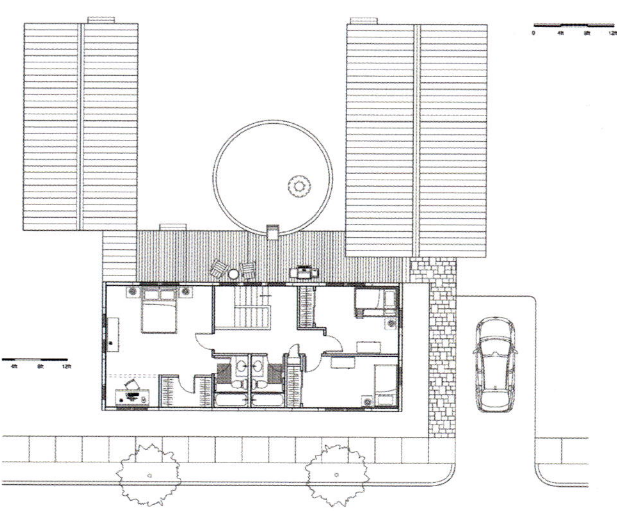

Small home, first-floor plan

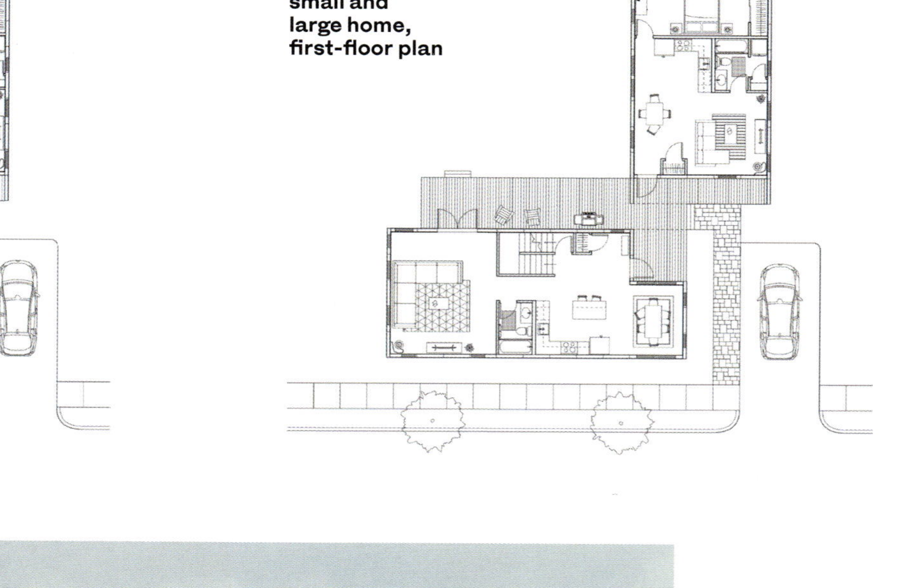

The Courtyard: small and large home, first-floor plan

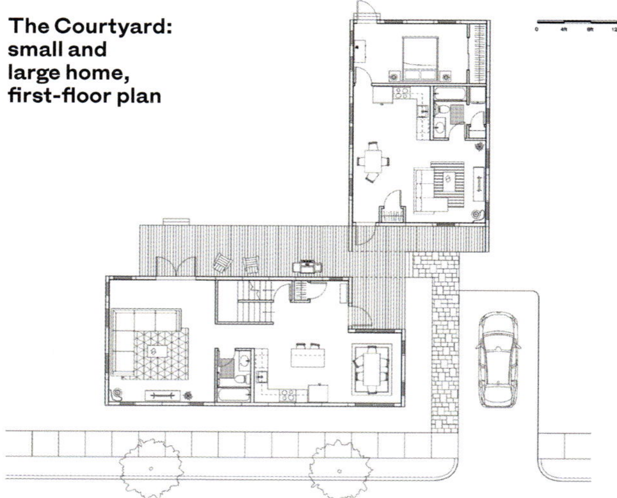

Visualization of community garden looking north

constructed as a whole without the capacity for future change. The comfort they sell is static; it cannot adapt over time to respond to ever-changing definitions of comfort.

Williston, an unofficial suburb of Burlington, Vermont, has seen a surge in demand for dwellings in the National House style. This trend has escalated the town's affordable housing shortage and incited a cultural shift away from the vernacular Vermont home, which emphasizes adaptability, physical comfort, and an amalgamation of built additions and renovations. Vermont's newly developed housing needs to maintain these traditions to allow for social insulation without the total isolation perpetuated by the National House.

This project offers residents the means to modify the dwelling at will to fit individual physical, social, and economic comfort needs. There are four distinct and adaptable dwelling types—the Passage, Courtyard, Inverted Ell, and Wing—and a masterplan that develops over time. The flexible home addresses all three constructs of comfort in a method consistent with Vermont's building tradition while still embracing the prevalence and familiarity of the National House. Without hindering a sense of community, the four typologies recognize cultural trends by physically varying levels of privacy, both within the unit and within the broader neighborhood. With the capacity to modify dwelling units to fit each life stage, the extended tenure of the residents further strengthens community connections. The dwelling configurations progressively increase the size of the residence, and thus the value of the home grows, adding to the social and economic diversity of the neighborhood. Each type promotes Vermont's heritage of self-proclaimed resourcefulness while also embracing future development.

The Passage, front elevation (left); side elevation (right)

The Wing, front elevation (left); rear elevation (right)

The Inverted Ell, front elevation (left); side elevation (right)

fort in Vermont

The Courtyard: fully developed, isometric

The Courtyard: fully developed first-floor plan

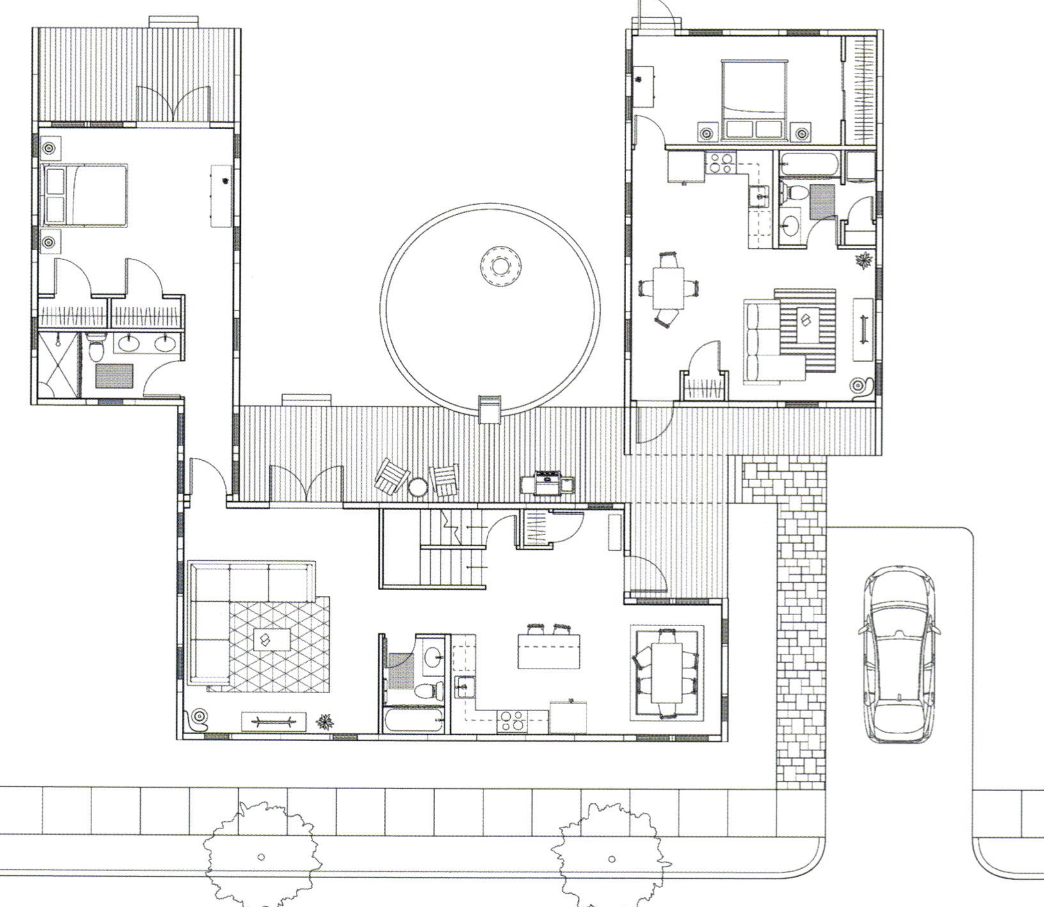

mikelasumner.com

Avril Teo (B.Arch)

A Part Apart: Disassembling Interiority in Singapore's Public Housing

Reviving a style of communal living without prescribing proximity, a model for public housing emerges through a history of its parts.

A Part Apart: Disass

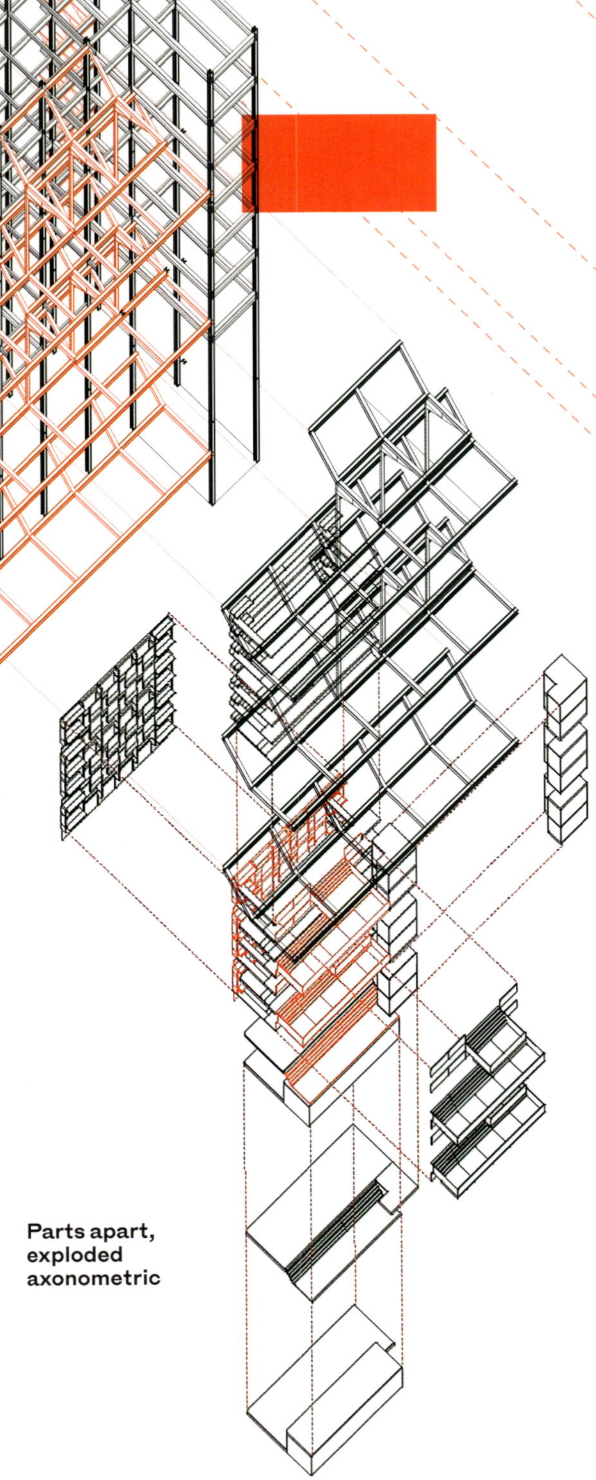

Parts apart, exploded axonometric

Margins, exploded axonometric

Precolonial Singapore predominantly featured Malay kampong villages, a typology characterized by traditional post-tie wood construction. Buildings responded to the tropical climate with ventilation and shading, connecting private and public space. The agrarian Singaporeans built incrementally, responding to environmental context. A tropical climate called for air flow, and the idiosyncracies of life required adaptability.

When Singapore separated from Malaysia in 1965, its contextualized buildings were immediately a thing of the past. Eager to introduce modernist ideology, government publications characterized urban kampong residents as "squatters," defining them as both illegal and socially inert.[1] The kampongs themselves were

1 Loh Kah Seng, "Dangerous Migrants and the Informal Mobile City of Postwar Singapore," *Mobilities*, no. 2, 2010, 197–218.

Interior corridor and one-bedroom unit

Multipurpose room between corridors

typecast as "an insanitary, congested, and dangerous squatter area."[2] The state-owned Housing Development Board (HDB) demolished existing kampongs and built high-rise apartments in their place, "separating, purifying, demarcating, and punishing transgressions … [to] impose systems on an inherently untidy experience."[3] In a moment when Singapore's aging population and waning birth rates posed an urgent problem, the HDB's design incentivized growing family size and class status to meet the state's population goals. Policies provided subsidies for those living close to their parents; bias for those expecting children; and racially segregated housing blocks. The house thus preceded the family that fit it—if you wanted cheap housing, you needed a family that aligned with the ideals of the state.

My thesis acknowledges the needs of public housing in Singapore but embraces occupants' agency. Avoiding the state's prescriptions, my proposal for mass housing revives the adaptable systems of the Malay kampong houses to foster a sense of authorship. Rather than demolish and build anew (as the government did), my design recognizes the temporality of family structures, where neighbors are an extension of the family and multigenerational living is an asset to the community. The exploded axonometric drawings representationally reject models of isolated components; even pulled apart, the drawings show a possibility of coming together. Units re-introduce public shades, and the spaces between aggregated units are designed to facilitate ventilation, so that singular buildings can function together as community space. The proposal employs casual, permeable relations among intimate families and neighbors, where the humid tropical climate supports a humanist lifestyle.

2 HDB, Bukit Ho Swee Estate, *Singapore: Housing and Development Board*, 1967, 39.

3 Mary Douglas, *Purity and Danger: An Analysis of Concepts of Pollution and Taboo* (London: Routledge Classics, 2002), 5.

Axonometric of front door

avrilavril.com

Above the basement and below the corridor

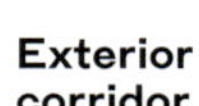

Exterior corridor

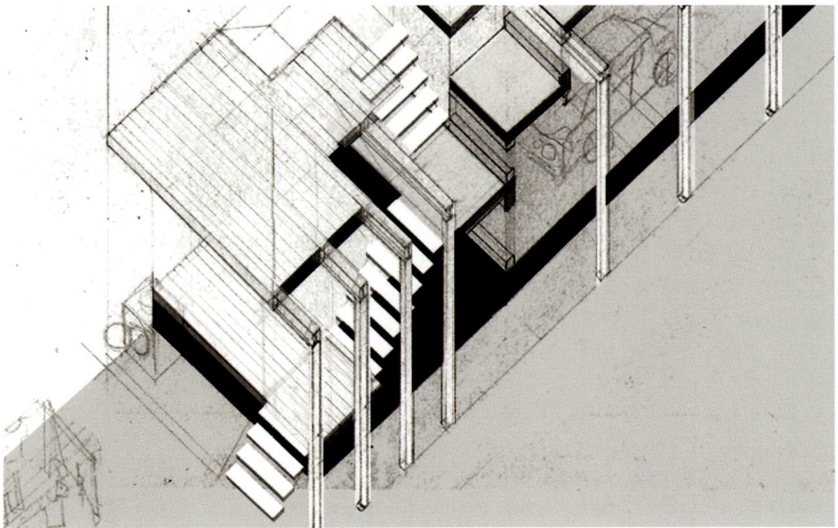

Axonometric of back stair

Axonometric of drop ceiling

Section through a landscape of public programs

Ventilation joint of the kampong house, wood model

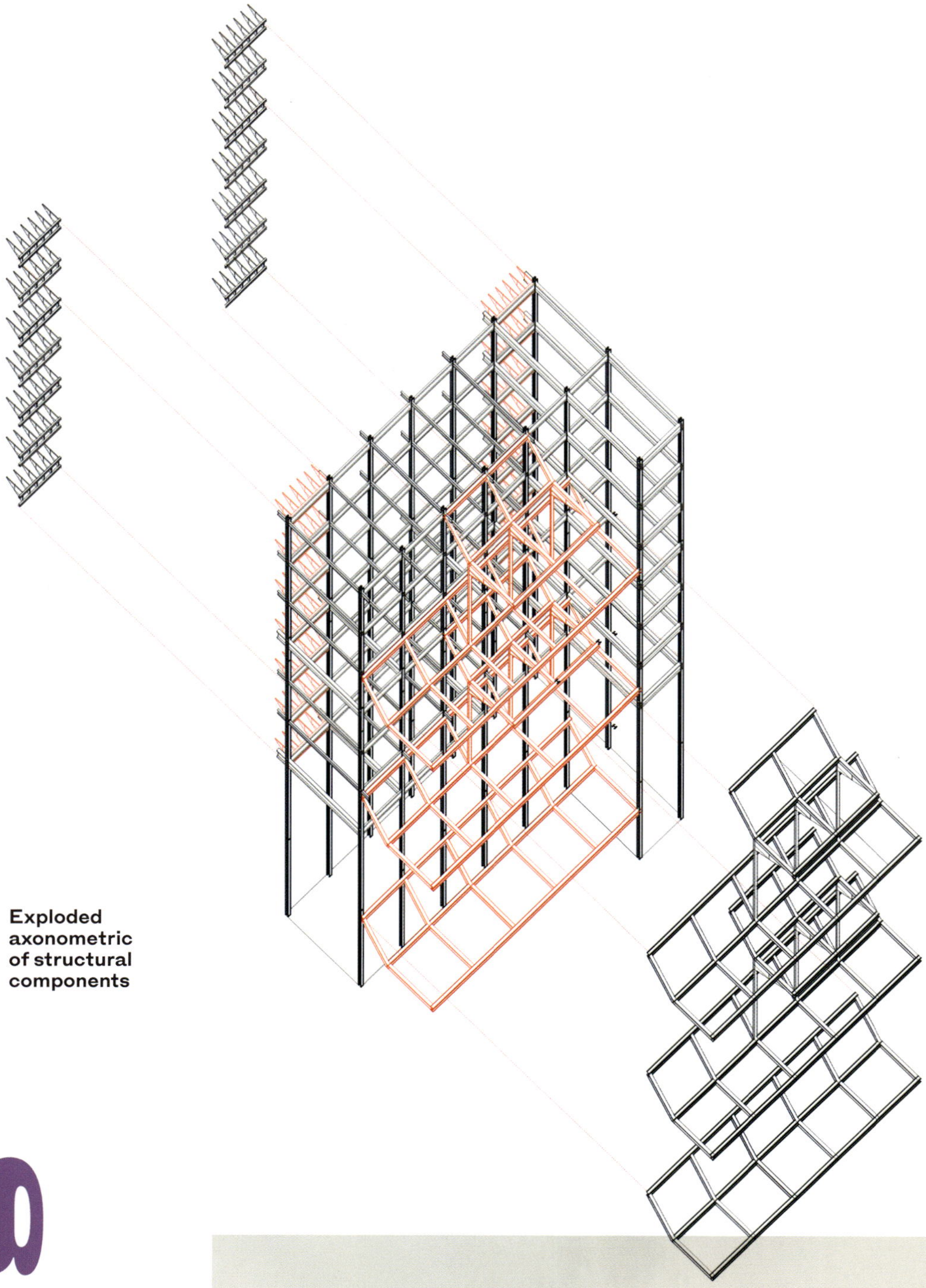

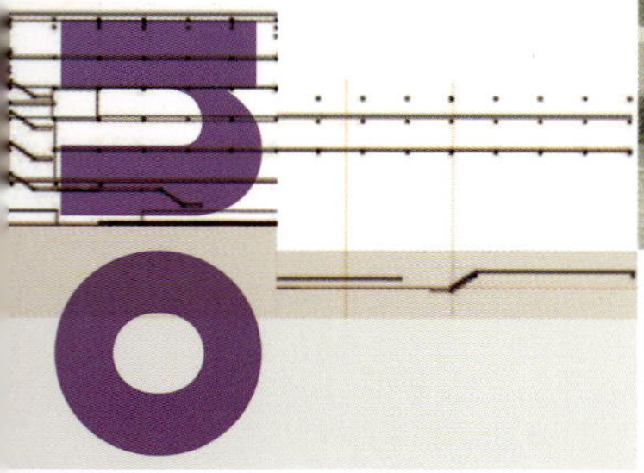

Exploded axonometric of structural components

Pavement

Housing

Masterplan: Consistent with Cherokee siting techniques, southeast sun exposure determines building location

Blue Ridge Livin': Environmental Development and Suburban Sprawl

Cherokee Indian construction evolved in specific topographic, geological, climatic, ecological, and socioeconomic contexts. These techniques and traditions provide alternative housing approaches that relate to the current natural context and the identity of the Blue Ridge Mountains.

Blue Ridge Livin': Env

Wood barn at the Oconaluftee Mountain Farm Museum, Cherokee, NC

Native Americans built with locally sourced, renewable materials and regional specificity in ways vastly different from contemporary construction. My thesis draws from this tradition and develops a process, workflow, and design methodology that respects both landscape and culture. I focus on precolonial Cherokee spatial practices, technologies, and locally sourced building materials specific to the Blue Ridge Mountains. Western colonists also influenced Cherokee architecture, as they integrated log cabin styles into their vernacular, while still holding onto traditional aspects of construction like site orientation and inhabitation rituals.[1] Today, this hybrid continues to provide a model for regional specificity that is both respectful to existing landscapes and resilient to climate.

1 See Brett H. Riggs and Thomas N. Belt, "Cherokee Housing in the North Carolina Mountains during the Removal Era," in *Native American Log Cabins in the Southeast* (Knoxville: University of Tennessee Press, 2019), 111–41

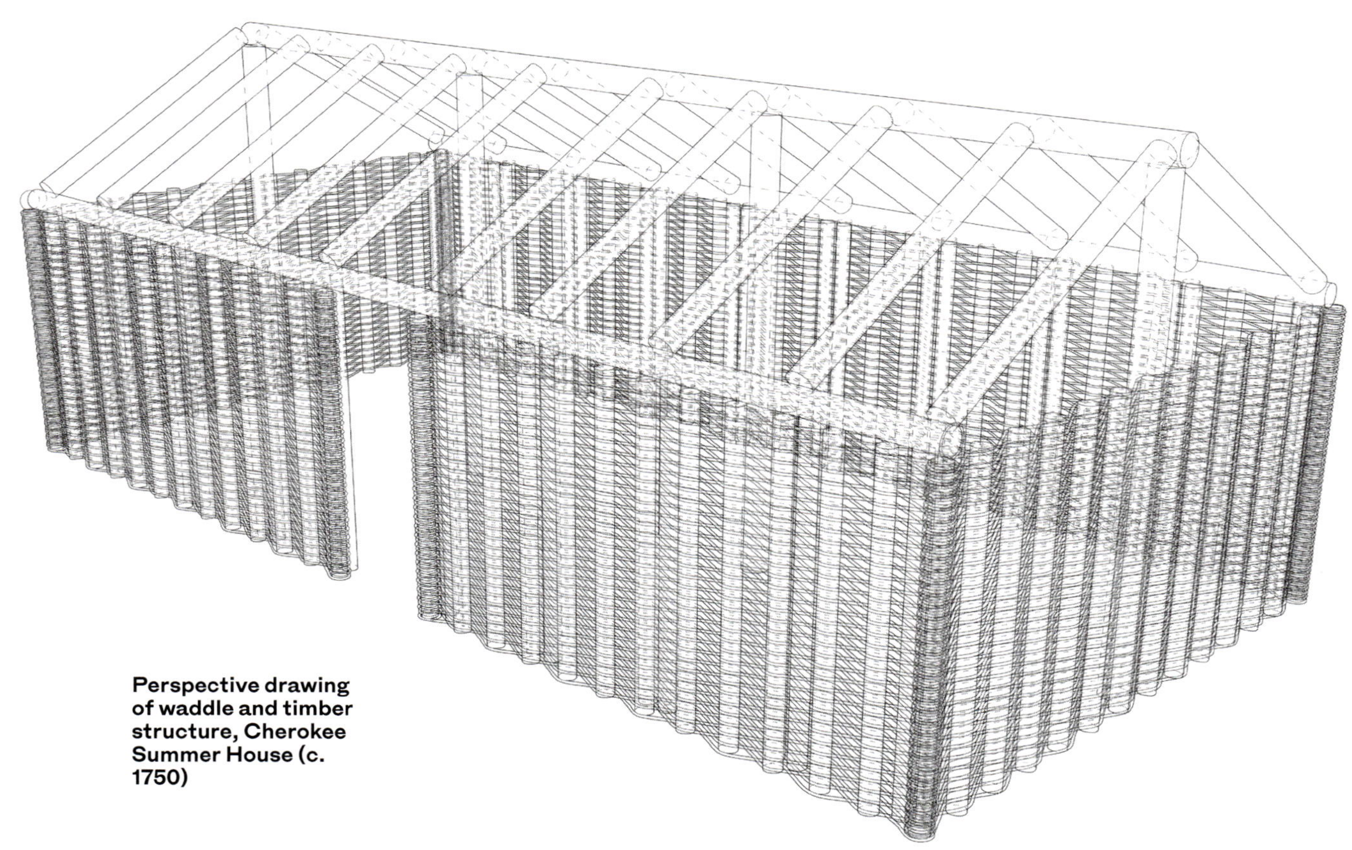

Perspective drawing of waddle and timber structure, Cherokee Summer House (c. 1750)

Model of Cherokee waddle building techniques; styrofoam, plasticine, basket round reed, willow, and birch stems

My site is located on the west side of HWY107, which runs north-south through the town of Cullowhee, North Carolina, home to Western Carolina University. The 100-acre site is isolated from the main campus, as busy highways, steep topography, and a lack of pedestrian crossings and sidewalks separate residents from the university. It is adjacent to apartments, student-occupied single-family homes, and a medical center to the west. Difference in elevation, from the bottom to the summit, reaches 400 feet. So, it was important to determine areas away from watersheds and terrain with a southeastern exposure—constraints faced by the Cherokee.[2] A more current capability includes the technology to build on locations of up to a 20% slope. The site is facing the threat of overdevelopment and suburban sprawl coming from nearby Asheville, an hour away. In response to the study of Cherokee

2 See Christopher Rodning, *Center Places and Cherokee Towns: Archaeological Perspectives on Native American Architecture and Landscape in the Southern Appalachians* (Tuscaloosa: University of Alabama Press, 2015).

design ethos, I developed a new housing prototype for the region, as well as a central civic center that serves the needs of an active community. Working sectionally emphasized a dialogue between construction and landscape, topography, soil condition, and the vegetative context. In plan, construction negotiates long-established proportions, traditions, rituals, and inhabitation. Interior spaces shift from public to private and back again, ending in bedrooms with views out to the surrounding landscape. As with Cherokee construction, the house uses locally sourced materials, including hickory, pine, and locust.[3] Additionally, the longer lasting foundations and retaining walls, integrate newer Cherokee craft

3 See Benjamin A. Steere, *The Archaeology of Houses and Households in the Native Southeast* (Tuscaloosa: University of Alabama Press, 2017).

Interior view of wood barn, Oconaluftee Mountain Farm Museum, Cherokee, NC

Isometric parti drawing, Cherokee Summer House

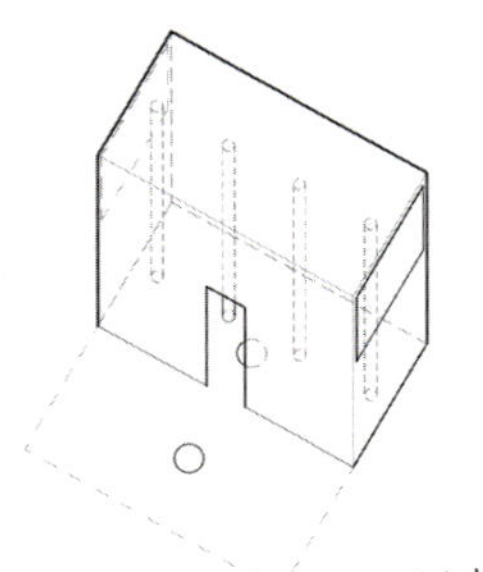

Summer House Elements

- Open Air Overhead Open to East/West Indirect Light
- Multiple Hearths Inside and Outside
- Four Central Posts in a Line (Black Locust)
- Outdoor Workspace

Isometric parti drawing, Cherokee Winter (Hot) House

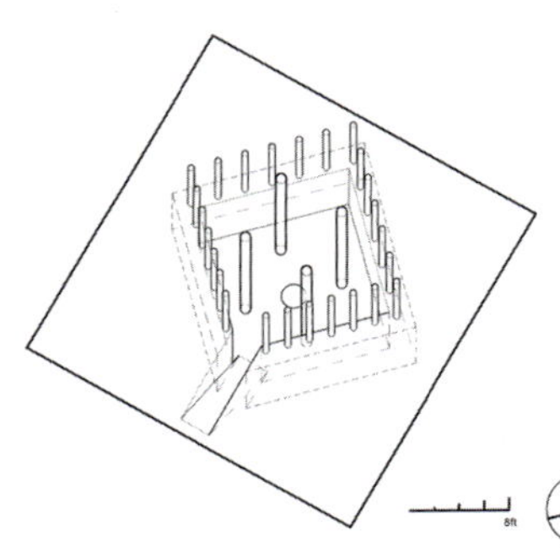

Winter (Hot) House Elements

- Dark, Cavelike, Submerged Experience
- Continuously-Burning Central Hearth
- Earthen Floor
- Four Central Posts in a Square, supporting Roof (Black Locust)
- Seven Perimeter Posts on Each Side

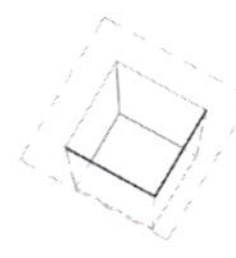

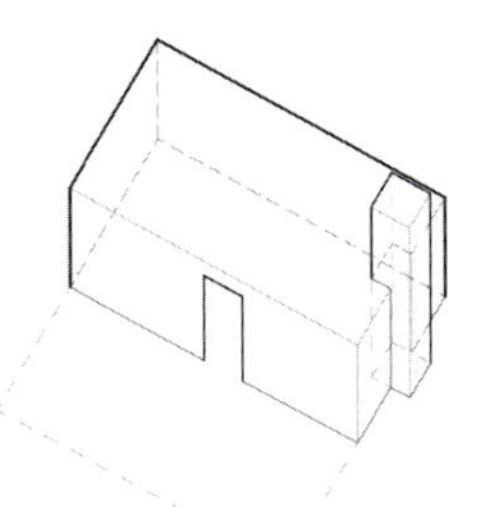

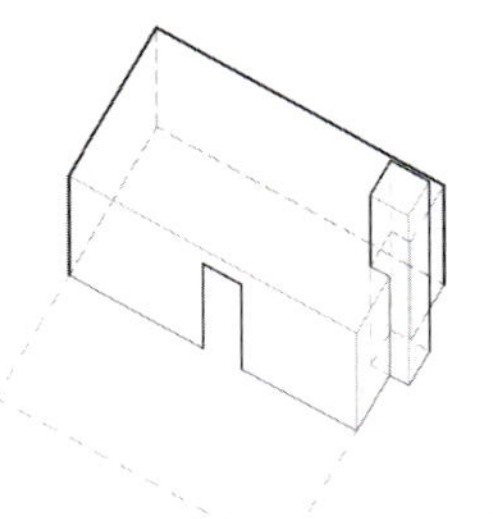

Isometric parti drawing, Cherokee Log House

Cherokee Log House

- No Windows for Natural Light; the Doorway Allows Light in
- Attached/Detached Potato Cellar for Ritual Space with Earthen Floor to the Southwest
- Outdoor Workspace
- Fireplace at End Wall (Northwest or Northeast Wall)

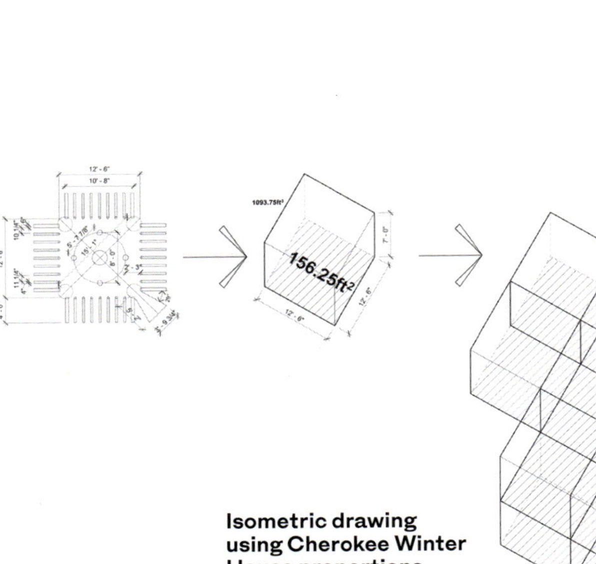

Isometric drawing using Cherokee Winter House proportions as massing blocks for housing prototype

traditions in stone masonry.[4] The textures of rammed concrete exterior walls are a nod to old wattle-and-daub surfaces. Throughout the prototype, windows open to indirect northeast and southwest sunlight to illuminate the open spaces connected to the Summer House.

Blending Cherokee construction traditions with contemporary building practices promotes a reciprocal relationship between construction and regionality, where people, place, and landscape thrive. My intent is to eliminate sprawl with better-designed houses that alleviate rising costs of living, and also to serve local housing markets with new community spaces that can welcome and inspire evolving regional values.

Perspective rendering, top of entry stair near the kitchen

4 **Benjamin A. Steere, interview by Christopher Pak Villalta, Cullowhee, NC, January 17, 2020**

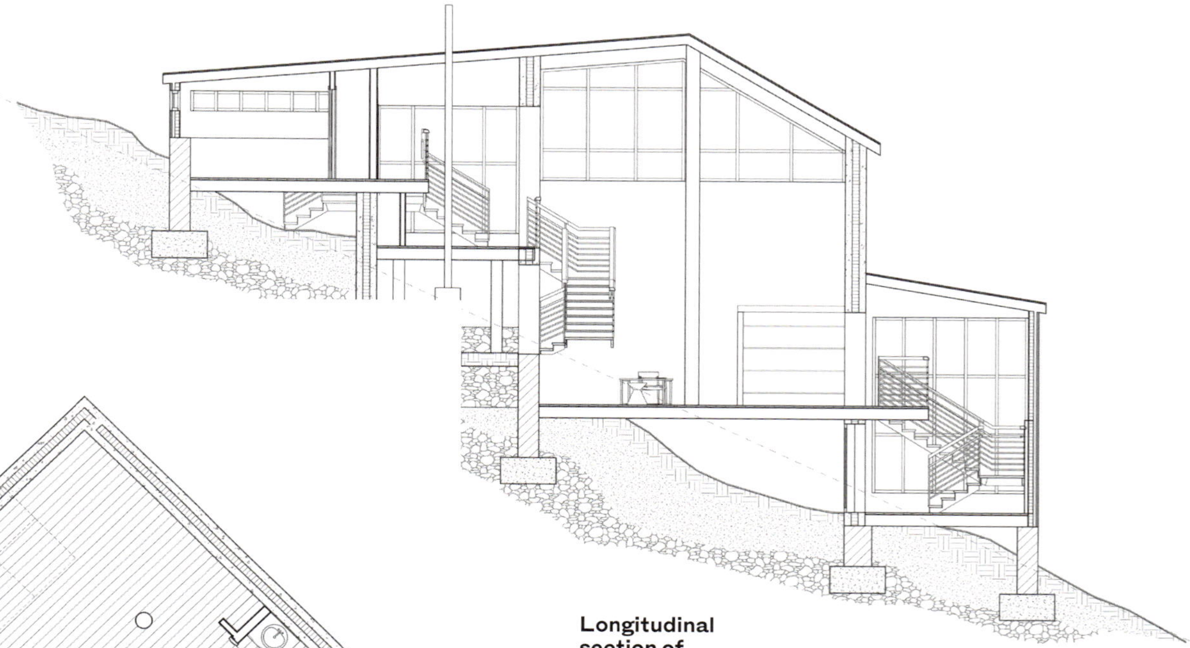

Longitudinal section of housing prototype

Plan drawing of main (second) floor

Revisionist Histories
Introduction

Primary Advisor **Amy Catania Kulper, Associate Professor, Head, Department of Architecture, RISD**
Secondary Advisor **Carl Lostritto, Associate Professor, Graduate Program Director, Department of Architecture, RISD**

Students **Hugo Caldwell (M.Arch), Sophie Weston Chien (B.Arch), Nathalie d'Hennezel (M.Arch), Benjamin Han (B.Arch), Julie Kress (M.Arch), Zachary Schumacher (M.Arch), Aaron Teves (B.Arch), Eamon Wagner (M.Arch)**

Revisionist history is no longer just an academic concept, it is a milieu, a culture, a contemporary way of life. It is materialized in Tweets, Photoshopped images, fake news, commissioned and decommissioned monuments, hearsay, reproductions, decoys, duplicates, facsimiles, forgeries, clones, reflections, and simulations of every kind. Although the proliferation of revisionist histories in this moment often makes it difficult to distinguish the real from the fake, its presence functions like a cultural and disciplinary litmus test, indicating a long overdue need to revisit singular canonical narratives and pervasive disciplinary monocultures. As a conceit for work on the architectural thesis, revisionist histories demand both the disciplinary and cultural positioning of the students' work. They require an explicit acknowledgment of whose shoulders they are standing on and whose work their theses are in dialogue with. It also anticipates the inclusion of disparate points of view, practices, and voices that form alternative narratives about, and approaches to, the design of architecture.

The students in this thesis cohort each have their own take on revisionism and architecture's possible imbrications with it. Hugo Caldwell's revisionism (see pp. 195–198) questions the top-down operations of planned communities, catalyzing a bottom-up strategic suburbanism that unleashes a kit of subversive parts, rethinking Columbia, Maryland. This planned community was the site of four early projects by Frank Gehry, so his work supplies the language of elements for these strategic interventions. Sophie Weston Chien's revisionism (see pp. 199–202) targets the practice of architecture, cultivating a new figure—the architect-organizer—whose practice taps local knowledge and fosters regional constituencies, addressing long-term spatial issues through engagement with enduring community partnerships. Her thesis asks: What can architectural design practice learn from the work of community organizers, and how will this transform the discipline's relationship to the communities it serves. Nathalie d'Hennezel's thesis (see pp. 203–206) explores that which literally flies under architecture's disciplinary radar—sound—and her revisionism resides in imagining acoustic signatures as the elementary building material for provocative spatial compositions. Though sound canceling and optimizing are architecture's typical *modus operandi*, this thesis challenges the primacy of the visual in architecture, asking whether sound can play a more generative role in design.

Benjamin Han's revisionism (see pp. 207–210) reimagines architecture's relationship to the machinic. Through the design of architectural machines with the capacity to both assemble and dismantle, his thesis alludes to global economies of extraction while contributing to speculative imaginaries of architectural futures. Julie Kress's revisionism (see pp. 211–214) positions animation and the skeuomorphic recovery of cinematographic techniques as a critical tool in the architect's arsenal, facilitating a conspicuous expansion of our discipline's representational capacities. This translation of cinematic techniques into digital animation sets the stage for the potential transformation of virtual affects into unique spatial inventions. Zachary Schumacher's revisionism (see pp. 215–218) considers the roles of the texture map in post-digital architectural design. Sampling from a broad array of surface registration techniques in other fields, this thesis repositions a technique originally associated with pictorial fakery, aligning it instead with the operations of realism and literalism. Aaron Teves's thesis (see pp. 219–222) provides an alternative narrative to the roles of craft and detail in the discipline of architecture, positioning the jig as the designed interface between existing building systems and future spatial innovations. In this project, the jig operates structurally across numerous registers—organizational, conceptual, material—anticipating and reinventing future craft practices. Eamon Wagner's thesis (see pp. 223–226) takes up, perhaps, the most unlikely vehicle for revisionism in his consideration of the generic object and its myriad sociocultural formats, examining their uncanny capacity to organize space and imbue it with atmosphere. Poised between the ubiquity of such objects, captured through reductive line drawings, and their potential misuse through unintended cultural practices, this thesis explores how the aggregation and accumulation of objects transforms potential readings of space.

When it was determined in March 2020 that RISD would continue our spring semester remotely, it was fascinating to observe how the revisionist histories framework empowered the students in the cohort to pivot and reconsider their projects through the lens of the remote economies through which they would now be operating. Within the context of revisionism, the students had cultivated well-calibrated radars, attentive to emerging disciplinary and cultural issues that needed addressing. In the case of each thesis in the cohort, the pivoting was subtle but significant. For Hugo, this pivot consisted in returning to the site of his thesis, Columbia, Maryland, and it resulted in a rediscovery of the playful tone of his early work through experiments in digital representation. For Sophie, our cohort's compulsory remoteness made the need for architect-organizers more concrete, more immediate, and more real, validating the premise of her re-design of our disciplinary practice. Nathalie's sudden return to Dallas narrowed the scope of her ruminations on acoustic signatures to a single typology—the apartment—transforming her into the living subject of her own research. In Ben's case, the pandemic amplified the urgency of the global crisis his thesis was tackling, making visible the insufficiency of the tools we have as architects to the scale of problems our discipline is called upon to address.

Over the course of final reviews, it became apparent to the assembled critics that digital animations were one of the most effective tools in architecture's disciplinary arsenal for communicating remotely. Digital animation was the focus and area of inquiry for Julie's thesis, and one of the discoveries occasioned by remoteness in her work is that beyond communicating, this medium can also radically transform the architectural imaginary. An integral dimension of Zach's thesis construction was the premise of outsourcing architectural labor, like the hydro-dipping of his models, so under conditions of social distancing, he tapped into the fictional dimension of revisionism, "faking" the subsequent outsourcing to maintain the integrity of the visibility of labor underwriting architectural practice.

For Aaron, remoteness offered the opportunity to avoid the stereotypical aesthetics associated with the topic of architectural craft; instead, after going remote, his thesis operated digitally and systemically in the work, critically emulating the operations of a jig. And finally, the currency of Eamon's thesis on the organizational capacity of generic objects to confer spatial legibility became images, rather than objects, which was an interesting byproduct of remoteness, allowing the work to dwell in the territory of spatial commodification through images like real estate, Craigslist, and Airbnb.

One final note about this incredible cohort of students points to their compassion and resilience beyond their collective agility as designers. In the early days of quarantine, when the headlines featured bad actors hoarding masks and hand sanitizer, and grocery stores with empty shelves, their initial impulse was to support and care for each other in isolation. Perhaps this speaks to the virtue of studio culture and to the ethos of mutual respect they had cultivated over the course of the year, but as proud as I am of the resilience they demonstrated in their work, it is their humanity and empathy that will make them great architects.

Hugo Caldwell (M.Arch)

Change of Plans: The Subversive Kit in the Planned Community By extracting latent possibilities in existing environments, a subversive kit of parts is implemented to challenge the prescriptive forces of urban planning in Columbia, Maryland.

Change of Plans: The

Frank Gehry at his office, 1972

Suburban homes

In the late 1960s, James Rouse developed a planned community in Columbia, Maryland, a town set midway between Baltimore and Washington, DC. After years of developing shopping malls, Rouse shifted his ethos toward designing for human value. Columbia served as an experiment in eliminating the segregated suburb, raising standards of living for a population diverse in race, religion, and class. Rouse's design, however, had a flaw: he designed not with diversity but with sameness in mind, homogenizing the buildings and streets into repeated forms and instilling unremittingly programmed spaces. I grew up in Columbia, and can now observe how Rouse's propensity for top-down urban planning alienated his ideals. Succumbing to modernist values

James Rouse, Columbia New Town plan, 1960s

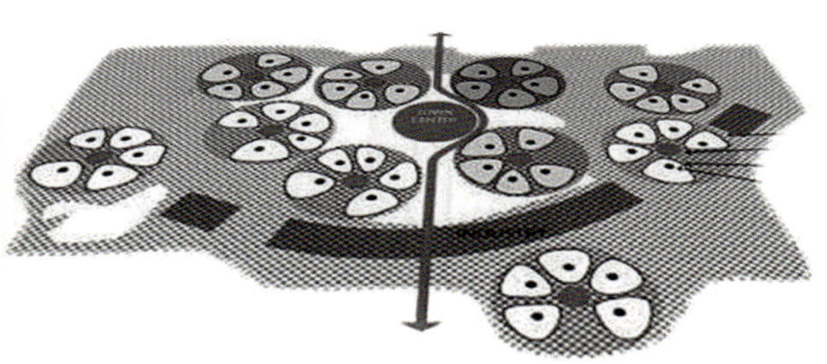

of prescriptive usage, planned communities like Columbia collapse scalar shifts into a singular, isolated environment. My project seeks instead to scale architecture down to an individual, intimate level, to the scale of urban planning.

Some of Columbia's buildings were designed by Frank Gehry—a fire station, exhibition hall, concert venue, and development company headquarters—and provide a fertile starting point for extraction. Using their existing conditions, I formulated a subversive kit of parts, working with each building's unique typology to apply a bottom-up design approach based in extracted symbolic objects. For example, while maintaining its utilitarian purposes, the fire station supplies domestic services, like a pizza oven or a fountain. The exhibition center exposes the disparity between exhibit and exhibition, and the objects it renders highlight these incongruities through picture windows and VR headsets. Merriweather, the concert venue, provides a major gathering space for the community, its commodifiable objects staying true to its aesthetic and iconicism. The headquarters acts as a gateway into Columbia, a role I emphasize with symbolic objects such as mailboxes and fences.

While derived from four buildings, the kit is not bound to them, as the parts also embed into the domestic landscape. These elements are multi-scalar and through everyday use develop the user's command over the kit. Houses engage the street and interiors become blended colorful collages. My kit of parts is a revisionist history of a top-down design ethos, providing subversive tools for citizen and visitor engagement.

Banneker
fire station

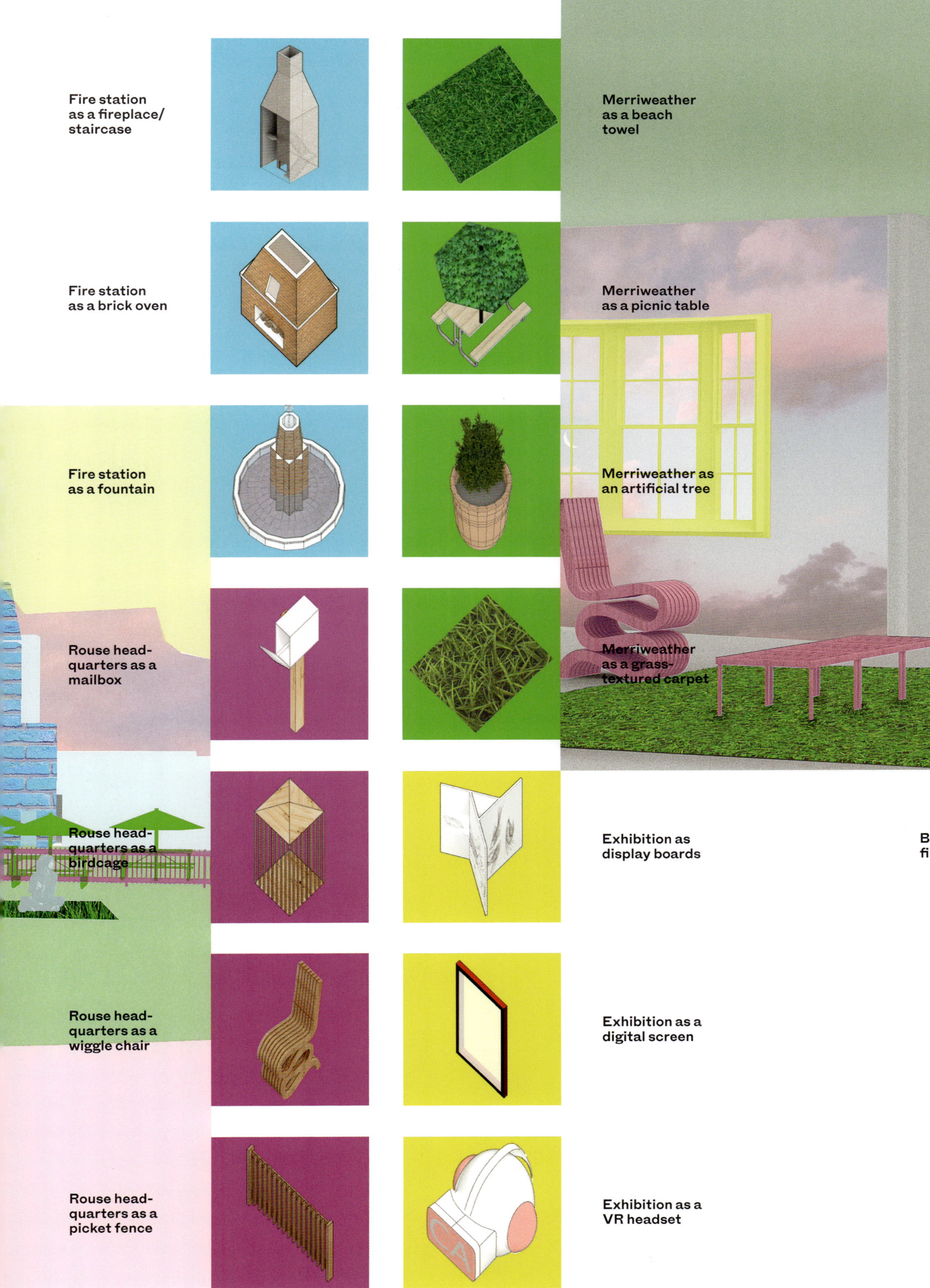

Banneker fire station

Merriweather Post

Former Rouse headquarters

Exhibition center

Sophie Weston Chien (B.Arch)

Practice: A Designer-Organizer Framework for Community Power

Recasting structures, envisioning futures, and fortifying community agency form the heart of both a single project and a holistic, emerging practice.

Ice fisherwoman, aerial view illustration

My thesis work creates structures that enable communities to be agents of their own change. This work is grounded by my own experience in Nome, Alaska, where in 2016 I was a summer intern for the National Park Service in Bering Land Bridge National Park. In Alaska, I learned how people live remotely and precariously, and through them, understood the importance of being connected to our natural world.

This thesis is both a project and a practice. The project inhabits this work in a real place, envisioning community power in a remote city in Alaska. It speculates on a justice-oriented future for the island community of Kigiqtaq (formerly known by its colonized name, Shishmaref) as its residents mitigate encroaching sea-level rise—the island they live on is being eroded away. The city of Kigiqtaq is remote but urban, the population is indigenous and young, similar to many other communities in Alaska.

The project starts by redrawing the boundaries of the state to reflect local ecological systems. Alaska is divided into watershed states, which bound jurisdictions according to how water drains in a basin. Within the new

-Organizer Framewo

Bureau of Subsistence meeting (muskox and elders), aerial view illustration

Governing hierarchy, diagram

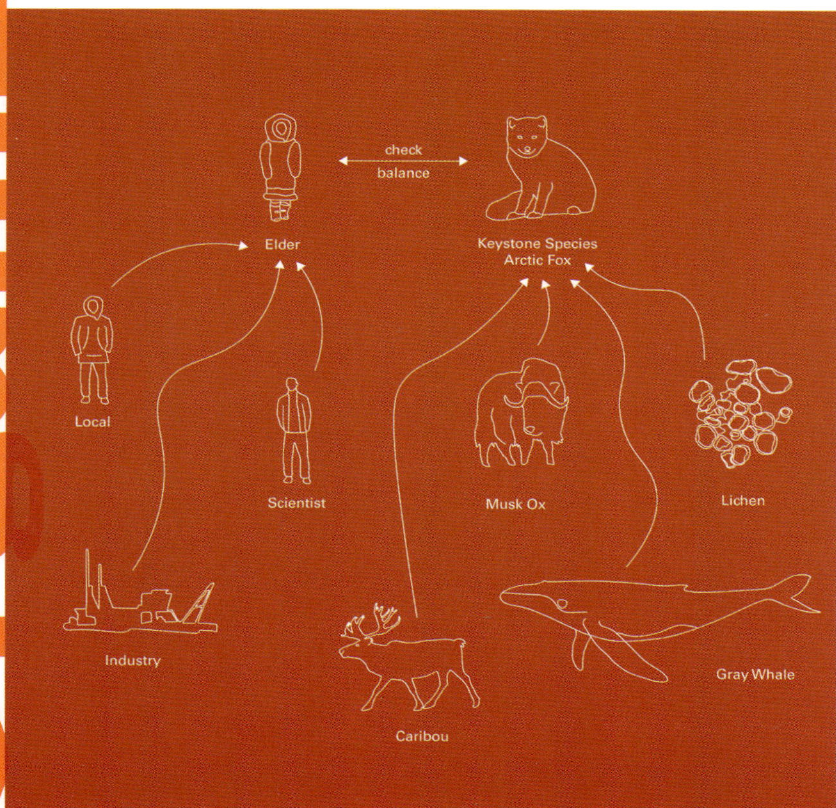

Salmon drying cycle, illustration

rk for Community Po

Caribou calving season, aerial view illustration

jurisdictions, private property is abolished and land trusts govern land use. This model shifts the power from a remote governing structure to a hyper-local one. Community power is also located in new agencies such as the Ways of Knowing Agency, which replaces the Department of Education and prioritizes indigenous knowledge taught by elders to younger generations.

The practice learns from the project and creates the framework for developing my role as a designer-organizer, a practitioner who focuses on redesigning relationships of place and power. It interrogates architectural conventions such as project timelines, scope, expertise, and the limits of the discipline, offering a template for future design engagement. The role of the designer-organizer is to amplify local perspectives and create spaces of care, attentive to the existing lifeways, and to critically examine not just what is created (project), but how (practice). Revisionism is at the core of this thesis work, which overturns conventions, clients, and buildings in favor of spaces inhabited by human and nonhuman beings, through social and physical structures, toward just futures.

Watershed states, map

Migrated Kigiqtaq, illustration

New bureaus, illustrations

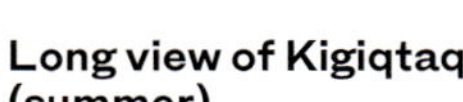

Long view of Kigiqtaq (summer)

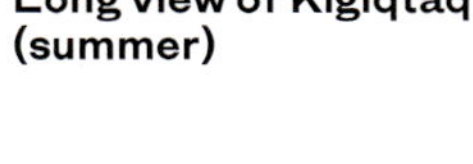

sophiewestonchien.com

Nathalie d’Hennezel (M.Arch)

Acoustic Signatures: The Agency of Sound in Designing Architectural Spaces

A visual language representing acoustic signatures informs a building’s program and elevates impromptu and adaptable auditory experiences.

An acoustic signature is the inherent relationship between a space’s size, form, and material composition, and one’s experience of sound within it. A common, recognizable manifestation of acoustic signatures occurs in cathedrals, which are highly reverberant and radiate echoes throughout the space. That echo enhances the spiritual quality of religious experiences and triggers the crescendo of the organ and resounding Gregorian chants.

Most architecture handles acoustics reductively and primarily in response to programmatic needs. Vague noise control measures are applied in simple ways, resulting in dull auditory experiences. Program-driven optimization of sound can work, but only in abstract, mathematically calculated scenarios. When spaces are used for anything other than their initial purpose—when a library becomes a music recital hall, for example—the room’s acoustics are unfit. Today’s acoustic design standards fail to address the impromptu and require significant resources to design and fabricate. Historically, acoustic signatures have remained the mere byproduct of common construction practices

Acoustic signatures, Dallas apartment, charcoal on vellum

Sounds of/ with/in architecture, charcoal on vellum

Step echo,
charcoal on vellum

and programmatic requirements. For example, tile, mirrors, porcelain tubs, and glass shower doors are elements commonly found in bathrooms, and consequently, bathrooms reverberate. Innately, acoustic signatures inform our interactions with architectural spaces.

Sound's engagement with architectural design relies on a representational translation of its invisibility. Since the physical environment defines acoustic signatures and we experience them as a phenomenon, I designed a language that offers an experience-based depiction of sound. I represent the fading of sound in space through time by gradients and with charcoal overlaid onto plans, sections, and perspective drawings. I used this language to study the acoustic signatures of my apartment in Dallas, Texas. Then, I altered those signatures to inform different ways in which similar spaces can be used and experienced. Sound replaces program as the material and formal driver of design, engaging with a variety of rooms designed for reflection, blending, containing, and moving.

My thesis designed specific acoustic signatures to engage with the myriad of unplanned and imperfect sounds that traditional acoustic practices overlook. It emends the disciplinary norms of program, materiality, and construction practices, elevating audio-spatial experiences through careful acoustic composition.

Composition of acoustic signatures, charcoal on vellum

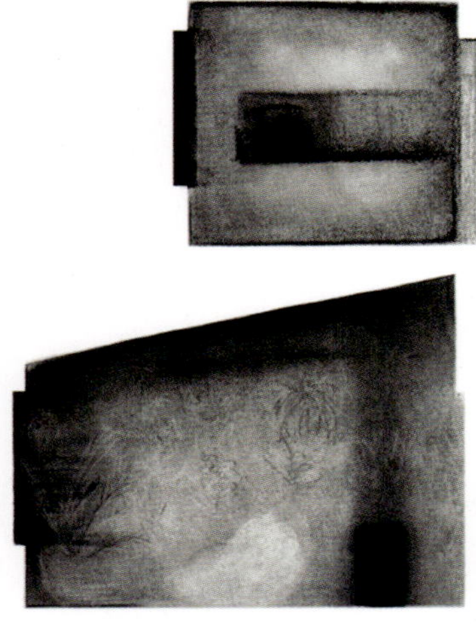

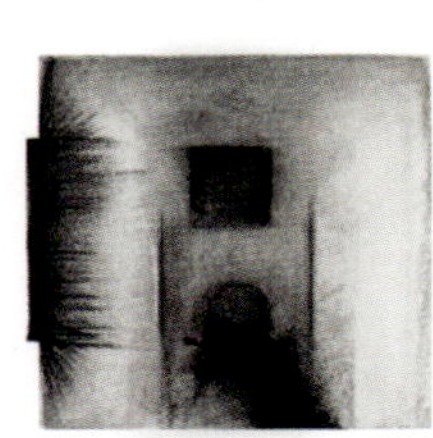

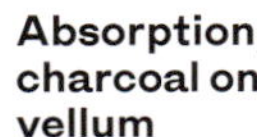

Absorption, charcoal on vellum

Clap: sound in

Step: sound with

tectural Spaces

Benjamin Han (B.Arch)

Inside the Machine of Re-excavation, radiograph elevation

We—humans and our machine constituents—irreversibly disturb our environment. We enlist systems and pipelines to disentangle landscapes, alienating resources. We enable natural mechanisms of destruction such as weather and fires to proliferate, manufacturing the end of the environment that we fundamentally rely on.

Responding to the climate crisis and our abuse and denial, my thesis projects into a future to examine our contradictory acts and highlight opportunities for collaborative resurgence ahead. It is sited in Vancouver, Canada, which is touted by ecocapitalists as a prime example of green planning and development. By 2080, with sea level having risen by five feet, Vancouver will be one of the last coastal cities in North America to flood.

Dismantling Usefulness

Dismantling Usefulness: Degrowth, Collaborative Resurgence, and Life after Manufactured Productivity Speculative fiction reveals two current truths: we are perpetually caught in irreversible disturbances of our environment, and we urgently need to imagine a set of productive frictions for a future of collaborative resurgence.

New ecologies formed from urban fires, flooding, and soil displacement

City ravaged by fire from infrastructure breakdown

Nonetheless, many affluent residents here are ready to flee when the inevitable disaster strikes.

Writing a speculative narrative, I invented two characters sprung from my research interests. Mycelium, the fungi network we associate with mold, decay, and decomposition, is a mediator between life, death, and regeneration, a producer of collaborations between life and the environment. Mycelium offers the conceptual grounding for my thesis, while Machine is its foil. Machine is both ally and enemy of human civilizations, an accomplice of modernity and modernization, a construct associated with productivity, efficiency, and simplified ecologies. Machine dismantles its permanence on the environment.

In the narrative, a small community is left to fend for itself in a Vancouver ravaged by climate disaster. As the affluent residents flee, the remaining citizens devote their lives to collective survival. They enlist machines and their modern knowledge to reconcile with the landscape. When machines are liberated from capital, they can and will generate unexpected human worlds, new assemblages of decentered technology and environment, a future of capital degrowth and coexistence.

My thesis refrains from a romanticized return to technology and destruction-free pasts. It is willfully optimistic. Through representational techniques and a projective narrative, I counter the prototypical Master

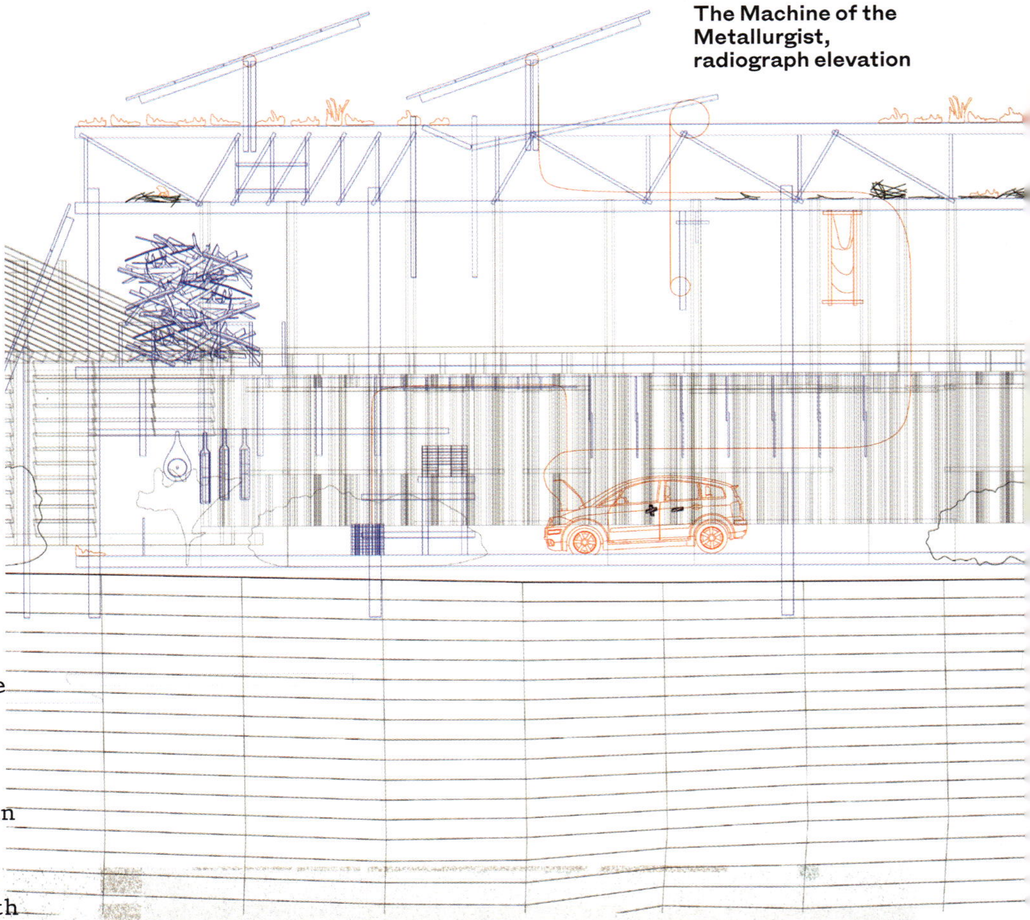

The Machine of the Metallurgist, radiograph elevation

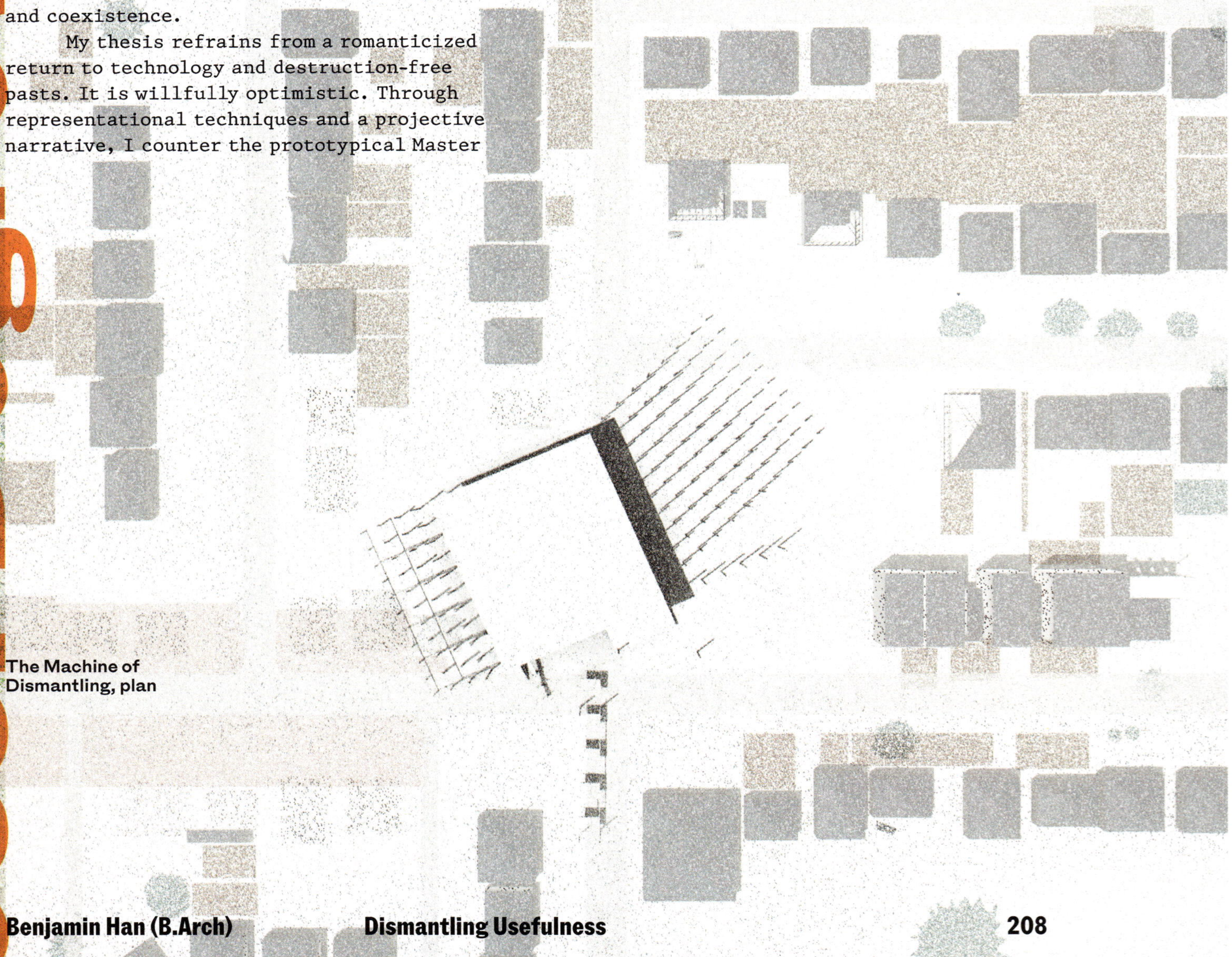

The Machine of Dismantling, plan

borative Resurgence

Mycelium, mediator between life, death, and regeneration

New condos being erected in Banff, Canada, 2080

The Machine of Re-excavation, digitally scattered pixel-screenprint plan

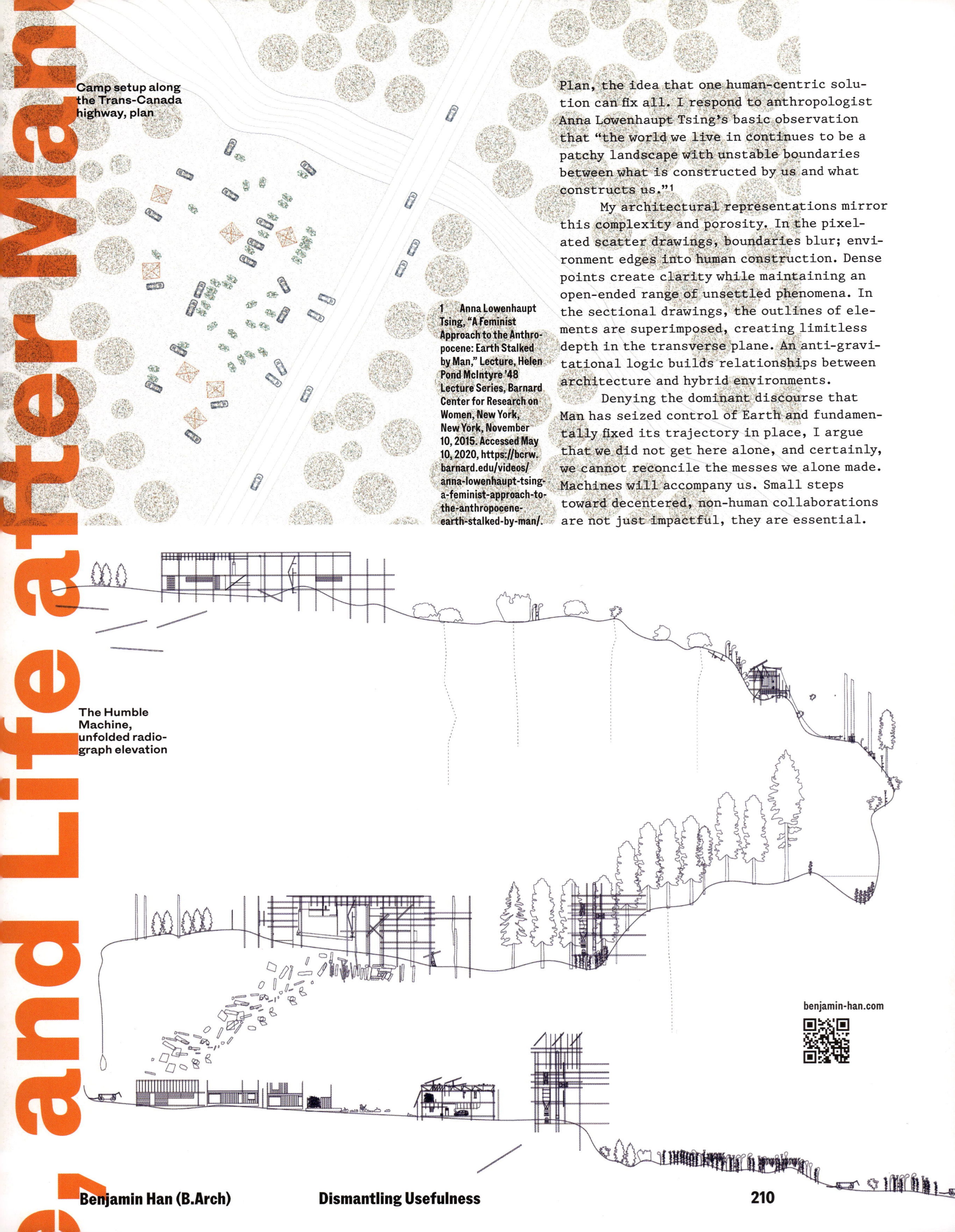

Camp setup along the Trans-Canada highway, plan

Plan, the idea that one human-centric solution can fix all. I respond to anthropologist Anna Lowenhaupt Tsing's basic observation that "the world we live in continues to be a patchy landscape with unstable boundaries between what is constructed by us and what constructs us."[1]

My architectural representations mirror this complexity and porosity. In the pixelated scatter drawings, boundaries blur; environment edges into human construction. Dense points create clarity while maintaining an open-ended range of unsettled phenomena. In the sectional drawings, the outlines of elements are superimposed, creating limitless depth in the transverse plane. An anti-gravitational logic builds relationships between architecture and hybrid environments.

Denying the dominant discourse that Man has seized control of Earth and fundamentally fixed its trajectory in place, I argue that we did not get here alone, and certainly, we cannot reconcile the messes we alone made. Machines will accompany us. Small steps toward decentered, non-human collaborations are not just impactful, they are essential.

1 Anna Lowenhaupt Tsing, "A Feminist Approach to the Anthropocene: Earth Stalked by Man," Lecture, Helen Pond McIntyre '48 Lecture Series, Barnard Center for Research on Women, New York, New York, November 10, 2015. Accessed May 10, 2020, https://bcrw.barnard.edu/videos/anna-lowenhaupt-tsing-a-feminist-approach-to-the-anthropocene-earth-stalked-by-man/.

The Humble Machine, unfolded radiograph elevation

benjamin-han.com

Julie Kress (M.Arch)

Framed Familiarity in Four Acts Skeuomorphic strategies engage with animation, realism, and cinematographic techniques to provide alternative conceptual frameworks for making architectural imagery.

Various architects, from Greg Lynn to Mark Rakatansky, have promoted animation as a generative, playful tool. Rakatansky, in fact, proposed a speculative architecture that would only be possible when animated. *Framed Familiarity* likewise delights in the visual ambiguities that are only possible through animation, that cannot exist as a single frame or image materialized through a static form. Taking inspiration from skeuomorphs—a digital replication of a physical object, like digital Post-it notes or recycling bins—I investigate historical and analog prototypes as operative metaphors to expand on sampled 3D models.

Act 1: Paper Promenade

Act 1: Paper promenade through an architecture of frames

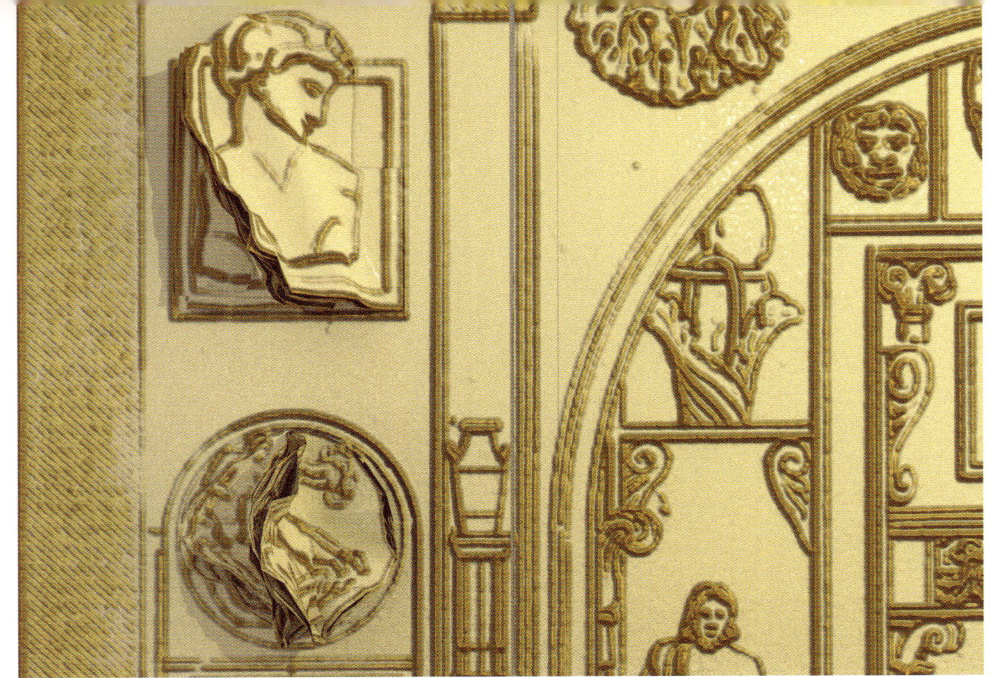

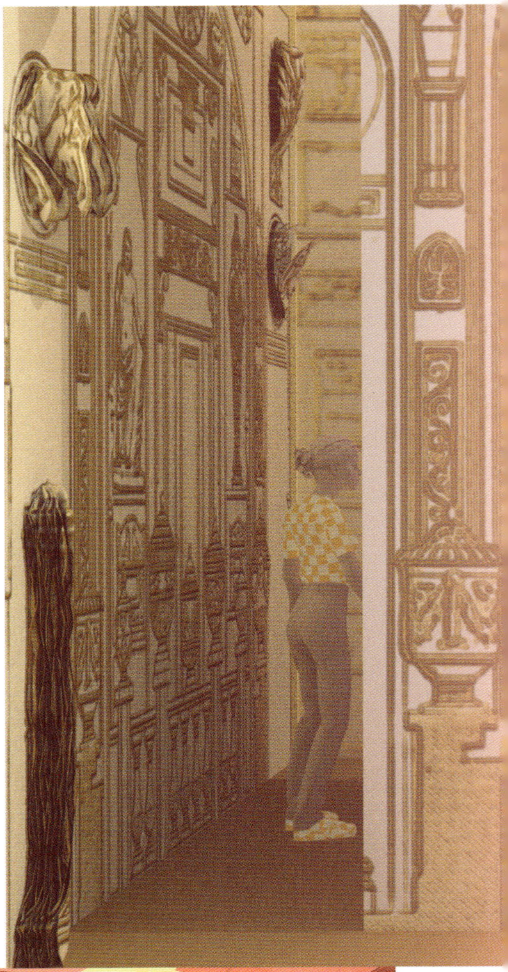

Act 3: Delamination, a skeuomorphic page turn

Act 2: Ribboned frame lines in the breakfast room

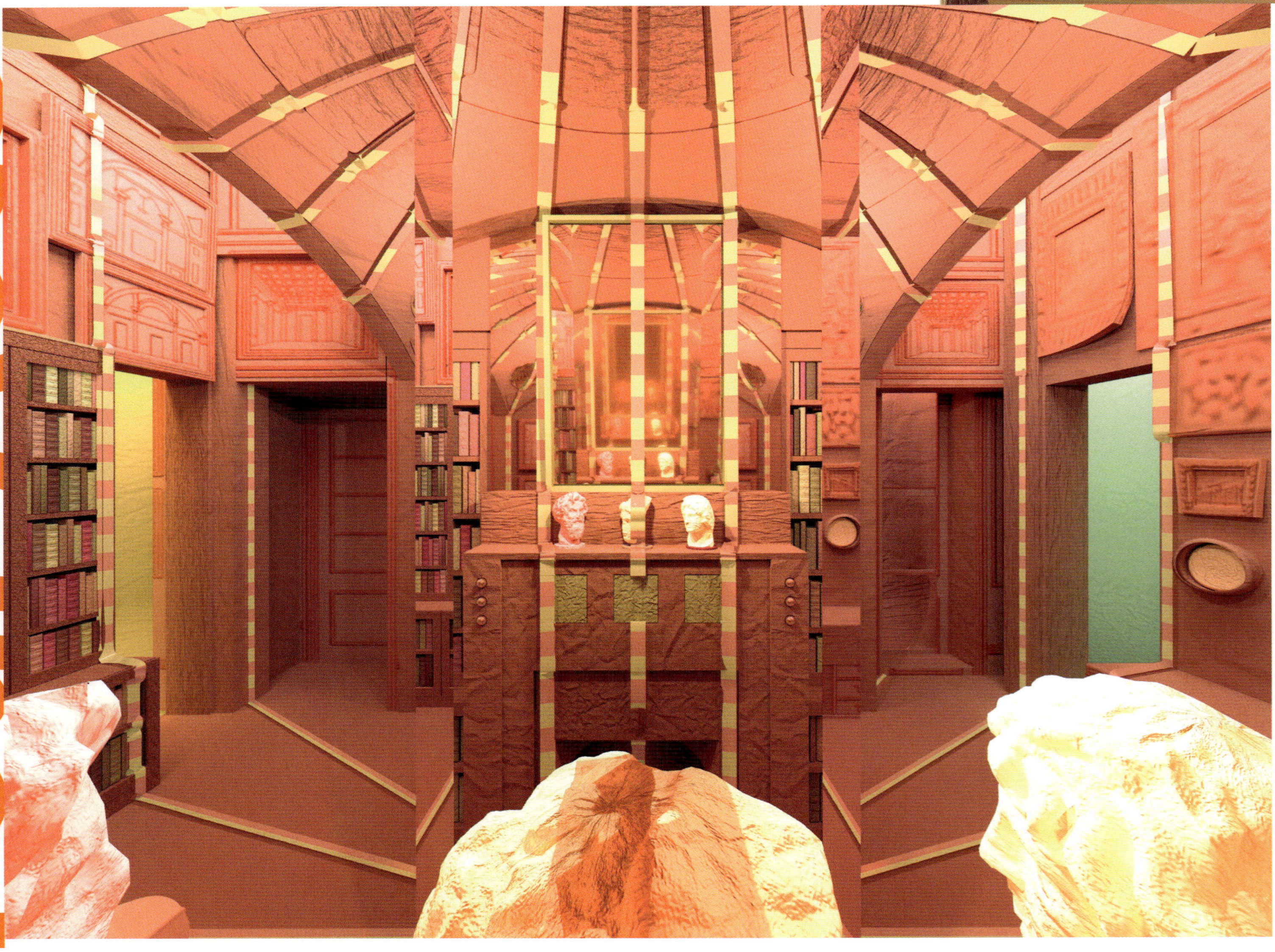

Four Acts

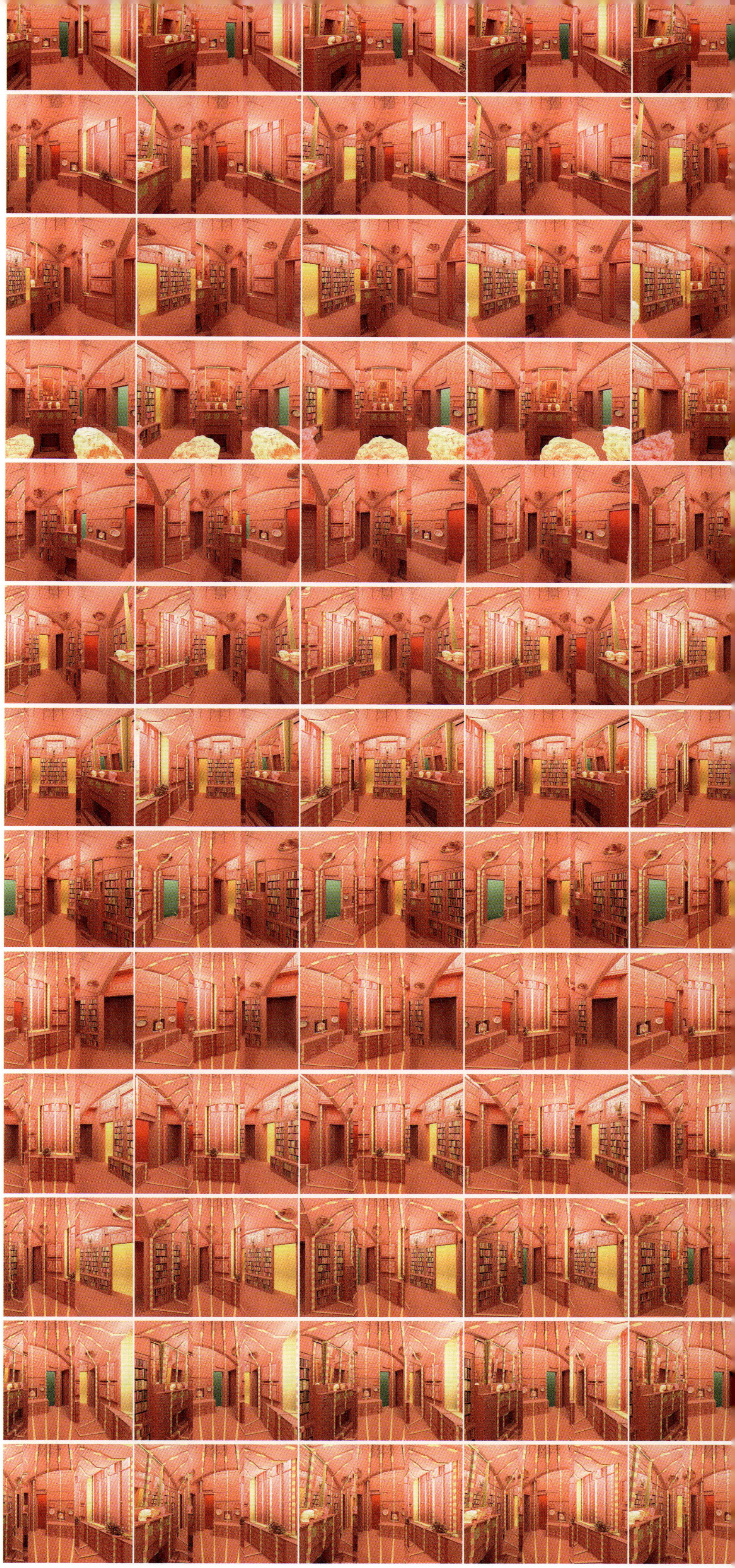

Act 3: A story within a story

Act 2: Zoetroped breakfast room in motion

My thesis amalgamates four animated acts through a color palette drawn from Wes Anderson's *Moonrise Kingdom* to create an anachronistic whole. Referencing Shigeru Ban's Paper House as a skeuomorphic approach to a papered curtain wall, Act 1 acclimates the viewer to the skeuomorphic concept of digital paper. The paper-thin surfaces replicate the John Soane Museum—the London house of the neoclassical architect—highlighting an architecture of frames made even more visible by collapsing one room against another. The user-controlled zoetrope of Act 2 acquires the optical behaviors of the prefilmic device to engage with the frame rate of my design. Act 3, enrolling Megan (a standard character from the Mixamo Asset library), draws inspiration

Act 2: Zoetroped Breakfast Room

Act 3: The Rigged Sepulchral Chamber

Act 4: Framed jump-cutting

from puppeteering and rotoscoping by rigging behaviors into objects and surfaces in ways as dynamic as modeling people. Act 4 considers the spatial displacements and coherences made possible by jump-cutting and dolly shots.

Integrating everything from architectural illustrations of the John Soane Museum to open-source motion-captured body movements to digitally scanned objects from museum archives, I create a cross section through history, time, and place. Through this hybrid treatment of analog and digital realities my thesis suggests how a skeuomorphic understanding of animation can recover techniques of the past and build a vocabulary for the future.

Act 4: Paperfied Dollyshot

Framed Familiarity in Four Acts: The full compilation of animations

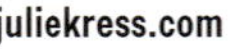

juliekress.com

Zachary Schumacher (M.Arch)

Digital Duck An experiment with hydro-dipped texture-mapping, a technique common to contemporary car design, makes the rendering of an 1850s house model literal.

Digital Duck

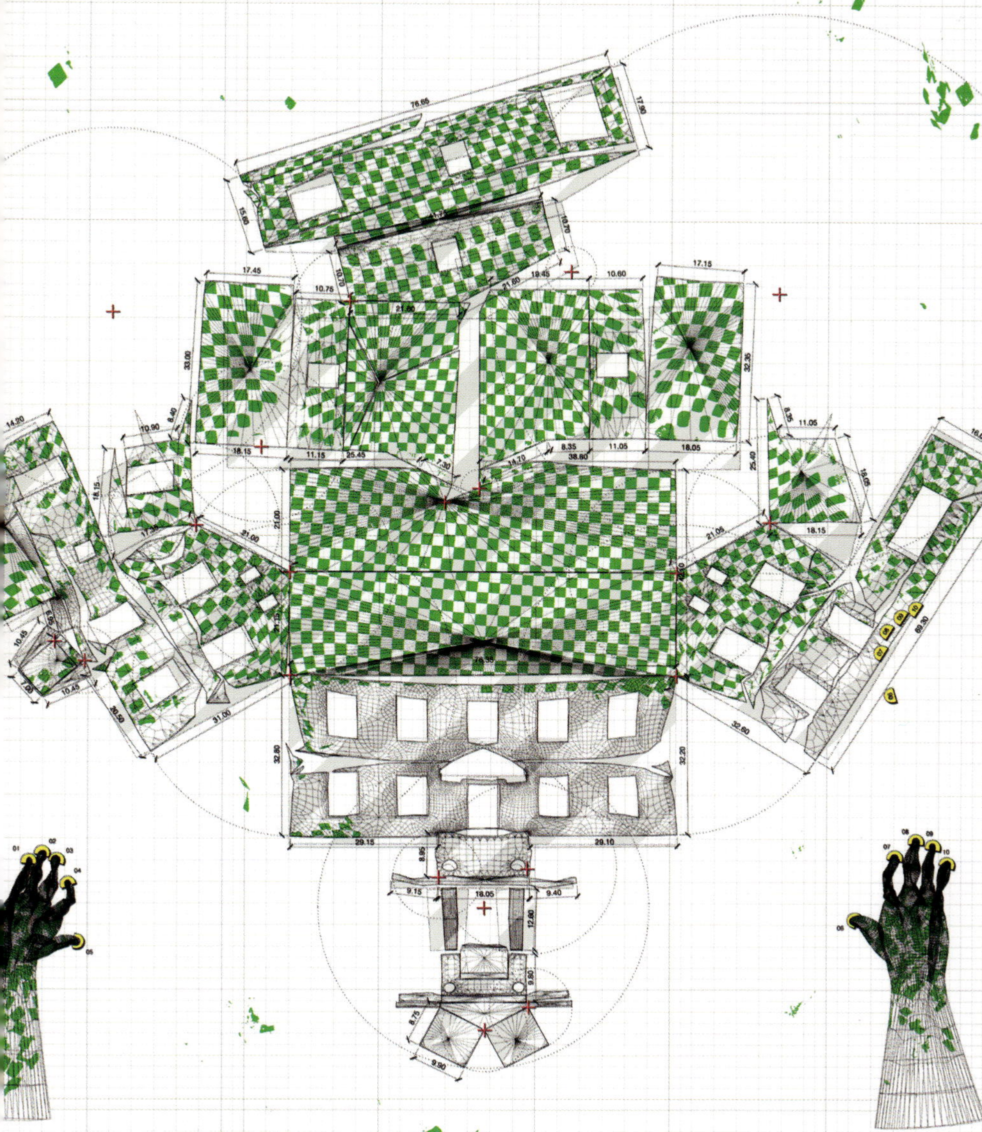

Unrolled, developed surface drawing of the deflated hydro-dipped house, loose floaters within the bath, and hydro-dipper's hands

Off of U.S. 44 there is an automotive repair shop with a large bath in a back room, above which hang a series of gun accessories and car parts tattooed with a variety of images: multicolored camouflage, wooden textures, Playboy Bunnies, and perhaps the possibilities and potentials surrounding the architectural surface. A nearby worker and his green-and-white-checkered sandwich paper sit near the hydro-dipper, a colloquialism that architects would ignore. Instead of dismissing them, I commissioned these characters to submerge a 3D-printed version of my 1850s family home into green-checkered water. His hands emerged tattooed with the same pattern. My thesis forces these characters to confront the gap between the computationally described object and the digitally constructed surface, between material composition, application, and fabrication method; they literalized texture mapping.

My thesis project, *Digital Duck*, recalls several precedents. The most current use of texture mapping applied to cars is camouflage, which is used to prevent spies or spy cameras from stealing new designs before their official

zachschumacher.com/Digital-Duck.

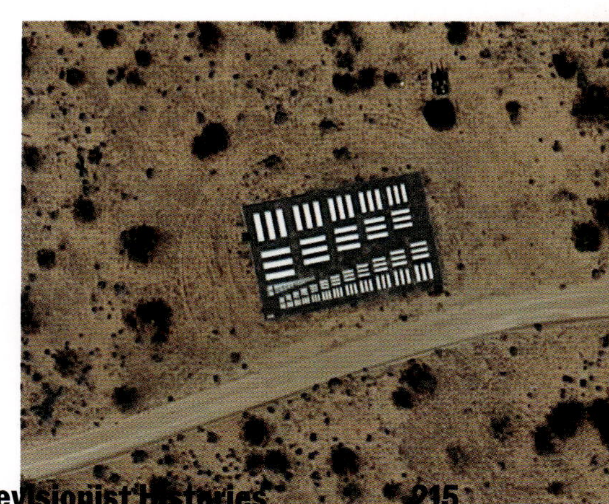

Resolution target used for aerial photographs and videos during the 1950s by the U.S. Air Force in California

December 2019

16 Google images of my family's now fifth
generation house built sometime around 1850.

This is a photogrammetric massing of the house's
16 available Google images

The results are endless and varied.

When 3D printed the object appears topographical

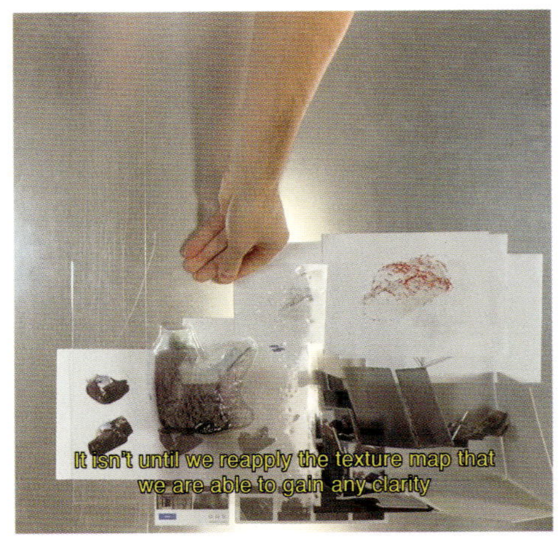
It isn't until we reapply the texture map that
we are able to gain any clarity

An architectural skin no longer dependent on
an interior.

Photogrammetric scanning by projection prefers
multicolored matte surfaces.

Inflated or deflated to better hold a projected
image

Entangled with the digital, the architectural skin
has become a space of constant flux.

Similar to the sandwich paper...

Literalism, Realism, Surface, and Hypertext

Hypertext video demonstrating the objects association with one another

release. The checkered wrapper mimics the patterns of photogrammetric resolution targets applied to the earth's surface by the U.S. Air Force in the 1950s, a motif revisited by German artist Hito Steyerl in her 2013 video *How Not to Be Seen: A Fucking Didactic Educational .MOV File*. In 2004, the Roman statue *Augustus of Primaporta* was rebuilt in polychrome using ultraviolet scans, which successfully repainted the original color. The "duck" in *Digital Duck* references Denise Scott Brown, Robert Venturi, and Steven Izenour's seminal book *Learning from Las Vegas*, which defines a "duck" building as one "where the architectural systems of space, structure, and program are submerged and distorted by an overall symbolic form."[1]

The exaggerated form of my unrolled wrapper connects to a history of architectural discourse around rendering form with applied graphics. In some ways, texture mapping argues for a biased realism in architecture, one commonly associated with forgery. In other ways, it productively sutures realism with literalism, challenging architecture's stable values. Literalism connects architecture and material composition, preventing realism from playing the gambit of architectural representation.[2] The transaction between

1 Robert Venturi, Denise Scott Brown, and Steven Izenour, *Learning from Las Vegas: The Forgotten Symbolism of Architectural Form* (Cambridge, MA: MIT Press, 1977), 87.

2 Mark Linder argues that this quote from Michael Cimino's 1978 film *The Deer Hunter* is the most literal statement one can make: "See this Stanley? This is this. This ain't somethin' else. This is this." Mark Linder, *Nothing Less Than Literal: Architecture after Minimalism* (Cambridge, MA: MIT Press, 2007).

Deflated house being hydro-dipped

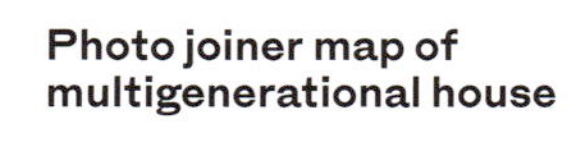

Photo joiner map of multigenerational house

Literalized normals map, engraved PVC with airbrush painted finish 42 × 22 in.

the green sandwich paper, the hydro-dipper, and the architectural surface uses a documentary tool historically used to perpetuate forgery but this time as a generative experiment that sutures architecture with pop culture.

Increases in computation literacy and extradisciplinarity have made architects active participants in the flow and evolution of representational techniques that formalize ideas into the physical environment. Yet we continue to cheat architectural content in fear of being too literal at the expense of the discipline. Realism and literalism are equally invested in material representation. To paraphrase architectural critic Mario Carpo, those interested in post-digital architecture favor representational tools and techniques that are (at times) aloof toward content and "don't care about technology."[3] My thesis looks outside the discipline to expand the post-digital conversation for architecture in the 2020s.

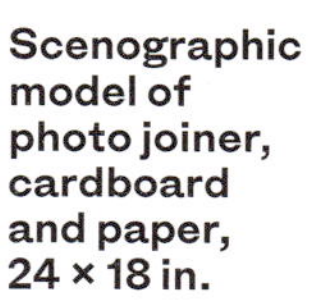

Scenographic model of photo joiner, cardboard and paper, 24 × 18 in.

3 Mario Carpo, *The Second Digital Turn: Design Beyond Intelligence* (Cambridge, MA: MIT Press, 2017)

zachschumacher.com

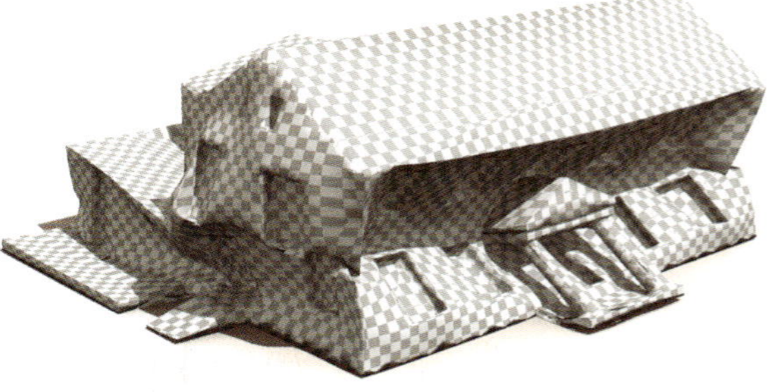

3D model of deflated house with texture map

Aaron Teves (B.Arch)

The Archi-Jig, or: A Manual for a New Craft Collective

The jig as an architectural typology—existing between tool and method—reframes the ambitions of the discipline and the practice of construction.

The Archi-Jig, or: A

The Backyard Prototype, 1:1 prototype, frames taken from film. Constructed in Providence, Rhode Island.

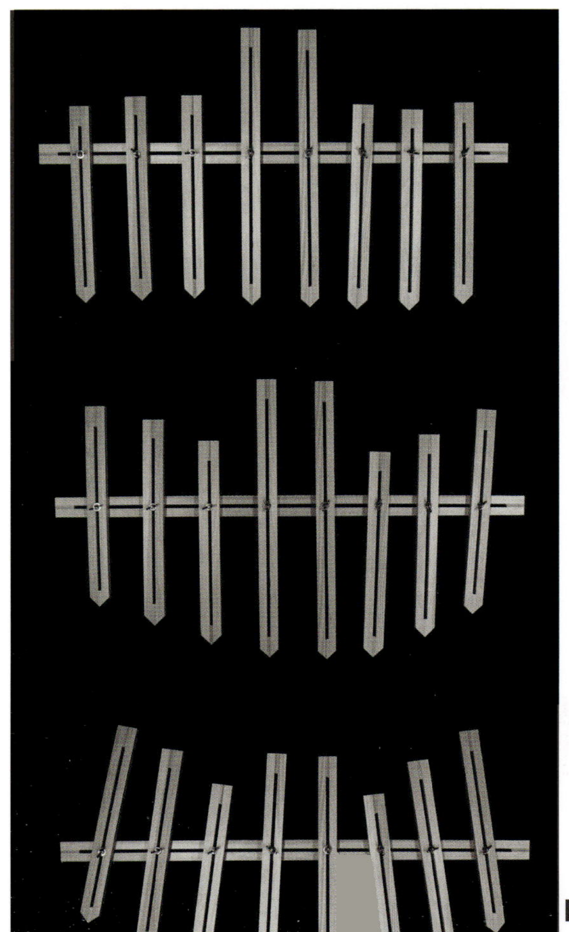

Primitive Jig No. 1, 1:1 model, frames taken from film.

Archi-Jig animations

Craft is the embodiment of skill: a proficiency in precision; a material understanding; and a comprehensive set of methods for making. Skill reflects the human desire to produce good work. Nonetheless, craft has been commodified for its aesthetic value and delegitimized by commercialism. As such, a new definition for craft could be, "labor, with dignity."[1]

Modular constructions like the Sears catalog house or the General Panel System developed by Konrad Wachsmann and Walter Gropius exemplify a commercialized aesthetic of craft. Though the comprehensive classification database for the Sears home was diverse, ultimately it presented an unfounded sense of individuality in a mass-marketed product. The General Panel System made use of an

1 Ezra Shales, *The Shape of Craft* (London: Reaktion Books, 2017).

The Backyard Prototype, 1:1 prototype, frames taken from film. Constructed in Providence, Rhode Island.

interlocking assembly module. This penchant for over-systematization led to the ubiquitous spaceframe, succeeding in scalar shifts but curbing spontaneity. Both present a franchise of pseudo-adaptability, a farce of craft and individuality.[2]

My revisionist history rethinks the jig as a post-aesthetic vehicle for craft, emphasizing dexterity in design. A jig is an apparatus to hold or guide a piece of work, a representational system, and an assembly logic. As an architectural typology, it exists between tool and method. It reframes key ambitions of the discipline, engaging the process of making and physical structure.

Operating as a kit of parts, the Primitive Jigs and the Modular Detail establish a

The Modular Jig, axonometric.

2 See Gilbert Herbert, *The Dream of the Factory-Made House: Walter Gropius and Konrad Wachsmann* (Cambridge, MA: MIT Press, 1986).

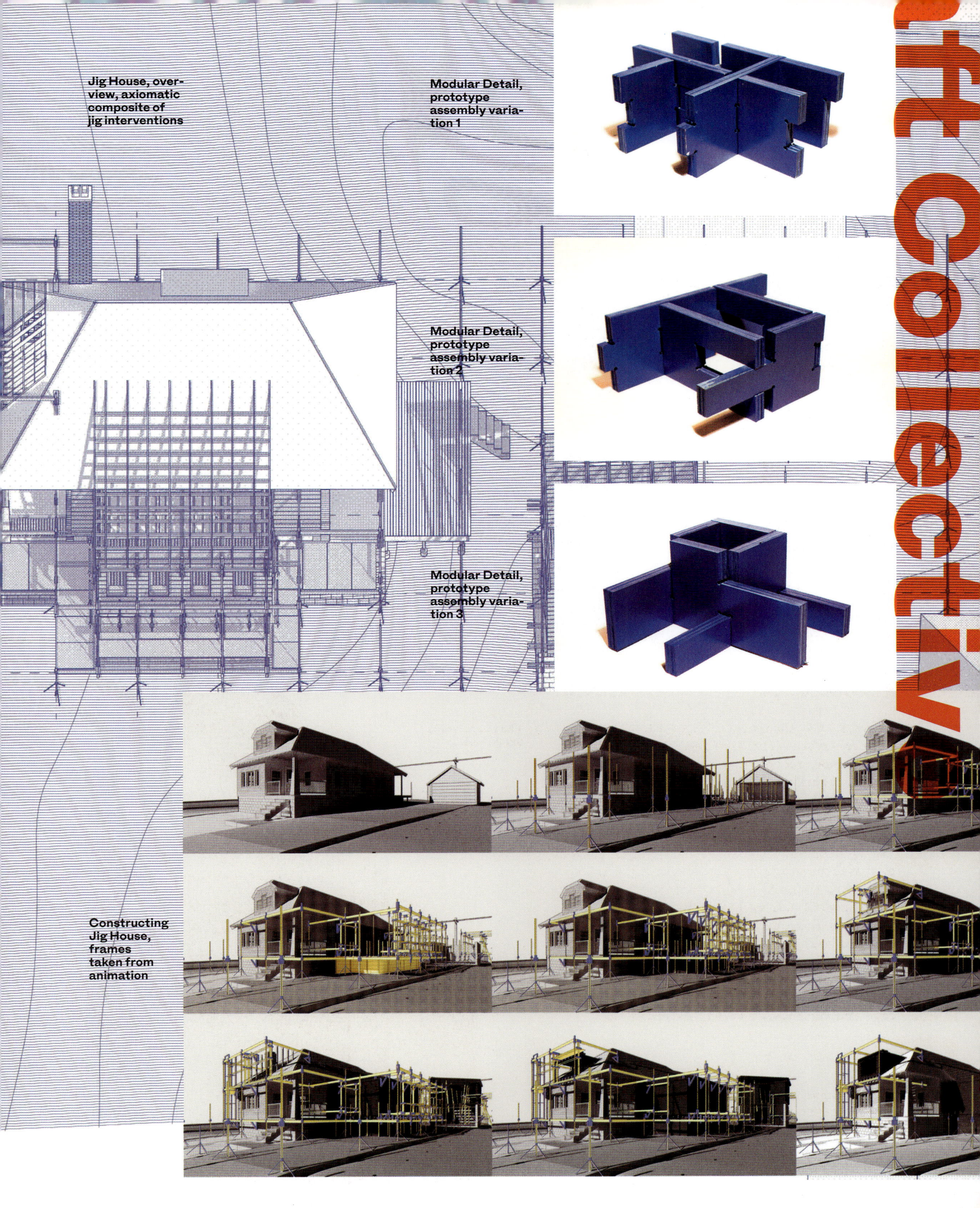

Jig House, overview, axiomatic composite of jig interventions

Modular Detail, prototype assembly variation 1

Modular Detail, prototype assembly variation 2

Modular Detail, prototype assembly variation 3

Constructing Jig House, frames taken from animation

language of standardized parts and frequent uses. The Primitive Jigs aim to decontextualize and defamiliarize established woodworking methods. Reanimating traditional jigs emphasizes patterns of repetition and adaption gestures. Similarly, the Modular Detail expands building standards and common parts (here, dimensional lumber) to anticipate the myriad prospects of use and utility.

Jig House enacts the open-ended jig system upon a construction site, operating as a constant working drawing. The many jigs are cataloged, revised, and prioritized to form a collaborative and cumulative craftsman's manual. The Site Jig facilitates a scope of work and registration marks upon the ground, acting as a node to attach other jigs. The Jig of Utility is an operable scaffolding, gauging materials with key areas of work. The Modular Jig adds new components to its growing repository of assemblies and material compatibility. The Provisional Jigs reorder and recycle jig parts, often permanently embedding jigs into the construction.

When used as a system for design, jigs shed their utilitarian impermanence; they begin to manifest in the built architecture. These jigs have not just a physical but a human function; they project toward a future for architecture as a craft collective. Reconnecting what often is lost in translation between architect and maker, this process activates an ethos of understanding unique goals. The craft collective—a knowledge and experience database, coupled with unique physical innovations—produces an aggregated collection of information. It shifts the architecture discipline toward craft-driven making; the construction site becomes a craft symposium.

The Site Jig, axonometric

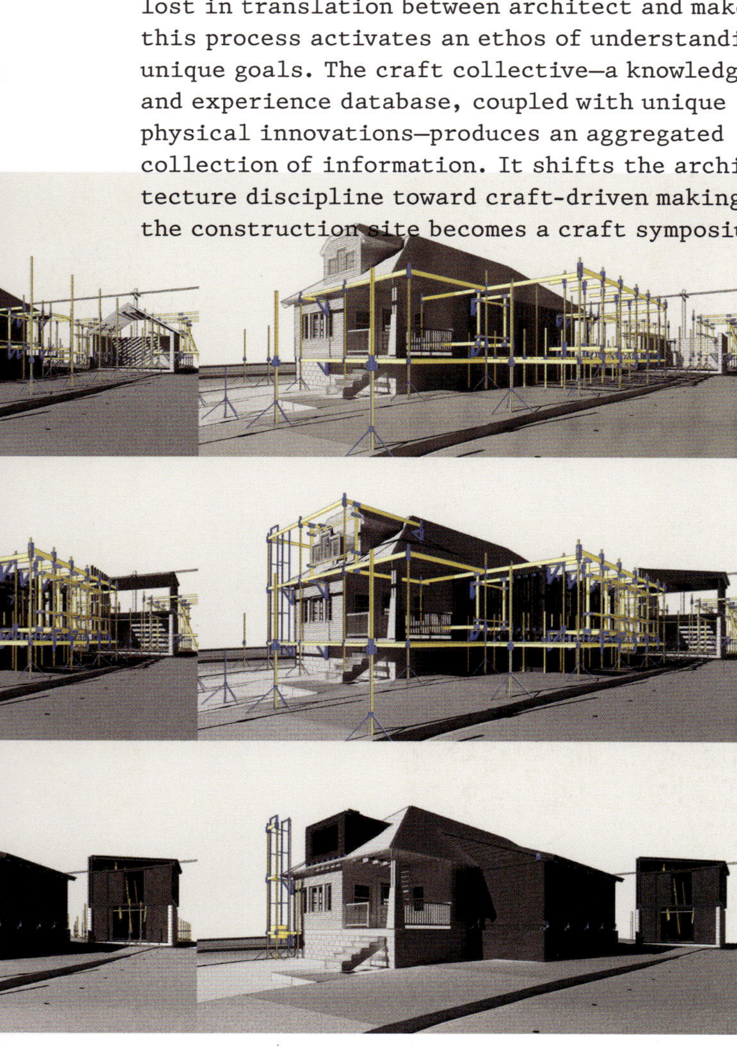

Constructing Jig House, frames taken from animation

The Numerical Jig: a database of parts numbers from the Sears Catalog House.

Eamon Wagner (M.Arch)

Uncanny Genericism: The Productive Misuse of Things

When objecthood evades definition, the generic and its representational techniques offer a generative authorship in spatial form.

Vertical scroll, film still

Uncanny Genericism

Craigslist-developed surface drawing

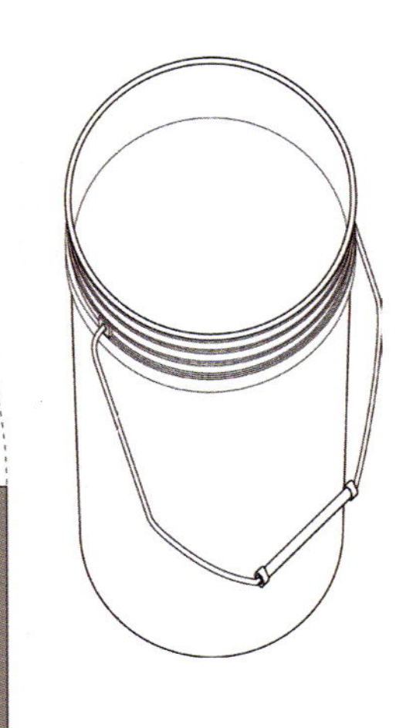

Plastic bucket and drum

Box fan and Bitcoin mine

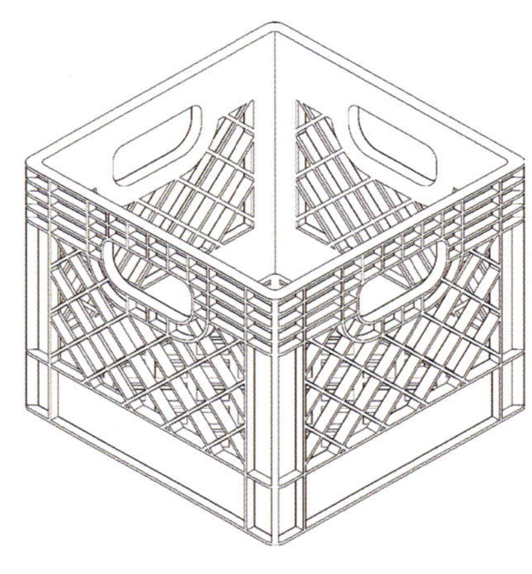

Milk crate and seat

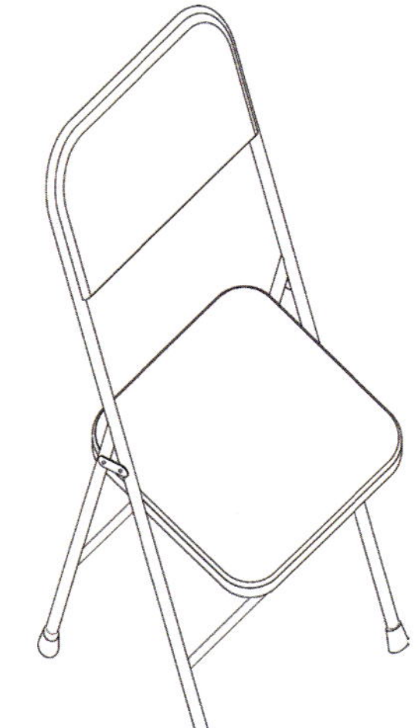

Folding chair and wrestling

use of Things

1 See Pier Vittorio Aureli, "A Room Without Ownership," in *Hannes Meyer: Co-op Interieur*, ed. Aristeidēs Antonas (Leipzig: Spector Books, 2015), 33–39.

In 1926 the soon-to-be Bauhaus director Hannes Meyer sent a photograph titled *Co-op. Interieur* from his home in Basel to an editor in Berlin.[1] The image, of a sparsely furnished bedroom, polemically frames inconspicuous components—a bed, two chairs, shelving—as radical anonymity. One exceptional object, a gramophone, hints at leisure and possession. A century later, Meyer's room bears new significance; every *thing* has a meaning, and architecture is only the container. My thesis reconsiders the role of representation relative to generic objects, and understands these objects as sources of authorship.

The notion of objecthood has been ceaselessly probed since the advent of mechanical reproduction. Our consumer-driven society privileges the object as the primary driver of self-expression and personal identity. For the past two decades, disciplinary discourse on consumerism has been largely focused on vast commercial spaces—the shopping mall, the airport—the "junk food" of architecture. As predictable floor plans increasingly define urban dwelling in climatized, glass box extrusions, the assemblage, storage, and accumulation of objects profoundly defines spatial characteristics. Architecture is no longer seen as a *thing* but as *things*. Meanwhile, the role of the digitally rendered image in representation compounds the assemblage of things as architecture. One need only search the profligate real-estate listings in which low-contrast images depict characterless spaces as part and parcel to the objects inside.

My thesis catalogs an array of everyday, generic objects—box fans, cinderblocks, milk crates—and arranges them in a generic, rendered room, forming a contemporary *Co-op. Interieur*. The renderings iteratively exploit genericism, hiding and highlighting the spatial constraints of the room. The selected objects are designed with such programmatic exactitude that the space for authorial display or geographic specificity is compressed, if not eliminated entirely. It is only in their misuse that they begin to exhibit the potential for an act of architecture. When a milk crate becomes a seat or a bucket turns into a drum, my authorship generates architectural form. In a time when objecthood evades definition, the renderings represent a reactive architecture, demonstrating the impossible conditions of objects and their uncanny effect on the architecture itself.

Endless interior, film still

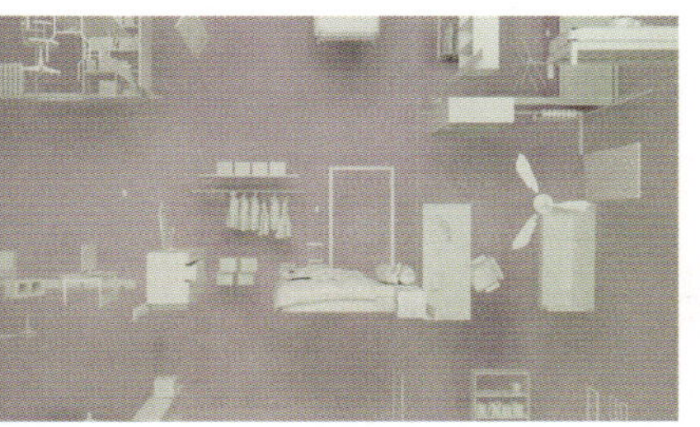
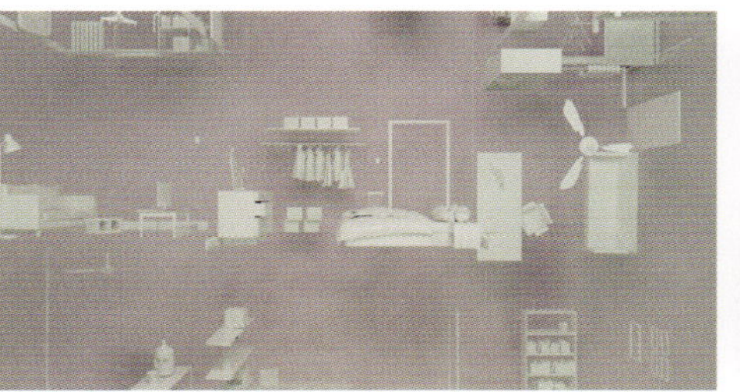
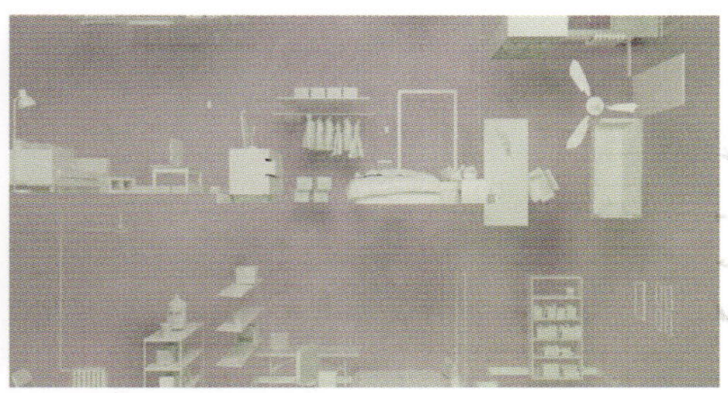

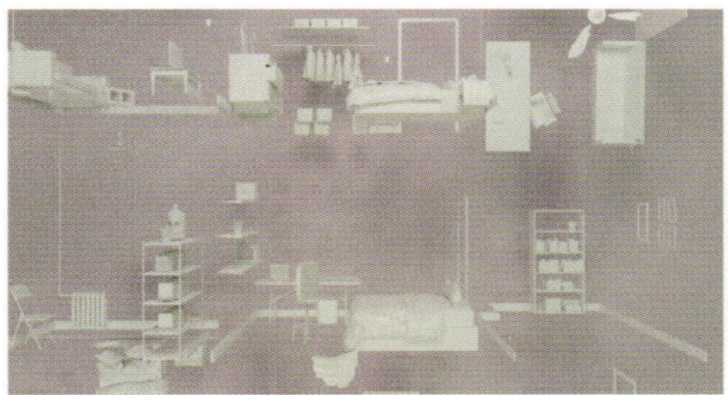
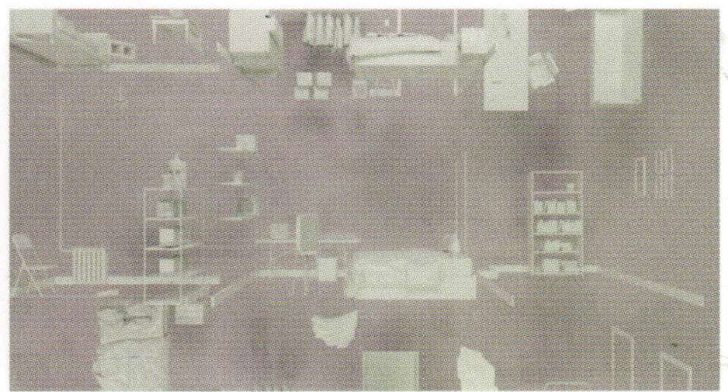
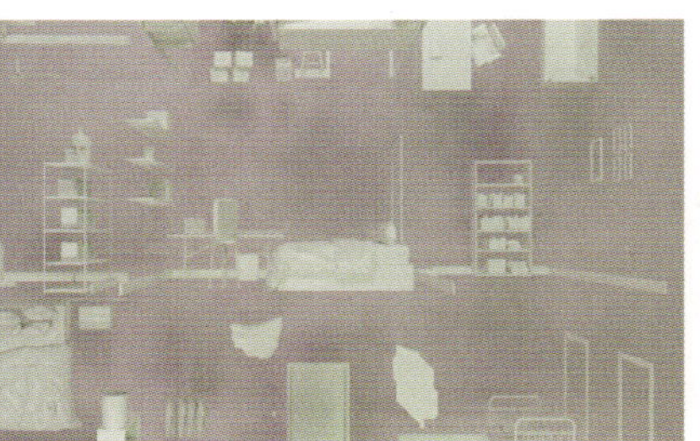

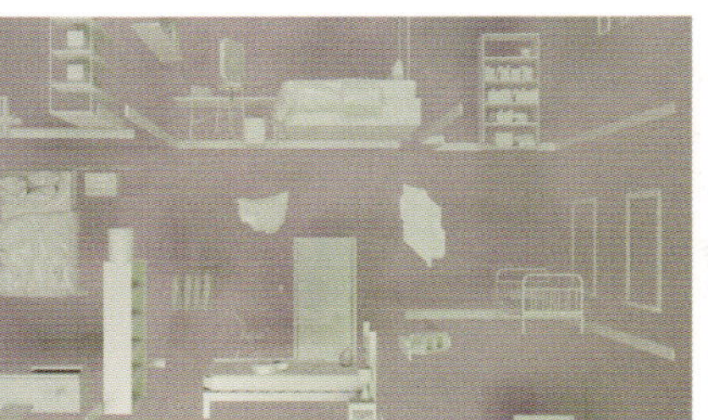
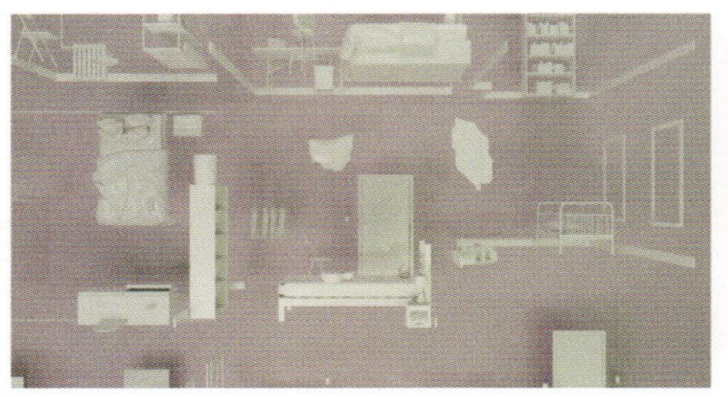

reply favorite hide

$1100 / 2br - 120ft² - Spacious

Spacious bedroom available for

Apartment is newly renovated with stainless
UNIT. and hardwood floors throughout.
windows facing North. and can be furnished
Room dimensions: 9'6" by 12"

Roommate is a kind. clean. and respectful

Apartment is located on the 4th floor of a
walk to fun restaurants and bars on
walk to 2/3 4/5 trains and 10

Available May 15 - July 31.

- do NOT contact me with

post id: posted:

Please flag

eamonwagner.com

Thesis Miro Board

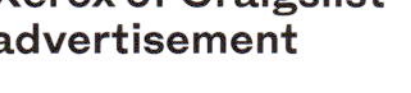

◀ prev ▲ next ▶

Posted 6 days ago

print

Sunny Sublet in Crown Heights, Brooklyn (Brooklyn, NY)

1 of 3

© craigslist - Map data © OpenStreetMap

Prospect Place near Nostrand Avenue

(google map)

2BR / 1Ba 120ft² available may 15

apartment

w/d in unit

no smoking

street parking

private bath

private room

edroom, 1 bathroom Crown Heights apartment!

eel appliances including dishwasher, washer/dryer IN
oom is ~120 sq ft with a large step-in closet, two large
ith a full-sized bed, linens, lamp, and AC unit if desired.

ale grad student in mid-20s.

o-op apartment building. 15 minutes walk to Prospect Park, Brooklyn Museum, Brooklyn Library. 5
anklin Avenue. 1 minute walk to Key Foods grocery store.
walk to A/C/E trains. 1 minute walk to B-44 bus line.

lexible but lease ends July 31. Rent can be pro-rated, utilities not included in rent price (vary by usage).

ated: about 11 hours ago email to friend best of

g. Western Union), or buy/rent sight unseen

Xerox of Craigslist advertisement

Rendering A:
Control

Rendering B:
Geometric orientation

Rendering C:
Spatial impossibility I

Rendering E:
Mesh configuration

Rendering D:
Lighting anomaly

Rendering F:
Spatial impossibility II

Essays & Interviews

Daniel A. Barber

"The Great Age of Doors Is Behind Us!": Architectural Histories, Design Imaginaries, Thinking the Unthinkable

1 Doomsday Machine

The current conjuncture is overwhelmed by three intersecting crises: the Covid-19 pandemic, centuries of racial oppression, and the looming disasters of climate instability. Some of these intersections are countervailing. We are, for example, on one side more deeply embedded in our interior spaces—what were once homes are now places for work, for schooling, havens against the invisible virus—and on the other, drawn into the righteous unrest in the streets, called with a searing urgency into a reenergized urban realm, striving to make voices heard. Architecture finds itself to be a crucial arena for mediating, and perhaps mitigating, these multiple converging complications.

At stake in any conjuncture: What are the prospects for increased liberation? Where are the necessary tools? In the U.S., many are simultaneously heartened by the renewed insistence on equality and also dismayed by the rank idiocy of national leadership, as we fall once again into exponentially rising viral spread. Hopes for the future abound, but are clouded by the now familiar anticipation of the unfamiliar—that, from here, it is difficult to know what will happen in the coming days, weeks, or months. That the future, or at least our collective ability to determine it, has been foreclosed by forces, biological or geophysical, seemingly out of our control.[1] Through the virus, we are beginning to recognize our collective reliance on comfortable delusions. Through the protests for racial equity, we are suspending our reliance on a stable "we," as a capacity for discomfort, alongside deranged anticipations of a knowable future, are more clearly seen as conditioned by racial, gendered, and economic stratifications. At stake, in architecture and in theory, is how we have relied on this stable "we"—a delimited range of future constituents—and how this embedded bias needs to transform.

I am struck now by the productive entanglement of two resonant voices. First is that of historian Dipesh Chakrabarty, who, in his celebrated essay "The Climate of History," now more than a decade old, notes that the epochal instabilities of climate change can "precipitate a sense of the present that disconnects the future from the past by putting such a future beyond the grasp of historical sensibility."[2] In other words, an assumed temporal continuity, often the spectrum on which theory seeks to take hold, is no longer viable. Tomorrow may not look like today, and we don't even know the terms of possible transformations. The pandemic was, in this sense, for most of us, something of a surprise, if not precisely a shock. Likewise, the vitality of the recent protests—monuments coming down, emergent legislation around abolishing the police—while clearly rooted in centuries of protest, is striking in its urgency, in the pace with which statues have fallen.

Chakrabarty's imperatives are followed more recently by Arundhati Roy's reflections in "The Pandemic Is a Portal," her widely read text from early April 2020, and the conceptual

1 See Jennifer Wenzel, "Evicted from the Future," in *Alienocene*, no. 1 (December 2019): 1–16.

2 Dipesh Chakrabarty, "The Climate of History: Four Theses," in *Critical Inquiry* 35, no. 2 (Winter 2009): 197.

basis for this volume. Responding to the chaos of India's forced Covid migration, Roy proposed that "the pandemic is a portal, a gateway between one world and the next." The lockdown, Roy continues, "worked like a chemical experiment that suddenly illuminated hidden things." Where Chakrabarty outlined an obstacle for collective thought, a barrier, Roy suggests a way to see through, a portal extending from the present into the unknown future—and celebrates the potentials embedded in this unknowability. Indeed, in the U.S. we have rapidly seen new contours of historical and theoretical thought, now more powerfully inflected by a dependence on migrant, compromised, and "essential" labor; a radically unequal health system; and a racially biased and violent police force. However, Roy also acknowledges the challenges we face. "Our minds," she writes, "are still racing back and forth, longing for a return to 'normality,' trying to stitch our future to our past and refusing to acknowledge the rupture. But the rupture exists." For Roy the rupture is not prohibitive, but prospective. "In the midst of this terrible despair," she concludes, "[the rupture] offers us a chance to rethink the doomsday machine we have built for ourselves. Nothing could be worse than a return to normality."[3]

3 Arundhati Roy, "The Pandemic Is a Portal," *Financial Times*, April 3, 2020.

4 Chakrabarty, 208.

5 See Walter D. Mignolo, "Epistemic Disobedience, Independent Thought and Decolonial Freedom," in *Theory, Culture & Society* 26, no. 7–8 (2009), 159–81.

2 Architecture as Petroculture

"The mansion of modern freedom," Chakrabarty also writes, "stands on an ever-expanding base of fossil-fuel use."[4] Here then is another challenge and point of discontinuity: How does architecture—as a discipline, a pedagogy, and a practice—imagine a future built environment in which mansions become housing collectives, powered by wind or solar rather than oil and coal? At stake is an epistemological shift in the historical framing of architecture and its relationship to the sociopolitical conditions in which it operates. Architecture is a crucial part of the global energy system, both as medium (material infrastructure) and media (system of representation). It modulates the throughput of the global energy metabolism and gives it cultural form. The data on carbon emissions inserts an imperative (however often ignored) to change the way we build, to reverse our logic of extraction, violence, and increased inequity.

Recent research and collaborative scholarly efforts have focused on redressing the discursive aporia through which "the environment" has been systematically elided, as a topic or matter of concern, from the historical discussion of architecture. Ecosystems, waste production, resource use, and the social impacts of these and other environmental aspects are beginning to receive more attention in the field. A substantive reconsideration of how to view histories of architecture after climate change is part of a broader intersectional tumult that is toppling many assumptions, lineages, and notions of what constitutes a significant disciplinary intervention—following, albeit here quite loosely, Walter Mignolo's call for epistemic disobedience.[5] The terms and the values have changed; architects, and architecture schools, are still catching

Any understanding of "architecture and climate" is also an understanding of architecture and race, gender, and equity, of a legacy of social and environmental injustice. The distribution of comfort and the terms of its social construction are indelibly gendered and racialized.

up. Any understanding of "architecture and climate" is also an understanding of architecture and race, gender, and equity, of a legacy of social and environmental injustice. The distribution of comfort and the terms of its social construction are indelibly gendered and racialized.

Two essential framing devices help us to reinterpret the history of architecture, in order to reconstruct a different future, on carbon terms. The first is asserting the basic premise that "architecture" (not just "building") contributes to carbon emissions. The material conditions of "architecture" as the production and maintenance of the built environment are implicated in the causes, effects, and the possible futures induced through climate instability. Populations process energy through buildings, turning fuel into regionally and culturally specific conditions for labor and leisure. While methods of analysis differ, the construction, maintenance, and demolition of buildings is generally seen to account for between 40 and 60 percent of carbon emissions in the U.S.[6] The recent Intergovernmental Panel on Climate Change report suggests that continued production of buildings is harmful to the future of the species, or at least that "architecture" as understood today can be pried open toward a range of discursive and professional reconfigurations aimed directly at reducing carbon emissions.[7] Implications from the Green New Deal also directly call on the field to swiftly change its practices, and its discourse, toward retrofit and energy conservation.

The second framework is historiographic: histories of architectural modernism have not simply ignored energy (and the environment more generally) but have been articulated, at least in part, as a means to discursively mask the role of energy in the production of the built environment. Think back to your survey course in Modern Architecture—was energy mentioned? Even later attempts to reframe architecture as an environmental practice have reasserted rigid disciplinary boundaries that keep "the environment" isolated from historical and critical discourse; the project of persistently reinscribing and reifying a framework for an autonomous architecture under threat from the facts and forces of environmental knowledge remains a potent trope in the field. "Sustaining Architecture in the Face of Sustainability" is how a recent volume put it.[8] The new path is clear: we must identify specific discursive and disciplinary strategies that can disrupt well-worn rhetorical patterns and criteria, and begin to rethink how historical narratives and critical approaches can help to define a new purview for architecture and allied forms of cultural inquiry.

Two students' projects at RISD in particular helped me to understand the "doomsday machine" as the conceptual infrastructure of the building industry, awash in not only the capitalistic contours of the "mansions," but also in the theories, practices, and pedagogies that have operated, at least since the 1970s, as a cover, a mask, a distraction from the building as a system of energy and cultural management rooted in carbon excess. Ece Cetin's *Critically Reimagining the Overt* (see pp. 27–30) deftly applies a parasitic method to existing buildings, using design strategies to uncover the compromised conditions, what is often seen as given, in designed activity. In other words, Cetin reveals the deranged condition of business-as-usual, large-scale projects by exploring with searing precision how other desires can be reflected in the dramatic reimagining of existing buildings. Taylor McCabe's pattern book for Baltimore (see pp. 43–46) inserts doors, portals, and mechanisms for opening toward a new

6 Oswaldo Lucon, Diana Ürge-Vorsatz, et. al., "Buildings" in: *Climate Change 2014: Mitigation of Climate Change. Contribution of Working Group III to the Fifth Assessment Report of the Intergovernmental Panel on Climate Change* (New York: Cambridge University Press, 2014): 671–739, 675.

7 Lucon and Urge-Vorsatz, "Buildings."

8 Preston Scott Cohen and Erika Naginski, eds., *The Return of Nature: Sustaining Architecture in the Face of Sustainability* (New York: Routledge, 2014).

conception of the right to the city, pointing up the embeddedness of racism into the built environment and the difficulties of overturning it. How to imagine, in this case, a city that is not subject to capital, white supremacy, and the horror of "development"? Is there a vision of the city that can change without growing? This sort of opening, the doors that are imagined, albeit often implicitly, reach toward extreme, and extremely welcome, possibilities.

Other disciplines face challenges similar to that of architecture in their sublimation of environmental implications, and critics in other fields have embarked on a thorough investigation of petroculture, in particular of the "oil encounter" and the problem of oil's invisibility.[9] Literary critics have emphasized the extent to which the absence of oil in literature reflects more general cultural and economic patterns. As Graeme Macdonald explains, "A strongly developed strain of petrocultural theory focuses on the way in which the means and effects of oil are structurally occluded from its mass of consumers, making it less apparent as an *explicit* object in social life and thus a specific topic in and for capitalist production."[10] This occlusion, and its structural condition, operate not simply as important tropes for renewed literary analysis but also for how this specific form of cultural articulation resists and restructures other possible energo-technological trajectories. In other words, the effect of oil's invisibility is to form something of a phantom cultural logic, one that dominates and determines, and that excludes other forms of expression. "Oil produces," as Macdonald writes, "the most violent logic of all energy forms and in doing so militates against alternative imaginative forms of representation." He continues, "Part of the point in theorizing energy as cultural is, therefore, to expose and determine reasons for our acculturation to its hierarchy of material (and, increasingly, immaterial) forms and the manner in which they dictate fundamental aspects of social life and organization."[11]

Patricia Yaeger discusses a potent and familiar example: oil is not evident in Jack Kerouac's *On the Road*, despite the fact that it structurally determines the narrative. Kerouac's characters are, as Yaeger puts it, "gasaholics. … Oil dependency created their world, each city, suburb, truck stop, and bite of pie depends on Standard Oil, Shell, Mobilgas, or Phillips 66." She goes on to ask, "Are the gas station's empty pumps a premonitory metaphor for resource anxiety, for what Pierre Macherey calls 'that absence around which a real complexity is knit'?"[12] Kerouac's novel is an extreme example. It is worth noting it was published in 1957, the same year Mies's Seagram Tower was completed—an energy-hungry building that became a template for carbon profligacy worldwide. Yaeger suggests the broader prospects of analyzing petro-literature in a general reframing of culture and energy, as she writes, "What happens if we sort texts according to the energy histories that made them possible … what happens if we rechart literary periods and make energy sources a matter of urgency to literary criticism?"[13] Indeed, what happens if we reveal architectural history relative to the sources of energy that made, and make, buildings possible? For one, we are reminded that buildings are not novels; in fact, the relationship between buildings, material flows, and political economies renders even more extreme the occlusion of energy from narratives of historical development.

The oil encounter in literature came to something of a discursive apex in the work of novelist and critic Amitav Ghosh. Ghosh's 1992 article in *The New Republic* on "petrofiction" expanded petrocultural interest *avant la lettre*, and serves as a touchpoint for much of the critical literature that follows.[14] His more recent text, *The Great Derangement: Climate Change and the Unthinkable*, follows on the logic of ubiquity and invisibility and also emphasizes the violence embedded in the energy/climate nexus.[15] Ghosh argues that oil's narrative absence has led to a general condition in which the drivers and consequences of climate change are difficult to integrate into cultural discourse writ large.[16] He points directly at discursive practices, such as architectural history, that don't simply ignore oil, or climate, but in fact operate to hide them. As he writes: "In a substantially altered world, when readers and museum goers turn to the art and literature of our

9 See Imre Szeman and the Petrocultures Research Group, *After Oil* (Alberta: Petrocultures Research Group, 2016); Imre Szeman and Dominic Boyer, *Energy Humanities: An Anthology* (Baltimore, MD: Johns Hopkins University Press, 2017); Imre Szeman, Patricia Yaeger, and Jennifer Wenzel, eds., *Fueling Culture: 101 Words for Energy and Environment* (New York: Fordham University Press, 2017); Imre Szeman, *On Petrocultures: Globalization, Culture, and Energy* (Morgantown, West Virginia University Press, 2019); Jennifer Wenzel, "Petromagic-realism: Toward a Political Ecology of Nigerian Literature" in *Postcolonial Studies* 9, no. 4 (2006): 449–64; and Peter Hitchcock, "Oil in an American Imaginary," in *New Formations*, no. 69 (Summer 2010): 81–97.

10 Graeme Macdonald, "Research Note: The Resources of Fiction," in *Reviews in Cultural Theory* 4, no. 2 (2013): 1–24, 6; see also Macdonald, "'Monstrous Transformer': Petrofiction and World Literature," in *Journal of Postcolonial Writing* 53, no. 3 (2017): 289–302, and Macdonald, "Oil and World Literature" in *American Book Review* 33, no. 3 (March/April 2012): 7–31.

11 Macdonald, "Research Note," 10.

12 Patricia Yaeger, Laurie Shannon, et. al., "Editor's Column: Literature in the Ages of Wood, Tallow, Coal, Whale Oil, Gasoline, Atomic Power, and Other Energy Sources," *PMLA* 126, no. 2 (March 2011): 305–26, 306.

13 Yaeger and Shannon, 306.

14 Amitav Ghosh, "Petrofiction: The Oil Encounter and the Novel," in *The New Republic* (March 2, 1992), 29–34.

15 Amitav Ghosh, *The Great Derangement: Climate Change and the*

How can resistance to carbon emissions be effected through the design and redesign of the built environment? What sort of discursive and historical frameworks, and pedagogical practice, can focus on and facilitate this transformation?

time, will they not look, first and most urgently, for traces and portents of the altered world of their inheritance? And when they fail to find them, what should they—what can they—do other than conclude that ours was a time when most forms of art and literature were drawn into the modes of concealment that prevented people from recognizing the realities of their plight?"[17] Literature and its forms of analysis, much like architecture and the discourse that surrounds it, have struggled to articulate the "unthinkable": they function as modes of concealment rather than mechanisms to reveal and evaluate the embedded conditions of a given text, building, or landscape in relation to energy use and climate disruption.

Ghosh makes two references specifically to architecture and its participation in the "great derangement." Indeed, he frames it as central to both causes and effects. First, in making his seminal point that cultural practices are an essential aspect in understanding and mitigating climate instability, he writes that climate change "is perhaps the most important question ever to confront *culture* in the broadest sense—for let us make no mistake: the climate crisis is also a crisis of culture, and thus of the imagination. Culture generates desires—for vehicles and appliances, for certain kinds of gardens and dwellings—that are among the principal drivers of the carbon economy."[18] A bit too general perhaps, but nonetheless an indication of the ongoing absurdity of discussing architecture without taking its climatic effects into account. A second reference is more pointed: "If contemporary trends in architecture," he asks, "even in this period of accelerating carbon emissions, favor shiny, glass-and-metal-plated towers, do we not have to ask, What are the patterns of desire that are fed by these gestures?"[19] This, in sum, is the tenor of the unthinkability in the present discursive challenge. It clarifies the correlate ambition for the field: What kind of architecture can solicit and affirm other patterns, other desires? Or, more explicitly: How can resistance to carbon emissions be effected through the design and redesign of the built environment? What sort of discursive and historical frameworks, and pedagogical practice, can focus on and facilitate this transformation?

3 Doors and Portals

If the pandemic is a portal, it is a designed object, an aspect of our cultural history, open to engagement or reinterpretation. First, we might ask: What does it look like? Is it a physical door, or simply an opening? Is it ornamented? The first definition of a portal in the OED defines it as "a doorway, gate or other entrance, especially a large and imposing one."[20] According to whom is it imposing, and how is this affect suggested? Whose history does it reflect? How does it relate to the street? Perhaps most simply and essentially: If the pandemic is a portal, does it have a handle? How does it open? Can it be closed?

Unthinkable (Chicago: University of Chicago Press, 2016).

16 Rob Nixon has discussed the historical progress of climate instability as one of "slow violence" that also operates across this visibility/ invisibility nexus: "By slow violence," Nixon writes, "I mean a violence that occurs gradually and out of sight, a violence of delayed destruction that is dispersed across time and space, an attritional violence that is typically not viewed as violence at all." Rob Nixon, *Slow Violence and the Environmentalism of the Poor* (Cambridge, MA: Harvard University Press), 2–3.

17 Ghosh, *The Great Derangement*, 11.

18 Ghosh, The Great Derangement, 132.

19 Ghosh, The Great Derangement, 5.

20 "Portal," *Oxford English Dictionary Online*, https://www.oed.com.

Bernhard Siegert, in his essay "Doors: On the Materiality of the Symbolic," suggests the gravity of possible answers to such questions, the deep implications of doors as an aspect of ever-evolving forms of sociability. Noting that social mores seem to elide how to "close a door quietly and discreetly, yet firmly," he recalls Theodor Adorno's observation that now "one has to slam car doors and refrigerator doors … while other doors snap shut on their own." Adorno sees this as acquiescence to a machine logic, as "nothing less than a prelude to fascism"; in Adorno's own words, "Already the violent, hard-hitting, unresting jerkiness of Fascist abuses" are at work."[21]

Siegert's point, the cause for Adorno's misgivings, is that the door had transitioned: it was no longer a physical object infused with culturally specific habits and expectations, but now, rather, a machine, with a fascist jerkiness that might premediate Roy's "doomsday machine." For Adorno this is distasteful, a fall into a cultural abyss; for Siegert, it is something else entirely: an opportunity to assert "a different concept of culture … a plurality of cultures that abandons a one-sided conception of human–things relations that privileges human beings."[22] Siegert introduces a "concept of cultural techniques," which "comprises a more or less complex actor network that includes technical objects and chains of operations (including gestures, among other things) in equal measures."[23] The machine then, is not outside of us but is rather part of our gestures, desires, habits, and aspirations. Human agency is constituted alongside technologies and techniques—not before, above, or in reference to a stable concept of culture. As we change, our gestures, our capacity to open and close doors, changes with us.

Siegert later focuses on the revolving glass door of office towers and shopping malls—"the only original door," Siegert notes, quoting Robert Musil, "conceived in our time."[24] The revolving door refigures without destabilizing the portal's capacity for cultural distinction, and inserts a climatic aspect. This is magnified, increasingly since Musil's reflection in 1926, by the importance of such revolving doors for the thermal stability of the interior; it "manifests," as Siegert notes, "a conception of architecture as a thermodynamic machine."[25] The brushes at the edge of the revolving portal allow for ingress and egress while minimizing disturbance to the conditioned interior volume; it is a device of climate efficiency, and thereby feeds into and supports the ubiquity of climate control systems—an aspect, no doubt, of the "doomsday machine" we are still building.

Musil's interest was in the continuous flow of people this new door allowed, its uniform treatment of disparate subjects, its unwillingness to block or prevent entry, a door that was not a filter, not imposing. There is always a subtle negotiation, a sort of power play, on entering the revolving system—assessing its speed, relying on others to not push it too hard, make it move too fast. Socially complex, perhaps, but for Musil refreshingly so. "In former times," he wrote, in the essay "Doors and Portals" that Siegert is referencing, "the door was an entrance into the society of privilege, which was opened or shut in the face of the new arrival, depending on who he [sic] was; generally it decided his fate." The machinic revolving door offers a new kind of cultural trajectory; "The great age of doors is behind us!"

21 Bernhard Siegert, "Doors: On the Materiality of the Symbolic," in *Grey Room* 47 (Spring 2012): 6; Siegert is quoting from Theodor Adorno, *Minima Moralia: Reflections from a Damaged Life* (London: Verso, 1997), 40, with a slightly modified translation. See also Bernhard Siegert, *Cultural Techniques: Grids, Filters, Doors, and Other Articulations of the Real* (New York: Fordham University Press, 2015), esp. 192–205, and Reinhold Martin, "Unfolded, Not Opened: On Bernhard Siegert's *Cultural Techniques*," in *Grey Room* 62 (Winter 2016): 102–15.

22 Siegert, "Doors," 7–8.

23 Siegert, "Doors," 8.

24 Siegert, "Doors," 15; quoting Robert Musil, "Doors and Portals," in *Posthumous Papers of a Living Author* (London: Penguin, 1995).

25 Siegert, "Doors," 18. Siegert also references the original appellation of "the new revolving storm door," resonating with these heightened climatic distinctions.

Open the door! Or better, dismantle it all together: dismantle our collective derangement. What is the architectural pedagogy of an open portal? So much unlearning to do.

Musil concludes, "We don't even slam the door in anyone's face anymore."[26]

Circling back to Adorno's anxiety, some misgivings may emerge: the revolving door has no latch, handle, or recognizable human interface. It is, as Siegert quotes from an early advertisement focused on its thermal efficiencies, "Always Closed." It is all machine, a vital part, as a definitive barrier, of Roy's "doomsday" prognosis, evidence of "the 'state of emergency' in which we live," now following Benjamin, that "is not the exception but the rule." Is this what we are trying to escape, this constant state of panic? Or is it something else? The revolving door reveals the ongoing catastrophe of daily life *before the pandemic*. Benjamin reminds us that "the tradition of the oppressed teaches us" about the delusions of any nonemergency condition, that in fact the emergency has always already been here.[27] "We," the tenured professoriate, the architectural historians, are—in the face of racial unrest, augurs of climate disasters, and the widespread discomfort, at best, of the pandemic—recognizing that the stories we tell of architecture are discursive sites for unveiling centuries of oppression: celebrated buildings constructed by slave labor; office towers dedicated to resource extraction; housing estates that offer a minimum condition for existence. The chemical experiment of the pandemic then, *pace* Roy, is a leeching out of the toxins behind the wall. As a growing stain of embedded bias and systemic racism emerges, we, as a discipline, must steadfastly resist the pressure to just add another layer of paint and hope it goes away.

We must ask: Who goes through this portal, escaping the doomsday machines we have built? Architecture, as a profession and a discipline, is a mansion built on a foundation of exclusion. Theory has been an essential gatekeeper: what one has read, with whom and in what context, determines who is let in, or out. The architecture profession's racial inequities have been the subject of much discussion in the U.S. in 2020. We know that only around 2 percent of registered American architects are Black. The percentage of Black Ph.D.s in Architectural History and Theory is even smaller; when we get to faculty, tenured faculty, school leadership positions, vanishingly (literally) few. Some (far from all) U.S. schools are beginning to reassess the pathways and pipelines that lead an individual to study in the field, then to practice or advanced research; that this happens alongside continued celebrations of participation in biennials, or the hosting of a Pritzker winner, for example, is an abstract contradiction that is not yet being confronted. "Business-as-usual" persists despite and alongside the urgency of the moment. "Still far more outdated than the door," Musil muses, "is the doorframe."[28]

The institutional apparatus of architectural academia can now revel in the outdatedness of practices put in the past, and focus on a future that emerges, with no small relief, as unfamiliar to the present. Open the door! Or better, dismantle it all together: dismantle our collective derangement. What is the architectural pedagogy of an open portal? So much unlearning to do. Our collective imperative: listen, read, and reflect on material seen to be outside of the disciplinary purview and strive to bring those writings, perspectives, and individuals into the center, to make discursive space for voices that have been implicitly or explicitly ignored. Honor the women and the people of color in the room, to be sure, but also elicit and explore the range of perspectives from the dynamism of world cultures, dismantling the implicit core (or frame?) of "Western thought" as essential to any way forward.[29] Perhaps Roy's portal is not an imposing gate; it could just as easily be thought of, in reference to numerous indigenous traditions, as an indelible opportunity achieved through knowledge and consciousness, rather than scaffolded by buildings and frames, or opened with levers. We arrive there by a careful extension and expansion of our ways of thinking. We, in architecture, have much catching up to do—reading, listening, learning—so that we can be as open as possible to the coming transformation.

26 Robert Musil, "Doors and Portals," in *Posthumous Papers of a Living Author* (London: Penguin, 1995), 59–63, 62.

27 Walter Benjamin, "On the Concept of History" in *Walter Benjamin: Selected Writings Vol. 4 1938–1940* (Cambridge, MA: Harvard University Press, 2003), 392.

28 Musil, "Doors and Portals," 62.

29 See Mark Rifkin, *Beyond Settler Time: Temporal Sovereignty and Indigenous Self-Determination* (Durham, NC: Duke University Press, 2017).

Three Station Points: A Conversation with Jason Young

Somewhere between Brooklyn, Providence, and Knoxville, Jason Young, the Director of the School of Architecture at the University of Tennessee, Knoxville, found time to Zoom with Amy Kulper and me on August 13, 2020. While he has traveled to RISD thesis critiques for three years, this year's Zoom reviews revealed what he described as the three "station points" of RISD Architecture: projects invested in architecture's representational nature, artistic ruminations, and the political economy of global culture. Young suggests RISD's pluralistic viscerality and intellectual grounding can move the discipline forward. He also challenges us to both "keep more layers on" and open up to our vulnerabilities as designers. **KC**

Amy Catania Kulper **In response to the pandemic, students worked from home, crafting digital presentations through portals and screens, regardless of their propensity for analog drawing and model making. From your perspective as a recurrent visitor to the department, what does RISD Architecture offer to this realm of education?**

Jason Young In my experience, the RISD Architecture Department has a particular institutional ethos stemming from being situated within a college of the arts. Student work advances a strong sensibility for the artifact within a robust culture of making. The conversations I've participated in at RISD have been diverse in many ways: geographical, area of study, faculty interests, and student demographics. Combined with a mixture of architectural thinking and artistic practices, the resulting plurality—the RISD quality of fusing art and design—was remarkable even through Zoom reviews. For example, Sina Erol's project (see pp. 143–146) exemplified that pluralism as he clearly and artistically pursued drawing by hand *and* navigated the translation of his work into Zoom beautifully.

ACK **What modes of engagement and production do you see within RISD Architecture?**

JY Specific to the thesis work, I see an interest in architecture's political economy alongside more abstract and productively obtuse artistic production. Three years ago, on my way home from my first trip to RISD, I created a list of transformations and themes I observed in the student work: finely crafted things; the value of taking care; making things without anxiety; participate; do the little things well; the carrying capacity of design; adjacencies and proximities; imprint and erasure; finding yourself versus losing yourself; inventory things and pull things forward; finitude; euphoria; delirium of the tedious; live better; affect and be affected; relational assemblies; conditions of humanity; deep structures; secondary and tertiary spatialities; listen to whispers; evacuate the narrative; secrets are spatial. The list stands in my sketchbook as a testament to being inspired by the messiness and unevenness of the work, both in terms of engagement methods and the diverse subject matter across the group of projects; it's a testament to the elasticity of the school.

The fragility and vulnerability of architecture is an emerging aesthetic, in which messiness and unevenness might prove to be more useful and productive than well-established practices of consolidation and reduction. Virtual learning can animate architecture as an uneven discipline and proliferate that asymmetry. The pluralism embedded in RISD is not solely an ambition or a solvable problem but is recursive to how the projects are produced, represented, and discussed.

ACK **Can you unpack this characterization of the unevenness in our discipline?**

JY This past fall, when thesis and directed research students were beginning their work, I presented a lecture at a RISD colloquium called "Building as Moving Project," explicating architecture as the product of a diverse array of negotiations and transactions. My thinking about architecture's implicit variability and unevenness came from framing this talk. The presentation engaged students in thinking about the many actors and actions involved in design research and the architectural thesis. We often see students get mired down in the idea that their design work is simply a solution to a particular problem that they hook onto. Reading the act of building as profoundly transactional, ripe with its contradictions and moments of interpretive confusion, could help us break away from some unacknowledged limits with thesis work. I noticed this during final reviews in the spring, not only in how digital culture impacted the projects; it was also the sensibility in the value of disagreements, negotiations, and migrations.

Kevin Crouse **In your essay that you shared with students at the colloquium, "Polyseamseal: Or, How I Learned to Stop Worrying and Love Caulk," you use caulk as a vehicle to critique architecture's propensity for monocultures that create "airtight arguments through linear strings of causal decisions." What is RISD's relationship to the architectural monocultures you describe?**

JY I think you can see evidence of linear causality in every school of architecture, given that this is a prevalent pedagogical mode, even if it is ambient and unspoken. This notion of producing airtight arguments creates a false teleology to bolster the defensibility of a given project. But based on what I experienced at RISD, I don't think the school is anything close to a monoculture; the pluralistic set of working disagreements exploits the lack of a singular modality. I see a triangulated, inclusive relationship between three distinct station points of the

The fragility and vulnerability of architecture is an emerging aesthetic, in which messiness and unevenness might prove to be more useful and productive than well-established practices of consolidation and reduction. Virtual learning can animate architecture as an uneven discipline and proliferate that asymmetry.

school: projects that explore architecture's representational nature, artistic and poetic ruminations, and projects that invest in the

political economy of global culture. Students like Julie Kress and Zachary Schumacher (see pp. 211–214 and 215–218) overtly experimented with

representation, revealing the discipline's bias and a need to test dominant assumptions. Those projects sit vibrantly next to others that are profound expressions of artistic consciousness, such as the work of Nathalie d'Hennezel (see pp. 203–206), which seems committed to the exigencies

of making. And those projects are positioned next to socially and politically informed speculative work that questions architecture's

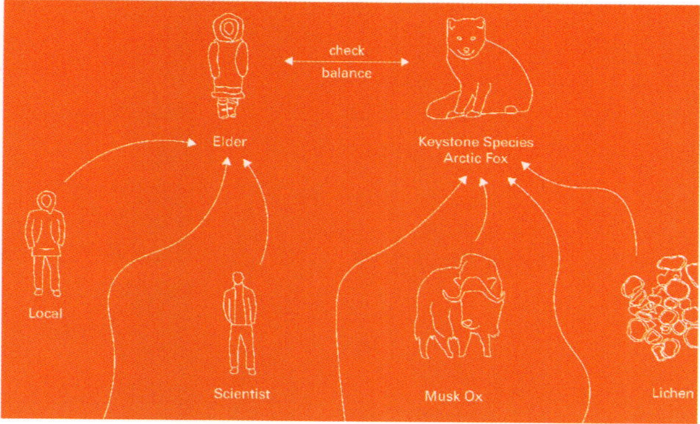

boundaries, evidenced by Sophie Weston Chien (see pp. 199–202). RISD Architecture permits these ebbs and flows, resisting the monotony of internal consistency.

KC **With those three types of projects—let's call them discursive representational, artistic, and politically engaged—an intradisciplinary question is at work at RISD: How can the school adapt and pull from those three ways of thinking into its core principles, especially in thesis?**

JY The students' commitment to fusing art and architecture produces artifacts influenced by both the political economy of building and design research conventions, hybridizing the typical art and architecture school models. Unifying student work across this span could push the whole curriculum to the next level.

Yunchao (Derek) Le's project (see pp. 165–168) is a good example. Something disquieting and purposeful makes his renderings read as artifacts, but they also present architecture as a technical object steeped in global politics. Yunchao invented a hybrid housing server farm that, among other things, anticipates the possibility of an incredible technological meltdown in the same way that Paul Virilio describes the combustion engine as both the invention of American mobility and the resulting environmental problem of greenhouse gases, as an emergent accident that unleashes simultaneous invention and destruction. By slashing across these three categories of work, Yunchao's strategy dodges a typical polemical argumentation style.

KC **Polemics can effortlessly pit polarized thoughts against each other. How can designers avoid polarization while engaging the invention and vulnerability Virilio describes?**

JY The deeper I have gotten in my academic career, the more I have seen that design education is about acquiring vulnerabilities more than becoming an expert and wielding expertise as a weapon. The ability to be responsive comes from learning in an ungrounded formwork. If a student can move across various explicitly framed pedagogies, they collect a vulnerable pluralistic experience, digesting instead of regurgitating.

KC **How did RISD students present, cultivate, and mitigate unevenness even against an architectural monoculture?**

JY Aaron Teves's project (see pp. 219–222) comes to mind. He integrated the jig system into the project's finished state, instead of the more expected result of the final construct leaving the jig behind. The jig itself is an exciting model for unevenness: a planned construction that pools things together for further elaboration. For Aaron, the jig becomes a vehicle for experiencing the project, nodding toward this differentiation that other projects work to hide.

Jake Lefeber's techniques (see pp. 69–72) for measuring natural systems articulate another novel approach to unevenness. He seems invested in constant environmental change, looking at singularities and inflection points while avoiding thinking through polarized ends within a system. He straddles a few disparately precise worlds by putting forward a technically structured object to penetrate and participate with concepts of connection between architecture and its surroundings. Again, it questions the boundaries of the discipline, asking, "What else might architects do?"

Another compelling example of productive unevenness is in Avril Teo's thesis (see pp. 185–188), which questioned what it means to

complete a project. Her drawings and renderings probed the necessity for enclosure as a

On the other side of the pandemic, we will need to return to making things physically as a way of testing and developing our thinking. And we will need to recapture the spontaneous sociability of studio culture. We will reestablish the viscerality of being simultaneously spatial and temporal.

fundamental question on the limits of architecture. I think this project lives in the school's folds. It could be an emergent type of condition, and we should, as educators, hone its skepticism of the discipline's boundaries. She labels her spaces—Front-Door Room, Stair Room, Head Room, and Void Room—as a way to reconceptualize typologies. This project struck me as a convergence of what I articulated earlier as the three station points, or positions, or pedagogies within RISD Architecture.

All of this makes me think about being in Marfa, Texas, perplexed by why Donald Judd liked John Chamberlain's work. Why would someone so ascetic have such an appreciation for crumpled sheet metal? Judd wrote about Chamberlain's work: it has an immediate visceral quality that enrolls the viewer in an experience. When that initial draw subsides, something deeply intellectual still sustains a longer entanglement with the work. If something lacks that immediate connectivity, the esoteric intellectual dialogue is less vibrant. But, if the project only has that quickdraw without the long tail unfurling, it evaporates quickly.

ACK **Reflecting on Judd's appreciation of Chamberlain, what is your advice for sustaining the visceral within the deadening screen world of remoteness that we currently occupy?**

JY Physical thinking has long defined the architecture studio. With the pandemic's arrival, studio culture got away from us, and I think it is waiting for us when we return to in-person classes. After finishing the semester remotely, one of my students told me, "I get done with class, I leave the meeting, and I'm all alone in my apartment." He was lamenting the loss of all the contact we have with one another in between things. On the other side of the pandemic, we will need to return to making things physically as a way of testing and developing our thinking. And we will need to recapture the spontaneous sociability of studio culture. We will reestablish the viscerality of being simultaneously spatial and temporal.

If you scroll back on Instagram to six months ago, you'll see abstract, singular, geometrically simplistic drawings. There was an argument for reducing an entire project down to one autonomous image posted as a response to too many images. But then what? I think the pandemic has unsettled this type of reductive architectural thinking, and what we will experience now is a return to the visceral, profoundly uneven, and also contextualized strangeness of building. In my Reading Architecture class this summer, one of my colleagues at the University of Tennessee at Knoxville, Scott Wall, started his lecture on Alvar Aalto's Villa Mairea by situating Finland as a nation-state. According to Scott, to understand Villa Mairea, you have to know something about Finland's history. Before the pandemic, I think we had forgotten about that type of deep contextualization because we were making images to end the making of images in architecture. The other side of this portal could offer us the chance to be robust with the plush, contingent, and indeterminate qualities of architecture that many architects have always been invested in, even as they refused to bound their discourse with them.

KC **Is architecture's trajectory a matter of recovery?**

JY I'm not trying to drag us back. Architecture is complex, and I want to get thoughtfully invested in its physical dimension. At the same time, I don't want to seem like a school administrator against those singular drawings. As an administrator, I don't want to beat someone over the head until they are more like me. That is a miscalculation. I'd rather open our thinking to the width and breadth of architecture's vitalism.

ACK **In Arundhati Roy's essay for the *Financial Times*, she frames the pandemic as a portal, and our conversation suggests the portal as a threshold to our discipline's disaggregation. How does architecture's agency navigate the contradictions inherent to a pandemic?**

JY The carrying capacity of global infrastructure is now radically on display through Zoom and the internet bandwidths that allowed everyone to pivot to virtual engagement at roughly the same time. To some extent, the way we used institutions—their spaces and resources—hid an incredible unevenness, and our exodus made hyper-visible a powerful inequity. Students were now encountering their education from the comfort (and discomfort) of their childhood bedroom. Or, they stood in a hallway for internet access. Or, at times, they were "learning" while driving a car. Temporality and the politics of accessing the virtual world became as prevalent as the institution's spatial logics. Instead of trying to shy away from unevenness, why not partner with it and look for new types of projects and new ways of working? It seems more urgent now to encourage design explorations that jump wildly between scales of engagement, multiplying the types of ambitions a designer can target in a single project. Being more accepting of incompletion and partiality might encourage more robust, diverse workflows and approaches to a project. Perhaps the pandemic is a portal toward more tolerance for the instabilities embedded in design and architecture. And through having more tolerance, maybe we can collectively see architecture as a bundle of migrations and negotiations, less so rendering design as a solution to a problem and more as a necessary correspondence with diverse issues prompting us to action, less as something experts craft through defensible arguments and more as a dialogue among variously prepared participants. I'm searching for conversations between the inequities we see so clearly during a pandemic and architecture as a dynamic cultural medium capable of reorganizing the future.

KC **Roy also describes the pandemic as a way to respond more broadly to many global issues: economic instability, class wars, xenophobia, racial injustice. If these are nodes of broad-scale injustice, clarifying our precarious position as a discipline, how can architecture schools use an administrative portal to transform their pedagogies, and as Roy puts it, "walk through lightly" into the future?**

JY The way I think about institutions is a result of my position in one. Capitalism wants me to either be a vampire or a zombie, but I don't want to be either. Administrators can look for an undisclosed third position and change institutions' cyclical behavior. As long as I'm in a central position, I will try to redefine what it means to be there and be less defensive in the power dynamic. I remain open to the fact that someone will make a run from the perimeter to the center sooner or later. This pandemic reminds us that the limits of agency are contested and temporal. Generally, you don't figure out things like curriculum once and just run with that. It should be continuously invigorated and turned over. Institutions can be very dehumanizing, but alternatively, we can build them around conversations and dialogues.

Iñaki Alday

Becoming Accountable: The Project as Thesis

I spent three years, with varying degrees of intensity, completing my thesis/final degree project: an exploration of the bullring typology and its possible future in the context of the reversal of the specialization process of architectural typologies that culminated in the nineteenth century. At the same time, my sister, Dr. Victoria Alday-Sanz, was working on her Master's thesis, studying the novel white spot virus. When I asked her why she wanted to study this virus, her answer was concise: "We are expected to make a contribution to science." My own objective was much more nebulous, and I was struck by doubt about the architectural thesis as a whole. What was its ultimate purpose? I tried to resolve this question in my own thesis and, since then, to analyze it in all those I have directed and witnessed in Barcelona, at the University of Virginia, at Tulane University, and in reviews at schools such as RISD.

In Spanish and many European schools of architecture, the thesis or final project typically combines three purposes. Inevitably and primarily, it is expected to demonstrate disciplinary competence in all technical and complementary aspects: structures, facilities, construction, materials, and, additionally today, sustainability, accessibility, or related social issues. Oftentimes, the thesis is also an opportunity to reflect on a hot topic or place of special importance or urgency. Finally, on some occasions, the thesis aspires to make some kind of contribution to the field, either through typological or technical explorations, and open an alternative path.

The thesis in American schools offers a fourth possible orientation: toward individual subjective expression. This expression takes multiple forms, from the social or philosophical comment to the "artistic" proposal, often formulated under the umbrella of "theory." Timothy Hyde, in "Turning the Black Box into a Great Gizmo," describes the first and fourth orientations—professional competence and artistic will—as the thesis's two historical limits.[1] The spring 2020 theses at RISD gave us the opportunity to analyze proposals exemplifying the four possible approaches. Least frequent was the demonstration of disciplinary competence that, in the American curricula and following the National Architectural Accrediting Board criteria, tends to be resolved in the "Integrated or Comprehensive Studio." Most if not all of the proposals approached thesis in one of the other three lines—significant site or topic, knowledge development, or individual expression—under the apparent influence of the advisors.

Katie Chizuko Solien's project (see pp. 77–80) perfectly exemplifies the fourth orientation,

1 Timothy Hyde, "Turning the Black Box into a Great Gizmo," *Thresholds*, no. 38 (Fall 2010): 80–83.

exploring a topic of intimate interest and historical, social, and political significance—the imprisonment of Japanese-American citizens during World War II—with an "artistic" resolution. The topic is pertinent—even more so at a time of deep social crisis around racial justice—and not widely known outside (or perhaps even inside) American borders. Reflecting on a tragic historical event, the thesis proposes an ephemeral memorial—a wooden structure that reproduces an original barrack and incorporates objects of daily use (clothes, footwear, kitchen utensils, etc.)—accompanied by delicate collages and drawings. One can perfectly imagine the fleeting life of this memorial, with its deterioration filmed and exhibited in a gallery, along with graphic materials, testimonies, original documents, and rescued objects. The proposal may raise doubts regarding the aestheticization and sterilization of a historical drama. It does not transmit the cold or heat of the desert, the acrid smell of sweat and fear, the hunger, the dirt, or the misery of incarceration in subhuman conditions. While graphicly exquisite, the spatial proposal also lacks a formal resolution, reproducing the banality of the barrack structure rather than aspiring to make an architectural statement or explore a typology. Solien's thesis focuses its undeniable value on artistic expression—as an articulation of a personal obsession and a historical-social commentary.

Several of the theses in Ben Pell's group share an autobiographical component, or at least the student's commitment to his or her place of origin and its critical issues that require strategic and urgent interventions. Yemo Koo (see pp. 121–124) and

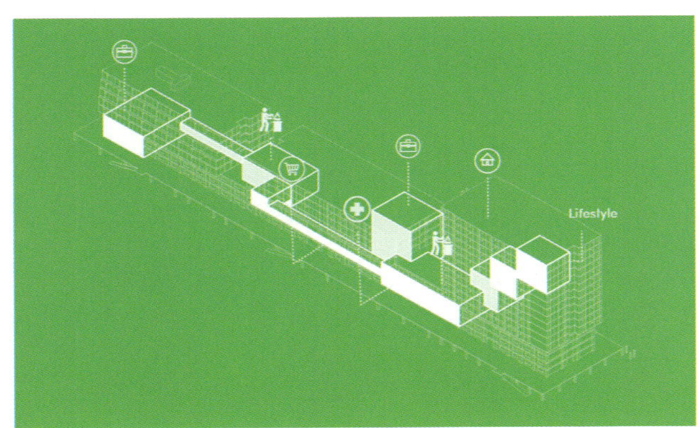

In many European schools of architecture, the thesis or final project typically combines three purposes. Inevitably and primarily, it is expected to demonstrate disciplinary competence. Oftentimes, the thesis is also an opportunity to reflect on a hot topic. Finally, on some occasions, the thesis aspires to make some kind of contribution to the field. The thesis in American schools offers a fourth possible orientation: toward individual subjective expression.

Zhan Zhang (see pp. 137–140) identify failed urban and architectural conditions with severe social impacts that are at the same time typological expressions in multiple Asian cities. The reconceptualization of macrostructures and the reenvisioning of vertical settlements for former farmers are rigorously analyzed and correctly diagnosed. The projects honor the scientific idea of a thesis—one that explores the verification of a hypothesis without guarantee of success—but aren't necessarily fully convincing as architectural proposals. As such, they merit further development, systematic review, and synthesis for application in similar cases.

The theses of Daniel Ibañez's directed research group most clearly activate the thesis as an opportunity to contribute to the fields of architecture and urban planning. Each student's involvement is total, but their topics do not spring from personal obsessions. Self-sufficient

collective housing (Anya Drozd; see pp. 31–34), new forms of collective housing (Elizabeth Parker; see

pp. 47–50), or the recovery of rural settlements in decline and depopulation (Diyi Zhang; see pp. 55–58) are urgent and thus far underrecognized topics for our discipline. In all three cases, the process of diagnosis, the formulation of the hypothesis, and the proposed architectural resolution are equivalent to the ambition of the scientific thesis in generating new knowledge.

Zhang's protean proposal, with its convincing and sophisticated formal resolution, bears the seeds of a systematic approach, easily independent of the chosen programs, which should be expanded and combined. The thesis integrates economic production strategies and the spatial recovery of existing structures, adapted to new productive programs. The problem Zhang addresses—a rural world losing population due to lack of economic opportunities—is common to several Mediterranean countries and to the whole world: The proposal's intuition to identify specific, small-scale programs (for farming and cooking, for example), while well adapted to the rural environment, would require the immediate engagement of economists and anthropologists to be calibrated and acquire the appropriate "tone." Zhang takes on the role of the architect in exploring society's problems with ingenuity and appropriateness, using design as a walking cane for the blind that helps our shortsighted societies to explore unknown and probably treacherous paths. Testing a hypothesis on the architectural integration of new programs and new structures in delicate settings with significant historical and cultural heritage, the work also passes the ultimate test of future value in the excellence of its design.

With less formal resolution, but with equal or greater graphic delicacy, Parker's proposal for a new collective housing concept goes a step further in claiming the legitimacy of the architectural thesis as a generator of knowledge, while, like any breakthrough, building on prior knowledge. Parker works explicitly on the history of a typology—the single-room occupancy (SRO) hotel—and reinterprets and projects it toward a potential future in response to contemporary social problems. The difficulty of her challenge is counterbalanced and perhaps contradicted by the seductive beauty of her graphic resources. Beyond that, the project deviates from a precise or daring resolution. However, like Drozd and Zhang, Parker identifies the insufficiently known "viruses" in contemporary society and suggests strategies to understand and "treat" them.

This is an appropriate, indeed an urgent, moment to rethink the thesis project in architecture schools in relation to the very concept of "thesis," in how architectural theses have been formulated in the history of the discipline and in the response to the demand for radical innovations in our time. First, we must acknowledge our broad oversights. Architecture has often avoided the accountability to which other fields of knowledge adhere. We struggle to formulate clear parameters on architectural and design research, often playing the victim in a way that justifies the misunderstanding of our science by universities, governments, and society in general. One could argue that our withdrawal and self-justification is a significant component of the difficulties the discipline faces in maintaining a social leadership role.

The lack of clarity about what constitutes a thesis and about the criteria for its evaluation is a specific step in the same unfortunate direction. In other fields—sciences, humanities, social sciences, etc.—the mission of the thesis is to develop specific knowledge, whether projective or retrospective, and to launch a professional career. The Spanish singer Rosalía rose to international fame in 2018 with an album that originated in her thesis in music studies. *El Mal Querer* recovers the idea of a conceptual album with twelve songs that form a unit, proposing an innovative fusion of flamenco, pop, Latin rhythms, and street culture. Hers is a hybrid street, one in Catalonia peopled by immigrants from the south of Spain and Latin America. Put another way, Rosalía transcends personal expression to make a global impact, her music resounding for millions and clearing a new path. Architectural theses might learn from her example.

Architecture, in addition to its cultural value as a reflection of the society of its time and intimation of the future, has a unique ability to engage with complexity and to visualize alternative futures. But architecture should not merely reflect the reality around us in all its complexity, conjuring up myriad conflicting interests. As Hyde proposes in his essay on the "gizmo," the thesis could distill complexity instead of creating it.[2] Indeed, the creation of complexity is, at best, an arbitrary imposition of complications and obscurities. However, applying the concept of the "gizmo" to the thesis may have a deleterious effect: it continues to position architectural practice in a world of mystery. Rather than claim that the "gizmo" reinvents the practice of architecture, I propose that the thesis be subjected to systems of evaluation and demand just like any other field of knowledge, with which, of course, architecture overlaps.

I would also propose an alternative way of setting the initial parameters of the thesis. Typically a thesis begins with a very personal choice of site, program, and issues that makes it supposedly unique and idiosyncratic from the start. While any relevant project in the history of architecture contains, explicitly or implicitly, a thesis, the programs and places of the vast majority were not chosen by the architects. The Unité d'Habitation by Le Corbusier, or the Igualada Cemetery by Miralles and Pinos, for example, were opportunities for the architects to test hypotheses cultivated over years prior to the project's inception. Miralles and Pinos did not invent an industrial area with a hidden stream in its backyard, or a funeral program. Instead, they seized an opportunity placed in an improbable, extremely banal and generic site and a program in which they had no previous expertise to propose a new way of anchoring architecture to topography and place and a new typology of Mediterranean cemetery that adds Nordic quietness to the

2 Hyde draws from Reyner Banham, "A Black Box: The Secret Profession of Architecture," in *A Critic Writes: Essays by Reyner Banham* (Berkeley: University of California Press, 1996), 673.

Today, the clear need is for architects to progress from being service providers to becoming leaders—from serving popes and kings hundreds of years ago, and corporations and developers more recently, to leading the reform of our built environment. We need new knowledge, and the thesis is where we start producing it.

dense and lively Southern cities of the dead. In her Vietnam War Memorial, Maya Lin, still a 21-year-old undergraduate, formulated a radical thesis. The monument is not only an architectural or sculptural piece; it is embedded in the ground until it becomes part of it. The meeting of the landscape—the topography, the water, the vegetation cover, the people circulating and reflecting on the wall—with the architectural abstraction, geometry, and materials responds to a thesis that reconceptualizes the idea of memorial and, more broadly, the monument. Rather than imposing and claiming its gravitas by standing out, it embraces visitors and melts into the surroundings. These contemporary examples are part of a long history of exploration, of testing and innovation, in which the great works and the great architects of history participate. Gothic cathedrals show the struggle to achieve lightness with stone (culminated by Paxton with steel). Saint Peter's Basilica in the Vatican is the result of the Platonic carving of a massive mountain of white marble that results in one of the greatest temples using the same principles that unveiled the David. These are just a few examples of advances in the field of architecture that emerged through formulating and successfully completing a thesis statement whenever the opportunity arose, even if the site or program were apparently unconducive or unlikely.

Architecture's relevance depends on our contribution to society and, specifically, on how we draw from our disciplinary knowledge to approach humanity's great and dramatic challenges. The most effective way to meet these challenges is, as always, through educating new generations, who themselves have to reformulate the mission of architecture. Today, the clear need is for architects to progress from being service providers to becoming leaders—from serving popes and kings hundreds of years ago, and corporations and developers more recently, to leading the reform of our built environment. As the culmination of this education, the thesis is the final test, not so much of professional competence but of the aspirations of each graduate to impact the world and claim an essential role for architecture. As repositories for the science of inhabitation, the new graduates have to reformulate the way we inhabit the earth. We need new knowledge, and the thesis is where we start producing it. As in any other discipline, the thesis cannot give up on examining and confronting what we know so far and, from there, generating new knowledge. Avoiding this commitment would be self-indulgent suicide. Taking it on promises a future both for our field and for our planet.

Peggy Deamer

Teaching Architecture in the Time of Covid-19

Whatever it is, coronavirus has made the mighty kneel and brought the world to a halt like nothing else could. Our minds are still racing back and forth, longing for a return to "normality," trying to stitch our future to our past and refusing to acknowledge the rupture. But the rupture exists. And in the midst of this terrible despair, it offers us a chance to rethink the doomsday machine we have built for ourselves. Nothing could be worse than a return to normality. Historically, pandemics have forced humans to break with the past and imagine their world anew. This one is no different. It is a portal, a gateway between one world and the next. We can choose to walk through it, dragging the carcasses of our prejudice and hatred, our avarice, our data banks and dead ideas, our dead rivers and smoky skies behind us. Or we can walk through lightly, with little luggage, ready to imagine another world. And ready to fight for it.
Arundhati Roy, "The Pandemic Is a Portal"[1]

Arundhati Roy's statement is so inspiring. And, as it pertains to how we teach architecture—which needs to be awakened from its self-satisfaction and increased irrelevance and move into a space of projective thinking—I so agree with it. Both the academy and the profession must change but the academy has the better chance of rethinking the definition of architecture in today's world than does insecure and compromised practice. The Covid-19 health crisis, along with the others we are currently experiencing—BLM, climate change, financial instability—insists that change in architectural pedagogy happen; we cannot let this opportunity pass by.

I reflected on this opportunity recently for a series published in *Places Journal* called "Field Notes on Pandemic Teaching."[2] *Places* asked, "How will the current adaptations inflect our understandings of studio and seminar instruction, in which the tools might be digital but the teaching is individualized and immersive, grounded in time and place, and rooted in embodied encounters that allow for serendipitous discovery?" Here is what I wrote:

The move to remote instruction may have been forced, but it is nonetheless bringing into sharp relief what has been true for years: that relevant education is not being delivered inside the academy. Students are realizing not only that their online studios and seminars are impoverished versions of their traditional courses but also that neither is enabling them to develop the skills, information, and relationships that are vital to being effective citizens. Rather they are learning about the precarity of higher education from social media, online forums, journals, and newspapers, and, within the architecture community, from online exchanges generated by journal-forums like *Archinect*, activist organizations like the Architecture Lobby and discussions like that generated by Yale School of Architecture students in their publication *Paprika*. Because students are no longer sheltering in their cloistered campuses, they are able to see how provisional, arbitrary, and temporally limited these communities are. As students increasingly organize to ask for either tuition reimbursement or representation in decisions pertinent to their expensive education, they are getting a lesson in realpolitik. As demonstrated by recent protests of Yale architecture students who are demanding that "resources

1 Arundhati Roy, "The Pandemic Is a Portal," *Financial Times*, April 3, 2020.

2 See https://placesjournal.org/article/field-notes-on-pandemic-teaching-1/, and the additional installments.

be generously allocated to those most in need and most affected by the crisis in order to ensure that our education continues in an equitable way," and also by the increasing number of graduate students and contract teachers joining unions in many universities, academia's young student-citizen-activists are finding expansive communities that offer more than their individual schools.

This is not bad news. It is the start of a new commons, one that is less precious, more relevant, and more empowering.[3]

I wrote this before being on a number of final reviews that exposed projects—many from RISD students—that were thoughtful and clearly not impoverished. They and the call for this paper led me to read all seventy-three of the *Places Journal* responses to see where my opinion sat among others and what I may have missed. While almost all acknowledged how whiplashed they, as faculty members, immediately felt by the pain of needing to learn new teaching software and then needing to give extra support to students for *their* pain, about 30 percent of the respondents were clear that even if they admitted (and many did not) that there were pleasures to teaching remotely, they were anxious to get back to in-place, embodied teaching; about 25 percent were noncommittal—they either wanted to write about other things, couldn't get past the weariness of Covid-19 altogether, or were undecided about how the pros outweighed the cons; and 45 percent, in which I put myself, embraced the new procedures, either for opportunities that came with the inevitable or with a half-exasperated, half-hopeful "*finally* ..."

The complete reading of the responses made me qualify my enthusiasm in a number of ways. I, in fact, hadn't been teaching studio during the pandemic, so I missed some of the insight that comes from the experience. I believed those who pointed out that if online learning was at all successful, it depended on the fact that prior to dispersion, students and faculty had physically met and gotten to know each other. Likewise, we need to guard against the possibility that our financially strapped and neoliberal universities will see online learning as an opportunity to cut funding for their programs in the name of economization with architecture, a notoriously expensive discipline given the spatial needs of studio and the one-on-one teaching, being particularly vulnerable. Despite these cautions, I am still hopeful that we academics are up to the task of combatting the forces of capitalism, xenophobia, and racism. The politicization of students and faculty who now see that neither the government nor our institutions have our backs is evidence of willingness to fight. Moreover, I believe that students will vote with their feet when choosing schools and that those programs that deliver a rewarding (spiritually, socially, and financially) education vs. one that is hollowed out and merely efficient, even if it means going abroad, will succeed.

The majority of contributors to the *Places* field notes expressed their love for the traditional studio context, which made me confront my own love for studio and how to balance that love with my critique of it. I now think of my love as half worthwhile and half problematic. The worthwhile part is getting to know a student and helping them establish their design voice. Both students and their designs are sources of profound pleasure. The problematic part is being so infatuated with love's affect that it precludes acknowledging the compromised systems in which studio operates. One is the false assumption of shared privilege that masks the often highly divergent backgrounds of each student. As Aaron Cayer, teaching theory at the University of New Mexico, pointed out in his contribution to the *Places* series, "the contrast that was evident on the screen—the beaming faces, the silenced voices—was underscoring the structural inequalities that already limit access

3 See Peggy Deamer, https://placesjournal.org/article/field-notes-on-pandemic-teaching-5/.

The politicization of students and faculty who now see that neither the government nor our institutions have our backs is evidence of willingness to fight.

to higher education in America"; this as some students returning to reservations couldn't find access to the internet and others drove cars looking for hot spots. "Meeting" students outside of the wholesome, homogenous space of the physical classroom and inside the tiles of Zoom, perhaps ironically, alerts us to differences that impede equal access to online education and should not remain hidden and hence unaddressed.

Another compromise is the buddy-like one-on-one teaching that masks the material power dynamics (students pay/teachers don't; students get grades/teacher give them) at play. In Italy, architectural design, in the second half of the twentieth century, was taught in an amphitheater, with students presenting their designs at the end of the semester. Students never saw their professors as their best friends. Just as Slavoj Žižek says the best gift employers can give employees is not pretending to be equals, the Italian context made clear who was and was not in control. Knowing this, the students pursued more relevant, sophisticated, and political goals than buddying up with their professors, the result being some of our more iconic, student-initiated practices—Superstudio and Archizoom. And of course, this plays into sexual politics as well. The proximity of bodies in veiled but nevertheless asymmetric power relations has always lingered in our discipline. Until our current crises, the #MeToo movement in architecture and its roots in our studio context were under investigation and their being on hold now shouldn't imply that the issue has been solved.

And finally, the prohibitively expensive education that studio participates in is no small matter. Making architecture less expensive and therefore more accessible to more people from diverse backgrounds is an essential goal. In Auckland, where I have taught at two different schools, hot desking is the norm; sharing desks not only doesn't diminish the quality of the work, it yields conversations between students about their work as they gather and encourages them to listen to each other's desk crits. Less expensive need not be less effective, and the Covid experience opens up possibilities that we previously thought were unthinkable.

Even without the context of Covid-induced pedagogy, many of the conditions that it has exposed—the inequalities; the masking of student intersectionality; the superficiality of our "normal" pedagogy in the face of multiple crises—call for change and stepping bravely into the future. As I (and others) have written elsewhere, it is crazy that our studio teaching still follows a Beaux-Arts format, especially given that that format was a response to economic demands particular to its time—emerging professionalization; a division of labor in the construction industry; a newly emerging intellectual class; new building trades associated with new construction materials.[4] Our current crises surely warrant an architectural pedagogy more appropriate to contemporary challenges.

My recommendation: have students design not objects but scenarios, while also addressing objectives that broaden the design intent. This broadening of intent would work on three axes.[5] The first, or X-axis, has the student consider those for whom the spaces are being designed and how those spaces function in producing subjectivity. The institutional powers that affect those identities would be examined. The normal student appeal to cultural/design hegemony would be replaced with concerns for social needs and desires. The various players impinging on the proposed scenario—politicians, developers, community leaders, unintended users, bankers—would be identified and queried. Architecture would be seen as a bridge between the communities we hope to serve and the spatial and institutional systems in which they reside.

The Y-axis in designing scenarios concerns the procurement and labor process. Students would consider who builds, with what materials, coming from where, and by what means. What suppliers, fabricators, and laborers are or should be set in motion? What software/apps expand access to relevant information and invite—no, insist on—collaboration? What experts from architecture, engineering, and construction industries would be invited into the studio to teach beside the architect? How are design decisions being made, in what context, under what time constraints, and for whose gain?

The Z-axis in designing scenarios describes form and visual representation. Formal thinking begins with abstraction, with intuiting the organizational diagram implicit in a given solution. For the design of a building, this means seeing the relational dance between the

4 I made this point in my keynote address at the 2019 National Journal of Architectural Education conference in Pittsburgh, PA, and in numerous papers. See as well the introduction by Tsz Yan Ng and myself to *The Journal of Architectural Education* 73, no. 2, "Work" (London: Taylor & Francis, 2019), 138–40. See also Chapter 13, "Coda," in my book *Architecture and Labor* (London: Routledge, 2020), 164.

5 The idea of these axes in scenario construction is described in a forthcoming paper, "Design Pedagogy: The New Architectural Studio and Its Consequences," in *Architecture_MPS* 18, no. 1, "Special issue: Re-Design Teaching Design," eds. Lohren Deeg, Taylor Metz, and Richard Trusky (London: University College London Press, 2020).

Even without the context of Covid-induced pedagogy, many of the conditions that it has exposed—the inequalities; the masking of student intersectionality; the superficiality of our "normal" pedagogy in the face of multiple crises—call for change and stepping bravely into the future.

spaces, elements, and walls; between plane/volume, solid/void, big/small, twisted/straight, repetitious/distinct; between structure and surface and surface in ornamentation. For the design of a scenario, however, abstraction means intuiting the organizational framework by which to calculate a scenario's unfolding over time. So, the student might ask: Change in use motivated by what contingency? Change in notions of "the public" determined by what forces? Change in climate caused by what actions? Change in a transformation of a type caused by what social reconfiguration? Change in aesthetics resulting from what new digital technology or structural technique? This type of design doesn't preclude traditional design—places are still being envisioned—but it emphasizes modes of representation that go beyond shape and material disposition. Charts, maps, and diagrams, numerical data, and literary narrative must be woven into a primarily visual form of communication.

There is no clear link between my suggestion of changed pedagogical content and a changed out-of-studio location. But the broadened scope of content does imply connecting with people, data, expertise, and communities that sit outside the confines of a given architecture school. It suggests that if one is addressing problems in the world, there are advantages to going out into the world. And so I think about, in the RISD thesis context, Zachary Schumacher's

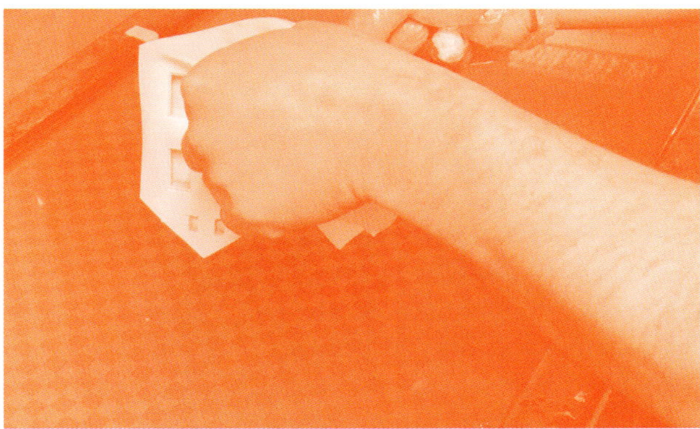

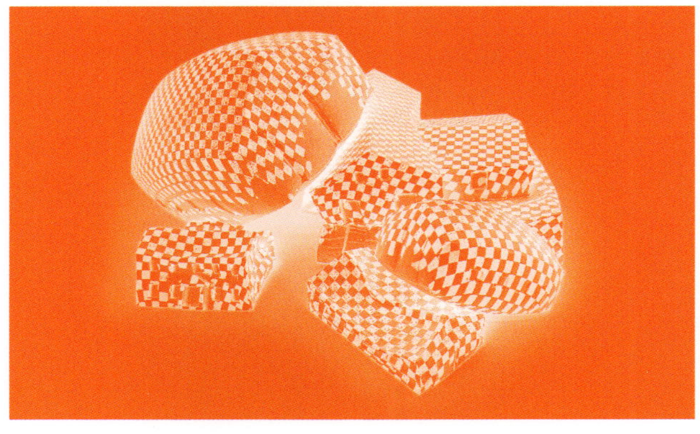

Digital Duck (see pp. 215–218), which explores the implications of applying a pattern/texture on a real object through hydro-dipping and which took advantage of his homebound, out of classroom situation to explore more than "design." Schumacher's query is not overtly political, but his probes into the implications of hydro-dipping—a process used to physically transfer an image onto an object, like the face of Jerry Garcia on a car door—throws into question the (false) realism, used commonly in architectural rendering, of digitally applying a texture onto a digital model and thereby the status of both objects and their surfaces. His video of a water bath with a viscous, thin, green-and-white pattern floating on its surface that gets transferred onto a funkily shaped white thing when dipped into the bath leads Schumacher to consider what, in the process and the result, is "literal" and what is "real." Partly a critique of applying simulacra of textures onto digital models to make them look "real" (a critique many of us on the review supported) and partly a promotion of the hydro-dipping technique to further advance the tensions façades play *with* and *as* a surface (also taken seriously by some critics, with a warning against techno-adulation), the project recognizes that one way or another, a thorn has been placed in the side of architectural representation and objecthood.

As a presentation, the cool-looking process revealed in the hydro-dipping video would not perhaps be so innovative if it weren't placed in a larger context of images and models exploring how 2D and 3D architectural digital operations get entangled in our digitally produced architectural images and objects. The final presentation then was a kind of additive time lapse of Schumacher's queries about the various ways we architects present reality to ourselves. A realtor's sixteen photos of his parents' house (where I assume he stayed during lockdown) is the basis of the seamed-together model that he hydro-dipped; the car shop owner who performed the hydro-dip was in his neighborhood; the lockdown made Schumacher's and the hydro-dipper's interactions its own kind of temporal dance. Schumacher may or may not have been aware of the theoretical traditions this query evoked—for me, Gottfried Semper's technique-based narrative of the origins of architecture that privileges planes/enclosure over space and structure; John Ruskin's plea that the designer not wholly control the process; and Colin Rowe's and Robert Slutzky's "Transparency: Literal and Phenomenal," but he clearly was aware that his exploration posed a problem for our normal narratives that divide designer from maker, architectural control from real-world arbitrariness, intended meaning from received impression. All in all, I can't help but wonder if the crisis of producing a "meaningful" thesis in these horrible times didn't affect choosing a theme that struck at the heart of our disciplinary tropes.

Whatever one feels about the pros or cons of Covid-induced architectural education, it is impossible to divorce this disruption from the larger economic and political context in which it operates. Indeed, how we teach architecture feels trifling in this new world of totalitarianism, economic inequality, disease, and global warming. Society and our planet need entirely different political and economic practices to ensure that we as a species survive and architecture matters at all. The real question for us architectural educators is how we ourselves understand the relationship between our architectural acts and the larger, deeply problematic context in which they operate. It is understandable that many feel that architecture can't and therefore shouldn't try to engage in this larger context. But I would suggest that we have the obligation to make the connection between our acts and the world order, not to change it but to prove our stake in an adjusted outcome. If we are not at least addressing the question of how architecture is produced and consumed in our current world and imagining relevant scenarios, we should not complain that all we are asked to do is decorate private developers' detritus.

Kevin Crouse & Jacqueline Shaw

Pastness: A Conversation with Dr. Mabel O. Wilson

On July 31, 2020, Jacqueline Shaw and I found Mabel Wilson, architect, designer, and professor at Columbia University's Graduate School of Architecture, Planning, and Preservation, on Zoom right after she participated in a panel discussion at the Society of Architectural Historians for the new book she coedited, *Race and Modern Architecture*. Mabel unearths the layers of displaced history in modern architectural discourse, and in our conversation reminded us that everyday usage, not architects, creates the value of architecture. **KC**

Kevin Crouse **In discussing Brittany Knowlton's thesis (see pp. 103–106), sited in Chicago, you noted the city's**

nineteenth-century Haymarket Riot alongside Theaster Gates's contemporary projects as a model for how to engage the community. In reviewing Sophie Weston Chien's

project (see pp. 199–202), you pointed to the tension between governance, ecology, and community. Within your current work, research, and teaching practice, which techniques and methodologies have most successfully revealed the discipline's complicit and complex entanglements?

Mabel O. Wilson When you encounter site, you automatically encounter history. As an architect, your intervention must navigate, negotiate, and take into account the context of existing materiality, dimension, structural condition, or community. Chicago has a complex history: precolonial indigenous history; histories of settlements; histories of migrations of people; technological histories (railroads and stockyards); economic histories; political histories with the Haymarket Riot; histories of segregation. And these layered histories are clearly reflected in the built environment. Theaster Gates, who lives and works in a community on the South Side of Chicago, engages these local architectural histories. He gives potent lessons in realized transformative interventions, revealing how one builds cultural institutions and resuscitates housing through material choices and ways of building. He works with found materials, which themselves have histories.

KC **What is the role of built form in relation to these histories over time?**

MW Buildings have afterlives. How the building transforms over time is out of the architect's purview. In the end, the built form always adapts to the protocols and habits of occupation; buildings are never static.

Jacqueline Shaw **How do you encourage students to recognize their power and take ownership of disciplinary consequences?**

MW Students need to recognize the inequality of who and what actualize buildings. Just as in professional practice, students' proposed drawings are rarely built. When something is built, though, you realize architecture's impact on people and our lives. We're now at the thirtieth anniversary of the Americans with Disabilities Act (ADA), which shows how much the environment presupposes non-disabled people. People with disabilities had been and continue to be neglected. The ADA asserted their right to be recognized and accommodated within the built environment. Yesterday I saw images of the Hajj, the Islamic pilgrimage to Mecca. During the pandemic, the Hajj has marked a series of concentric rings in color so people will move in a choreographed way. It demonstrates the power of borders and boundaries to define how people occupy space. There's no question about it: space dictates how people should move. Architecture has an incredible ability to do this, no matter our bodily type, especially in novel situations.

JS **Several theses directly enact the adage "the personal is political," moving freely between multiple scales, engaging students' personal identities while situating their work in cultural, historical, and ecological frameworks. The expanded reality of this work requires alternative forms of scholarship and representation—an attempt to capture complex narratives. Alexa Thorne's work (see pp. 81–84) transformed the site diagram by rendering it**

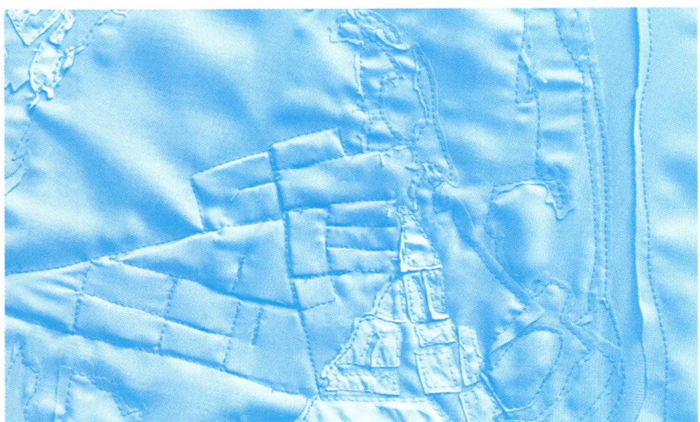

For all its attempts, architecture cannot claim universal truths. Universal Diagrams typically use white, able-bodied figures, which supposedly signify every human, but in actuality they were highly specific people. The discourse is saying *every*, but the reality is far more varied. These discrepancies are essential to understand in order to insert other types of bodies, experiences, or narratives.

in embroidery, embedding gendered layers and a familial history into her work's representational techniques. Katie Chizuko Solien (see pp. 77–80) rebuilt 1:1 structures to

directly confront the historical carceral experience of a Japanese-American concentration camp barrack. As the poet Audre Lorde has written, "the master's tools will never dismantle the master's house." Where do identity and the personal fit within projects of dismantling, uncovering, and situating work for public interest? Do we need new representational forms to express identity?

MW Architecture is a body of knowledge just as it is a set of practices; it's a discourse, discipline, and profession. For all its attempts, architecture cannot claim universal truths. Ernst Neufert's universal diagrams typically use white, able-bodied figures, which supposedly signify every human, but in actuality they were highly specific people. The discourse is saying *every*, but the reality is far more varied. These discrepancies are essential to understand in order to insert other types of bodies, experiences, or narratives. The master narrative of architecture—using Lorde's terminology—defines the rules of the discipline, and understanding the limits allows you to test them. A phrase like *the public* is another universal in architecture presumed to represent everyone, but it does not; the public typically means citizen, but what about undocumented workers? They are not citizens, so they are not part of the public. And expanding the public into public space ignores its political dimension, which is the public sphere—*polis*—or the space of politics. We are profoundly unequal, and we must recognize those inequalities.

The competition for transforming Monument Avenue in Richmond, Virginia, is fascinating. Those monuments, made of granite and bronze, were meant to be permanent. They privilege a dominant narrative of who gets to be visible in the city. The sense that these monuments should be preserved for "heritage" privileges the notion that one history can speak for everyone. Yet this is a mythology rooted in the "Lost Cause" of the Confederacy, and it is wholly antithetical to American values. When Monument Avenue's transformation turned to tagging, projection, and performance, the space was reoccupied in an architectural act that changed the public sphere.

Counter to that is Simone Leigh's *Brick House*, a huge ceramic construction on the spur of the High Line near Hudson Yards, and an unusual expression of Black female beauty unrecognized in Manhattan. For American and Confederate monuments, the masters are Thomas Jefferson and Stonewall Jackson, and the tools of power are precisely the granite and bronze. In the context of Hudson Yards, it's the glass curtain wall and steel as contemporary expressions of power, domination, and wealth. Through materiality and form, Leigh references spaces for Black bodies to counter the language of power in a city where high rises are made for parking wealth. She is not dismantling; she is adding another narrative and expression into New York's growing homogeneity.

JS **A thread found in many student projects was the responsibility and relevancy of architecture to question, push against, and depend upon history. In his thesis, Patrick Spence (see pp. 125–128) argues**

for thoroughness, pushing for an "unbiased story" of Market House and Market Square in Providence. He

proposes a bridge, echoing the old slave market's formal strategy, to foreground the site's racist history, which is currently masked. **Bobby Zhao (see pp. 111–114)** **explored**

monumentality of the ground plane, pointing to the immediate outdatedness of the Hive in Hudson Yards. In both projects, we see projected futures of obsolete monuments. How do we incorporate the endless newsfeed—the accelerated and ever-present historical shift—into constructing a narrative to engage deeply rooted histories?

MW Both Patrick Spence and Bobby Zhao took on different but equally loaded sites. Patrick's work with the Market House deals with its slaver's past and its siting as a divide between East and West Providence. For Bobby, Hudson Yards has a history of its own making. I think both fit within a lineage laid out by Michel-Rolph Trouillot in *Silencing the Past*. The production of history and its reliance on a particular set of protocols displays the relationship between the historical event and producing the historical narrative—a process of recall and return. All of that goes into history, which is also to say that history is not neutral. History, just like architecture, is a power relation. The formation of history in the West was dependent upon a determination of who was being rendered ahistorical. Someone like Hegel would say that Africans have no history; they live in the moment. He looked at narratives, journals, diaries; he's looking secondhand at firsthand accounts to formulate a theory of European progress in history, or Europe as the center of history and as leading civilization forward, the nexus of modern culture, which is racialized as white and classed. History has a history in and of itself and is not neutral in any way.

Hudson Yards's history within New York has a historical lineage that produces a certain kind of urbanism that is part and parcel of a modern city. Its history reveals that New York is no longer an industrial city, but has become a global city (using Saskia Sassen's term) over the last twenty years. Hudson Yards is a perfect example of how global finance, leisure, and the consumption of art and culture image a city. Bobby's contemporary plan is trying to understand and intervene in that. In the same way, Patrick's project on Market House embodies the layered histories through its multiple uses and physical change over time. It takes a certain understanding of history in the city—in this case, Providence—and operates on it through a different dimensionality of the historical narrative in time and space.

KC **Is it the task of the architect to choose which history to tell?**

MW In siting history, architects are hardly ever conscientious. For instance, indigenous histories are problematic because they are often represented through a colonial perspective. When offered a monument, some indigenous communities answer, "No, that's not how we engage the past; our *land* is how we understand pastness." But their land is now someone's private property. That's a very different type of lens to understand pastness. It assumes that history is linear and periodized, but we need to recognize the presence of multiple histories and, further, replace history with pastness. Ways of engaging pastness are diverse. History is a Western concept of pastness, the same way architecture is a Western concept of building.

JS **For many people of color, their familial history stops abruptly due to slavery. It is a particular type of censorship.**

MW Trouillot calls it the silence of the archive. There are some people whose histories are archival and archived, and there are a lot of people whose histories are not. In Europe, even if you were poor but white, there was a church record somewhere someone kept. Eventually, that became the state record books. For people of color, though, birth and death records were overlooked for hundreds of years.

When offered a monument, some indigenous communities answer, "No, that's not how we engage the past; our land is how we understand pastness." But their land is now someone's private property. That's a very different type of lens to understand pastness. It assumes that history is linear and periodized, but we need to recognize the presence of multiple histories and, further, replace history with pastness.

KC **We are in a literal pandemic. As Arundhati Roy describes in her essay for the *Financial Times*, the pandemic is a portal that responds to many global issues—economic instability, class wars, xenophobia, and racial injustice among them. If these are nodes in an infrastructure of broad-scale injustice, clarifying our precarious position as a discipline, how can architecture schools use an pastness portal to transform their pedagogies and, as Roy puts it, "walk through lightly" into the future?**

MW Global issues of economic instability, class war, xenophobia, and racial injustices are all historically produced. The pandemic is opportunistic; it will infect whoever is vulnerable. If you're going to attack racial injustice now, you must understand its historical origins. In my fall studio, we looked at an in-depth history of eighteenth- and nineteenth-century slavery in Manhattan up to the recent history of protesting gentrification, ranging from the Cross Bronx Expressway to the Tompkins Square Riots to Seneca Village. The areas of New York City that had very high infection rates, when overlaid with redlining maps, neatly fit around areas graded D. These are all areas densely populated with immigrant communities, in which the value of property was going down. These areas deal with the stressors of racism (which make you vulnerable to infection); they are historically overcrowded, and working-class folks cannot work at home. Histories produce these conditions of vulnerability in the built environment, and it is critical to recognize them as legacies of colonialism, imperialism, deep resource extraction, and labor exploitation. The redlining map devalues other people's lives and makes them vulnerable to things like the novel coronavirus. They have no choice. It's destructive: it destroys lives, places, and environment. And so, I think to walk lightly means to change that footprint, to extract less value, kill fewer people, and hurt the environment less. And I think that's worth learning in architecture school today.

Kiel Moe

The Difficult Whole Is Full of Difficult Holes

An architecture of complexity and accommodation does not forsake the whole. In fact, I have referred to a special obligation toward the whole because the whole is difficult to achieve. ... It is the difficult unity through inclusion rather than the easy unity through exclusion.
Robert Venturi, "The Difficult Whole"[1]

As positioned by Robert Venturi a half-century ago, an architecture of the "difficult whole" is a nonreductive, complex architecture, one based on "difficult unity through inclusion." However, at this stage in global history we can recognize that extremely palpable, contemporaneous social and environmental content was overtly excluded and externalized from Venturi's genre of architecture. Contrary to its own claims on inclusion and totality, this architecture—as well as that of Venturi's peers and acolytes in and out of the academy who would narrowly circumscribe architecture in similarly retrospective Anglo-European terms—openly forsook the looming, potent complexities of social, political, and environmental questions that characterized the 1960s. Venturi's "soft manifesto" was anything but indirectly polemical. It was a wildly successful and perhaps clever, if not cynical, rhetorical maneuver for Venturi to promote an articulate, but very constricted, exclusionary model of architecture through a language of complexity and inclusion. Today we can see the influence this willfully narrow view of a "difficult" whole had on pedagogical positions more generally in the ensuing decades of architectural education. This influence can still be felt in so many inward-looking, self-absorbed approaches to architecture that, even now, continue to appear and enjoy inexplicable attention, despite the voracious contradictions inherent to building in the late phases of capital and its hydrocarbon basis.

Venturi's antecedents in prior paradigmatic statements on architecture—from that of, say, Vitruvius through Alberti and to Semper—all posited in each their way a much more cosmopolitan and terrestrial account of architecture that overtly engaged its irrefutable social and environmental content. While Venturi stated that he was for "vitality as well as validity," he clearly eschewed ecological vitality and social validity. This is apparent not only in Venturi's neglect of such issues, but in the position of the book's sanctioning institution, The Museum of Modern Art. Although he claimed he was interested in the "richness and ambiguity of modern experience," there is no ambiguity that the book was intended to serve a rich and unambiguously elite audience. The March 13, 1967, MoMA press release announcing the publication of *Complexity and Contradiction in Architecture* claimed Venturi's "view that the complexity and contradiction in a technologically changing society are elements that the architect should embrace and utilize, rather than reject or try to alter." This advocacy of embracing, rather than critiquing or subversively

1 Robert Venturi, *Complexity and Contradiction in Architecture* (New York: The Museum of Modern Art Papers on Architecture, 1966), 88.

Decades of loyal architects and pedagogues forsook the possibilities of what architecture could be and do in this world as architecture utterly capitulated to a burgeoning neoliberal political economy model based on ethically inchoate, unequal ecological and social exchanges.

altering, the burgeoning technics of that era signaled a consequential withdrawal from the environmental and social potential of that transformative decade. We live and work in the architectural aftermath of that refusal to work on the difficult whole of terrestrial architecture: decades of loyal architects and pedagogues forsook the possibilities of what architecture could be and do in this world as architecture utterly capitulated to a burgeoning neoliberal political economic model based on ethically inchoate, unequal ecological and social exchanges.

By distorting and externalizing the totality of what architecture is and does, in other words, Venturi's "Difficult Whole" was in fact full of difficult holes: disciplinary blind spots, both overtly intentional and ambivalently unintentional, that today are impossible to ignore except in the most abjectly regressive and ethically destitute visions of the project of architecture in this century. On the threshold of other visions of the world, it is worthwhile to reflect on the difficult holes that architects have excluded in their attempts at putative virtuosity. These difficult holes are, themselves, portals not into other worlds, but rather portals back into the readily apparent contingencies and urgencies of our world. Looking forward, a more nuanced—and indeed a more complex—relation between virtue and virtuosity is at stake as architecture becomes a more terrestrial endeavor in the years and decades ahead.[2] For example, today a beautiful architectural object with an utterly vulgar program of unequal labor and extraction is nonetheless a vulgar architectural project.

Architecture can no longer escape its blind spots and difficult holes. In pedagogy and practice, the aesthetics of architecture in a context of global climate change, persistent racism, pandemics, and ever-vertiginous economic disparities will accordingly evolve beyond the capitulating fetishization of architectural objects—and thus inversely the sublimation of far-flung people and places—and instead begin to design more sane and just relations among the terrestrial realities of life. Once architects finally take the terrestrial reach of architecture seriously, then the immense difficult holes of architecture's actual difficult whole of more ecologically sane and socially just design suddenly becomes central to the discipline. To be clear, what I have in mind is not the criminal ecological failures, and neoliberal success, of "sustainability" and its forms of exceptionalism, or how "resilience" fails to prepare us socially and practically for adapting to the next states of this planet. Rather, deeper and perhaps less familiar discourses and methods enter—or in some cases reenter—the discipline and help *redescribe* what architecture is and does, and moreover what it could do, in this century.

Instances of this redescription of disciplinary assumptions and methods thus provided, for me, the bright spots among the projects reviewed in RISD Architecture

2 Today, we have begun to see sharp critiques of these blind spots, though largely from outside of architecture in the work of, for instance, urban theorist Neil Brenner and landscape architect Jane Hutton.

students' 2020 final projects. In particular, I noted: engagements with rurality; an ethics of care and repair; the energetics and material culture of building as a planetary activity; and finally redescriptions of architecture's media, as the following examples will begin to suggest.

Zi Ye (whose project *Externalized Dwelling: Living and Working in Rural China in the Age of Internet Plus* is not featured in this book) considers rural Chinese life as the source of a material, structural, and spatial composition, critiquing the dynamics of "underdevelopment," in which hinterland zones lose population to late capital's centers of agglomerated development. In contrast, Ye's project shifts modes of production so that the periphery now feeds off the core of urbanization. Amplifying rurality through design is one example of a compelling shift toward a more nuanced relation between virtue and virtuosity. Though it retreats into a genre of familiar scenographic regionalism in certain instances, it is clear that the designer is engaged in rurality relationships beyond the architectural object itself. This project points to a future wherein the métier of architecture is not bound to developer-driven exchanges focused on urban agglomerations, but rather architecting key relationships of material culture and shifting labor conditions in rural contexts.

As the social, ecological, and most recently, virological stability of our inherited world breaks apart daily, the recent model of an architecture based on stability starts to break apart as well. An alternative model for architecture in the coming decades might thus involve what computer scientist Steven J. Jackson calls "broken world thinking": "what happens when we take erosion, breakdown, and decay, rather than novelty, growth, and progress, as our starting points?" For Jackson, what ensues is "an appreciation of the real limits and fragility of the worlds we inhabit—natural, social, and technological—and a recognition that many of the stories and orders of modernity (or whatever else we choose to call the past two-hundred-odd years of Euro-centered human history) are in the process of coming apart, perhaps to be replaced by new and better stories and orders, but perhaps not."[3] Design follows, and produces, a different set of orders in broken world thinking. An alternative model emerges, in part, from practices of care and repair.

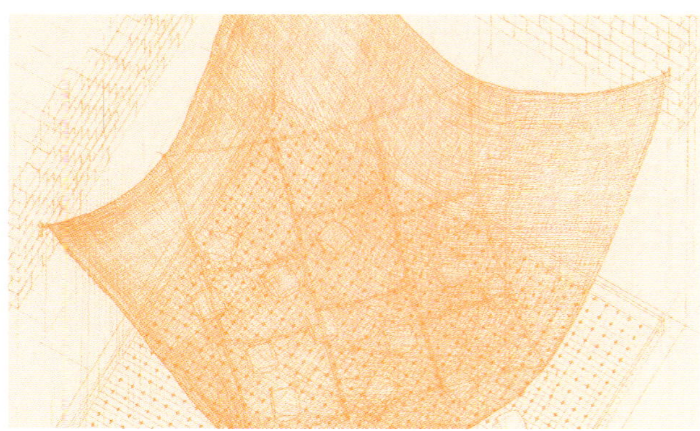

In Sina Erol's project (see pp. 143–146), an ethic of care and repair guides design methods and decisions. Erol's meticulous documentation of site—both hand drafted and drawn at a very large scale—is emblematic of a genre of design care that makes the actual intervention interdependent with the matrix within it is projected. If, for instance, a contemporary architect finds it impossible to draw the irregularities of a rock—that is, to make an electro-numeric simulation of a rock—with the regularizing suite of current software and their smoothing algorithms, here the method of actual drawing through the systematic distribution of graphite on paper, enables and literally draws attention to the irregularities of actual conditions rather than smoothing them over. The intense but convivial documentation of a place through the labor of large-format drawings affords the designer something that more regularizing and normalizing design techniques could not. Once carefully documented, what is necessary in the difficult whole of such a place might indeed demand very little

3 Steven J. Jackson, "Rethinking Repair," in *Media Technologies: Essays on Communication, Materiality, and Society*, eds. Tarleton Gillespie, Pablo J. Boczkowski, and Kirsten A. Foot (Cambridge MA: MIT Press, 2014), 221.

design in any conventional sense of that verb. This outcome is itself the intended product of a larger vision of design: that of designing the way one works, and designing what is documented as already itself a potent design position and endeavor. A compelling relationship between virtue and virtuosity is evident, refreshingly tacit, in the methods of this project. This is a major lesson for emerging designers.

A project that took aim at one of architecture's deepest, most difficult holes was Yangchuan (Niko) Tian's speculations (see pp. 51–54)

about the adaptive reuse of hydrocarbon modernity's perhaps most symbolic infrastructure: a petroleum extraction platform rig in the Gulf of Mexico. The intense research and documentation of this project's contexts and imagined futures compellingly extends the project of architecture into multiple simultaneous spatial and temporal realms, positioning architecture much closer to its actual difficult whole of simultaneous ecological, social, and political realities. Tian's design attempts to internalize and symbolize the metabolic rifts and shifts monumentalized in the project's site. The project of architecture thusly is redescribed, no longer hocking spectacular, cynical objects and renderings for developers or municipalities but rather literally designing the aftermath of hydrocarbon modernity and optimistically inverting the futures of modernity's abundant failures and externalizations. The project's mixture of research, documentation, design, and speculation frames rich redescription of what architecture might be, what it takes as its possible contexts, and what it could accordingly do in this century.

Though perhaps less overtly engaged in social, political, and ecological realities of

In the present context of the interconnected concerns and outright rage about architecture's racist history and tendencies, its persistent climate change denials, and cynical servitude to neoliberal development, questioning fundamental disciplinary assumptions and routines has never been more vivid and absolutely necessary.

contemporary architecture and its terrestrial contingencies, one other project merits discussion in terms of redescribing the discipline. While Zachary Schumacher's project (see pp. 215–218)

covered some familiar ground regarding recent techniques of representation in architecture, the presentation of that representational content was one of the most well-suited to the new abnormal of remotely reviewed and discussed design projects. His scrolling website felt like an ideal and highly accessible format for this genre of review, and for his project in particular. It is, as such, a redescription of some of the most staid and counterproductive assumptions of architectural education—in particular the way that architectural education suddenly adopts a juridical metaphor to present and review work that was paradoxically developed through alternately quasi-artistic and quasi-scientific modalities. Schumacher's format and media evaded many of the assumptions and tropes of those metaphors and modalities in favor of a fluid and clear explication of a project that seemed to perfectly suit the known manner in which his audience would engage his project. The loose, scrolling format lent a playful but cogent mode of engagement with the project thesis, its content, and its outcomes. There was a refreshing ease with which the architecture was presented. The ability to move image and objects around forced an interactive engagement with the project content not possible in most other review formats. It made compelling work even more compelling. Few projects, at RISD or beyond, acknowledged the fundamental shift in mode in engagement and feedback triggered by sudden remote learning, production, and critique. This basic cognitive act alone merits design recognition.

There are as many permutations of "thesis" programs as there are schools of architecture. The most engaging of those programs—and the projects its students and faculty collectively cultivate—are those that question basic disciplinary assumptions and routines. In the present context of the interconnected concerns and outright rage about architecture's racist history and tendencies, its persistent climate change denials, and cynical servitude to neoliberal development, the importance of questioning fundamental disciplinary assumptions and routines has never been more vivid and absolutely necessary. The most resonant projects in this cohort of final projects identified dormant assumptions, researched and developed alternatives through at times novel methods, and designed astute responses that are remarkable for how their often ambitious modesty transmits important queries about the status of the project of architecture in this century.

The lives, work, and faces of present and future architecture students will increasingly look unlike that which shaped the lives and careers of current school of architecture faculty and design firm principals. While prior generations of architects and academics actively excluded important topics, concerns, places, and people from architecture, future citizen architects warrant fresh frameworks with which to develop novel practices that better suit this century. The best projects in this volume offer probes into these disciplinary holes and corresponding insights for a much more generous and inclusive vision of the difficult whole of architecture and its terrestrial potential. They redescribe what architecture is and can do.

Ana Miljacki

Future-Catching in Our Times

See p. 207

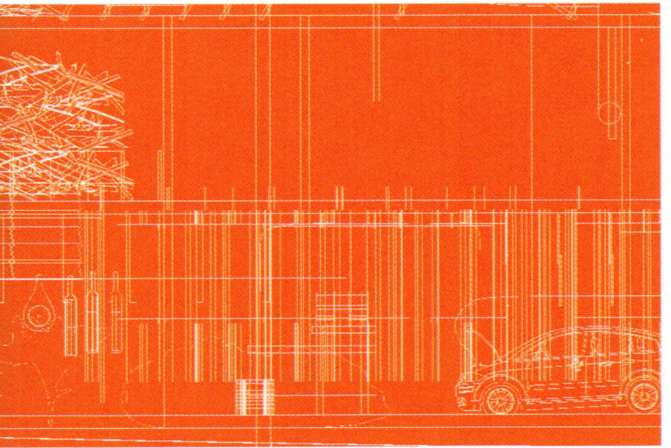

Somewhere north, in a hilly landscape, wooded, lush, and now warming beyond anything in living memory, a community of walkers with aptitudes for mechanical things has begun to put together a constellation of new, house-scaled, collective tools. Repurposing the leftovers they have collected along the way and starting from scratch, they are settling down with new resolve, guarded optimism, patience for mistakes. They will have to reinvent all social relations and some architecture, initiate regional exchanges of goods and knowledge and maybe new forms of governance. Stories of the old ways still circulate among them as cautionary tales, and luckily some know how to make use of them.

Cut. New scene.

Caretakers of the excavation roam it slowly in the hot midday sun. They measure, draw, and redraw plans, three-dimensional records, sketches. They keep meticulous diaries. They live in a three-dimensional, archeological puzzle. As they are putting its pieces together, they discern, theorize, and project—by hand—what it was and what it could be. The blue Mediterranean sky reflects off the polished concrete floors of their living and lived-in museum. The year: could be now, could be two hundred years ago, or maybe it's just after electricity went out the last time in all of Balkans and the Middle East.

See p. 69

See p. 143

Cut. New scene.

Off the coast of Rhode Island, just down the street from the big, lavish houses that tell their own stories on kids' audio guides, is a new installation of measuring devices. They bob, ebb, and flow with the sea, melt into the landscape, becoming part of it, just like the fishing pier or the old changing rooms on the beach once did. Every day, their caretakers read out the measurements, make small repairs, collect wandering buoys that got caught in the grid in the storm the night before. They know the sea has gotten less predictable lately. Everyone here knows, just by glancing at the installation.

Cut. New scene.

In this new Library of Babel everything is now an immersive story. The space twists, pans, unfurls, and dollies, with mysterious wall devices activating portals into other stories. Visitors stitch the pieces of the library, of stories, together in acts now known as revisions. Perhaps we all wear goggles to see this architecture and to see each other in it. This is where we gather now, each beaming in from our own stationary spot,

See p. 211

See p. 89

from our respective sofas and chaise lounges. We meet to experience hyper architecture and our collective making of it. My favorite story to revision collectively is the one about revisioning an old piece of architecture, which once, in the olden times, played with physical and pictorial puns. It gives us so much to work with.

Cut. New scene.

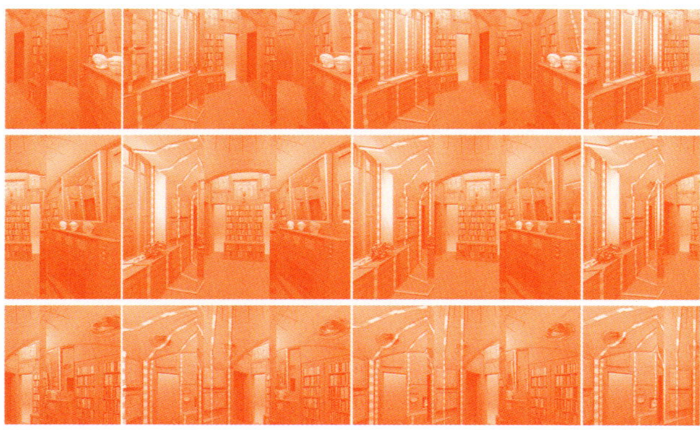

At some point someone managed to build an architectural loophole into the drab uniformity of rapidly built housing. Tall, dense housing stretches as far as the human eye can see, and probably as far as the new battery charge will take the medium-range surveillance drone. But when there is a gap, a space left open for imagination and life in that gray mass, life finds it, and fills it, and often with joy. And things go from there, the way a single ice crystal can catalyze a reaction in supercooled water. If one plants enough of these pauses, spaces that invite human agency, a whole reality might unravel, and go not-as-planned. An architect came up with that loophole.

The worlds I've sketched here—and so many others imagined in final architecture thesis projects—are whispers from the future, "barely audible messages from a future that may never come into being."[1] Thinking of them this way makes the architecture students (especially in their final year of school) the invaluable "catchers," articulators of messages from the future. But what use do these messages, or any aesthetic works set on articulating future prospects, have? Jameson cautions that utopian and sci-fi texts are delimited by the imaginations that created them. Following this line of reasoning, we might glean that the scenes above and students' work are not an image of the future, or of utopia, but rather evidence of the impossibility of imagining it, or of one age's limits in thinking it.

Jameson, however, found his own point enough of a downer to attempt to reorient it a

1 Fredric Jameson, "The Politics of Utopia," *New Left Review* 25 (January/February 2004): 54.

The temporal and ethical orientations materialized in architectural thoughts of various types, and in different media, are, by definition, both prospective and, in line with our historical moment, only precariously hopeful.

This is not the optimism of modernism, the optimism of an era that did not worry about losing the prospect of its future. We and our future catchers don't have the luxury of that kind of stable image or stable concept of the future.

bit, at the last minute. In the final paragraph of his essay, he quotes from Marge Piercy's sci-fi novel *Woman on the Edge of Time*, words uttered by a future farmer, a visitor from a (utopian) twenty-second-century village in Massachusetts called Mattapoisett.[2] The main character, Connie, living in the twentieth-century present, is a kind of "catcher," open to "sendings" from the future. She is surprised to find out from the future farmer that the future she was "sent" is in danger, that its members are reaching out to her because they are afraid. One of them tells Connie: "You may fail us … You individually may fail to understand us or to struggle in your own life and time. You of your time may fail to struggle altogether … We must fight to come to exist, to remain in existence, to be the future that happens. That's why we reached you."[3]

Thesis work shares something of the possible-yet-not-inevitable status of the Mattapoisett "sendings," of the fragile and properly utopian—just, equitable, conscious of resources and other species—futures they represent. The temporal and ethical orientations materialized in architectural thoughts of various types, and in different media, are, by definition, both prospective and, in line with our historical moment, only precariously hopeful. The whisper of the future that vibrates through the student work is a gift. It is a confirmation of and a return on the trust required for learning and teaching. On one end, learners must trust that all the teaching is in good faith. On the other, teachers can only embrace the future by trusting their students with it. That contract enables generation after generation to push the boundaries of the discipline, as well as break the walls within it. An architecture school then, prepares students not only to harness uncertainty toward accomplishing urgent tasks ingeniously, but also to sidestep expectations and think up new ones. And it does so by transmitting measurable skills and expertise, allowing room for the impractical, the improvised, and the sideways, inviting critique of its own ways, and with trust as a precondition for it all.

Now, if the post-apocalyptic collective machines, living and breathing museums, climate-measuring infrastructures, and hacked housing in urban villages in China are whispers of futures, all produced in our historical moment (regardless of the distance from which they were sent), Jameson's limit test might invite the student work to express something important about our own moment. Not singularly, not authoritatively (keep in mind the "whisper" of the future as a special type of presence), but still, if we read them together across a cycle of final projects or multiple cycles, or final projects across an entire landscape of schools, we might be able to discern the limitations they tend to highlight collectively.[4] This in turn might allow us to characterize better the

2 See Marge Piercy, *Woman on the Edge of Time* (New York: Penguin Random House, 1979). In this complex and difficult novel, the narrator is a poor, incarcerated woman of Mexican origin, Consuela, or Connie. She taps into a twenty-second-century reality, in which cities have been abandoned, the population is completely racially mixed, children are mothered by three "mothers" of any gender, and all are birthed from a tube. Everyone works at producing food, does what they are good at, and learns by finding people to study with.

3 Piercy, 213.

4 On and off, but mostly on, over the last decade I have directed the M.Arch thesis at MIT and have been lucky to participate in thesis reviews at architecture schools around the U.S. and in Hong Kong. There is nothing quite like that enchanted circuit to get a sense of the general mood shifting.

precarious optimism that the student works have granted us access to. This is not the optimism of modernism, the optimism of an era that did not worry about losing the prospect of its future. We and our future catchers don't have the luxury of that kind of stable image or stable concept of the future. Everything coming our way is tenuous like that future Mattapoisett.

Not so long ago Timothy Morton described climate crisis (one of the things directly threatening our future) as a hyperobject.[5] He described a hyperobject, in turn, as a kind of coherence so complex, so far beyond any single human life, that it is hard to see and comprehend from the vantage point of that life and its temporality. The climate crisis hyperobject is made up of an immeasurable number of small-scale, daily, individual acts, of both social and political agency as well as of so far unthinkable geological agency of us, humans. The capitalocene we inhabit is populated by many more hyperobjects (think: the patriarchy, white supremacy). In the case of each hyperobject, the daily lives of humans are deeply implicated and eventually cohere into a thing, on a plane far, far away—away from private failures to recycle, from the exhaust generated by the family car, from a group's routine tolerance of a mansplainer in its midst, away from the advice to a female colleague to ingratiate herself, away from daily rations of privilege, from condoning the acceptance of "slightly dirty" money … and so many other small, individual contributions.

Morton suggests that in the presence of or from within hyperobjects, irony structures the experience of reality. This is not the postmodern, sloganeering, plastic irony, but a dimension of living with the awareness that there is no distance (and no innocence) to be had. Sincere Irony. Morton likens it to "being Jonah in the whale realizing that he is part of the whale's digestive system, or Han Solo and Leia inside the gigantic worm they think is the surface of an asteroid."[6] Postmodern irony required distance, or an illusion of distance. But irony that structures the experience of reality is closer to "the feeling of waking up inside a hyperobject, against which we are always in the wrong."[7] To catch glimpses and whispers of the future from within it is perhaps to navigate a sincere experience of irony. From within the belly of the whale, our future catchers have to handle hope and rations of optimism with extra care. Our self-awareness about being caught within that belly is vital—it needs to be felt simultaneously by many in order to become transformative.

5 See Timothy Morton, *Hyperobjects: Philosophy and Ecology after the End of the World* (Minneapolis: The University of Minnesota Press, 2013).

6 Morton, "The Age of Asymmetry," in *Hyperobjects*, 184.

7 Morton, 173.

Kevin Crouse & Carl Lostritto

Media and Archives: A Conversation with Nicholas de Monchaux

Carl Lostritto and I met Nicholas de Monchaux, the Department Head of Architecture at Massachusetts Institute of Technology, over Zoom on August 10, 2020. Drawing on Robin Evans's take on architecture as a mediated discipline, we ruminated over this year's wholly digital thesis presentation—on how both significant and insignificant the medium of the screen turned out to be. De Monchaux's multimedia practice, *modem*, and his expertise in new media root his efforts to archive every bit of work so that architecture can find a democratic, inclusive, and expansive way forward. **KC**

Carl Lostritto **During the Super Jury, you noted that if anything in the discipline needs to be comprehensive in providing social agency and corrective in handling environmental pressures, it is digital media rather than physical space. Daniel Barber complicated this position by insisting that if we learned anything from the last decade, it is that digital media is not separate from physical space; it occupies hidden physical conditions and resources, like server farms and fiber optic cables. Did any of the student projects engage with the discipline's digital discourse in compelling ways?**

Nicholas de Monchaux Yes, Zachary Schumacher's project (see pp. 215–218) resonates especially

with the architectural media discourse. It accepts that in the Western tradition since the fourteenth century (where, sadly, much of our work still resides), architecture has been a discipline of media. We do not build; instead, we produce forms of media—blueprints, models, and narratives—that cause things to be built in different ways. Yet, as Robin Evans famously points out in *Translations from Drawing to Building*, most architects deliberately pretend, perhaps because we must, that we construct buildings. Understanding architecture as a mediated discipline helps us recognize why media thinking and innovation often develop from architecture, like the influence of the Bauhaus on film and culture, or the development of the Media Lab out of the Architecture Machine Group at MIT. These are not separate conversations, as generations long before mine have known.

Zachary's project also recognizes the triumph of media in our contemporary condition. The space shaped by architects with media is becoming substantially a space of media *and* a space of matter. Whether in the latently dystopian narratives of smart cities or the overlap between Tahrir Square and Facebook, the feedback loop between spaces of media is faster, sharper, and more inextricable every day as governments and activists continue to understand its capacity for both change and control.

Media—from the Latin word for *lens*—allows you to see something differently by distorting your vision. In that way, Zachary's project is a tour de force in the deep, uncanny physicality of ephemerality as the hydro-dipper sinks his hairy hand into a grotesque liquid with precision among imprecise, humming machinery. It's beautiful! The hydro-dipping film has the literal thinness of an image, and it warps and distorts our vision of space and the building, even as it becomes inextricable from it. What is remarkable about the film is you see all of that in a single, seemingly everyday cinematic moment. The rest of the thesis surrounds that moment like a decorated proscenium; it exists to help us understand that single clip without getting in the way.

CL **Julie Kress** **(see pp. 211–214)** **established a similar distance from architecture itself in the way she operated on the John Soane Museum. It was not a proposal**

for a new museum, but a discursive exploration of skeuomorphic animations. What are architecture's disciplinary limits within media studies? Can architects claim any type of media?

NM Julie's thesis, a performance in architectural media, presents a profound and unsettling truth by divesting from the fiction of building. When Julie shows the film during the animation, it's like the moment in Dziga Vertov's *Man with a Movie Camera* when the camera pulls out to see the sprockets at the side where the editor does her work inside the movie. With the artifice acknowledged, we look more attentively and deeply to enjoy the nature of the illusion.

Julie creates an environment that turns Zachary's thesis on its head; she presents architecture as a medium, a set of experiences divorced from structural purpose. While they might be interesting, the anamorphic animations would not work if it were a Big Y supermarket—they rely on Sir John Soane's house as a space of experience over structure. The work sustains a commentary on high architectural history by specifically connecting one architectural mediation to another.

Kevin Crouse **Even though Julie worked entirely digitally from the onset, Covid significantly affected her presentation. Whether intended or not, her project and others were designed not just *through* screens, but *for* screens. We found ourselves in a 2020 version of a paperless studio. Since the digital turn, the screen has held a position between image and drawing. Do you believe that the pandemic repositioned the screen?**

NM Julie clearly designed her project for the medium in which it was shown. Even though my screen is slightly different than hers—perhaps a different dimension or color temperature—

In the Western tradition since the fourteenth century (where, sadly, much of our work still resides), architecture has been a discipline of media. We do not build; instead, we produce forms of media—blueprints, models, and narratives—that cause things to be built in different ways.

the intimacy of sitting in front of a monitor recapitulates her relationship to the work as she crafted it. It thus strangely offers greater intimacy.

I would also push back against the idea that the screen is new. Even Soane would be familiar with the camera obscura, capturing reality and presenting it differently. Looking at screens, capturing reproduction, miniaturizing, and copying are all part of a long condition of modernity: the view as a commodity. Understanding the miniaturization and reproduction of architecture through measurement, tone, and color on a screen is old, but the virtuosity of its scale and the endless repetition and layering in Julie's project expands on something more subtle than its digitality.

CL **The spectacle of zooming in and out of images on a Miro board over Zoom showed that the internet mediated projects more than the screen. When we zoomed into Sina Erol's large-scale hand drawings (see pp. 143–146), we**

saw not a pixelated version of the drawing, but deeper, layered nuances of the multiplicity of resolution. Similarly, when Benjamin Han (see pp. 207–210) realized his detailed

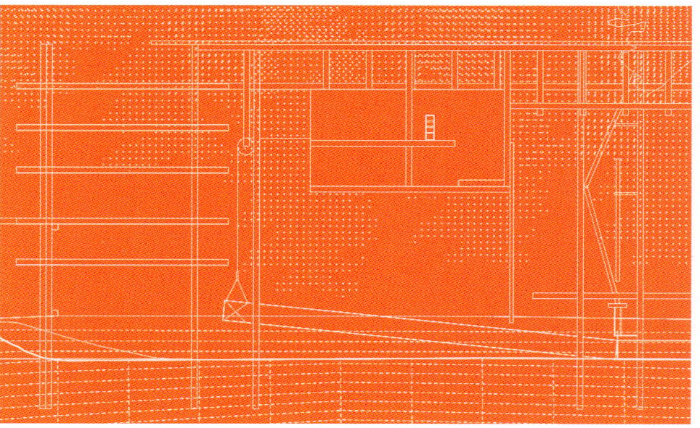

sections would be seen on the screen, he began to change the colors and line weights to sustain zooming in and out. Do you think the internet as a medium for architecture will become genuine instead of an analogy of space?

NM I lived through the first generation of paperless studios and attempts at communicating through resolution. I was always exasperated by the hand versus computer debate; paper versus screen is more interesting, or at least more clear, because it merely frames resolution as an ability to move in and out. And one of the profound stupidities of in-person critiques is sitting twelve feet away from detailed drawings and talking about the work as if you can see it. Yunchao (Derek) Le (see pp.

165–168) allowed the user autonomy to zoom in and out, which established intimacy astonishingly well. He embeds a rhetorical clarity with Easter eggs in every scale of the project, like a Pieter Bruegel painting as architectural rendering. I can imagine a student using this technique as a disciplinary joke, but the way Yunchao discussed and presented it earnestly was a real pleasure.

CL **As an educator, how do you advise students on the necessity of archiving your work and reflecting on the process?**

NM I often use others' archives, which informs decisions about archiving oneself. Ideally, you should save everything for a long time and then make decisions; a simple project or a page of offhand correspondence can be the most essential thing decades later. The nature of digital archiving allows us to take a more political attitude toward what we save and highlight. In these students' lifetimes,

The archive hoards things that do not seem essential but prove significant later. The intellectual content, work, and embedded labor that it represents are equally valuable to the future. The angel of history only looks backward.

curation's role went from finding to filtering. The work archived before architecture schools' digitalization was a political act by professors to highlight projects that legitimate their success. This is no longer the case—but still, only one thesis wins the Thesis Prize. It is hard to argue that the historic selective process has advanced architectural discourse, but it is easy to argue that it was inhibitive. The critical theses that challenged their milieu were often not the prize-winning ones. But they are the ones, most of all, that should be saved.

KC **The Super Jury is a compromise between both approaches: while it picks a "best thesis," it also presents a group of twelve students equally across each section to flatly discuss the year's work.**

NM My ideal process for a Super Jury would be perhaps that the students vote on which projects to review, then the faculty select additional projects if they wish, and then the students get to add one more. The selection itself should be a conversation. One productive element of the current moment is the blunt skepticism toward the way authority, selection, and, let's be honest, racism, perpetuate each other: architecture is a culture of patronage and capriciously ties itself up in networks of authority. Not by coincidence, our current racist, authoritarian president is a real estate developer and builder. Structural racism is about structures, not just institutions, and manifests in both by centering whiteness. Today, for this reason especially, we should question how our schools apply standards for admission, selection, and critique.

KC **We are in a literal pandemic. As Arundhati Roy describes in her essay for the *Financial Times*, the pandemic is a portal that responds to many global issues: economic instability, class wars, xenophobia, racial injustice. If these are nodes of an archive into broad-scale injustice, clarifying our precarious position as a discipline, how can architecture schools use an archival portal to transform their pedagogies, and, as Roy puts it, "walk through lightly" into the future?**

NM The archive hoards things that do not seem essential but prove significant later. The intellectual content, work, and embedded labor that it represents are equally valuable to the future. The angel of history only looks backward. Revolutions have always changed much more and much less than they promised. I do not presume to know the exact nature of the transformations that await us on the other side of our current portal, but I know that grounding work in the cycles of history and their reimagining is a piece of essential luggage to take through the door.

Kevin Crouse & Ryan McCaffrey

Design Research: A Conversation with Lola Sheppard and Mason White

From across the west and east sides of Massachusetts, Ryan McCaffrey and I Zoomed with Lola Sheppard and Mason White at their Toronto-based firm Lateral Office on July 24, 2020. Their book *Many Norths* highlights their roots in both landscape urbanism and Rem Koolhaas's research studios, and extends the architect's role to include ethnographic studies. In conversation, they expanded on the role of design research during the pandemic, arguing that architects need to think humbly as we question the infrastructures of systemic injustice. **KC**

Kevin Crouse **Mason, during the Super Jury you noted a common theme: that many thesis projects begin with an individual student's interest, but do not necessarily extend to a conventional structure in the built environment. Did you pick up on any other tendencies?**

Mason White RISD's binary approach to thesis—the directed research and the independent thesis (or undirected research) running in parallel—speaks to the interplay between dogmatism and individualism in design research. There was a powerful push and pull between those two methodologies across the various thesis work. Most projects leaned into one approach or another, yet some had properties of both. For example, Benjamin Han's project (see pp. 207–210) is half cynical, half optimistic,

combining individuality (narrative exploration) and directed research methods (in his case, mycelium) in a post–climate change world. In terms of representation, his architecture explored ephemerality with a pointillist style composed of one dot at a time.

Many of the thesis projects became a highly personal journey, whose internal narrative was enhanced even more during the isolation from studio in an unfolding pandemic. The hyper-individuality emerging in real-time through the projects was an effective rallying

technique. I remember Sina Erol (see pp. 143–146) referring to analog drawings' therapeutic quality in his thesis as he drew stone by stone and room by room. For Diyi Zhang (see pp. 55–58),

the emptiness of the new Italian domestic landscape and everyday rituals, like cooking or cleaning, reactivate the village for visitors. Aaron Teves's *Archi-Jig* (see pp. 219–222) is

a love letter to the architecture of supports, formwork, and nodes and an homage to scaffolding. I certainly sensed a celebration of the small, domestic, and individual, revealing friction between individuality and collective (or shared) research.

Lola Sheppard The pluralism at RISD is invigorating. The range of work we saw powerfully represented a broad spectrum of disciplinary preoccupations. Students increasingly recognize that history is more complex than the singular narrative that marquee architecture would imply; often, you need other tools and strategies for engaging in and solving a spatial challenge. The student work understood doing less could do more.

KC **Is that the tendency you saw in the department?**

MW Yes, there was a suggested interest in how little could be done and yet still have an impact. For instance, Taylor McCabe's thesis (see pp. 43–46) oscillated between adaptive

reuse, demolition, and façadism of unoccupied Baltimore buildings. He orchestrated these minor acts cohesively, countering the heroic, single authorship of modernism.

KC **How is Lateral Office organized, and how does this structure serve your interests in the built environment?**

MW Actually, we embedded the idea of non-hierarchical horizontality literally into the name—*Lateral* Office—to honor a collective approach. We are also interested in the possibility of modesty and simplicity in a project, which is exciting to see in many of the students' work.

To design for a given urban or suburban site is fathomable and what we have historically been trained to do. But with larger scales and global networks of economic flows, we need to develop new analytic and representational drawing types.

Ryan McCaffrey **Lola, about Min Jin (MJ) Kook's directed research project (see pp. 39–42), you asked in**

the review, "How do we represent the sublime scale of infrastructure? How does it relate to the public realm?" Much of your work represents a similarly sublime scale by presenting a wealth of data, maps, and information on how global conditions shape specific sites. Why are these new representational strategies important?

LS For about fifteen years, there has been a disciplinary interest in large-scale landscape and infrastructure projects that operate beyond the single object. It's still relatively new territory. To design for a given urban or suburban site is fathomable and what we have historically been trained to do. But with larger scales and global networks of economic flows, we need to develop new analytic and representational drawing types that evoke the sense of urgency and synergy of various issues. How do you tell the story of a network of processes and stakeholders that is beyond scalar comprehension? Representation is a political project and a graphic one, especially when dealing with geopolitical and ecological conditions.

It is also essential to recognize that representation is a tool of "storytelling" in architecture, particularly when the issues are complex. In MJ's project, capturing three global sites through animations effectively described the temporality of people and

objects' international flows. Yangchuan (Niko) Tian's project (see pp. 51–54), which explored the possibility of repurposing oil rigs to ecologically remediate the Gulf of Mexico, successfully avoided a representational dogma. She recognized the need to draw oil rigs as a technological megastructure, but she evoked the sublime postindustrial landscape in other drawings. MJ was clear and consistent in her representational methods, while Niko intelligently explored a range of techniques to delve into the tectonic details.

KC **Your *Many Norths* project bridges an ethnographic study of Northern Canada with the architectural method by gathering regional spatial strategies through interviews with locals and collecting resource data to visualize a "distinct Northern vernacular." In the face of globalized crises, several thesis projects addressed similar issues around sociological and ethnographic physical constructions. How do projects incorporate specific communities' everyday existence to confront the homogenizing forces of architecture as it is typically practiced?**

MW Interviews, case studies, essays, and timelines intentionally eradicate our singular voice. The task of the architect is that of a detective, teasing out modes of spatial practice. Our approach to *Many Norths* was informed by vernacular inquiries such as *Learning from Las Vegas*, although obviously with different forces at play in the Canadian Arctic. A few thesis students pursued work with a similar "learning from" approach. Avril Teo (see pp. 185–188) was detective-like in

observing how modernism adapted to Singapore's locality and cultural specificity. Her precision in exploring Singapore's housing typology, even down to the dimensionality of the roof overhang and how rooms get partitioned, compellingly paired local knowledge with contemporary innovation. Also in the "learning from"

spirit, Sam Wesselman's project (see pp. 133–136) took a psychogeographical approach to peri-urban infrastructural spaces, making subtle and modest interstitial modifications to common spaces along feral expressway lands and embracing imperfect moments in his representation. Avril's project is overtly regional; Sam's reveals an infrastructural vernacular. They both touch on ways in which vernacular is a bottom-up enterprise produced by society and culture, countering the modernist ethos of hyperarticulated programming for the occupant.

RM **You mentioned you want to eliminate the singular author in *Many Norths*, yet you set the research agenda, and research projects necessarily deal with ethical questions about authorship and legitimacy. Lateral Office is a part of Koolhaas's lineage of research-led practices. Is it possible to conduct real, ethical engagement through research? Or, in a more optimistic framework, when do you know a project has become larger than yourself so that the label of researcher, designer, or presenter expands our disciplinary boundaries?**

LS I would argue that research—both empirical and data-driven—keeps fantasy in check. It helps ground a project without negating speculation and design as an essential enterprise. Research forces architects to expand beyond the discipline and engage more complex forces that shape our built environment, especially when architects operate in unfamiliar contexts. In our work and teaching, we deal with this idea of detective work, a euphemism for research, in which you follow leads that are uncertain and indeterminate. Research goes beyond a linear relationship, such as "I'm studying this because it will help answer this predetermined question." Being open to uncovering unexpected leads is often where innovation—be it programmatic, material, or social—begins.

Koolhaas's project on the city set a standard for design-research approaches—whether it be on cultural activity (shopping), on a city (Rome), or a region (Pearl River Delta). I'll go on record to say that when you look at his research on "Countryside"—a topic we also work on extensively—it primarily reads as shock value for public consumption. Research isn't just finding the phenomenon and putting an image to it; it's about unpacking the phenomenon and its nuanced systems. The countryside is not homogenous; it is highly specific. Research allows you to dig down to hyper-specificities. I talk a lot about this in thesis: narrowed specificity will uncover phenomena and resonate across much larger questions. It's only in getting specific that you can find a meaningful response.

Sophie Weston Chien's project (see pp. 199–202) is a great example. She documents seasonal patterns of use in Kigiqtaq, Alaska, while investigating various stakeholders from species to government agencies. She eloquently recognizes the many complex actors in this community. Similarly, Rashi Lalaji's investigation of Mumbai's

It is increasingly important to train architects to listen and observe patiently. This wasn't always encouraged in my education, and it's not often promoted in design culture. Research is listening.

housing typologies (see pp. 161–164) represents the challenge of documenting daily domestic use and culture. She employs more familiar figure-ground drawings of building types, but she also documents, through collages, people living in the housing. We're still developing ways to research and document political and ecological forces in our work, so it is encouraging to see students exploring the implications of research in design.

MW It is increasingly important to train architects to listen and observe patiently. This wasn't always encouraged in my education, and it's not often promoted in design culture. Research is listening. Without it, Lateral Office would only be a practice. Architecture is a service industry; research makes architecture a discipline. The question today isn't so much, should we have research? It's more about its form and agency and how it influences work.

LS Even with thorough, meaningful research, however, architects still have to design. The role of research is to close the gap between context—whether it's social, political, spatial, or otherwise—and the response, with an active, creative leap of design. The research will never provide the full spatial answer nor the material manifestation of the project. As Mason noted, the role of research is to listen humbly. With recent events and a growing social and political awareness, we are seeing students who feel disempowered assert authorship in design, and in some cases, decide against design entirely. I would argue that it is still better to speculate in research and design and get it wrong than not take that risk. That is how the discipline moves forward. I look at projects we did in Lateral from ten years ago and think, I don't know if I would do it that way again. But that doubt is more useful than avoiding the risk. Design is an optimistic act of speculation.

KC **We are in a literal pandemic. As Arundhati Roy describes in her essay for the *Financial Times*, the pandemic is a portal that responds to many global issues: economic instability, class wars, xenophobia, racial injustice. If these are nodes in an infrastructure of broad-scale injustice, clarifying our precarious position as a discipline, how can architecture schools use an infrastructural portal to transform their pedagogies, and, as Roy puts it, "walk through lightly" into the future?**

MW We know from Reyner Banham and contemporary thinkers like Keller Easterling that infrastructure relies on architecture to act politically. Whether social, physical, atmospheric, or data, infrastructure is complicit in the problems of today's world. Landscape architects have been more effective in embracing that responsibility because they understand the need to enmesh systems into the design. Architecture, however, literally hides systems within cavity walls and ceilings to try to make them invisible.

Equally, architects often claim to have limited agency in delivering social infrastructure, asking: "What can I do? I'm just an architect." But increasingly, many architects actually ask: "What can an architect do to combat social, racial, and environmental injustice?" This was evident in many of the RISD theses this year, which called for the discipline to address economic instability, class wars, rampant injustice, and ecological impacts. It's clear this generation wants to climb through this portal and is willing to get messy and raise the ire of powers. We can walk through lightly environmentally, but we can walk through with great noise and energy to finally address longstanding injustice and oversight.

LS The political and social acts of architecture that all our institutions must address are the discipline's infrastructures. The pandemic and recent protests will open new discussions and finally challenge antiquated discourse. Our academic infrastructures of history, representation, studio, and technology courses focus on independent (albeit interrelated) knowledge portals; thesis offers a moment of convergence of knowledge. As we unpack the legacy of architectural pedagogy, I imagine thesis will be ground zero to reflect on changing disciplinary priorities.

Increasingly, many architects ask: "What can an architect do to combat social, racial, and environmental injustice?" This was evident in many of the RISD theses this year, which called for the discipline to address economic instability, class wars, rampant injustice, and ecological impacts. It's clear this generation wants to climb through this portal and is willing to get messy and raise the ire of powers.

Sean [illegible]anty

New Adjacencies of Discourse and Practice

I've had the great pleasure of participating in the end-of-year thesis reviews at RISD for the past three years. This year, through the Super Jury process, I noticed students positioning their thesis projects on one or more of the following spectra: strategy vs. technique, typology vs. program, and anachronism vs. novelty. Their pursuits toward critical engagement with the discipline and with retooling the canon—however sincere or ironic—make room for the overlooked, forgotten, and not yet considered. They give hope that the arduous, extremely personal endeavor of thesis, which actively shapes one's engagement with the profession, will lead in important new directions.

Two thesis projects in particular stood out in addressing qualities of the discipline that obfuscate questions of equity, justice, and how our tools shape architectural practice. While these two theses, on the surface, have very little in common—one emphasizes digital tools and the other formal typologies—they are tethered through the willingness of both students to engage with difficult issues while remaining self-aware and critical of received paradigms and ideologies. Rather than reaching beyond the discipline for answers, these two theses turn their focus inward to its tools, techniques, histories, and subjects. They highlight the merits of métier and skillfulness in service of change and transformation.

Zachary Schumacher's *Digital Duck* (see pp. 215–218)

tests representations of function through shape, geometry, and form and asks what it means to mine technical and representational tools for aesthetic and spatial cues. Schumacher's thesis engages a range of analog and digital techniques native to the tools that transform, calibrate, or measure geometry through the protocols of literalism (things as they are) against interpretation and realism (things as they are constructed and embodied). His thesis points out that whether pre-digital, digital, or post-digital, the architectural surface is an active mediator between literalism and realism. Further, in the context of our contemporary advancements and computational literacy, these paradigms aren't necessarily distinct from one another; the literal and the real are intertwined.

Digital Duck elicits an immediate conversation with Denise Scott Brown and Robert Venturi's "duck" building and the "decorated shed," whose adornment is applied independently of the structure.[1] Zach's questioning of literalism and realism also relates to work by Preston Scott Cohen, John May and Zeina Koreitem of MILLIØNS, and Anna Neimark and Andrew Atwood of First Office. All of these practitioners question the relationship between form, representation, and architectural images, implicating them equally. In "Elliptical Congruencies: The Tubular Embrasure of San Carlo ai Catinari," for example, Cohen presents a case study that demonstrates the complexities and possibilities of representational analysis. Analyzing perspectival images of the sacristy at San Carlo ai

1 Robert Venturi, Denise Scott Brown, and Steven Izenour, *Learning from Las Vegas: The Forgotten Symbolism of Architectural Form* (Cambridge: MIT Press, 1977), 17.

Catinari, he discovers an odd schism between the interior and exterior. A pair of elliptical windows that define an exterior corner are represented by only one window on the interior. Thus the two windows on the exterior pass light to a single interior window.[2] The elusive line between inside and outside, in Cohen's observation, falls outside the norms of embrasures, which typically provide direct passage through a wall to an interior or exterior opening.[3] This anomalous corner of geometric rarity and adaptation is conspicuously concealed. A close reading of perspectival images led to its discovery, which spurred a series of speculations on how such a condition came to be. Cohen built a series of digital analytical models from photographs through the use of the Taylorian Perspective Method to produce orthographic projections from perspective images. In this process, the reverse engineering of perspective—a format meant to represent subjective and embodied experience—is refocused to reveal a hidden exceptional condition. In exemplary ways, Cohen leverages the tools of the architect to reveal perspective as a system of production, a hegemonic construct that can be appropriated for new modes of discovery. The project implicates images in both the construction and the understanding of architectural form.

Schumacher's interrogation of representation focuses most explicitly on texture mapping, a digital modeling tool that enables a two-dimensional surface to be wrapped around a three-dimensional object. Schumacher created

Preston Scott Cohen's Taylorian Perspective Method, which produces orthographic drawings from perspectives

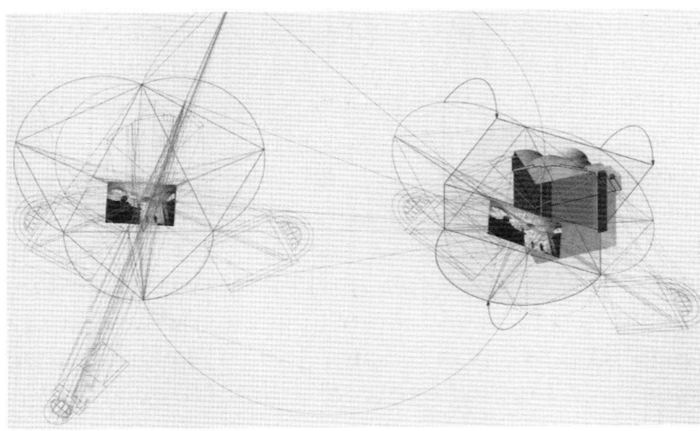

an analog to this digital process by using hydro-dipping (a way of mapping a two-dimensional design to a three-dimensional object through water transfer) to index and visualize surface shape and deformation. His surface is the simple checkerboard pattern of sandwich paper, which recalls the "empty" background of a Photoshop file—an implied lack of content or information. However, in this application, the checkerboard pattern conceals content and information presented not in two dimensions but in three—specifically those of a vernacular home, which are articulated via a gridded lattice. The process reveals formal and geometric idiosyncrasies, calling attention to the assumptions inherent in texture mapping and to the smoothness of the implied result.

Schumacher's thesis draws our attention to computational frameworks embedded in three-dimensional modeling packages, like the cage edit command or force simulations, which play a significant role in defining a surface

2 Preston Scott Cohen, "Elliptical Congruencies: The Tubular Embrasure of San Carlo ai Catinari," in Cohen and Laurence King, *Contested Symmetries: The Architecture of Preston Scott Cohen* (London: Laurence King, 2001), 36–53.

3 Cohen, 36.

"Schumacher's thesis enables us to see the "digital duck" of our present by translating between mediums and media. His thesis builds an appreciation for literalism (in both tools and context) as well as for the elisions embedded in tools and the frameworks that shape them.

through a graphical device. A digital metaphor for the sandwich paper might be the .png and its inherent qualities: its agility in accommodating different image and graphic types, its support of transparency, its edge fidelity, and its ability to preserve image quality and resolution even after successive compressions. In contrast, the .jpeg selectively deletes information with each compression, a form of digital ruination that perpetually approximates and excludes content. In effect, the .jpeg ages the image, exchanging youth for portability. The temporality and fidelity of these image formats are one analogical version of digital ducks and decorated sheds.

Andrew Atwood, in his essay "Rendering Air: On Representation of Particles in the Sky," illuminates parallels between traditional image making (like the English picturesque) and more contemporary forms of image production (the technical image). Atwood refers to an early picturesque concept practiced by the landscape gardener William Gilpin called "keeping," or techniques of creating distance and depth in images of the picturesque.[4] Drawing attention to the representation of air in images, he notes that for a picture to be considered "picturesque" in Gilpin's terms, it has to have an effect of keeping distance between objects in the painting as the composition moves from front to back and from one object to the next.[5] This concept catalyzed a variety of representational techniques to distinguish objects and space represented within the frame. The technical image folds these traditional techniques into rendering and photo-editing software, as Atwood notes: "[Digital] techniques are not simply analogous to processes found in traditional image making but are sampled representations of processes of traditional image making that operate as abstractions of their traditional counterpart." An appealing turn for Atwood is that technical images, unlike traditional images, offer opportunities to make visible the steps of an image's production.[6]

In this spirit of the English picturesque, wherein space is organized in the likeness of a picture, Schumacher's project gestures toward preoccupations with the likeness of images, real and perceived. Donato Bramante's Church of Santa Maria presso San Satiro would be a classic example of the way in which a compromised contextual situation uses perspectival distortion to fake the extension of the choir within a shallow depth. In Francesco Borromini's Palazzo Spada, materials and architectural elements are literally distorted to construct an ideal image. More recently, in Jennifer Bonner's Haus Scallop and Haus Sawtooth, bricks from two Mies Case Study houses are imaged and scanned and then retextured through a combination of bit maps and bump maps. The result is a literalization of imaging processes that questions the affective quality of the bricks as they appear without structural implications.

To return to Scott Brown and Venturi, Schumacher's thesis enables us to see the "digital duck" of our present by translating between mediums and media. His thesis builds an appreciation for literalism (in both tools and context) as well as for the elisions embedded in tools and the frameworks that shape them. What is to be gained by reconsidering the way in which modes of image production, like the English picturesque movement, shape architects' tools? What might other canons of image production contribute to shaping the discipline for contemporary purposes? If air is a shared medium, open to interpretation and rendered in many forms and many cultures, how might we pluralize its representations?

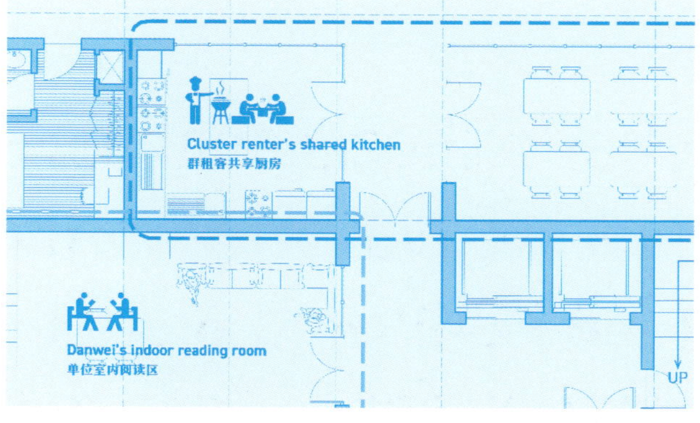

Wei Xiao's thesis, *Resettling Urban Villages* (see pp. 89–92), signals a return to typological thinking as a way of resisting the market pressures of development within global urban centers and promoting inclusive development

4 Andrew Atwood, "Rendering Air: On Representation of Particles in the Sky," *Log*, no. 31 (2014): 47.

5 Atwood, 47–48.

6 Atwood, 49.

Xiao's research aligns with Sarah Whiting's idea of an engaged form of architectural autonomy, a legible project that eludes iconicity while engaged in a diffused form of context through nuanced form and program.

practices. Xiao's project is critical of urban renewal projects in many parts of China, which push to rapidly modernize traditional regions by replacing dense and nuanced vernacular forms of dwelling and commerce with efficient, homogenous vertical structures. Responding to the increase in these projects throughout the country, Xiao's project seeks to preserve a dense urban housing community in Zhejiang, China, insisting on preservation and rooted spatial practices of place.

Xiao's research aligns with Sarah Whiting's idea of an engaged form of architectural autonomy, a legible project that eludes iconicity while engaged in a diffused form of context through nuanced form and program.[7] His approach strategically shifts typological thinking from governing only the plan, which is often driven by monetary value, to implicating the elevation and the section. Three levels of type unfold in the project: the plan, governed by efficiency and market forces; the elevation, governed by the graphic and symbolic residue of typology; and the section, which preserves spatial residues embedded deep within the site. The project functions in two ways: concentrating density to further alleviate incursion on neighboring areas, and smuggling the specific into the generic to preserve vernacular types while allowing for new programmatic use. The latter proposition is the more disciplinary of the two. It is catalyzed to resist and protest normalized, exclusionary, and insincere forms of development.

Xiao's thesis also explores Venturi and Scott Brown's idea of superadjacency, or the superimposition of various elements as related to the façade. In *Complexity and Contradiction in Architecture*, Venturi writes:

> **Superadjacency is inclusive rather than exclusive. It can relate contrasting and otherwise irreconcilable elements; it can contain opposites within a whole; it can accommodate the valid non sequitur; and it can allow a multiplicity of levels of meaning, since it involves changing contexts—seeing familiar things in an unfamiliar way and from unexpected points of view.[8]**

This is the strategy at hand in Xiao's research: a means of reconstituting holistic types not only for their configurative characteristics (organization) but also for their figurative potential (spatial and formal) by smuggling in new spaces between stacked types within the section. In effect, this operates by the same logic of vertical extrusion and sameness often seen in residential towers in Asia, but he slips in a heterogenous section and elevations and negative spaces that are socially aleatory. Think of New York's Downtown Athletic Club without its envelope, MVRDV's Dutch Pavilion, Kengo Kuma's Asakusa Culture and Tourism Center, or Jennifer Bonner's Best Sandwiches. In each case, the heterogenous stack is a reconstitution of extrinsic spatial paradigms, bound in the tightness of an exterior wrapper. The section is made legible by elevation—a graphic, spatial, or symbolic residue of the plan—

7 Sarah Whiting and Peter Eisenman, "I Am Interested in a Project of Engaged Autonomy," *Log*, no. 28 (2013): 109–18.

8 Robert Venturi and Vincent Scully, "Contradiction Juxtaposed," in *Complexity and Contradiction in Architecture* (New York: The Museum of Modern Art, 1966), 58–59.

while embracing the technical support of architecture, successive stacking, and volumetric extrusion. Xiao's thesis carefully balances the graphic and the spatial as a form of preservation to maintain a sense of formal and social togetherness while embracing the inevitable large-scale development.

Both Schumacher's and Xiao's theses draw on Venturi and Scott Brown, whose practice was a radical one that forced our discipline to see the overlooked, the normal, the ordinary, to closely read and understand architecture as not only a profession but a social and cultural practice. Both ask disciplinary questions and answer those questions through disciplinary experiments. Both also ask how we might reexamine our profession and the métier of the architect to engage with the issues of today, to find opportunities to build a more inclusive, equitable profession and set of spatial practices. It goes without saying that reaching into the canon of architecture to find a broader range of diverse voices has proven difficult. The methodologies proposed within the final reviews at RISD offer suggestions, however small, that the discipline can make space for new perspectives, certainly an essential task in the time to come.

Both Schumacher's and Xiao's theses draw on Venturi and Scott Brown, whose practice was a radical one that forced our discipline to see the overlooked, the normal, the ordinary, to closely read and understand architecture as not only a profession but a social and cultural practice.

Georgeen Theodore

Creative Collaboration in the Time of Covid-19

Architectural practice, by its very nature, is collaborative. The solitary hero-architect drafting alone at his desk—most famously epitomized by Howard Roark in *The Fountainhead*—represents a bygone myth. Designing and constructing a building typically requires a team of people with different expertise, including not only a group of architects, but also structural and MEP engineers, lawyers, bankers, zoning and code consultants, landscape and lighting designers, and so on. Within this network of professional actors, the task of the architect is to synthesize the inputs of the various contributors into a coordinated project, in which the whole is greater than the sum of its parts. Given that this creative collaboration is at the heart of architectural practice, it is puzzling that schools of architecture don't explicitly teach collaboration. Architecture faculty typically organize studio curricula so that each student conceptualizes and creates their own, individual design in conversation with one instructor. The architectural thesis, which remains the academic capstone at many institutions, represents the apotheosis of the independent, individually driven student project. Why is the creative process as practiced in architecture school so often autonomous rather than collective?

I am both a practitioner and an academic, and in my creative work in the office and the classroom, I directly engage creative collaboration. In my professional practice, I typically take on projects in the urban, public realm, from small public spaces to regional plans. Such projects require intense engagement with many different stakeholders and constituencies—from city departments and agencies to special interest groups, community organizations, and individuals. To be successful, such projects require engaging with conflicting ideas and desires, working synthetically, and moving toward creative collaboration. I believe that these practices can provide useful models for a more collaborative architectural education. As a professor at New Jersey Institute of Technology, where I have taught studios for the past fifteen years, I have experimented with various models of collaborative work to simulate the complex interactions that occur outside of the academic studio. After many iterations and tests, ranging from fully individual projects to entirely group-based endeavors, I now work with a hybrid model organized through a pyramid of tasks. A design challenge serves as the basis of the studio, and I typically choose one that is so complex and multilayered that it would be daunting for one person to do on her own. We start out with each student working individually, and with each successive task, the students join larger and larger groups until we have one group and one shared project. This process requires dialogue, listening and learning from others, advocacy, compromise, and creative synthesis among all participants, including me.

Since the onset of the coronavirus pandemic, the fundamental practices of creative collaboration have been turned upside down.

Social distancing and working from home have forced us to reconsider nearly every aspect of architectural practice, and we have had to adopt and invent different ways of communicating, creating, and critiquing. Both the office and the classroom are now online, remote, and conducted virtually. Interactions are no longer face-to-face, but screen-to-screen. Presentations, project meetings, and casual conversations all happen via Zoom, Webex, and Slack. How have these modes of communication affected creative collaboration? What are the best practices for remote collaborative work? And, what have we learned while working remotely that will change post-pandemic practice?

The experience of the spring 2020 RISD Super Jury prompted me to reflect on these questions, offering a special lens through which to consider the state of the discipline. The three-day jury was an intense experience unlike any other year-end review. Like other studio reviews at schools of architecture in the spring of 2020, all of the proceedings happened on Zoom. It is worth noting that the Zoom review completely changes the relationship between the presenter, the reviewers, and the work. Unlike the traditional final review, where the work is pinned on a wall, and the student stands between their work and the jury (lined up in the first row of chairs like a firing squad), the Zoom review places all participants—the invited reviewers, students, faculty, guests—in a nonhierarchical, perhaps even egalitarian, grid. During the RISD reviews, each student presented their work through a short prepared video in which their body was not visible, so the reviewers focused directly on the work. This also resulted in a less hierarchical review space. Experiencing the student presentations in this format eliminated the kinds of biases that come with judging people by their physical characteristics, their clothes, and their posturing, all of which certainly influence the proceedings and outcomes of traditional in-person reviews.

As we reviewed students grouped by studio instructor, the range and originality of the projects impressed me. While the faculty framed specific studio challenges,

The architectural thesis represents the apotheosis of the independent, individually driven student project. Why is the creative process as practiced in architecture school so often autonomous rather than collective?

students in the same studio pursued very different projects, suggesting they had the space and support to develop their own voice. Their projects were original, personal, and fully developed. While I cannot compare this year's cohort to those of previous years, my sense was that studying from home may have had some benefits. The students were prodigious in their outputs, which aligns with recent reports, mostly from tech fields, of increased productivity in working from home, due mostly to fewer distractions and less time commuting.[1] But beyond breadth and quantity, qualitatively many of the projects expressed an inner focus likely borne out of quarantine and working from home. For example, in Zachary Schumacher's project (see pp. 215–218),

the digital space of his presentation *was* the architecture, an alternative realm through which the viewer moved from photograph to video to sculpture to surface. Such sophisticated and thought-provoking projects express the involuted spirit of our quarantined times. While the projects are inwardly focused, these students did not pin their drawings on a wall and let the work "speak for itself"; instead, they borrowed narrative techniques from storytelling and filmmaking to convey the project and its surrounding ideas. This represents a long-overdue shift toward empowering students to take charge of the messaging and reading of their projects and advocate for what they think is important.[2]

While this emphasis on narrative is praiseworthy, I'd also like to express my concerns about this format. Like film watching, where the visual story and sound emanate from a screen and the viewer receives the information, the narrated Zoom presentation is mostly one-way. What's missing is the two-, or three-, or five-way conversation in which multiple voices and ideas ping-pong back and forth as shared discoveries are made. Zoom, not only as a presentation platform, but perhaps more importantly, when used for collaborative discussions, hinders the casual banter that is at the heart of creative design thinking. In productive, in-person conversation, speakers provide signals and cues to each other to confirm that they are in sync, which encourages and positively reinforces back-and-forth discussion. However, Zoom impedes these signals and cues. Sound in Zoom is not perfect. When a person speaks, listeners experience unintended delays in the spoken words that result in vocal distortions, awkward pauses, and cut-outs, all of which contribute to a feeling of disconnection among the participants. To improve audio fidelity, many Zoom users "mute" themselves when they are not speaking and politely wait for others to complete their sentences before beginning theirs, slowing down the conversation and formalizing verbal exchanges. Poor fidelity and self-muting discourage the use of interjected affirmatives, such as the "mm-hmm" and the "uh-huh," that typically create a back and forth between speakers. Additionally, forms of nonverbal communication, such as observing and responding to body language, are limited or just not there. The Zoom speaker's screen has a landscape orientation, which focuses on the face and occludes the body. The slouch that suggests "I feel comfortable with you," or the upright posture that posits "I'm listening because what you're saying is important!" or the fiddling of fingers, or the crossing of legs, and so on, all are withheld. The Zoom "gaze," frontal and focused on everyone and no one, furthers feelings of isolation and disconnection.[3]

In architectural practice, conversational brainstorming occurs not only in words but in drawings. Collaborative sketching mixes spoken and visual language into a hybrid form of communication. Done around a table, side-by-side at a desk, or on a job site, sketching is a core skill that enables architects to develop new ideas, solve problems, and cultivate consensus. Of course, even before

1 See Clive Thompson, "What If Working From Home Goes on … Forever?" *New York Times*, June 9, 2020. However, from my own observation, I would add that increases in productivity that result from working from home do not seem to accrue in households with young children.

2 See Fabrizio Gallanti, "Pan Scroll Zoom," in *Drawing Matter*, July 30, 2020, https://drawingmatter.org/pan-scroll-zoom-1/, for a reflection on the relationship between student Zoom presentations and cinema.

3 Thompson (n.1) informed some of my analysis here.

We have turned our teaching and pedagogy upside down and inside out over the past few months, demonstrating that we can adapt, pivot, and change. Moving forward, why not radically rethink the review? Why not bring more perspectives and different expertise into review settings, shifting from one-way design-star soliloquies to multivoiced dialogues among a network of equal actors, including the student?

the pandemic, architectural collaboration through sketching had shifted and changed, with some offices and designers moving toward computer-based processes. But Covid has laid bare the essentiality of collaborative sketching. In architectural education, the day-to-day method of instruction is the "desk critique," the spoken and sketched conversation between studio professor and student. Already there is experimentation on how to best simulate collaborative sketching in a remote context, testing tools and techniques such as the "annotate" and white board functions in Zoom, document cameras, and digital pen tablets. Since March 2020, we have adapted and become more adept, but digital, remote sketching remains slower, clumsier, and less effective than in-person practice. We have not yet been able to invent an equal or better online replacement. Whether or not we do, because collaborative sketching is crucial to architectural education, we should pay more attention to, and seek opportunities to improve, its in-person practice after the pandemic. As educators, we should take a closer and more critical look at how to create new and improved settings for these creative exchanges. We might consider both the physical spaces of the exchange and the exercises and tasks we give to our students. To encourage creative and collaborative design thinking, we should foreground processes that require conversation, multichannel dialogue, and teamwork.

I believe that one of the most important factors in encouraging creative conversation is the studio itself. Studio culture, the basis and bond of a group working together toward a shared goal, typically develops endogenously in the space of the classroom, borne partly out of shared interests and partly from spending sleep-deprived hours together in cramped quarters. Since studios shifted from in-person to remote in spring 2020, faculty and students have developed different techniques to cultivate a sense of community while working exclusively from home. RISD students, keenly aware of the value of studio culture, actively sought ways to simulate it remotely, including the use of Slack channels, student-only "working in studio" times, shared Spotify playlists, and Instagram stories. Given that remotely conducted studios will continue for most of us for the foreseeable future, we as educators should actively support students in creating and sustaining studio culture during these challenging times. However, communication through digital applications and social media threatens the commons of a school. The tools used to create mediated studio culture (Zoom, Slack, etc.) work within closed, self-selected groups. Face-to-face, chance encounters—those that come from walking by a pin-up of another studio, small-talking in the print room while you wait for a plot, looking over someone's shoulder in the library—introduce new ideas, techniques, perspectives, and people into one's smaller studio circle. These externalities are unfortunately eliminated in remotely run architecture school and result in less resilient social networks and weaker design thinking. We only have to look at the world in which we live today for evidence of this fragility; our current crises are a consequence of economic and racial segregation, as well as political and cultural isolation.

Designing spaces and processes that allow for the coexistence of different voices, perspectives, and experiences should be central to architectural education. The specific conditions of the pandemic have diminished the open, multichannel dialogue—both in the day-to-day life of studio and in the more formal settings of reviews—that is so central to creative collaboration. We have turned our teaching and pedagogy upside down and inside out over the past few months, demonstrating that we can adapt, pivot, and change. Moving forward, why not radically rethink the review? Why not bring more perspectives and different expertise into review settings, shifting from one-way design-star soliloquies to multivoiced dialogues among a network of equal actors, including the student? Certainly, many studio professors and schools already invite experts from outside of architecture into the studio and the studio review. However, this expansion of perspectives, this embrace of multiplicity, could serve as the foundation of an intentionally collaborative studio pedagogy. The "comprehensive" or "integrated" studio can be team-based and guided not only by an architecture critic but by regular input from an expanded group of experts. Open, multichannel dialogue among different actors prepares students for the variety of voices and inputs that they will encounter in the collaborative *practice* of architecture. In academia, we should insist on having that conversation now.

Kevin Crouse & Ijlal Muzaffar

Performance: A Conversation with Mario Gooden

On August 14, 2020, Ijlal Muzaffar and I, calling in from Providence and Brooklyn, connected via Zoom with Mario Gooden on Long Island. We began our conversation with a grounding in Gooden's 2016 book, *Dark Space: Architecture, Representation, Black Identity,* a collection of essays underlining the spatial resistance integral to Black American identity and liberation. There and here, Gooden highlights the limits of the discipline, argues for breaking the boundaries of typological studies to upend the modernist myth of universality, and points optimistically toward the future of architecture: with strategy and ceaseless rehearsal, we can expand the discipline's boundaries. **KC**

Ijlal Muzaffar **Architecture is necessarily political, shaping the threshold between public and private identities. The recent protests in the streets in response to police killings of Black people were a powerful manifestation of people asserting, making, and performing their identities. How can we expand architecture to provide a platform for performing identity at the scale of the city? Are there forms and spaces architects can deliberately shape toward this end?**

Mario Gooden Forms and typologies are complicit with subjugation, oppression, and regimes of power. Our goal should go beyond finding new forms; we should instead learn how existing architecture enables performances. Having said that, even though the protests happened within city infrastructure—streets, highways, bridges, intersections, plazas—they weren't conceptualized through architectural form. Protesting is a form of resistance, but it is not architecturally formal. Put another way, architecture is a medium for the performative aspects of identity, unrelated to typologies. Therefore, I would say just the opposite regarding a search for new architectural forms, and I would argue that liberation is a spatial practice independent of typology. Black people have always been fluid, dynamic, and agile in negotiating social, political, infrastructural, and economic barriers in the struggle for freedom in this country.

IM **Should we move our pedagogical focus away from finding new forms to identifying the limits of formal typologies? In that way, we accept that we will not resolve architecture's reliance on systems of power. It can never actively perform the spatial qualities of protest but instead create friction with those systems.**

MG Architecture has agency and a role to play in modes of resistance, and it's productive to understand architecture's historical complicity with regimes of power. Audre Lorde wrote "The Master's Tools Will Never Dismantle the Master's House." We must understand, however, how the master's house operates. It's not merely rebuilding another type of house, but reimagining the concepts of shelter and comfort entirely. The results may not be typological at all; they emphasize understanding domesticity as relationships among people. The next step would be to

Black people have always been fluid, dynamic, and agile in negotiating social, political, infrastructural, and economic barriers in the struggle for freedom in this country.

foreground those relationships to determine how architecture enables domesticity.

IM **Historic precedents go beyond typology and into the relations they produce. In that way, architecture is a form of surfacing the exclusion of identity performance, and students' goal is to bridge that gap legibly. Where is the legible line of representing forms of identity?**

MG Legibility is a tricky word. There was a period in the academy, about thirty years ago, when typology went away as a reaction to postmodernism. Architects strayed from the discipline; they were interested in film, literature, and discursive modes of representation, followed by a period of digital formalism. For some people within the academy, those dalliances with extra-disciplinary theory had somehow muddled architecture as illegible. In the last decade, there has been a resurgence of typology and the desire for legibility within the re-disciplining of architecture.

Often in the floor plans of modernist houses, we see spaces labeled "maid's quarters" and "butler's room" without raising questions. There is also the modernist axiom of "served and servant spaces." Well, who were these maids and butlers? What was the division of labor within these spaces? And how did that manifest in the floor plan? The modernist myth of the universal subject takes these questions for granted; however, we know that there was a division of labor that was often highly racialized, socially stratified, and infused with the spatial representation of capitalist barbarism (to borrow from Walter Benjamin). Legibility articulates hierarchies, order, and clear spatial boundaries and borders. It showcases inclusion and exclusion, possession and non-possession, and compliance and dissent.

IM **Legibility, then, is one of the tools that enable the relations of power. By giving a legible corner for servants, the rest of the plan can appear neutral and universal as a code of operations.**

MG Yes, but, on the flip side, for students, the prompt might be otherwise. For example: design a space for reading. A space for reading could be the window in the space where you sleep. The bedroom, living room, or kitchen typology can go away because you could eat in your sleeping space or cook in the same space that you read. Those overlaps of programming enable non-static events and performances.

IM **Does reframing typologies as overlapping programs have a definite political undercurrent? Can it give students a different understanding of architecture as a political practice?**

MG You can give architecture a clear political agenda *and* a clear social and material agenda. For example, if we design a reading nook in a window, the window would have the depth to accommodate various body types. The sill might be two feet deep such that you can sit in the window, or the window is five feet wide so you can lounge in it. Designing with multiple people and purposes in mind opens architecture to be more imaginative about what it can do.

Kevin Crouse **During the Super Jury, there was a conversation on engaging identity to counter modernism. You said that identity has always played a critical role in modernism, but it was a white, European male identity. For instance, the suppressed dimension in Le Corbusier's sketches of Algerian women inform his planning for Algiers. How can architects dodge similar dominating voices in designing something like a window for reading?**

MG They can by reinscribing the body within architecture, but not in the Vitruvian sense. The window can accommodate different bodies so that it's not necessarily the male body; it can be wholly asymmetrical. The mere act of considering varied bodies projects differentiation into space. The architecture becomes an instrument for liberation.

KC **One reason for the upsurge in typological studies is a response to the ambiguity of neoliberal politics. Typologies are articulate and transparent, and thus digestible. Yet, with their ease in comprehension, typologies become caricatures, proliferating open-ended programming for vacant spaces. How can we provide inclusive programming that avoids such clichés?**

MG The architectural profession has given away its agency to neoliberal capitalism and thereby to the politics that it fosters. Architecture has become a product. Experimentation within the academy twenty to twenty-five years ago was coopted into the profession to the extent that it is difficult to distinguish a commercial building by a corporate firm from a design by an architect that was once considered cutting-edge. The market for that commercial client has turned architecture itself into a sellable image, which has now boomeranged back into the academy, where we no longer produce renderings but renders. That verb, render, has something to do with marketability. In this neoliberal condition, it is the academy's job to teach students how to resist the glossy rendering.

IM **The Providence River's contours trace a harbor designed for slave and opium trade that was led by benefactors of Brown and RISD. Sites like Market Square, a slaver's market space now in the center of RISD's campus, are unacknowledged markers of this fraught history. How can tools of architectural research bring back historical memories? How can the city itself become a reading nook?**

MG Instead of designing a singular structure, designers can strategically excavate particular locations and moments to uncover, interpret, and intervene in layers of history at multiple points. Material tactics can reveal the layers of history as an index of historical relationships. Bringing in our typological discussion, I'm thinking of Alexa Thorne's project on domesticity (see pp. 81–84). The

embroidered maps created a material strategy—a way of making—that countered the typological study in the proposed design. Her grandparents' home as an adaptable, modifiable precedent physically manifested material layering in her embroidered map, but the typological design primarily dealt with geological layering.

KC **How can students utilize that moment of transference between rich material explorations and "real" architecture?**

MG The definitions of architecture are entrenched; students learn how to make architecture, which is a static activity. It is not critical to make that actualized house but to question it. How can we remake that domestic thing? What can space accommodate on its independently defined terms? What would an architectural floor plan look like if Alexa embroidered it? That prospect is incredibly exciting. "House" can go away. At some point, there comes a period of unlearning architecture, and that takes time and experience. Alexa's embroidered landscape study takes longer than a semester. It is often the non-architectural objects that are most exciting because they break the boundaries and show new limits. When it shifts to designing a building, we are discouraged by the limitations of the discipline again.

KC **We are in a pandemic. As Arundhati Roy describes in her essay for the *Financial Times*, the pandemic is a portal that responds to many global issues: economic instability, class wars, xenophobia, racial injustice. If these are nodes of broad-scale injustice, clarifying our precarious position as a discipline, how can architecture schools use a *performative* portal to transform their pedagogies, and, as Roy puts it, "walk through lightly" into the future?**

MG Performance can mean something very prescriptive, but the agile and flexible aspects of performance art represent the opposite. Improvisation, however, requires expertise; it derives from extensive practice. Before Donald Byrd could actually improvise on the trumpet, he trained to know the capacity of the instrument; he learned and digested myriad musical possibilities. Rehearsing shows us the limits of discipline, and we do that rehearsal in architecture school. Students shouldn't necessarily have to wait until they graduate to loosen and improvise if the institution emphasizes agility and maneuverability. Architecture is a mentally and conceptually iterative practice. When you make a drawing, the whole plan doesn't show up at once, even digitally. Iteration and learned agility enable facile ways of working, where one learns the potential of architecture as an instrument for the next thing coming.

IM **Improvisation is always in friction with what it's improvising. In the same sense, architecture must be in dialogue with what it criticizes. How can we integrate that dialectical way of teaching into studios?**

MG Going back to where we started, the protestors made thorough contingency plans to elude police barricades. We may not be aware of that planning, but it shows that improvisation doesn't just happen. Harriet Tubman successfully evaded capture on the Underground Railroad through all the trips from the South to the North. She learned how and where to cross rivers and circumvent boundaries through those journeys. She shared the experience that enabled others the agility to maneuver and subvert systems and infrastructures. Hers is an example of tactical pedagogy, showing how architecture can reclaim its subversive techniques.

Students shouldn't necessarily have to wait until they graduate to loosen and improvise if the institution emphasizes agility and maneuverability. Iteration and learned agility enable facile ways of working, where one learns the potential of architecture as an instrument for the next thing coming.

Timothy Hyde

Action and Stillness

It is only stating the obvious to note that undertaking an architecture thesis project during the spring of 2020 was an enormously imposing challenge for any student. Not simply because of the now-familiar difficulties of working remotely, using digital tools almost exclusively, having conversations on Zoom instead of in a studio, and all the many other constraints on design thinking. And not simply because of the emotional and intellectual trials of navigating the sudden onset of the pandemic and the subsequent quarantine. All that encumbrance would be intimidating enough, but thesis students in the spring of 2020 faced an additional burden in the suddenly surrounding urgency of providing solutions to crisis—practical solutions or speculative solutions, present-day solutions or future solutions, amateur or expert, as long as oriented toward solution.

Almost any architecture program envisions its thesis program as a challenge to its students to imagine the very contours of possibility. RISD certainly presented its cohort with this task starting in the fall of 2019, a time, of course, when such an assignment seemed reasonable and appropriate, merited by the discipline's need and desire to replenish its terms and interrogate its presumptions. This effort is what any thesis should attempt, as I have argued previously and as I argued (blithely, in retrospect) to the RISD students once again last fall.[1] But the spring of 2020 arrived and changed the calculus entirely. Now the need for new terms, for rigorous disciplinary scrutiny, was even more pressing, and the goal even more obvious. The crisis of the pandemic made the slower-moving cataclysm of climate change even more apparent than it had been, and brought also the parallel crisis of global social and economic inequality sharply into focus.

I spoke with the RISD students last fall about my conceptualization of the architecture thesis as a type of "great gizmo"—a process of producing new, legible arrangements of disciplinary knowledge. While I think the gizmo model still has relevance for conceptualizing the architecture thesis, the circumstances of the current moment obviously demand some qualifications and some significant reconsiderations. The gizmo, not easy in any circumstances, is all the more challenging to pursue when the relevance and authority of the discipline itself cannot be taken for granted, and—to put it bluntly—amid the surrounding turmoil of crises, it is not yet clear what, if any, indispensable role architecture has to play, at least as it is conventionally taught and practiced. Before it is possible to think of disciplinary scrutiny undertaken through the gizmo, then, it would be necessary to articulate some possibility for the persistence of the discipline itself.

It is plainly unfair to set this task to thesis students, but then again it seems that many thesis students have taken on the task of their own volition—perhaps as an inquiry into the capabilities of the profession for which they see themselves training; perhaps as a test of connections between academic thought

1 See Timothy Hyde, "Turning the Black Box into a Great Gizmo," *Thresholds*, no. 38 (Fall 2010): 80–83.

Thesis students in the spring of 2020 faced an additional burden in the suddenly surrounding urgency of providing solutions to crisis—practical solutions or speculative solutions, present-day solutions or future solutions, amateur or expert, as long as oriented toward solution.

and social realities; perhaps inadvertently. Regardless of motive, glimpses of a particular irresolution, or productive actions of irresolution, appear in several of the spring 2020 thesis projects, actions of irresolution that I would discern as the manifestation of compelling forms of stillness.

Jake Lefeber's project **It's Not a Sport** (see pp. 69–72) populates part of the shoreline

of Newport, Rhode Island, with an array of architectural instruments, each calibrated to respond to the kinetic action of environmental factors. Wind and waves provide the primary inputs for these instruments, which then translate those inputs into fields of data, legible to expert eyes as information. Each of these architectural instruments appears to a viewer as an assembly of discrete and quite delicate parts, fastened and joined into a larger structure comparable to a small building. And it is as small buildings, or small pavilions, that these instruments would present themselves to a casual observer, for whom the translation of environment into data would manifest not as information but as experience—experience of movement, of gradual oscillations, of a machine at work.

We are fully cognizant, in our present moment, that the translation of environment into data is a vital action, critical for catalyzing our urgently necessary decisions on addressing the climate crisis. This thesis clearly attaches itself to this moment and to this urgency, and it would of course be understandable, and fair, to analyze the thesis in terms of the adequacy of its contribution to the movement toward change and melioration and solution. In those terms, is the architectural presence too modest and the architectural function too slight? Does the very delicacy of the assembly of frames, cables, and planks dissemble the scale and urgency of the problem with its atmosphere of slow, subjective contemplation?

But it is not the obligation of this thesis (or any other) to provide a solution as such, but rather to attempt to craft a disciplinary perspective. Seen though this lens, the actions created by the array of shoreline instruments are indeed actions, but actions that cumulatively produce a kind of stillness. Their delicacy of repetitive movement would enact, in experiential terms, a stillness in contrast to the relatively urbanized surroundings, but this is a literal sense, and the kind of stillness toward which the project points is more profound. Through its architectural machines and the experience of encountering those machines, Lefeber's thesis reduces the translation of environment into data into discrete and singular events; one arc at a time, one rise or fall at a time, one measurement, one point of data. Accumulation may be the eventual outcome, but it is stillness that is highlighted here, the pause or gap between one registration of data and the next.

It would be no surprise to see any particular thesis project adopt utopia as its focus, and perhaps this familiar thesis framework should be even likelier to appear in the context of the overlapping crises of the present moment. But Sam Wesselman's project **Generally Specific** (see pp. 133–136) points toward a different no-place,

a no-place through which we regularly traverse with only glancing notice. The *terrain vague* surrounding and woven throughout postindustrial cities appears in patches small and large, overgrown or bare, dense with ruins or empty. Terrain vague is our contemporary no-place, owned by someone but unused, demarcated by zoning and property maps but unregulated, an abundant but unrecognized resource.

This thesis takes terrain vague as its site of action, beginning with a meticulous inventory of its characteristics, its materials, artifactual remains, and environment. From this inventory, the thesis descries a set of potentialities, or possible future actions. Many are modest in scale—re-fittings of existing abandoned objects or something as simple as paint upon asphalt. The thesis prioritizes strategies of intervention and invention over any definitive outcome. As architectural actions, each is limited in itself but holds the promise of accumulation over time into a larger framework of change. And each in itself places deliberate and intense focus upon a specific architectural action in order to reveal the general possibility of that action if undertaken over time—the definition of a boundary, the conjunction of two differentiated materials, the construction of a roof plane.

The material consequences of these actions, and even more so the labor that would undertake them, render them visible and concrete, but they nevertheless contribute to a kind of stillness. The simplicity of some of the actions is one factor, as they refrain from installing a dramatic physical transformation on the existing terrain vague. But the more powerful factor is that the thesis deliberately and decisively presents the actions as actions in themselves. That is to say, each action is complete in itself, and whether it offers a coordinated addition to another action is of little concern. The focus is upon each direct and minimally defined specificity. One strategy, for example, which would seem to offer the most consequential and most legible transformation through its actions, is the architectural site proposed for use as a training area in building trades. Here, actions would presumably be undertaken hour after hour, with an atmosphere of busyness and possibly something like a building as the result. But it would not in fact be a building, but rather the repetition of actions, and in this unceasing action, a certain kind of stillness.

Alexa Thorne's thesis project, **Mended Fields** (see pp. 81–84), considers the juxtaposition of two

scales, the very large and the very small, as the framework for exploring repair and maintenance. The large scale is the landscape surrounding Badin, North Carolina, a landscape that has been damaged by the processes of industrial production and which the thesis sees as an impetus toward repair through remediation and new protocols of environmental maintenance. The small scale is a single-family house in the same location, which the thesis sees as an impetus toward a new approach to design that takes repair and upkeep as its initial requirements. In both of these scales, the thesis sharpens a focus on action, but action that acknowledges and embraces the circumstance of impermanence.

Action here might take forms that are familiar within the contemporary discourses of both environmentalism and architecture—filtration or replacement or cleaning. But there is another vital action undertaken by the thesis, the action of representation, and in this the thesis challenges its audience to see that maintenance is a critical yet unremarked foundation of architecture and architectural thinking. To see maintenance should not be difficult, yet architectural discourse has elided it, and elided it to such an extent that the discipline has, for example, struggled even in recent years to locate preservation and conservation within its disciplinary boundaries; has, for example, struggled to see how refraining from building might be an architecture strategy appropriate to our moment of climate crisis.

One set of representations within this thesis project captures not only the decision to render visible, but also the full subjective depth of meaning that maintenance might carry. Four startling and compelling representations—or "embroidered geographies"—capture an image of the landscape within the confines of an embroidery hoop. Each embroidered panel shows not only an abstracted scaled plan of the selected landscape, but also marks out the damaged areas within that land, outlined in stitches of red thread. These elegant representations conjure their own paradigm of stillness, and here again, stillness is not an antagonist of action but is rather a different category of action. This stillness is the pace and dimensions of an embroidery needle and stitch, the slow fashioning of shape and image with a line of thread and a background of fabric. This stillness is also the continuity of familial generations against a landscape that is changing and unchanged. This stillness is the stillness of maintenance, the persistence achieved through repetition, replacement, and repair. Architecture's disciplinary past may not hold lessons, much less solutions, for the successive waves of crises that have broken over the past few months, and architecture, we should remind ourselves, is not the answer to every question. But if the disciplinary past is mined for insights, an introspective,

Glimpses of a particular irresolution, or productive actions of irresolution, appear in several of the spring 2020 thesis projects, actions of irresolution that I would discern as the manifestation of compelling forms of stillness.

Stillness is not inaction; stillness is not a withdrawal into disciplinary introspection; stillness is neither an unthinking performance nor a contemplative subjectivity. The stillness evident in these thesis projects is a tool.

distracted architectural interior might seem a peculiar choice of prospect. Yet in turning to Sir John Soane's house in Lincoln's Inn Fields, Julie Kress's thesis project, **Framed Familiarity in Four Acts** (see pp. 211–214), transforms

its architecture into an action of inaction through the careful crafting of distortions and dissimulations. The house, as the thesis title suggests, is familiar to the architectural mind; indeed, it has often been taken to be the singular example of the manifestation of an architectural mind, an unmediated reflection of the designer who occupied it. One curator of the house museum, in the early twentieth century, despaired of ever being able to overcome the defining presence of that architectural mind, of ever being able to reveal the house in any other terms.

This project endeavors exactly such an attempt—to overcome the defining architectural presence in order to make space for other thoughts, other intentions, other consequences. The medium for the attempt is animation, with a painstaking re-rendering of the interior spaces of Soane's house as spaces of instability and uncertainty. One room is transformed into a succession of paper frames; another becomes a zoetrope. The key to this innovative rewriting of the house is to see the house, and architecture itself perhaps, not as the substantiation of ideas in material objects but the instantiation of materiality into the register of concepts. Through this reorientation, the animation (or reanimation) of the materiality of the house offers a way to revalue its conceptual framework.

In one act of the short film that is the final thesis project, the disruption of the house is quite minimal. The actual house is dense, filled with a cascade of objects, but they are all at rest. In the reanimation, however, the ornamental figures begin to peel away from the walls, begin to flutter like the pages of a book. Like the pages of a book lifted by a breeze, these figures draw out a sensation more of stillness than of motion, simply because of the momentary and contingent nature of their animation. The background, to which they will shortly return, remains in place, remains still, but with a newly charged sense of significance now that its potential animation has been established, now that any future moment may be the moment that ends the suspension of stillness.

In drawing a focus upon—and admiring—the kinds of stillness evoked and created by these thesis projects I do not mean to conjure up in the reader's mind an idea of inaction, much less an idea of inaction in the face of necessity. Quite the opposite, for these modes of stillness seem to me to be very much modes of action, and important ones, in the spring of 2020. There is no question that action is urgently needed in response to encompassing crises, those that have arrived, those that have long been forewarned, those that will soon emerge, and surely architecture will need to respond to those crises, at the very least, and in some cases will have to contribute toward their mitigation. So, yes, inaction would be all but unforgivable. A withdrawal into disciplinary introspection such as the movement toward autonomy in the 1970s could not now be sanctioned much less applauded. Nor can a veil of pragmatism such as that summoned in response to architecture's theoretical bent be employed now as a means to move ahead with blind technical determination.

But stillness here is not inaction; stillness here is not a withdrawal into disciplinary introspection; stillness here is neither an unthinking performance nor a contemplative subjectivity. The stillness evident in these thesis projects is a tool, a tool with the potential to create a space within disciplinary busyness and rapidity, within disciplinary presumptions and existing definitions. Stillness was of course a widespread experience for many in the days of quarantine, so it is perhaps not surprising to witness its appearance in thesis projects developed under the conditions of spring 2020. But this stillness is less a response than a potential, a potential to recalibrate one by one many aspects of disciplinary thinking.

Acknowledgments

As John Donne famously said, no man is an island, and by extension, no book is produced in isolation. This book—miraculously written, assembled, and designed during lockdowns, pivots to online teaching, illness, and at least one international move—is the product of one of the most collegial, creative, and productive collaborations of my professional life. I want to take a moment to thank all of the individuals who have contributed to this project. It has been a silver lining in the dark crisis of a pandemic that has brought to visibility the racial, political, and environmental inequity in which we currently operate. As a result, this project stands in stark contrast to the moment that produced it, and the generosity and commitment of the team who made it happen is all the more remarkable for the circumstances within which they operated.

First, a big thank you to the design and editorial team that made this book possible. To James Goggin (RISD Graphic Design) and Shan James of Practise, thank you for celebrating our RISD Architecture Class of 2020 with your exquisite graphic design of this book. Your support of our students and their work is so appreciated, and your responsive, representative design perfectly captures and concretizes their work in this ephemeral moment. Thanks to Jennifer Liese (Director of the Center for Arts & Language at RISD) for her thoughtful and prescient editing of the book's texts, and for her capable and steadfast collaboration throughout the process. To Kevin Crouse (RISD M.Arch '18), it was such a pleasure to finally have the opportunity to collaborate on a writing project, and I so appreciate your thoughtful edits of the student submissions and your skillful crafting of the interviews in this volume. Chloe Bennie (RISD M.Arch '21), as graduate assistant for the thesis and directed research class of 2020, along with Yash Gupta, saw this project through from beginning to end with consistent and flawless work as managing editor for this volume. Thanks, also, to Vrindha Vijay (RISD M.Arch '21), whose superhuman archival work with the book's images contributed to its visual potency. Finally, to Sarah Kramer, many thanks for your meticulous proofreading.

In the planning and execution of this book, I am extremely grateful to three RISD Architecture colleagues without whom this project might never have been realized. Thank you to Daniel Ibañez, a wonderful colleague and collaborator, who skillfully coordinated the seven studio cohorts represented in this volume and was instrumental in developing the Directed Research degree path over the last three years in the department. Dani was instrumental in the initial brainstorming about this volume, and introduced me to Ramon Prat at Actar, who graciously agreed to publish the book. Many thanks, also, to Carl Lostritto, RISD Architecture's Graduate Program Director and secondary advisor to the Revisionist Histories thesis cohort. To his credit, when the idea for this book emerged in the midst of the chaos of a global pandemic,

Carl greeted it with his characteristic good-natured and enthusiastic support, and he has generously taken up the slack as this project developed. Additionally, Jacqueline Shaw's meticulous development of the Thesis Discursive Workshop over the past three years has underwritten the robust disciplinary positioning of the student work and fastidious attention to the design of the thesis books. This book was supported in the department by our Senior Coordinator, Katy Rogers, and our Coordinator, Karen Bell. Katy and Karen were crucial in the department's sudden shift to remote learning in March 2020, and they have thoughtfully supported this project, with all of its details and logistics, ever since.

I am fortunate to undertake this work at RISD with a teaching team dedicated to the intellectual and creative growth of our students, and to creating a milieu within which their design aspirations can thrive. Many thanks to Hansy Better Barraza, David Gersten, Daniel Ibañez, Ryan McCaffrey, Ben Pell, and Rachely Rotem for their collegiality and tireless efforts in support of our graduating students. Each of these advisors was supported by a secondary advisor tasked with bringing alternative perspectives to the work and acting as a sort of continuity editor for the project. Thank you to Silvia Acosta, Damian White, Jacqueline Shaw, Lauren Bordes, Ijlal Muzaffar, and Carl Lostritto for riding shotgun while substantively contributing to the quality of the design work and its discursive depth.

While RISD Architecture colleagues contributed to creating conditions to support and grow the student work, architecture colleagues and friends from other institutions collaborated to build a context around the projects, both verbal and written. In a summer of chaos in higher education, these colleagues stepped up in support of our students, helping us to interpret the work and its meaning in this unprecedented moment. Thank you to the participants in the Super Jury—Iñaki Alday, Daniel A. Barber, Sean Canty, Peggy Deamer, Nicholas de Monchaux, David Gissen, Mario Gooden, Timothy Hyde, Ang Li, Ana Miljački, Kiel Moe, Ronald Rael, Katerina Ruedi Ray, Lola Sheppard, Georgeen Theodore, Mason White, Mabel O. Wilson, and Jason Young. Your critical feedback charted possible future trajectories for our discipline, and your supportive engagement of our students and their work at a difficult time will not be forgotten.

And finally, to the RISD Architecture class of 2020, thanks seem insufficient to the gracious and agile ways each of you have navigated a set of unimaginable circumstances. Your commitment, your humanity, and your creativity amid protracted adversity speaks to your individual resilience and collective stamina. It has been an honor and a privilege to work with you, to learn from you, and to witness the strength and character that will contribute to your future success.

Amy Catania Kulper

Contributors

Iñaki Alday is a registered architect, landscape architect, and urbanist. After graduating from the Polytechnic University of Catalonia in 1992, he founded aldayjover architecture and landscape with Margarita Jover in 1996 in Barcelona. The innovative multidisciplinary, research-based practice is renowned for its approach to the relation between cities and rivers, in which the natural dynamics of flooding become part of buildings and public spaces, eliminating the idea of "catastrophe."

Alday has been Dean and Richard Koch Chair in Architecture at Tulane School of Architecture since 2018. Before that he was Quesada Professor and Chair of the Department of Architecture at the University of Virginia and Associate Professor at the Vallès School of Architecture, Universitat Politèchnica de Catalunya. Both in academic research and in practice, Alday addresses the role of architecture and architects, the integration of disciplines and scales, nontraditional programs as hybridized infrastructures, and social and environmental ethics to promote a new attitude toward the transformation of our environment and toward re-imagining how architecture can contribute to the inhabitation of the most challenged areas of the planet.

Daniel A. Barber is Associate Professor of Architecture and Chair of the Ph.D. Program in Architecture at the University of Pennsylvania. His research examines historical relationships between architecture and global environmental culture, reframing the means and ends of architectural expertise toward a more robust engagement with the climate crisis. His book *Modern Architecture and Climate: Design before Air Conditioning* (Princeton University Press, 2020) explores how modern architects incorporated climate-mediating strategies into their designs and shows how regional approaches to climate adaptability were essential to the development of the field. His first book, *A House in the Sun: Modern Architecture and Solar Energy in the Cold War* (Oxford University Press, 2016), documents mid-century experiments in solar housing. Together, the two projects reassess the role of environmental factors in the historical development of modern architectural principles and practices.

Barber is focused on providing conceptual tools for architects to better address the climate crisis. He has published in *Technology and Culture*, *Grey Room*, *Public Culture*, and forthcoming in *South Atlantic Quarterly*; in numerous edited volumes; and through podcasts and online venues. Recent articles in *Log* and on *e-flux Architecture* encourage designers to take the future into account. He edits the ongoing *Accumulation* series on *e-flux Architecture* online and is a cofounder of *Current*, a platform for the discussion of environmental histories of architecture, launching summer 2020. He has held fellowships at the Harvard University Center for the Environment, the Princeton Environmental Institute, the Sydney Environment Institute, and through the Alexander von Humboldt Foundation.

Hansy Better Barraza earned her B.Arch from Cornell University and MAUD in Urban Design from the Harvard Graduate School of Design. She joined RISD's faculty in 2002 and served as Graduate Program Director from 2014 to 2017. Born in Barranquilla, Colombia, Barraza focuses her research on the intersection of design methods, social practices, and equity. She offers students an intense focus on design methods that embrace social responsibility. In 2016 she was awarded a grant from the Graham Foundation for Advanced Studies in the Fine Arts to support the research, writing, and publishing of her book *Where Are the Utopian Visionaries?: Architecture of Social Exchange* (Periscope, 2012).

Barraza is also an editorial board member of the journal *Critical Productive*, which examines the intersection of architecture, culture, and theory.

In 2007 Barraza cofounded BR+A+CE: Building Research + Architecture + Community Exchange, a nonprofit dedicated to creating new spaces through community partnerships. In 2002 Barraza founded Studio Luz Architects in partnership with Anthony Piermarini. Based in Boston, Studio Luz's designs have received international honors including the Architectural Record Design Vanguard Award, a Progressive Architecture Award, multiple AIA Design Excellence Awards, the Architectural League Prize for Young Architects, and the Chicago Athenaeum's American Architecture Award.

Chloe Jenny Bennie is in the final year of the M.Arch program at RISD. Having grown up in Scotland, she received her Bachelor of Environmental Design from the University of Hawai'i at Mānoa, where she was the recipient of the AIA Honolulu Scholarship, took home first place at Hawaii's Wood Show, and traveled to Shanghai to participate in the Tongji University International Construction Festival, where she took home third place. Bennie's thesis will explore women's and women-identifying sexuality through weaving applied to domestic architecture.

Sean Canty founded Studio Sean Canty, a design practice that activates environments by conjoining discrete geometries, materials, and architectural types, in 2017. Canty is Designer and Assistant Professor of Architecture at the Harvard Graduate School of Design, where he teaches architectural design in the Core Design Studios. Prior to joining the faculty at the GSD, he held teaching positions at The Cooper Union, University of California, Berkeley, and California College of the Arts. In addition to architectural design, Canty has taught classes on descriptive geometry and design media.

Canty is one of the founding principals of Office III (OIII), an experimental architectural collective that spans New York, San Francisco, and Cambridge. Selected as a finalist for the 2016 MoMA PS1 Young Architects competition, OIII has completed a Welcome Center for Governors Island and exhibited work at the Museum of Modern Art in New York. Prior to founding these studios, Canty was a Senior Project Designer at IwamotoScott Architecture in San Francisco, where he led commercial projects for clients including Pinterest, Bloomberg, and Heavybit and oversaw residential projects including the Goto House and Noe Valley Residence. Canty received an M.Arch from the Harvard Graduate School of Design and a B.Arch from California College of the Arts.

Kevin Crouse is an architectural and lighting designer living and working in Brooklyn, New York. He holds a Bachelor of Arts in Architectural Studies from Hampshire College and received his M.Arch from RISD. At RISD, Crouse was the recipient of the Graduate Architecture Thesis Award for his work on problematizing American consumerism and fraught altruism. He co-taught and developed the class Writing as Architecture, in which students investigated the role of writing in the design process, and which later evolved into a studio course. Crouse is the cocreator of *Modern Usage*, an interview archive that invites professionals across multiple disciplines to speak frankly about how their practices contribute to conversations surrounding theory, pedagogy, and professional methodologies. Currently, Crouse is participating in a series of conversations at the interface of architecture, ethnography, and anthropology.

Peggy Deamer is Professor Emerita of the Yale School of Architecture, principal in the firm Deamer, Studio, and the founding member of the Architecture Lobby, a group advocating for the value of architectural design and labor. Deamer is the editor of *Architecture and Capitalism: 1845 to the Present* (Routledge, 2013) and *The Architect as Worker: Immaterial Labor, the Creative Class, and the Politics of Design* (Bloomsbury, 2015) and the author of *Architecture and Labor* (Routledge, 2020). Her articles have appeared in *Log*, *Avery Review*, *e-flux*, and *Harvard Design Magazine* among other journals. Her theory work explores the relationship between subjectivity, design, and labor in the current economy. Her design work has appeared in *HOME*, *House and Garden*, *Progressive Architecture*, and the *New York Times*. In 2018 she received the Architectural Record Women in Architecture Activist Award.

David Gersten is an artist, architect, writer, and educator based in New York City. He is Distinguished Professor and Director of Interdisciplinary Learning at The Cooper Union for the Advancement of Science and Art, where he has taught since 1991 and has served as Associate Dean and Acting Dean of the School of Architecture. Gersten is currently a visiting professor at RISD, an International Visiting Scholar at the Central Academy of Fine Arts (CAFA) in Beijing, a fellow of the Royal Society of Arts in the UK, and a member of the Board of Directors of Big Picture Learning.

Gersten is the founding Director and President of Arts Letters & Numbers, a nonprofit arts and education organization dedicated to expanding the experiences understood as education through creating new structures and spaces for creative exchange across disciplines. He works in collaboration with international organizations, educational and cultural institutions, and education policy groups including UNICEF, the United Nations Academic Impact division, and Education Reimagined, and recently presented a keynote address titled "Unlocking the Creativity of Youth" at the UNICEF–EXPO and at the Chancellors Summit at CAFA in Beijing.

Gersten's works, which include drawings, stories, essays, films, prints, performances, buildings, and constructions, have appeared in international exhibitions and performance spaces and are held in the collections of the Canadian Centre for Architecture, the New York Public Library's print collection, and private collections. He has published on topics ranging from emergent disciplinary geographies to the links between embodied experience, cognition, memory, perception, language, space, and education.

James Goggin is a Providence– and Auckland, New Zealand-based British and/or Australian graphic designer from London via Sydney, Stockholm, Copenhagen, Arnhem, and Chicago. He received a master's degree in Graphic Design from the Royal College of Art in London and founded a design practice named Practise in 1999 with partner Shan James. Between 2016 and 2021 James taught BFA and MFA Graphic Design as an Associate Professor at RISD in Providence. He previously taught at Werkplaats Typografie in Arnhem, The Netherlands, and at ÉCAL (École cantonale d'art de Lausanne) in Switzerland.

Alongside Practise, Goggin has worked as a design consultant to Tate Modern and Tate Britain (2003–2010), art director of British music magazine *The Wire* (2005–2008), and Director of Design, Publishing, and New Media at the Museum of Contemporary Art Chicago (2010–2013). He designs type for various projects, with a number of fonts available from Swiss foundry Lineto. Goggin has run workshops, lectured, and served as critic at architecture, art, and design schools in Europe, the U.S., and Australasia. He contributes writing to a range of international publications, serves on the editorial board of architecture magazine *Flat Out*, and was inducted as a member of Alliance Graphique Internationale in 2010. Works by Practise are included in the permanent collections of the Victoria & Albert Museum, the Art Institute of Chicago, and the Chicago Design Archive.

Mario Gooden is a cultural practice architect and founding principal of Huff + Gooden Architects. His practice engages the cultural landscape and the intersectionality of architecture, race, gender, sexuality, and technology. His work crosses the thresholds between the design of architecture and the built environment, writing, research, and performance. Gooden's performances include *Working on Water*, presented at Columbia University in October 2019, and *Black Holes Ain't So Black*, presented at the Museum of Modern Art's Pop Rally *Studio Visit: Practice as Ritual* in 2018. His work has been exhibited at the International Architecture Exhibition Biennale in Venice, Italy; Architekturmuseum der TU München; the Netherlands Architecture Institute (NAi); Storefront for Art and Architecture; the National Building Museum in Washington, DC; and the Municipal Art Society of New York. His work has been featured in publications including *Artforum*, *Architect Magazine*, *Architectural Record*, *Metropolis*, *Wallpaper*, *Architecture & Urbanism* (*A+U*), and the *New York Times*.

Gooden is a Professor of Practice at the Graduate School of Architecture, Planning and Preservation (GSAPP) at Columbia University, where he teaches advanced architectural design and theory and is codirector of the Global Africa Lab (GAL). He is a 2012 National Endowment for the Arts Fellow, a MacDowell Fellow, and a 2019 American Academy of Arts and Letters Award in Architecture recipient. Gooden is the author of *Dark Space: Architecture, Representation, Black Identity* (Columbia University Press, 2016) as well as numerous essays and articles on architecture, art, and cultural production. He is also Research Associate at Visual Identities in Art and Design (VIAD) at the University of Johannesburg, South Africa.

Timothy Hyde is a historian of architecture and Associate Professor at the Massachusetts Institute of Technology whose research focuses on the political dimensions of architecture from the eighteenth century to the present, with particular attention to the relationships between architecture and law. His books include *Ugliness and Judgment: On Architecture in the Public Eye* (Princeton University Press, 2019) and *Constitutional Modernism: Architecture and Civil Society in Cuba, 1933–1959* (University of Minnesota Press, 2012). Hyde is a founding member of the Aggregate Architectural History Collaborative and coeditor of the first Aggregate book, *Governing by Design*. His writings have appeared in journals including *Perspecta*, *Log*, *El Croquis*, *The Journal of Architecture*, *Journal of Architectural Education*, *arq*, *Future Anterior*, *Architectural Theory Review*, and *Thresholds*.

Daniel Ibañez is an architect and urbanist, Doctor of Design candidate at the Harvard Graduate School of Design, and research fellow at the Harvard Office for Urbanization and the Urban Theory Lab. Ibañez's research seeks to frame the design disciplines in relation to broader socio-ecological interdependencies through cross-disciplinary studies in the field of urban metabolism. He has organized conferences including *Projective Views on Urban Metabolism* (Harvard GSD, 2014) and his books include *New Geographies 06: Grounding Metabolism* (Harvard University Press, 2014), *Third Coast Atlas* (Actar, 2017), and *Wood Urbanism: From the Molecular to the Territorial* (Actar, 2019). Ibañez has received academic research grants from the Graham Foundation for Advanced Studies and Fundación La Caixa Fulbright Fellowship, among others.

Ibañez is currently Assistant Professor at RISD in the School of Architecture, a codirector of the Master in Advanced Ecological Buildings and Biocities (MAEBB) at the Institute for Advanced Architecture of Catalunya in Valldaura Self-Sufficient Labs, Barcelona, and Senior Urban Specialist consultant at the World Bank, advising on housing and urban development at the intersection of urbanism and climate change. He cofounded and directs the design firm Margen-Lab, a transcalar-targeted office invested in developing ecologically powerful and materially exuberant architecture and urban design. Ibañez received his master's of Architecture from Escuela Técnica Superior de Arquitectura de Madrid in 2007 with honors. He holds a master's in Advanced Architecture from IAAC with distinction. In 2012, he completed a master's in Design Studies in Urbanism, Landscape, Ecology with distinction from the Harvard Graduate School of Design.

Before assuming the role of provost at RISD in 2019, **Kent Kleinman** was the Gale and Ira Drukier Dean of the College of Architecture, Art, and Planning at Cornell University as well as professor in the Department of Architecture from 2008 to 2018. He has taught at institutions including the Academy of Fine Arts in Vienna, the Hochschule der Kunst in Berlin, the Royal Danish Academy in Copenhagen, and ETH Zürich, and was also a faculty member at the University of Michigan, chair of architecture at the State University of New York at Buffalo, and dean at Parsons School of Design, The New School.

Kleinman received his professional degree in architecture from the University of California, Berkeley. His scholarly focus is twentieth-century European Modernism, and his books include *Villa Müller: A Work of Adolf Loos* (Princeton Architectural Press, 1994); *Rudolf Arnheim: Revealing Vision* (University of Michigan Press, 1998); and *Mies van der Rohe: The Krefeld Villas* (Princeton Architectural Press, 2005). He was awarded a Mellon Foundation Senior Public Goods Fellowship in 2002 and was a visiting scholar at the Canadian Centre for Architecture in 2005. He has received four Graham Foundation grants, the national Bruner Award, two *Architects' Journal* 10 Best Books awards, a New York State Council for the Arts grant, and (with Eric Sutherland) a Progressive Architecture Design Award. In 2012 Kleinman received the American Institute of Architects New York State Educator Honor Award and was recognized as a Top 25 Most Admired Educator by *Design Intelligence* in both 2016 and 2018. He is a coprincipal investigator on a grant from the Mellon Foundation focused on integrating architecture and the humanities in the study of urbanism. He is a registered architect in California.

Amy Catania Kulper is an architect, theorist, and curator whose teaching and research focus on the intersections of history, theory, and criticism with design. Kulper has taught at Cambridge University, the University of Pennsylvania, UCLA, SCI-Arc, the University of Michigan, and RISD, where she is currently an Associate Professor and Head of the Department of Architecture. At the University of Michigan, she was a four-time recipient of the Donna M. Salzer Award for teaching excellence.

Her curatorial work includes framing and cochairing the 107th Annual Meeting of the Association of the Collegiate Schools of Architecture in 2018 with Grace La (Harvard GSD) and Jeremy Ficca (Carnegie Mellon). The conference, *BLACK BOX: Articulating Architecture's Core in the Post-Digital Era* recorded the highest submission rate for an ACSA conference in the last decade, and included an exhibition, *Drawing for the Design Imaginary*, positioning the role of drawing in post-digital practice, at the Carnegie Museum of Art. In 2019 she cocurated and designed *Drawing Attention* at the Roca London Gallery.

Kulper's writings are published in *Log*, *The Journal of Architecture*, *arq: Architectural Research Quarterly*, *Candide*, *Journal of Architectural Education*, and numerous edited volumes. Kulper has served on the editorial board of the *Journal of Architectural Education*, where she served as the Design Editor for six years, and in 2017 received the Distinguished Service Award from the ACSA for her work on the journal. Kulper holds master's degrees from the University of Pennsylvania and Cambridge University and a Ph.D. in the History and Philosophy of Architecture from Cambridge University.

Jennifer Liese is director of the Center for Arts & Language at RISD, where she teaches courses on graduate thesis writing, professional practices, and publishing. She has presented at College Art Association, Association for Independent Colleges of Art and Design, and Society for Artistic Research conferences. Liese's anthology of contemporary artists' writings, *Social Medium: Artists Writing, 2000–2015* (Paper Monument, 2016), was named one of the best art books of the 2010s by *ArtNews*. Her writing has appeared in publications including *Artforum*, *Bookforum*, *Cabinet*, *BOMB*, *Provincetown Arts*, and *Paper Monument*, along with various exhibition catalogues. Liese was managing editor of *Artforum* (2000–2004) and is an independent editor for museums and publishers including the Museum of Modern Art, MIT Press, and Phaidon. She holds a master's in Art History, Theory and Criticism from the School of the Art Institute of Chicago.

Carl Lostritto is Graduate Program Director and Associate Professor at RISD Architecture. He has also taught at the Boston Architectural College, Massachusetts Institute of Technology, Catholic University of America, and University of Maryland. His research, practice, and scholarship focus on design computation and representation, especially with respect to drawing. Lostritto recently published *Computational Drawing: From Foundational Exercises to Theories of Representation* (AR+D, 2019), which frames computation and drawing as barely compatible technologies whose combination warrants reflection and speculation. In his work, drawing productively disrupts the ability to conflate digital media with computational ideas while computation disrupts the mythical status of drawing as territory for personal expression. At RISD, Lostritto's current studio, Eggshell Digital, seeks to conceive of speculative digital constructs that are slightly but meticulously rendered as physical form.

Ryan McCaffrey is an architect focused on the relationship between regional building techniques and contemporary environments. He works primarily on large cultural and residential building projects that incorporate rural planning, adaptive reuse, and culturally relevant building systems. Having worked extensively in China, in 2019 he established Regional Building Group to work on rural development projects internationally and to provide a structured approach to architectural research rooted in sociotechnical theory. His design and teaching practices leverage sociological research as the basis for material strategies in projects that serve specific communities. McCaffrey's collaborative projects that have received international recognition include Yangpu Riverfront (2018), Lin'an Museum (2017), and Wencun Village Renovation (2014). McCaffrey holds an M.Arch from the China Academy of Art and a B.Arch from RISD and has studied architecture history and theory at McGill University. He has taught design and construction at the China Academy of Art and lectured internationally on regional research methodologies and the ethics of regional practice.

Ana Miljački is a critic, curator, and Associate Professor of Architecture at Massachusetts Institute of Technology, where she teaches history, theory, and design. She directed the Master of Architecture Program at MIT from 2016 to 2020 and the Architecture and Urbanism group from 2017 to 2020. She was part of the three-member curatorial team, with Eva Franch i Gilabert and Ashley Schafer, of the U.S. Pavilion at the 2014 Venice Architecture Biennale, where their project, OfficeUS, critically examined the last century of U.S. architects' global contribution. In 2018 Miljački launched the Critical Broadcasting Lab at MIT, whose work, "Sharing Trainers" was included in the São Paulo Architecture Biennale in fall 2019. The lab also presented the work of the studio it hosted, Collective Architecture Studio, at the Seoul Biennale of Architecture and Urbanism in fall 2019, and curated and produced the Play Room exhibition and its Play Dates at MIT in spring 2020. Miljački is the author of *The Optimum Imperative: Czech Architecture for the Socialist Lifestyle 1938–1968* (Routledge, 2017), coeditor of the *OfficeUS* series of books, guest editor of *Praxis Journal* 14: *True Stories*, and coeditor, with Amanda Reeser Lawrence, of *Terms of Appropriation: Modern Architecture and Global Exchange* (Routledge, 2018). Her *Under the Influence* symposium proceedings were recently rereleased (Actar, 2019).

Kiel Moe is a practicing architect and the Gerald Sheff Professor of Architecture at McGill University. In recognition of his design and research endeavors regarding the energetics and material culture of building, he was awarded the Gorham P. Stevens Rome Prize in Architecture at the American Academy in Rome, a Fulbright Distinguished Chair in Helsinki, the Architectural League of New York Prize, and the American Institute of Architects National Young Architect Award. He has published ten books on architecture, including *Unless: The Seagram Building Construction Ecology* (Actar, 2020), *Wood Urbanism: From the Molecular to the Territorial* (Actar, 2019), *Insulating Modernism: Isolated and Non-Isolated Thermodynamics in Architecture* (Birkhäuser, 2014), *Convergence: An Architectural Agenda for Energy* (Routledge, 2013), and *Thermally Active Surfaces in Architecture* (Princton Architectural Press, 2010).

Nicholas de Monchaux is Professor and Head of Architecture at Massachusetts Institute of Technology, a partner in the architecture practice modem, and a founder of the design technology company Local Software. Until 2020 he was Professor of Architecture and Urban Design and Craigslist Distinguished Chair in New Media at the University of California, Berkeley. De Monchaux is the author of *Spacesuit: Fashioning Apollo* (MIT Press, 2011), an architectural and urban history of the Apollo Spacesuit, winner of the Eugene Emme Award from the American Astronautical Society and shortlisted for the Art Book Prize, as well as *Local Code: 3,659 Proposals about Data, Design, and the Nature of Cities* (Princeton Architectural Press, 2016). In 2012 he was named one of the "Public Interest Design 100" by *Good Magazine*. His design work has been exhibited widely, including at the Biennial of the Americas, the Venice Architecture Biennale, the Lisbon Architecture Triennale, SFMOMA, the Yerba Buena Center for the Arts, the Storefront for Art and Architecture, and the Museum of Contemporary Art Chicago and has been supported by

MacDowell, the Santa Fe Institute, the Smithsonian Institution, the Hellman Fund, and the Bakar Spark Fund. He is a Fellow of the American Academy in Rome.

Rachely Rotem has led MODU, an interdisciplinary design studio creating architecture, urban spaces, and interiors, since its founding in 2012. As founding director and studio futurist, Rotem has directed the design of projects including the Cloud Seeding plaza pavilion and the Heart Squared public artwork. Along with Phu Hoang, she was awarded the 2017 Founders Rome Prize in Architecture. She has also been awarded the Emerging Voices award from the Architectural League of New York (2019) and the U.S.–Japan Creative Artists fellowship from the National Endowment for the Arts (2018). Rotem holds a B.Arch (cum laude) from Technion in Haifa and a master's in Advanced Architectural Design from Columbia University. She currently teaches at RISD and has taught at Massachusetts Institute of Technology. Rotem is a fellow of the American Academy in Rome, a licensed architect in Israel, and a LEED Accredited Professional in Building Design and Construction.

Ben Pell is a founding partner at PellOverton Architects, an award-winning design and research practice based in New York and Providence. Pell received his M.Arch from UCLA and his B.Arch from Syracuse University and has previously taught on the design faculty of the Syracuse University School of Architecture and the Pratt Institute and as a regular member of the Yale School of Architecture faculty from 2005 to 2014. Pell's work as a principal at PellOverton Architects, founded in 2003, has been nationally recognized through publications and awards, including the Young Architects Award from the Architectural League of New York. The firm's work has been exhibited internationally, and Pell's writing on architecture has been featured in various publications. He is the author of *The Articulate Surface: Ornament and Technology in Contemporary Architecture* (Birkhäuser, 2010).

Lola Sheppard is Professor at the University of Waterloo School of Architecture and a founding partner, with Mason White, of Lateral Office, a Toronto-based practice. Her work operates at the intersection of architecture, landscape, and urbanism. Sheppard has been pursuing teaching, research, and design work on the role of architecture in rural and remote regions for the past ten years. She is committed to design as a research vehicle to pose and respond to complex, urgent questions in the built environment, engaging in the wider context and climate of a project—social, ecological, or political. Sheppard's work has been exhibited extensively and she has lectured across the U.S., Canada, and Europe. Lateral Office has presented at the Seoul Biennale of Architecture and Urbanism (2017) and the Chicago Architecture Biennial (2015), and they were awarded a Special Mention at the 2014 Venice Architecture Biennale. They received a Progressive Architecture Award in 2013 and the 2012 Holcim Gold for Sustainable Construction for North America for their work on the Arctic. Sheppard is co-author, with White, of the book *Many Norths: Spatial Practice in a Polar Territory* (Actar, 2017) and of *Pamphlet Architecture 30: COUPLING, Strategies for Infrastructural Opportunism* (Princeton Architectural Press, 2011). Sheppard is also coeditor of the journal *Bracket*.

Georgeen Theodore is an architect, urban designer, and Professor at New Jersey Institute of Technology's College of Architecture and Design, where she directs the Master of Infrastructure Planning (MIP) program. She received a B.Arch from Rice University and an M.Arch in Urban Design from the Harvard Graduate School of Design, where she graduated with distinction. Theodore is founding partner and principal of Interboro, a New York City–based architecture and planning research office. Since its founding in 2002, Interboro has worked with a variety of public, private, and nonprofit clients, and has accumulated many awards for its innovative projects, including the Curry Stone Design Prize, Social Design Circle (2017), the Rice Design Alliance Spotlight Award (2013), the MoMA PS1's Young Architects Program (2011), the Architectural League of New York's Emerging Voices Award (2011) and Young Architects Award (2005), and the AIA New York New Practices Award (2006). Theodore and her partners, Tobias Armborst and Daniel D'Oca, are the authors of *The Arsenal of Exclusion & Inclusion* (Actar, 2017), a book about accessibility in the built environment in the U.S.

Vrindha Vijay is in her final year of the M.Arch program at RISD. She received her B.Arch degree from Rajalakshmi School of Architecture in Chennai, India. Currently, she is starting her thesis, which will address the impact of the built environment on well-being and health, with a particular focus on the behavior and emotions of cancer patients and their families.

Mason White is Professor at the University of Toronto Daniels Faculty and a founding partner, with Lola Sheppard, of Lateral Office, a Toronto-based practice. His work operates at the intersection of architecture, landscape, and urbanism. White has been pursuing teaching, research, and design work on the role of architecture in rural and remote regions for the past ten years. He is committed to design as a research vehicle to pose and respond to complex, urgent questions in the built environment, engaging in the wider context and climate of a project—social, ecological, or political. White's work has been exhibited extensively and he has lectured across the U.S., Canada, and Europe. Lateral Office has presented at the Oslo Triennale (2019), the Seoul Biennale of Architecture and Urbanism (2017), and the Chicago Architecture Biennial (2015), and they were awarded a Special Mention at the 2014 Venice Architecture Biennale. They received a Progressive Architecture Award in 2013 and the 2012 Holcim Gold for Sustainable Construction for North America, for their work on the Arctic. White and Sheppard are coauthors of *Many Norths: Spatial Practice in a Polar Territory* (Actar, 2017) and of *Pamphlet Architecture* 30: *COUPLING, Strategies for Infrastructural Opportunism* (Princeton Architectural Press, 2011). White is also a founding coeditor of the journal *Bracket*, which just published its fourth volume, *Takes Action* (AR+D, 2020).

Mabel O. Wilson is the Nancy and George E. Rupp Professor in Architecture and a professor in African American and African Diaspora Studies at Columbia University. She also serves as the Director of the Institute for Research in African-American Studies and codirects Global Africa Lab, an innovative research initiative that explores the spatial topologies of the African continent and its diaspora. With her transdisciplinary practice Studio &, she is a collaborator on the architectural team that recently completed the Memorial to Enslaved African American Laborers at the University of Virginia. Studio & makes visible and legible the ways that anti-Black racism shapes the built environment along with the ways that Blackness creates spaces of imagination, refusal, and desire.

Wilson has authored *Begin with the Past: Building the National Museum of African American History and Culture* (Smithsonian Books, 2017) and *Negro Building: Black Americans in the World of Fairs and Museums* (University of California Press, 2012). She coedited with Irene Cheng and Charles Davis *Race and Modern Architecture: A Critical History from the Enlightenment to the Present* (University of Pittsburgh Press, 2020). In 2011 Wilson was honored as a United States Artists Ford Fellow in Architecture and Design. She received the prestigious Arts and Letters Award in 2019 from the American Academy of Arts and Letters for her work with Global Africa Lab. Wilson was also awarded in 2019 the Educator/Mentor honor from *Architectural Record*'s Women in Architecture Design Leadership Program.

Jason Young is Professor and Director of the School of Architecture at the University of Tennessee. In his academic career, he has taught architecture at the University of Michigan, at the University of California, Berkeley, in the Summer Institute for Architecture at The Catholic University of America, and as a Visiting Professor at the Schwerpunkt Holz in Murau, Austria, an international architecture workshop exploring the culture of wood. His academic research explores contemporary conditions of American urbanism in a post-city, digitally organized culture. Young was the 2012–13 Helmut F. Stern Professor in the University of Michigan Institute for the Humanities, where he worked on a project titled *Skirmishes with the MacroPhenomenal: Letting Go of the City*. This research explores franchise space, digital culture, and the emergence of a "database subject," a new type of urban subject. Young was a contributing coeditor for the anthology *Stalking Detroit* (Actar, 2001) and has lectured on his urbanism research at the Berlage Institute in the Netherlands, ETH Zürich, Politecnico di Torino, Università Luav di Venezia, and the University of California, Berkeley, among others. Young holds an M.Arch from Rice University and a Bachelor of Science in Architecture from the Georgia Institute of Technology.

Portals: Pedagogy, Practice, and Architecture's Future Imaginary (RISD 2020)

Portals: Pedagogy, Practice, and Architecture's Future Imaginary (RISD 2020)

Editors: Amy Catania Kulper, Kevin Crouse, Jennifer Liese

Department of Architecture, Rhode Island School of Design, Providence